Africa and Asia in Comparative Economic Perspective

Also by Peter Lawrence

WORLD RECESSION AND THE FOOD CRISIS IN AFRICA (*editor*)

RURAL COOPERATION IN TANZANIA (*co-editor*)

Also by Colin Thirtle

THE ROLE OF DEMAND AND SUPPLY (*co-author*)

AGRICULTURAL PRICE POLICY: Government and the Market, Training Materials for Agricultural Planning (*co-author*)

PRODUCTIVITY, EFFICIENCY AND LAND MARKETS IN SOUTH AFRICAN AGRICULTURE (*co-editor*)

SOUTH AFRICAN AGRICULTURE AT THE CROSSROADS: An Empirical Analysis of Efficiency and Productivity (*co-editor*)

Africa and Asia in Comparative Economic Perspective

Edited by

Peter Lawrence
Senior Lecturer in Economics
Keele University

and

Colin Thirtle
Professor of Agricultural Economics
Imperial College
University of London

in association with
the ESRC Development
Economics Study Group

First published 2001 by
PALGRAVE
Houndmills, Basingstoke, Hampshire RG21 6XS and
175 Fifth Avenue, New York, N.Y. 10010
Companies and representatives throughout the world

PALGRAVE is the new global academic imprint of
St. Martin's Press LLC Scholarly and Reference Division and
Palgrave Publishers Ltd (formerly Macmillan Press Ltd).

ISBN 0–333–79029–4

This book is printed on paper suitable for recycling and
made from fully managed and sustained forest sources.

A catalogue record for this book is available
from the British Library.

Library of Congress Cataloging-in-Publication Data
Africa and Asia in comparative economic perspective / edited by
Peter Lawrence and Colin Thirtle ; in association with the ESRC
Development Economics Study Group.
        p. cm.
Includes bibliographical references and index.
ISBN 0–333–79029–4
  1. Asia—Economic conditions. 2. Asia—Economic policy.
  3. Africa—Economic conditions. 4. Africa—Economic policy.
  I. Lawrence, Peter. II. Thirtle, Colin G., 1944–
  HC412 .A23 2000
  330.95—dc21
                                                  00–066881

10   9   8   7   6   5   4   3   2   1
10 09 08 07 06 05 04 03 02 01

Printed in Great Britain by Antony Rowe Ltd, Chippenham, Wiltshire

Contents

Acknowledgements

This volume brings together essays originating from a selection of papers first presented at the July 1998 ESRC Development Economics Study Group (DESG) conference entitled 'Is Africa different from Asia?' held at the University of Reading in England. The principal objective of the conference was to encourage comparative analysis across the two continents with a view to pointing out similarities and differences in particular subject areas and with trying to understand why the performances of these two country groups have been so different. We would like to thank Helen Stutley of the International Development Centre at the University of Reading for taking on most of the organisation of the conference, and without whom the conference would not have taken place. We would like to thank Michael Lipton for his plenary address which set the conference asking the right questions, all those who contributed papers to what was a very stimulating and successful conference, and to the contributors to this volume for making the editors' job so easy.

Finally, a word for our sponsors. We would like to express our thanks to the UK Economic and Social Research Council which has funded the DESG for almost three decades and part of that funding has supported the annual conference. We would also like to acknowledge the past support for these conferences of the former Overseas Development Agency (now the Department for International Development (DfID)), and the Royal Economic Society.

Notes on Contributors

Shaikh S. Ahmed is an Assistant Professor in the Department of Finance and Banking at the University of Dhaka, Bangladesh. He was a PhD researcher in the Department of Accounting and Finance at the University of Birmingham, UK. He has published papers on rural credit and development finance institutions and has been involved in many research projects in these subjects. His current research is in monetary and fiscal policy and economic growth.

Harvey W. Armstrong is Professor of Economic Geography at the University of Sheffield. He worked previously in the Economics Departments at the Universities of Loughborough, Lancaster and British Columbia. He has published extensively in the fields of regional and local economic development, EU and UK regional policy and the analysis of the performance of micro-states and autonomous regions. He has acted as an advisor to the European Commission and the Foreign and Commonwealth Office.

Sonia Bhalotra is Fellow of Newnham College and Senior Research Officer at the Department of Applied Economics in Cambridge and Lecturer in Economics at the University of Bristol. Her research is in labour economics and applied microeconomics and she has analysed data for India, Pakistan, Ghana and Zambia to study issues such as child labour, intrahousehold resource allocation, the impact of microcredit provision, wage-setting, productivity and unemployment. She has published several articles in leading economics journals.

Anne Booth is Professor of Economics (with reference to Asia) at the School of Oriental and African Studies, University of London. She has previously worked at Department of the Environment, UK, Hasanuddin University, Ujung Pandang University of Singapore Research School of Pacific Studies, Australian National University, and has acted as consultant variously for the International Labour Organisation, United Nation Development Programme and World Bank in Indonesia, Bangladesh and Papua New Guinea. She has published extensively on Asia and, especially, on agriculture and labour in Indonesia. She is an Editorial Board member of the *Journal of Development Studies*.

Christopher Heady is Professor of Applied Economics at the University of Bath. He was previously Assistant Professor at Yale University and Reader at University College, London. He has published widely on labour markets and public economics in developing, transitional and developed countries.

Raul Hopkins is Lecturer in Economics at Queen Mary and Westfield College, University of London, and Research Fellow at Suntory and Toyota International Centres for Economics and Related Disciplines (STICERD), London School of Economics. He has written extensively on Development Economics with special reference to Latin America and Asia. He is currently the co-ordinator of an international study about the impact of Oxfam Fair Trade on poverty alleviation. He is also consultant for various International Development agencies and Non-Governmental Organisations.

Raghbendra Jha is Executive Director, Australia South Asia Research Centre, Australia National University, Canberra. He was previously at Columbia University and Williams College in the USA, Queen's University in Canada, University of Warwick, UK and Delhi School of Economics, National Institute for Public Finance and Policy (NIPFP) Indian Institute of Management (IIM) and at the Indira Gandhi Institute of Development Research, Bombay in India. He specialises in Public Economics, Macroeconomics and Development Economics and has published extensively in the major international economics journals.

Colin Kirkpatrick is Director and Professor of Development Economics, at the Institute for Development Policy and Management, University of Manchester, UK. His research interests include financial sector development and policy, international trade issues and sustainable development policy on all of which he has published widely. He is a joint-editor of the *Journal of Asia-Pacific Economy* and an Editorial Board member of the *Journal of Development Studies*.

Peter Lawrence is Senior Lecturer in Economics at Keele University, UK. He has taught at the Universities of Dar-es-Salaam, Tanzania, Manitoba, Winnipeg and at Makerere University Kampala, Uganda. He has researched widely on development problems in sub-Saharan Africa and Eastern Europe. He is currently concerned with structural adjustment and the performance of agricultural exports in sub-Saharan Africa. He is a founding editor of the *Review of African Political Economy* and has published extensively in refereed journals and books.

Angela Lusigi is currently a consultant with International Fund for Agricultural Development (IFAD) in Rome. Her area of specialisation is the analysis of agricultural productivity in Africa. Her work experience includes examining returns to agricultural research expenditure in Botswana and South Africa, and project evaluation in Zambia.

Mark McGillivray is Associate Professor of International Development at RMIT University in Melbourne, Australia and a Fellow of the Centre for Research in Economic Development and International Trade at the University of Nottingham. He is also an Advisory Board member of the (Australian) Development Studies Network Inc. He has published numerous articles in academic journals, mainly on aid allocation, aid and public sector fiscal behaviour and inter-country development levels. His present research concentrates on the impact of structural adjustment and links between aid and trade.

Mahmood Messkoub lectures in economics at Leeds University Business School. He has also held a consulting position (1989–1996) on a UNFPA funded project in Population and Development, based at the Institute of Social Studies in the Hague, that took him on regular visits to Tanzania and Botswana on support/collaborative work. He also held visiting scholar positions at the Institute d'Etudes Politiques de Paris and Boston University. His publications include works on the social and economic impacts of adjustment programmes in Tanzania and developing countries in general. His current research interests are in the interface between population studies and economics, particularly in the areas of migration and population ageing. His paper on the 'Crisis of Ageing in Less Developed Countries' was published in *Development and Change*, in 1999. He is currently working on a project on the impact of population structures and ageing on savings in developing countries.

Oliver Morrissey is Director of the Centre for Research in Economic Development and International Trade (CREDIT) and Senior Lecturer in Economics at the School of Economics, University of Nottingham. He has published numerous articles in academic journals, notably on aid policy, trade policy reform and structural adjustment, and has co-edited books on poverty, inequality and rural development, economic and political reform in developing countries and evaluating economic liberalisation. His present research concentrates on the macroeconomic impact of aid; aid and trade policy linkages; non-policy barriers to exporting; and the political economy of economic policy reform.

Bilge Nomer is Lecturer in Economics at Marmara University, Turkey. She is currently writing her doctoral thesis at the Economics Department Queen Mary and Westfield College, University of London. Her research examines the impact of structural adjustment programmes on economic growth and the balance of payments using a cross-section panel of countries of Asia, Africa and Latin America.

Harald V. Proff is Assistant Professor at the Darmstadt University of Technology, Germany and was a manager for regional strategies with Daimler-Benz (1993–96) and a doctoral student with the department of Economics at the Darmstadt University of Technology (1990–93) after receiving a joint master's degree in economics and mechanical engineering (1985–90). His research covers international economics, industrial policy, theory of economic policy and the automotive industry. He has published widely in refereed journals.

Robert Read is a Lecturer in International Economics at the University of Lancaster. He has previously worked in the Economics Department of Unilever and the University of the South Pacific in Fiji (as a Visiting Fellow) and also as a Research Fellow in the Department of Economics at the University of Reading. He has advised the Foreign and Commonwealth Office, the African, Carribean and Pacific Group of States, the Maltese Federation of Industry and the Falkland Islands Government. He has published widely in the areas of the international banana economy, including trade policy issues and the activities of the banana multinationals, and economic aspects of growth and development in small states, including trade policy issues, structural transition and growth strategies.

Gareth Api Richards is Hallsworth Junior Research Fellow in the Department of Government, University of Manchester where he also teaches the politics of globalisation and international political economy of the Asia-Pacific. His research interests include South-East Asian politics (especially Malaysia); Asia-Europe interregionalism; and state-capital-labour relations in Asia's political economy. He has published on these themes in major journals.

Mridul Saggar is a PhD candidate at the Indira Gandhi Institute of Development Research, Bombay, India. He was educated at Delhi and Princeton Universities. He researches on money and banking issues and has published his work in several journals.

Peter Smith is Senior Lecturer in Economics at the University of Southampton, where he teaches development economics at undergraduate and postgraduate levels. He has also taught at the National University of Singapore, and acted as poverty consultant to the Bank of Uganda. His research interests include the use of social indicators in measuring human development, the flexibility of national economies, and poverty analysis and alleviation and he has published widely on these and other topics.

Kecuk Suhariyanto took his MSc in Applied Statistics at the University of Guelph, Canada and his PhD in Agricultural Economics at the University of Reading, UK. Currently, he is a researcher at Central Bureau of Statistics, Indonesia and a lecturer at Academy of Statistics, Indonesia.

Colin Thirtle is Professor of Agricultural Economics in the T.H. Huxley School of Environment, Earth Sciences and Engineering at Imperial College, University of London and Extraordinary Professor of Agricultural Economics at the University of Pretoria, Republic of South Africa. He has previously taught at Columbia, the University of San Francisco and the Universities of Manchester and Reading. He has researched and published extensively on the economics of agricultural development.

Matsuo Watanabe is a PhD candidate in Development Economics at the Institute for Development Policy and Management, at the University of Manchester. He was a Researcher at the Association for the Promotion of International Co-operation in Tokyo. His doctoral research is on regional integration in East Africa.

1
Comparing African and Asian Economic Development

Peter Lawrence and Colin Thirtle

The World Bank website devoted to economic growth research has a graph showing the path of East Asian and sub-Saharan African GDP per capita since 1960. Beginning from a relatively small gap, the picture is one of continued divergence thereafter. The obvious question to ask is why is there this increasing gap? What is it about sub-Saharan Africa (SSA) which makes its performance so different from Asia since 1960? The papers collected in this volume address these questions from three different standpoints. The majority of them compare particular aspects of economic behaviour in the two continents. Another group of papers examine potential lessons for Africa that might be learned from Asian, mainly East Asian, development. Finally, two of the papers address the issue of convergence and divergence between the two country groups.

The issue of convergence is often the starting point for comparisons across countries. Barro's work showed that, controlling for initial human capital endowment, there is a negative relationship between starting per capita income and growth (Barro, 1991). Driven by theoretical assumptions of diminishing marginal productivity of capital this result is comforting to neoclassical growth theory but also makes some concession to theories of endogenous growth by emphasising the importance of initial human capital endowments. As Mkandawire and Soludo (1999) observe in their recent survey of SSA's structural adjustment experience, trying to explain why SSA has not emulated Asia, or indeed suggesting that it can do so, requires some assessment of initial conditions. As they note, it is important not only to compare initial states of GDP per capita, but also to observe other characteristics such as human capital endowments in order to explain differences in subsequent performance.

Table 1.1 attempts to make this kind of comparison for eight countries, four of the so-called high-performing Asian economies (HPAE) and four

Table 1.1 Asia and Africa: selected countries' key indicators 1960 and 1997

	Year	GDP p.c. (USD)	Agric/ GDP (%)	Mfg/ GDP (%)	Exports/ GDP (%)	Energy cons	Mfg/ exports (%)	Urban pop/ total (%)	Life exp at birth (years)	Primary enrol (%)	Secondary enrol (%)	Tertiary enrol (%)	Adult lit (%)
Indonesia	1960	174	54	8	13	129	0	15	41	71	6	1	39
	1997	1110	16	25	28	442	53	37	65	97	42	10	84
Korea	1960	349	40	12	3	258	6	28	54	94	27	5	71
	1997	10550	6	26	38	3225	93	83	73	99	96	48	98
Malaysia	1960	547	37	9	54	242	6	25	57	96	19	1	53
	1997	4680	13	34	90	1655	65	55	72	91	57	7	84
Thailand	1960	218	40	13	17	64	2	13	51	83	13	2	68
	1997	2800	11	29	39	878	73	21	71	97	37	19	94
Kenya	1960	223	38	9	31	143	12	7	47	47	2	0	20
	1997	330	29	11	32	109	18	30	58	93	24	1	78
Nigeria	1960	296	63	5	15	34	3	13	39	36	4	0	15
	1997	260	45	8	15	165	3	41	53	93	30	3	57
Ghana	1960	426	41	10	28	106	10	23	40	38	5	0	27
	1997	370	47	9	25	92	23	37	59	75	39	2	34
Côte d'Ivoire	1960	538	43	7	37	76	1	19	37	46	2	0	5
	1997	690	27	18	47	97	17	45	55	69	23	3	60

Notes: 1960 GNP is in 1978 prices; 1997 GNP is in current prices; some 1997 data is for the latest year available.
Source: World Bank, *World Development Report* (various years).

SSA economies. Both sets of four countries fell, in 1960, across a similar range of GDP per capita levels and are chosen for that reason. Both sets of economies show similar initial conditions across other characteristics. They derived between 35 and 55 per cent of their GDP from agriculture. While the four HPAE countries derived between 8 and 13 per cent of GDP from manufacturing, the four SSA countries had a range of 5 to 10 per cent. Only Malaysia, out of the four Asian countries exhibited openness levels as measured by the ratio of exports to GDP, greater than the four African economies. Two of the African countries were well ahead of the rest in the proportion of manufacturing exports to total exports. Degrees of urbanisation were slightly higher in the Asian four. In measures of health and education, however, the HPAEs showed superior 'initial' conditions. Life expectancy averaged 10 years longer. All four African countries showed primary school enrolment rates of less than 50 per cent of the age group, while no HPAE scored below 80 per cent. Secondary and tertiary enrolment rates also showed the four African countries to be well below the four HPAEs, among which Korea was already demonstrating large differences from the rest. Adult literacy rates ranged from 39 to 71 per cent among the HPAEs, but only from 5 to 27 per cent among the four African countries.

Nearly four decades later the differences between the two sets of economies are stark. Korea's per capita GDP is now 40 times that of Nigeria, compared to one-sixth higher in 1960. Korea's GDP per capita, twice as high as Indonesia's in 1960, is now almost 10 times higher. Indeed the divergence among the four Asian economies is noticeably greater than that between the African ones, while the intercontinental divergence is even wider. Other indicators show the extent of the Asian–African divergence, especially in manufacturing growth and exports, and in human capital indicators. In the two West African countries, even primary school enrolment rates are still below the lowest of the Asian four in 1960. What is suggested by even this brief comparison of performance is that initial human capital endowments appear to be important.

What this or any more sophisticated statistical comparison cannot explain is why the Koreans have such a high rate of primary and secondary school enrolment in 1960 relative to other Asian countries and to Africa. As Michael Lipton noted in his plenary address to the conference, the more sophisticated comparisons which have been made between Asian and African performance are of two main types. First, there are the multivariate regression analyses involving a large number of countries and explanatory variables which ultimately test for a significant Africa or Asia 'dummy'. Comparing two continents in this way, as Lipton pointed out, hides the differences within the continental country groups. In the end there is no reason for believing that geographical location in and of itself explains the different outcomes across the continents. Trying to explain differences between the performance of different countries or groups of countries, within the same continent might be more instructive. The second type of comparative studies are the comparisons of small groups or even pairs of countries, or comparisons of particular issues, such as child labour in this volume, or sectors, such as agriculture, across the continents. This kind of comparative exercise has the virtue of greater depth and the possibility of greater historical understanding of initial conditions. However, it is more difficult to draw generalisable conclusions from such small sample comparisons.

The papers in this volume run the full range of approaches. There are large cross-country comparisons, there are sub-regional comparisons, there are comparisons involving a small number of countries, and some involving just two. The comparisons take place at the level of macroeconomic aggregates, especially overall growth performance, at the sectoral level, mainly agriculture, but also monetary and financial, and at the level of specific issues, such as child labour or ageing. We have grouped the papers under three broad themes. The first set of papers, Part I of this book, is concerned with possible lessons to be learned from the Asian experience for Africa's development. One important prerequisite of learning lessons is that we get the teacher's story right. In Chapter 2 Anne Booth presents a comparative account of the Asian success story, drawing attention to the differences between the four HPAEs of South-East Asia, and South Korea and Taiwan. As noted in Table 1.1, Korea outstrips the other three (South-East Asian) HPAEs listed there, particularly in the development of human capital endowments. Other differences appear, too, in the role of the state and in income distribution, reflecting the different historical experiences of these countries. Although the HPAEs have been successful relatively to most other developing economies, the differences between them make it problematic to speak of an 'Asian model'.

Nonetheless, there are features, not all common to all of the HPAEs, to which much of the success of these economies can be attributed. Starting from this position, Oliver Morrissey in Chapter 3 seeks to tease out the lessons from Asia for sub-Saharan Africa. Like Booth, Morrissey points up the developmentalist and distributive role of the State, especially in Korea and Taiwan. Here relatively authoritarian states have identified their maintenance of power with a successful economy, while in sub-Saharan Africa authoritarian states have become kleptocracies. Even now under the adjustment policies of the last two decades, there is an absence of policies which proved important for the HPAEs, such as more equitable income distribution, land reform and an industrial strategy involving directed credit. In the end, SSA's success may depend on more non-economic lessons from Asia: the existence of national identity and political commitment to growth with equity. Here Africa's record is weak.

One country in SSA which patently did not exhibit a strong national identity was Uganda. Peter Smith looks at the case of Uganda in Chapter 4. Approaching the issue in a slightly different way, he discusses the replicable and non-replicable factors responsible for Asian growth. Using Bank of Uganda household survey data he then examines how far Uganda measures up against these replicable factors. Once again, the low level of development of human capital is seen as an important area to attack, as also are the low rates of saving relatively to the Asian successes. All three authors note the importance of macroeconomic stability, now promoted as part of adjustment policies, but still subject to variable implementation. Confidence in governments' credibility requires a long period of stability, especially following the instability of previous years. This is one of those replicable factors which requires political stability alongside it, and this may be more elusive than its economic partner.

However, adhering to stabilisation conditions in adjustment programmes while necessary to achieve macroeconomic stability and government credibility is not sufficient. Attention needs to be paid to the allocation of structural adjustment lending. Taking the case of a poorly performing Asian economy, the Philippines, Mark McGillivray asks, in Chapter 5, what can be learned by other poorly performing economies, especially in SSA, from relative failure in Asia. Testing a model of public sector fiscal behaviour, his results suggest that aid following the implementation of adjustment programmes may lead to public sector behaviour which is the opposite of that associated with a reform programme and with the Asian successes.

One area of public expenditure which has received attention in developing countries over the last few years, has been pensions provision for ageing populations. As Mahmood Messkoub shows in Chapter 6, this is not only a developed country problem. As Asia is ageing to a greater extent than Africa now, Messkoub focuses on the lessons which can be learned from Asian provision for Africa. In particular, he sees an important lesson as being the preservation of traditional systems for in-family care of the elderly, in combination with some state support, especially in the form of incentives to families to maintain such care.

The second set of papers, Part II of the book, is concerned with comparisons of development experiences. Colin Kirkpatrick, Gareth Api Richards and Matsuo Watanabe compare African and Asian regional development strategies and experiences between Asia and Africa (Chapter 7). In the context of a renewed interest in Africa in regional trading arrangement, the authors take a critical approach to the idea that lessons can be learned from the Asian experience. The authors criticise both the orthodox explanation that African regionalism failed because it was inward looking, and the view that the Asian regionalism succeeded because it was 'outward looking' and therefore this is all African regionalism requires to succeed. As with other contributions to this volume, it is clear that there is a complexity and diversity in both Asian and African experiences of regionalism which denies the possibility of a simply 'toolkit' approach to learning lessons from success or diagnosing reasons for failure.

The issue of regionalism reappears in the comparative analysis of the performance of African and Asian micro-states which Armstrong and Read make in Chapter 8. Apart from analysing the determinants of performance in micro-states across the world, in which variables such as natural resources, tourism and financial services are highly significant, the authors compare the performance of African and Asian micro-states. In this case the relatively lower income of micro-states in Africa is a consequence of their location in relatively poor regions. What is interesting about the comparative analysis here is that it suggests, first, that there is no African dummy in the sense that African micro-states perform any differently than Asian ones to the same economic impulses, and secondly, that African micro-states perform much better than their larger neighbours, a feature also of micro-states in Asia. Data limitations preclude including determinants of success that figure in other models, particularly those associated with human capital development in micro-states.

A constraint on human capital development insofar as it constitutes competition with school participation, is child labour. In Chapter 9, Sonia Bhalotra and Christopher Heady compare child labour activities and their determinants across rural Ghana and Pakistan, using household survey data. Child labour comes in different forms and while much attention has been paid to child labour in its more dramatic forms on the streets and in the workshops of Asia, the authors concentrate here on rural child labour in which more meaningful comparisons can be made with child labour in Africa. Significant differences are found in participation in child labour, especially between girls and boys, in child labour outside the family farm and in levels of parental education between the two countries. However, the key negative influence on child labour in both countries is the mother's education. Raising levels of human capital both in Africa and South Asia will require policies directed at increasing access to education for females.

The next two chapters are concerned with comparative monetary policy. In Chapter 11, Raghbendra Jha and Mridul Saggar compare money demand functions for four SADC countries with other studies which have been made for the ASEAN countries. The stability of money demand functions is critical for monetary targeting. The authors find stability in two of the African cases which allow monetary targeting, but less stability in the other two. Comparing these results with those for Asia, they find evidence of significant money demand instability. Part of this they adduce to financial innovations and reforms which have already been found to affect the stability of demand for money in developed economies. This is a comparative analysis which offers some lessons from the ASEAN experience in the importance of moves towards financial liberalisation and innovation.

In Chapter 12, Shaikh Ahmed carries out a more traditional cross-developing country analysis of the relationship between central bank credit creation (to fund government expenditure) and growth. While finding that central bank funding for government expenditure was negatively related to growth across all developing countries in the sample, including Latin America, the results for Africa alone showed no significant relationship. This result may have to do with lower levels of credit creation in Africa connected to Africa's low level of income, especially as Ahmed finds that low amounts of credit creation have no significant impact on growth.

Some of the earlier chapters have included Latin America in the datasets from which African and Asian behaviour has been compared. In Chapter 10, Raul Hopkins and Bilge Nomer make an explicit comparison of the performance of African with Latin American agriculture. They find strong differences in the sources of agricultural growth between the two continents, with African output growth explained by increased irrigation and labour productivity, while Latin American growth is explained by increased fertiliser use. Contrary to the analyses in earlier chapters, they do find a significant Africa dummy which they suggest may have to do with levels of human capital and the quality of institutions, variables not included in their regression model.

The third and final part of the book is concerned with the issue of convergence. In Chapter 13, Harald Proff presents an analysis of convergence which involves taking the 27 countries of three regional trade groupings and arranging them into clusters, by various economic characteristics. He then shows that membership of clusters demonstrates intra-regional heterogeneity and inter- regional homogeneity. Regions break up into clusters, while clusters can contain members from more than one region. This suggests the emergence of 'convergence clubs' which cross continental boundaries. Analysing the development of convergence clubs might then be more productive than comparing continent wide groupings whose only common link is geography.

Finally, Kecuk Suhariyanto, Angela Lusigi and Colin Thirtle examine convergence of agricultural total factor productivity (TFP) in Africa and Asia. They find negative TFP growth for Africa, but positive for Asia. However, they find that regions of Africa had faster TFP growth than East Asia and that it is West Africa which drives down the African average. There is evidence of convergence in Africa, but not in Asia. The results here give support to the view that within continental differences and trends are as important and interesting as differences between them, a theme that runs through the contributions to this volume.

Whether there is much to be gained from a comparative approach is still an open question. In particular, engaging in comparisons, 'learning lessons', trying to model a country's economic policies in order to replicate the success of others, only tells part of the story. Initial conditions in every case are different, political and social cultures are different, and it may be mistaken to engage in comparative analysis in order to produce policy conclusions. Policies which 'work' in one economic environment may fail in another. However, there is an established body of research which tells us what does not work. Learning the lessons of strategies and policies which fail may be of considerable advantage in constructing strategies and policies which succeed. There is also a body of research which suggests a minimum set of policies which are necessary but not sufficient for rapid growth. This book is offered as a modest attempt to assist that continuous process of learning from failure and success, while respecting the specificity of history and initial conditions.

Part I

Lessons for Africa of the Asian 'Success'

2
Why is South-East Asia Different from Taiwan and South Korea?

Anne Booth

2.1 Introduction

The last decade has seen an explosion of work on the fast growing economies of East and South-East Asia, by individual scholars and by the international development institutions. Influential books by Amsden (1989) and Wade (1990), as well as the work of Johnson (1982, 1995) have explored the nature of the East Asian developmental state, and especially the role of government in determining the allocation of resources to particular industries, in building infrastructure and in the development of the educational system. The widely discussed report published by the World Bank (1993) on the East Asian 'Miracle' endeavoured to draw lessons not just from the experience of Japan, Taiwan and Korea but also from four fast-growing economies in South-East Asia, Singapore, Indonesia, Malaysia and Thailand. The recent growth experience of China was also discussed. This report and the large literature which it generated have tended to convey the impression that the huge area of the world which the term 'East Asia' embraces have all experienced rapid economic growth over the last three decades, and that from their experience a coherent set of 'lessons' can be drawn for less successful economies in other parts of the world.[1]

The available data show clearly that such an impression is wrong; indeed if we examine the growth experience of all the economies of East Asia for which data are available since the early 1960s it is clear that they fall into four groups. The first group of economies are those which had very low per capita incomes in 1960 and have experienced very modest growth rates since then; Cambodia and Burma fall into this category and so do Laos and Vietnam although in both these economies GDP growth has accelerated since the late 1980s. A second group of low achievers include Brunei and the Philippines, both economies which had relatively high per capita GDP in 1960 but which have grown very slowly since then. A third group comprise what are perhaps the true 'Asian miracles', those economies which had low per capita GDP in 1960 but which have grown rapidly (4 per cent per annum in per capita terms or more) since then. Into this group falls Indonesia, South Korea and Thailand. Last are another group of high achievers in the growth stakes who started from rather higher per capita GDP levels, but have grown fast since the 1960s; they include Taiwan, Malaysia and Singapore. Singapore had the highest per capita income in the region in 1960 and has grown very rapidly since then with the result that by the mid-1990s per capita GDP was higher than the West European average (World Bank, 1997b).

Although there can be little dispute about the broad facts of GDP growth in East Asia over the past 30–40 years, there is far more room for debate on the causes of the divergent growth outcomes. Several authors have argued that there is in fact no one 'Asian model' of economic success and that the World Bank-termed 'high performing Asian economies' (HPAEs) fall into several categories. Perkins (1994: 655–6) has argued that there were 'at least three models of East Asian development', a manufactured export-led, state interventionist model based on the experience of Japan, Taiwan and South Korea, the free-port, commerce and service dominated model of Hong Kong and Singapore, and the natural-resource model of Indonesia, Malaysia and Thailand. Amsden (1995: 794) in her discussion of the last model argues that, in the context of Malaysia, Indonesia and Thailand, rich natural resources allowed a:

> more modest initial role for the government than in Korea and Taiwan. The leading sectors of these South East Asian countries were agro-based and competitive in world markets without substantial productivity-augmenting support from government, and without significant reliance on imported inputs.

Elsewhere (Booth, 1999), I have argued that the causes and characteristics of the rapid economic growth of South Korea and Taiwan (and indeed Japan especially in the decades from 1955 to 1975), while sharing some similarities, are in a number of crucial respects different from those in the fast-growing countries of South-East Asia, especially in Malaysia, Indonesia and Thailand. I tried to spell out the nature of these differences, going beyond the rather obvious differences in natural resource endowments and their implications for economic policy, and examining the different historical legacies which have conditioned recent development policies in different parts of Asia. Here, I wish to develop further some of the arguments of the earlier work, paying particular attention to educational attainment, access to agricultural land, rural development policies, and linkages between rural and urban sectors of the economy, and the implications of these for distributional outcomes in different parts of South-East Asia.

2.2   Determinants of income distribution in East and South-East Asia: the historical legacy

A feature of the economies of South Korea and Taiwan which has attracted widespread notice is the apparently quite equal distribution of income and wealth which characterised both economies at the start of their era of accelerated growth, and which has persisted until the 1990s. Rodrik (1995: Figure 13) has argued that in both countries, the Gini coefficient for income and land distribution was unusually low, and that the 'relatively equal distribution of income and wealth was critical' in insulating the government from sectional pressure groups. Although the international data on which these comparisons are based may be flawed for a number of reasons, the basic point is probably correct. The peculiar historical conditions under which both Taiwan and South Korea began their process of accelerated growth undoubtedly did create an unusually even distribution of income and wealth (Perkins, 1994: 660). In Taiwan the period of Japanese colonisation, followed by an influx of migrants from the mainland, displaced and disempowered the indigenous elites while in South Korea the effects of the civil war and the large-scale migration from the north to the south was to create an economy where very few had access to more than the basic means of subsistence. Thus neither government had to contend with powerful landed elites, as in much of Latin America, and nor was there an established class of industrial or financial entrepreneurs to feel threatened by new directions in economic policymaking.

Much of the discussion of income distribution in Taiwan and Korea has focused on the personal distribution of income, but it also needs to be stressed that both societies were characterised by a high degree of ethnic homogeneity. Where there were ethnic minorities such as the aboriginal population of Taiwan, they were small and played very little part in the modern economy. The very sharp disparities in the distribution of income across ethnic groups so characteristic of South-East Asia has not been a feature of either economy, at least since the departure of the Japanese. In addition, regional disparities in income were quite modest in the initial phases of accelerated growth, and have not increased dramatically in either economy, in spite of rapid urban growth and substantial rural–urban migration.

In South-East Asia by contrast, marked disparities in income and wealth had emerged by the 1950s when one by one the colonial regimes departed from what had been the Netherlands Indies, French Indochina, the American Philippines and the British colonies and protectorates in Burma, peninsular Malaya and Singapore, Sabah (North Borneo), Brunei and Sarawak. These disparities also existed in Thailand, which had not been directly colonised. They were due to a number of factors but three stand out: the meagre educational legacies left behind by the colonial powers, the relative impoverishment of rural areas, partly through discriminatory tax measures and partly through lack of investment in infrastructure and new agricultural technologies, and the superior economic status of immigrant minorities from other parts of Asia, especially the Chinese.

Let us start by looking at access to education. There can be little doubt that, with the exception of the Philippines under American rule, the colonial regimes in South-East Asia left behind an extremely meagre educational legacy. Not only was there inadequate provision of educational facilities, but such facilities as did exist were mainly (at the post-primary level almost exclusively) in large towns and cities, and places were usually allocated on the basis of race and income, rather than academic merit. The well-known study by Furnivall (1943: 111) showed that in the late 1930s the proportion of the population enrolled in recognised schools was around 11 per cent in Taiwan and the Philippines, 9.7 per cent in Thailand, 6 per cent in Malaya, 4 per cent in Burma, 3.4 per cent in the Netherlands Indies and only 2.1 per cent in French Indochina.[2] Furnivall (1943: 119) pointed out that the good performance of the Philippines and Thailand in comparison with the rest of the region was due to 'specially favourable circumstances':

> In both countries the chief impulse to the progress of primary instruction has been the nationalist drive behind it. In the other countries foreign governments have inevitably been critical of nationalist enthusiasm, and nationalist leaders have had less zeal for primary instruction than for higher education, which, as they hope, will equip them for handling national affairs.

In British Malaya, the appointment of the noted scholar of Malay culture, Richard Winstedt, to the post of Assistant Director of Education in the inter-war years appeared to usher in a period of educational progress for rural Malays. But as Rudner (1994: 288) has pointed out, access to English language education continued to be restricted to a tiny minority, almost entirely in urban areas. For the rural Malay, the number of years in elementary schooling was reduced and the curriculum was oriented to such manual skills as basket weaving and horticulture. 'This benign, custodial outlook in education tended to reinforce the prevailing colonial assumption that the Malay peasantry should be retained, and improved, in their traditional kampung environment and saved from the disruptions of modernization'. A similar view prevailed among many colonial officials in the Netherlands Indies.

In colonial South-East Asia, as in most other parts of the colonial world, education in the language of the colonial power was the key to non-agricultural employment, especially in highly remunerated professional, technical, administrative and clerical occupations. The skewed access to secular, non-vernacular education inevitably resulted in substantial disparities in income between and within ethnic groups, and between urban and rural areas. But other factors were also at work which led to increasing disparities in income both within rural areas, and between rural and urban areas. In rural areas the distribution of land became more skewed especially in regions where large estates were established. In the very densely settled regions of South-East Asia (Java and Bali, the Red River delta in North Vietnam), a growing population could, by the early decades of the twentieth century, no longer be accommodated on the available land, and a landless rural proletariat emerged which depended mainly on wage income to survive. Given the large numbers competing for the available wage labour, wages and total incomes were extremely low, and a significant proportion of the population fell below even a modest poverty line.

In the more land abundant parts of the region, growing rural populations were accommodated through an expansion of the cultivation frontier. But often the land was of poor quality, and basic infrastructure such as irrigation and roads were not provided. In addition, in some frontier areas such as North-East Thailand, new settlers were in effect squatters with no title to land. Thus they could not use their land as collateral to borrow, even where rural credit facilities were available.[3] Those farmers growing export crops such as rice in Thailand, and rubber in Malaysia and Indonesia, were taxed very heavily via graduated export taxes. The burden of taxation on rural incomes earned from export crop cultivation was thus much heavier than on incomes derived from other sources (Booth, 1980). Over time the effect of such discriminatory policies was to widen urban-rural and inter-regional disparities in incomes and living standards.

As a result of these trends, substantial differentials had emerged within indigenous populations in South-East Asia by the 1960s, based on access to land, education and employment. In addition, the last phase of the western colonial era saw the emergence of growing disparities between indigenous populations and immigrant Chinese, especially in Indonesia and Malaya. In most cases these disparities were not greatly reduced in the early post-independence years. Thus most countries in the regions entered a phase of accelerated growth in the 1960s with greater disparities in income and wealth than was the case in either Taiwan or South Korea.

2.3   Trends in educational attainment since the 1960s

It might have been expected that given the poor educational legacy from the colonial era, the newly independent states of South-East Asia would have given high priority to educational expansion after 1950. To a considerable extent, this was the case, but given the low level from which educational expansion was starting in most parts of the region, great efforts and resources were required, and government revenues were not always sufficient. Thus private sector education played an important role in educational expansion, especially at the post-primary levels. In countries such as Indonesia, Malaysia and Thailand, universal primary education became a key government priority and was indeed largely achieved by the early 1980s. But progress in post-primary enrolments was much slower and more erratic. Even in Singapore, which had a higher per capita GDP than either Taiwan or South Korea by 1980, secondary enrolments lagged far behind these two economies (Table 2.1). In Malaysia, Thailand and Indonesia, enrolments were lower still.

In Thailand over the 1980s, the gross secondary enrolment ratio grew slowly but this was mainly due to falling numbers in the relevant age cohorts; numbers enrolled grew only very slowly and indeed at the senior high school level they contracted for much of the decade (Booth, 1997: Table 8). In 1992, when per capita GDP in Thailand was roughly equal to what had been attained in South Korea in 1984, or in Taiwan in 1978, gross enrolment ratios at the secondary level were still only 37 per cent, compared with 76 per cent in Taiwan in 1978 (Booth, 1999: Table 3). In Indonesia growth in secondary enrolments through the 1980s was very rapid, although upper secondary enrolments contracted in the early 1990s. Even so, in 1992, gross secondary enrolment ratios in Indonesia were higher than in Thailand, although still lower than in South Korea

Table 2.1 Educational indicators for fast growing Asian economies, 1980–92

Country[a]	Gross secondary enrolment ratio		Tertiary students per 100,000 people		Government education expenditures as % GDP	
	1980	1992	1980	1992	1980	1992
Singapore	58	68	963	3233[b]	3.1	4.4
Taiwan	80	96	2035	2604	3.6	5.6
South Korea	78	91	1698	4253	3.7	4.2
Malaysia	48	60	419	697	6.0	5.5
Thailand	29	39	1284	2029	3.4	4.0
Indonesia	29	43	367	1045	1.7	2.2
China	46	54	116	192	2.5	2.0
Vietnam	42	32	214	149	n.a	2.1

Notes:
[a] Ranked in order of per capita GDP, 1992.
[b] Data refer to 1991.
Sources: UNESCO, *World Education Report*, 1995, Tables 6, 8, 10; with additional data on Taiwan from the *Taiwan Statistical Yearbook*, 1995, Tables 47, 53 and *Taiwan Statistical; Data Book*, various issues.

and Thailand in 1980. Even in Malaysia, where government spending on education had risen to over 5 per cent of GDP in 1992, the gross secondary enrolment ratio was only 60 per cent, compared with 80 per cent in Taiwan in 1980 (Table 2.1).

It is clear from the available evidence that educational progress in the fast growing countries of South-East Asia has been much slower than in Taiwan and Korea. Singapore, Malaysia, Thailand and Indonesia all had lower levels of educational attainment than Taiwan or South Korea in the 1960s; and in spite of considerable expansion in enrolments at the primary and secondary levels, the gap had not closed in 1992, especially in Thailand and Indonesia. Indeed in both countries there were signs of falling educational enrolments at the secondary level in the 1980s, and early 1990s. The effects of this are clear when we look at the educational attainment of the labour force in Indonesia and Thailand in comparison with South Korea when levels of per capita GDP in the three countries were roughly similar (Booth, 1999: Table 2). Already by 1974, only 13.6 per cent of the male Korean labour force, and 29.6 per cent of the female labour force had five years of schooling or less. In Thailand in 1981 the corresponding figure was 83.3 per cent for males and 89.5 per cent for females.

Given that in most parts of South-East Asia enrolments in the higher levels of education increase sharply in the upper income groups, and given the evidence of a tight link between level of education and lifetime earnings, there can be little doubt that restricted access to higher education is a powerful reason for the transmission of relative deprivation across generations. Khoman (1993: 330) has argued for Thailand that 'this inter-generational perpetuation of inequality is likely to accelerate in future as production technology becomes increasingly more complex and employment shifts increasingly out of agriculture and into industry'. Certainly the successful implementation of the nine-year cycle in both Thailand and Indonesia could potentially be a vehicle for greater equality, especially if at the same time a generous scholarship programme is available to permit bright children from less affluent homes to progress to upper secondary and tertiary levels. But that will involve a sharp increase in government educational expenditures relative to GDP, especially in Indonesia.

Furthermore, the problem for Thailand and Indonesia, as for other countries which have only just committed themselves to the goal of universal nine-year education, is that many young people who left school with at most completed primary education will be in the labour force for years, or indeed decades, to come. They will find it increasingly difficult to compete in a labour market which will demand more skilled workers in order to permit the Thai industrial sector to move into export markets for more sophisticated manufactured goods and services. The Thai predicament can be contrasted with countries such as Taiwan and South Korea, where:

> educational expansion took place ahead of demand, delivering new cohorts of appropriately skilled workers for each phase of industrialisation. This allowed rising average wages to be underwritten by growing productivity, and moderate or declining wage differentials (Ahuja *et al.*, 1997: 53).

But providing education ahead of demand also has its problems as the Philippine case illustrates. Indeed the Philippines emerged into independence with probably the most favourable educational legacy of any of the former colonies in South-East Asia. This advantage was squandered by decades of macroeconomic mismanagement which meant that, by the mid-1990s, per capita GDP (in ICP dollars) was lower than in Indonesia, where the Dutch colonial legacy in the educational sector had been far more meagre. The Indonesian government has made considerable progress in increasing access to education at all levels in the five decades since independence, but government educational expenditures as a proportion of GDP remains low in comparison to most other Asian countries (Table 2.1). In Indonesia, critics of current educational policies argue that low expenditure per student leads to poor quality education, which in turn will affect the quality of the labour force for decades to come.

2.4   Trends in rural development since the 1960s

Following a classic paper of Myint (1967), it is often argued that the economies of South-East Asia can be divided into the 'inward-looking' and the 'outward-looking', depending on the trade and exchange rate policies they have adopted, and their stance towards foreign investment, and foreign aid and borrowing. In some respects this is a useful distinction, but as far as agricultural policies are concerned it is probably more helpful to distinguish between those governments which have treated the agricultural sector mainly as a source of tax revenues, and those governments which have viewed it as an engine of growth, to be supported through subsidies and other policy interventions. But even this distinction frequently breaks down as most governments in South-East Asia, in both colonial times and more recently, have adopted very different policies to different parts of the agricultural sector. Important export crops have been taxed through export taxes, which almost always depressed the prices received by local producers, while at the same time other producers (or even the same producers) have been assisted through provision of infrastructure at low or zero prices, subsidised inputs and subsidised credit. Indeed it has been said with some justification that no country in South-East Asia has pursued an integrated rural development policy. Rather, they have adopted an uncoordinated bundle of crop-specific policies, which have themselves often varied considerably over time.

The outcome of this very mixed approach towards agricultural and rural development since the mid-1970s is shown in Table 2.2. In per capita terms, agricultural output grew at close to, or over, 2 per cent per annum in most parts of South-East Asia from 1974 to 1984. In Malaysia agricultural output growth in per capita terms accelerated over the decade from 1985 to 1996, but in the Philippines the poor growth performance of the earlier decade continued. Elsewhere in South-East Asia there has been a trend towards slower growth in agricultural output per capita although only in Laos has growth actually been negative. The reasons for the trends shown in Table 2.2 vary considerably by country. In Thailand, where a high proportion of agricultural output growth in the past has been due to the expansion of cultivated area, rather than to yields growth, the slowdown of growth since the mid-1980s is in part attributable to the fact that there is now little land left with arable potential that is not already under some form of cultivation. Furthermore the Thai government, by the early 1990s, had become alarmed at the rate of deforestation and is now trying to reforest land which was earlier cleared for grazing or cultivation.

Table 2.2   South-East Asia: annual average growth of per capita agricultural output, 1974–84 and 1985–96

Country	Average annual growth rate of per capita agricultural output		Paddy yields tons/ha.
	1974–84	1985–96	(average 1994–96)
Indonesia	2.2	1.6	4.4
Laos	4.2	–0.5	2.6
Malaysia	1.0	1.3	3.1
Myanmar	2.8	0.7	3.2
Philippines	0.7	0.6	2.8
Thailand	1.8	0.7	2.4
Vietnam	2.8	2.4	3.6

Sources: FAO *Production Yearbooks*, 1985 (Vol. 39), 1996 (Vol. 50), Table 10.

Many Thai agricultural economists have urged that the government respond to these challenges by adopting policies designed to increase yields, especially for crops such as rice. In spite of some reforms through the 1980s which were intended to increase farm-gate prices and thus the profitability of using fertiliser and new varieties of seed, rice yields in Thailand remain well below most other parts of the region.

Most other countries in South-East Asia have been more successful in disseminating new yield-increasing technologies in smallholder agriculture, especially in the foodcrop sector, although Malaysia in particular has also had considerable success in increasing yields for smallholder treecrops such as rubber. Those countries which adopted the new rice varieties earliest (especially the Philippines) did experience rapid output growth but this slowed down once most farmers in well-irrigated areas were operating near the technology frontier. Further yields growth would have required investment in irrigation and through the 1980s successive governments were unable to make such investments. In Indonesia the rapid adoption of new rice and corn varieties led to rapid growth of output but again output growth slowed once farmers operating in the more favourable biophysical environments had achieved maximum yields. In Vietnam where dissemination of new rice varieties only occurred in the 1980s, and where government reforms after 1986 gave much greater production responsibility to individual households, output growth per capita has been sustained at a high rate until 1996.

While there is broad agreement about the main causes of agricultural output growth in South-East Asia since the 1970s, there has been far more debate about the consequences of that growth for income distribution and poverty decline in rural areas. Has agricultural growth led to growing disparities in income and wealth within rural areas? Or has the sluggish performance in the agricultural sector since the mid-1980s in rapidly industrialising countries such as Indonesia, Malaysia and Thailand led to greater polarisation between urban and rural areas? To what extent has rapid growth in the non-agricultural sectors created more off-farm employment opportunities, especially for the poorer groups in rural areas, as happened in Taiwan? And what have been the consequences for the proportion of the rural populations living below the poverty line? In fact, as will be made clear below, the evidence indicates that the answers to these questions in South-East Asia varies considerably by country and by region. But before looking at this evidence in detail, it will be useful to examine the consequences of the different rural development strategies pursued in different parts of South-East Asia for income disparities between urban and rural areas.

2.5 Trends in urban–rural disparities

Urban–rural disparities in household income and expenditures in most parts of South-East Asia were, by the early 1980s, substantial and in several countries appear to have been increasing over time. In Indonesia, urban–rural disparities in personal consumption expenditures increased through the 1970s but have stayed stable over the 1980s. But the disparity between the national capital district and the rest of the country has grown over the 1980s (Booth, 1998: Table 3). In other words, while consumption expenditures in all urban areas have not grown faster than in rural areas over the 1980s, those in Jakarta have grown relative to other urban areas. In most parts of South-East Asia for which data are available there has been an increase in the disparity between GDP per capita in the capital city and in the country as a whole (Table 2.3). In Thailand and Indonesia in the mid-1990s per capita GDP in Bangkok and Jakarta was over three times as high as the national average, while in Indonesia and the Philippines per capita consumption expenditures were over twice as high in the capital as for the country as a whole. In Vietnam the disparity in

Table 2.3 Ratio of per capita GDP and personal consumption expenditures (PCE) in capital city to national average

	GDP	PCE
Philippines		
1984	2.70	1.80
1994	2.49	2.05
Indonesia		
1984	2.29	2.07
1994	3.70	2.34 (1993)
Thailand		
1984	2.90	1.70 (1981)
1994	3.41 (1993)	1.74
Malaysia		
1987	1.74 (1988)	1.67[a]
Vietnam		
1993	n.a.	1.37 (2.60)[b]

Notes:
[a] Peninsular Malaysia only.
[b] Figure in brackets shows the ratio of personal consumption expenditure in Ho Chi Minh City (Saigon) to the national average.
Sources: National income accounts and household survey from the countries shown, as reported in Statistical Yearbooks, and national planning documents.

consumption expenditures between Hanoi and the national average was only 37 per cent but it was much higher for Ho Chi Minh City (Saigon).

There are several reasons for the wide (and often increasing) gap between capital cities and the national average, both in GDP and in per capita consumption expenditures, in South-East Asia. Capital cities are of course the seat of government and the great majority of politicians and senior civil servants are located there.[4] In addition most large companies, whether domestic, multinational or joint ventures, have their national head offices in the capital city, and thus a high proportion of senior managers are to be found there. Capital cities usually have a large number of high schools, universities, hospitals and research institutes and laboratories, and thus attract a disproportionate number of highly skilled professionals. In South-East Asia most capital cities are either ports or located close to ports, and have better transport infrastructure, and so attract a disproportionate number of manufacturing industries. The extreme example is the Bangkok Metropolitan Region which in the late 1980s accounted for 78 per cent of all manufacturing value added in Thailand. This concentration of the fastest growing sector of the economy in one region inevitably led to a faster growth of GDP, and of personal incomes in the Bangkok region. In 1988 Tinakorn (1995: Table 10.5) estimated that the Bangkok region accounted for less than 15 per cent of the total population, but 32 per cent of total household income.

A further aspect of urban–rural inequality in South-East Asia concerns the ratio of agricultural productivity (output per worker) to non-agricultural productivity, or the share of agricultural value added in GDP divided by the ratio of the agricultural labour force to the total labour force (Table 2.4). There are very considerable variations in this ratio across South-East Asia, and also in the extent to which it has changed over time, which reflect differences in both the agricultural share of GDP, and the agricultural share of the labour force. With the exception of Myanmar (Burma), every country in the region has experienced a decline in both these shares since the early 1970s. But the rates of decline in the output and labour force shares have been far from uniform so that by 1994 Thailand still had 56 per cent of the labour force in agriculture, but only 11.5 per cent of GDP accrued from agriculture so that productivity per worker in agriculture was only 21 per cent of output per worker in the economy as a whole.

In Malaysia the decline in the agricultural share of GDP between 1970 and 1990 was accompanied by a larger decline in the agricultural share of the labour force, so that output per worker in agriculture in 1990 was 72 per cent of the national average.

Table 2.4   Ratio of agricultural output per agricultural worker to average output per worker in South-East Asian economies

	Agricultural productivity ratio	Percentage of GDP agriculture	Percentage of the labour force in agriculture
Philippines			
1971	0.59	29.6	50.4
1994	0.49	22.4	46.1
Burma			
1976/77	0.73	47.5	65.3
1993/94	0.97	63.2	65.2
Vietnam			
1994	0.40	28.7	72.2
Malaysia			
1970	0.60	31.4	52.6
1990	0.72	18.6	26.0
Indonesia			
1971	0.67	43.6	64.8
1994	0.37	17.3	46.1
Thailand			
1971	0.36	28.6	79.2
1994	0.21	11.5	56.0

Source: National accounts data, as published in Statistical Yearbooks and Labour Force Surveys.

Given that output per agricultural worker in Thailand is such a small proportion of average output per worker in the economy as a whole, it is hardly surprising that rural–urban income disparities are high, and that overall household income inequalities have been growing. Of course it can be argued that many agricultural households in Thailand, and in other parts of South-East Asia, are deriving a substantial part of their incomes from non-agricultural sources and from remittances from family members working in cities, and this mitigates the impact of low agricultural incomes. This argument is examined further in the next section. It can also be argued, with some plausibility, that the agricultural labour force in Thailand is overstated relative to other countries in the region, not least because of the very high numbers of women reported as working in agriculture as unpaid family workers. But even allowing for these factors, there can be little doubt that economic growth in Thailand over the past four decades has exhibited a high degree of urban bias, although by the 1980s rural pressure groups had become more vociferous in defending rural populations against increasing urban encroachment (Pasuk and Baker, 1995: 84–6).

2.6 Changing employment patterns, income diversification, and urban–rural linkages

An important channel through which developments in other parts of the economy impact on the agricultural sector is through the provision of off-farm employment opportunities in rural areas, a topic which has generated a considerable literature in South-East Asia in recent years (see in particular the papers in Shand, 1986). In their study of linkages between the agricultural and non-agricultural sectors in the Philippines, Ranis, *et al.* (1990: 76–7) stressed that increased agricultural output increases rural non-agricultural employment and increasing modern non-agricultural activity leads to a rise in agericultural productivity. In a subsequent paper, Ranis and Stewart (1993) contrast the development of both types of linkages in Taiwan and the Philippines. They point out that the growth of rural non-agricultural employment was much faster in Taiwan than in the Philippines, and by 1980, 67 per cent of the rural labour force in Taiwan was employed in non-agricultural activities. The comparable figure for the Philippines in 1985 was 33 per cent. They argue that the more egalitarian distribution of rural income in Taiwan compared to the Philippines meant that a smaller proportion of total rural expenditures went on imported goods or luxury goods made in urban areas. The rapid expansion of Taiwanese manufactured exports also served to boost rural incomes, in that a significant proportion were processed agricultural products and even those produced in export processing zones and bonded warehouses used locally produced inputs supplied often from small industries located in rural areas.

Thus 'Taiwan's macro and sectoral policies were favourable to strong rural linkages, with good agricultural growth, a relatively egalitarian land and rural distribution of income, the generous provision of rural infrastructure, as well as an export orientation which was substantially rural-based' (Ranis and Stewart, 1993: 98). As a result, over the years from 1962 to 1980, rural non-agricultural incomes in Taiwan grew over three times as fast as agricultural incomes.[5] In the Philippines in the two decades from 1965 to 1985, agricultural incomes grew almost as fast on an annualised basis, as in Taiwan but the growth of non-agricultural rural incomes was very much slower. Thus what Ranis and Stewart term the 'linkage ratio' was much lower in the Philippines. The more skewed distribution of income in the Philippines, combined with the more capital-intensive, urban-biased nature of the industrialisation process, meant that a given amount of agricultural growth created fewer non-agricultural employment opportunities in rural areas.

There is evidence that what Ranis and Stewart found for the Philippines also applies in other parts of South-East Asia, even in those countries such as Thailand and Indonesia where overall growth rates have been more rapid over the past two decades. The data on growth of agricultural household income in Thailand cited by Onchan (1990: Table 2.13) show that income from non-agricultural sources grew about 66 per cent faster than income from agricultural sources over the 1970s (Table 2.5). In Indonesia, evidence from the 1983 and 1993 Agricultural Censuses indicates that the growth of off-farm income of agricultural households was only about 22 per cent faster than the growth in income from the agricultural holdings. A comparison of Indonesia and Thailand over these different time periods is justified because real per capita GDP (in 1985 dollars corrected for purchasing power difference) increased by a similar rate. In Taiwan, during the years 1962–72, the linkage ratio was considerably higher. As in the Philippines, it is probable that the skewed distribution of land and the pronounced urban bias of the industrialisation process in both countries explain the lower linkage ratio. In both Indonesia and Thailand, data from Agricultural Censuses show that a much lower proportion of land is in small holdings, and a higher proportion of agricultural land is in holdings over five hectares compared with Taiwan (Table 2.6).

The growth of non-agricultural employment in rural areas in both Indonesia and Thailand also appears to be following the Philippine rather

Table 2.5 Linkage ratios and the percentage of total farm income accruing from off-farm employment

Country/Years	Linkage ratio[a]	Per capita GDP (initial year)	Percentage of farm income from off-farm sources	
			Initial year	Final year
Taiwan (1962–80)	3.55	1364	25	60
Philippines (1965–85)	0.94	1248	45	56
Taiwan (1962–72)	2.28	1364	40	60
Thailand (1971/2–1982/83)	1.66	1507	46	59
Indonesia (1983–93)	1.22	1561	45	50

Notes:
[a] Growth in off-farm incomes over the period shown divided by growth in farm incomes.
Source: Taiwan (1962–80) and the Philippines: Ranis and Stewart (1993: Tables 9 and 14). Taiwan (1962–72): Ho (1986: Table 4.2). Thailand: Onchan (1990: Table 2.13); Indonesia: Central Bureau of Statistics (1987, 1995).

Table 2.6 Distribution of land by holding size: Philippines, Indonesia, Thailand and Taiwan

Holding size (hectares)	Philippines 1971	1980	Indonesia 1973	1983	Thailand 1978	Taiwan 1960	1975
Under 1.0	1.9	3.8	25.0	22.7	2.3	33.4	39.0
1–3	22.2	25.9	32.6	35.3	19.3	51.5	48.0
3–5	23.7	21.2	11.1	12.9	17.8	10.5	9.2
5–10[a]	18.3	23.1	8.8	9.8	36.3	4.6	3.8
Over 10	33.9	26.0	22.5	19.3	24.3		
Total	100.0	100.0	100.0	100.0	100.0	100.0	100.0

Notes:
[a] Data for Taiwan include land in all holdings over five hectares.
Source: Ranis and Stewart (1993: Table 10); Censuses of Agriculture for Thailand, Indonesia and the Philippines.

than the Taiwanese pattern. In Indonesia, the growth of the manufacturing labour force has been rapid since 1971 (although from a small base), but much of the growth has occurred in urban areas (Table 2.7). In Thailand (perhaps surprisingly, given the fact that such a high proportion of manufacturing value added accrues from the Bangkok region) the

Table 2.7 Annual growth of manufacturing employment, and the percentage of the rural labour force in agriculture

Country/Years	Annual growth of manufacturing employment		Percentage of rural labour force in agriculture	
	Rural	Urban		
Taiwan				
1956–66	5.0	4.9	1956	70
1966–80	10.3	9.4	1980	33
Philippines				
1967–75	0.6	1.4	1967	75
1975–88	2.0	4.8	1988	67
Indonesia				
1971–80	5.9	9.7	1971	75
1980–95	3.2	8.8	1995	61
Thailand				
1980–95	6.4	5.7	1980	82
			1995	64

Source: Ranis and Stewart (1993: Tables 5 and 8); Indonesia: Population Census of Indonesia, 1971 (Series D), 1980 (Series S2); Inter-censal Population Survey 1995, Series S2. Thailand: Report of the Labour Force Survey, July–September 1980, 1995.

growth of the manufacturing labour force has been slightly faster in rural areas than in urban areas between 1980 and 1995. But in both urban and rural areas the growth was markedly slower than in Taiwan between 1956 and 1980. The steep decline in the proportion of the rural labour force employed in agriculture in Taiwan over these years has not occurred in more recent decades in either Thailand or Indonesia. In spite of the fact that per capita GDP (in constant ICP dollars) in Taiwan in 1980 was about the same as in Thailand in 1995, the proportion of the rural labour force in agriculture was almost twice as high in Thailand (Table 2.7).

Another way of viewing different employment outcomes in South-East Asia compared with not only Taiwan but also Japan and South Korea is to look at the share of the non-agricultural labour force employed in services, rather than in industry. It has long been accepted that for any given agricultural share of the labour force, the service share of the non-agricultural labour force (SSNALF) has tended to be higher in modern industrialising economies compared with the historical experience of Japan, Western Europe and the USA. This is frequently attributed to the fact that manufacturing industry is inherently more capital-intensive in modern times than was the case in the nineteenth century; another reason given is that public services including education absorb a larger share of the labour force in many contemporary developing countries than was the case in Europe or the USA a century ago (Berry, 1978). While this may well be true, there is a striking difference in the SSNALF between the Philippines, Malaysia, Thailand and Indonesia on the one hand, and Taiwan, South Korea and Japan on the other in the post-1950 era. If we compare Thailand in 1978 with Taiwan in 1969, when per capita GDP was roughly similar, not only was the proportion of the labour force in agriculture much higher, but the SSNALF was considerably lower (Table 2.8).

The significance of the higher SSNALF in South-East Asia is that service occupations tend to be very diverse with a much greater variation in remuneration compared with industrial jobs. To the extent that people in Thailand or the Philippines are leaving agriculture for relatively poorly remunerated work in services, the overall distribution of earnings and income is likely to be more skewed than in Taiwan, where the falling employment share of agriculture was reflected to a greater extent in increased employment in industry. The greater capacity of the Taiwanese and South Korean industrial sectors to absorb labour is often claimed to be due to their high degree of export orientation, but in Thailand and Malaysia exports as a ratio of GDP were almost as high, or higher, than in South Korea and Taiwan by the early 1990s. Before returning to this puzzle in the final section of the

Table 2.8 Composition of the employed labour force in East and South-East Asia (per capita GDP of approximately ICP$2040, 1985 prices)

Country/Year	Percentage of employed labour force in agriculture	Percentage of non-agricultural employed labour force in services
Philippines (1995)	43.6	71.9
Indonesia (1992)	53.7	68.2
Thailand (1978)	66.5	64.3
Malaysia (1970)	53.5	68.7
South Korea (1978)	50.0	60.6
Taiwan (1969)	39.0	56.7
Japan (1955)	42.9	59.8

Sources: Philippines: *Philippines Statistical Yearbook* (Manila: National Statistical Coordination Board, 1996: Table 11.3); Indonesia: *Labour Force Situation in Indonesia* (Jakarta: Central Bureau of Statistics, 1992); Thailand: *Report of the Labour Force Survey*, (Bangkok: National Statistical Office, July–September, 1978); Malaysia: *Third Malaysia Plan* (Kuala Lumpur: Government Printing Office), 1976–80: Table 8.1): South Korea: *Korea Statistical Yearbook* (Seoul: Bureau of Statistics, 1976: 70); Taiwan: *Taiwan Statistical Data Book* (Taipei: Bureau of Statistics, 1972: Table 2.9b); Japan: *Japan Statistical Yearbook* (Tokyo: Bureau of Statistics, 1958: 44–5).

paper, it will be useful to examine in more detail the data on income distribution in various parts of Asia.

2.7 Distributional outcomes of the development process in Asia

I have already emphasised that an important part of the colonial legacy in South-East Asia was the substantial income disparities between urban and rural areas, between regions and between ethnic groups, which persisted in the immediate post-independence era. Most countries in the region embarked on a process of accelerated growth after 1960 with greater income differentials than in South Korea or Taiwan. Although international comparisons of inequality indicators are fraught with difficulties, the available data on the distribution of household income/expenditure show a less skewed distribution, with a lower proportion of total income accruing to the top decile in South Korea and Taiwan than in most parts of South-East Asia (Table 2.9). In Malaysia and Thailand in 1989 and 1992 respectively, the ratio of the percentage share of the top decile to the bottom two deciles was very much higher than in Taiwan in 1972, or South Korea in 1976.

Greater inter-personal disparities are only one facet of the differences in the distribution of income between South Korea and Taiwan on the one

Table 2.9   Distribution of income in East and South-East Asia by decile group and country

Country	Year	Per capita GDP ($)[a]	Percentage share of: Top decile	Bottom 20%	Ratio of top 10% to bottom 20%
Singapore	1982–3	8565	33.5	5.1	6.6
Japan	1969	6995	27.2	7.9	3.4
South Korea	1976	2584	27.5	5.7	4.8
Malaysia	1973	2504	39.8	3.5	11.4
	1989	4571	37.9	4.6	8.2
Thailand	1975–6	1813	34.1	5.6	6.1
	1992	3931	37.1	5.6	6.6
Taiwan	1964	1574	26.7	7.7	3.5
	1972	2698	22.7	8.9	2.6
Philippines	1970–1	1433	38.5	5.2	7.4
	1988	1699	32.1	6.5	4.9
Indonesia	1976	902	34.0	6.6	5.2
	1993	2142	25.6	8.7	2.9

Notes:
[a] Per capita GDP in 1985 international dollars adjusted for changes in the terms of trade.
Source: GDP data: Penn World Tables version 5.6 as published on the Internet; Income Distribution data: World Bank (1983: 200–1); World Bank (1997b: 222–3); Taiwan: Ho (1978: 141).

hand and South-East Asia on the other. We must also examine spatial inequalities and interracial inequalities. In Indonesia, interprovincial inequalities in GDP have been high since the late 1960s, largely because of the concentration of mining and manufacturing activities in a few locations. Although the decline in GDP in several oil-producing areas as a result of production cutbacks has led to some diminution in regional inequalities, the disparities in per capita GDP by province remained quite high in the early 1990s (Akita and Lukman, 1995: Table 2). Urban–rural differentials in per capita consumption expenditures have widened since 1980, and disparities in consumption expenditures within urban areas have also widened (Booth, 1992: 329–34).

In Thailand, where urban–rural and spatial income differentials have always been high, there is little evidence of any narrowing of the gap during the era of rapid growth after 1980 (Tinakorn, 1995: Table 10.7). In 1992, the share of total household income accuring to the poorest two deciles was 5.6 per cent, no higher than in the mid-1970s (Table 2.9). Similarly in Malaysia, rapid growth has been accompanied by only a modest narrowing of income disparities since the mid-1980s (Table 2.9).

In Singapore, a recent analysis of personal income data indicates that the Gini coefficient of taxpayer incomes has been increasing slowly since the mid-1960s and by 1992 was 0.48, indicating a fairly skewed overall distribution (Rao, 1996: 387). In 1982–3 the distribution of household income was far more skewed than in Japan in 1969, when per capita GDP was roughly similar (Table 2.9).

What are the consequences of these greater disparities? Studies using cross-sectional data from a large number of developing countries have reached the conclusion that 'inequality in income and land distribution is negatively associated with subsequent growth' (Alesina and Rodrik, *et al.* 1994: 485; see also Birdsall, 1995: 495). Clearly such a finding would have to be treated with great caution in the South-East Asian context where Thailand and Malaysia, starting from a fairly skewed distribution of income in the 1970s, have achieved rapid growth over the past two decades. But large income disparities can have destabilising effects. In both Malaysia and Indonesia, there are very considerable regional disparities in poverty, and some resource-rich regions such as Sabah in East Malaysia, and Irian Jaya in Eastern Indonesia have high incidences of poverty relative to the national average. This is partly due to the system of resource taxation which drains a large part of the profits from exploitation of minerals and timber off to the centre (Booth, 1996: 199–202). In the longer run such a system is bound to fuel regional tensions, and even lead to separatist movements.

2.8   Conclusions

This chapter has argued that it is unhelpful to think in terms of a single 'East Asian' development model; there are important differences in development strategies and outcomes between South Korea and Taiwan on the one hand and the four high-performing South-East Asian economies on the other. Although Perkins's categorisation into three distinct types has some value, even here one has to take some care in distinguishing different policies and outcomes. Among the three high-performing and 'resource-rich' countries, there have been significant differences in, for example, government expenditures on education and growth in post-primary enrolments. And although income distribution is more skewed in most parts of South-East Asia than in Taiwan, or indeed South Korea, there are significant differences between Indonesia and Thailand, especially in rural areas.

It can, of course, be argued that in spite of the obvious differences in their growth strategies compared with Japan, Taiwan and South Korea, the four 'high-performing' economies in South-East Asia have been over the past three decades exactly that, out-performing many economies in other parts of the developing world whose initial endowments of both natural and human resources were certainly no worse than theirs. They must therefore have been doing at least some things right. This is certainly true; all four economies managed to control budget deficits, keep inflation under control, and provide the right incentives to encourage rapid growth of manufactured exports. But at the same time the cumulative effect of the trends discussed in this paper have been serious, and in part at least contributed to the sharp falls in real GDP which occurred in 1998/99. For example, a severe shortage of educated labour in Thailand had emerged by the early 1990s; as wages for semi-skilled and skilled workers increased, Thailand became a less attractive location for many labour-intensive industries, while at the same time shortages of skills made it very difficult for Thai industrialists to move into medium-technology industries, as Taiwan and South Korea managed to do in the 1970s and 1980s. Indonesia also was by the early 1990s suffering from skill shortages in particular disciplines, while at the same time employers were complaining of the poor quality of many graduates from high schools, vocational colleges and tertiary institutions.

Improvements in access to education, although important, will not by themselves be sufficient to return Thailand, Malaysia and Indonesia to the kind of growth rates which they were able to sustain from the 1960s to 1996. There will also have to be major changes in regulatory regimes, especially regarding the financial sector, and in the relationship between policymakers and those implementing policies, in both central and local government. To discuss the nature and feasibility of these changes would take us beyond the scope of this paper, but it is worth pointing out that many other countries in other parts of the world have experienced prolonged growth cycles followed by periods of stagnation or even decline. Like most other things in life, sustained economic growth cannot be taken for granted; there is no magic shortcut to achieving it, and even when it has been achieved there is no guarantee that it will last forever.

Notes

1. As well as the countries whose experience formed the basis of the World Bank report East Asia includes China, North Korea, Vietnam, Brunei and the Philippines, Burma, Laos and Cambodia.
2. A detailed discussion of Japanese educational policy is given in Tsurumi (1977); Tsurumi (1984) contrasts policies in Taiwan with those in Korea. See also Woo (1991).

3. Tongroj (1990) discuss the problems of land rights and land titles in Thailand.
4. It is not true that the majority of civil servants are located in the capital city; in Indonesia only 9.4 per cent of the estimated 4 million permanent civil servants are located in Jakarta. But a much higher proportion of the senior ones are in the capital while many of those in the regions are relatively poorly paid teachers, health workers and so on.
5. Fei *et al.* (1979: 315) argue that non-agricultural income was more evenly distributed than agricultural income in Taiwan, and thus the growth in farm household income from rural industries and services made a considerable contribution to the decline in inequality in farm household income that occurred over the 1960s.

3
Lessons for Africa from East Asian Economic Policy

Oliver Morrissey

3.1 Introduction

The aim of this essay is in principle a simple one: to identify the reasons underlying the success (from the 1960s to 1997 at least) of the East Asian economies and derive any lessons for economic policy in sub-Saharan African (SSA) economies. The 1997–98 crisis notwithstanding, for some thirty years many East Asian economies enjoyed unprecedented economic growth rates. An understanding of the reasons for this can help inform economic policy recommendations for other developing countries. Furthermore, the reasons underlying the crisis also offer lessons, in particular regarding exchange rate and financial sector policies. Economic policy in developing countries can benefit from greater understanding of the successes and failures of the East Asian countries. We do not argue that African countries should emulate or copy the Asian economies. Rather, we ask what can African economies learn (or what can we learn, from the Asian experience, about prospects for African economies)?

Few would contest the dramatic scale of the economic success of the eight high-performing Asian economies (HPAEs) – Hong Kong, Indonesia, Japan, Malaysia, Republic of Korea, Singapore, Taiwan and Thailand. Over 1965–89, real GDP per capita annual growth averaged just over 5 per cent for East Asia, compared to less than 0.5 per cent for sub-Saharan Africa (*World Bank*, 1991: 30). The *East Asian Miracle* Report (World Bank, 1993) offered a number of reasons for such growth, in particular high savings and investment rates; a relatively high degree of equality; high growth rates of human and physical capital; high productivity growth, including agriculture; and high growth rates of manufactured exports. The question is to what extent these features contributed to the success and to what extent they were policy-induced. The latter is an issue of some debate (see Morrissey and Nelson, 1998). Was the success of East Asian economies due to the ways in which governments intervened in the economy, or were they successful in spite of government intervention?

Section 3.2 very briefly reviews the principal factors underlying the economic success of HPAEs drawing on Morrissey and Nelson (1998). Section 3.3 examines the interaction between political characteristics and economic policy, and draws on the political economy framework of Morrissey (1999b). Section 3.4, having contrasted the policies followed by the HPAEs with those proposed under World Bank adjustment programmes, relates the findings on East Asia to the features of SSA countries. Section 3.5 presents my conclusions.

3.2 Economic success in East Asia

Over the period 1965–90 the eight HPAEs grew faster than any reference groups and sustained their performance better than any other group of countries. There is no generally accepted single explanation of why these countries were so successful. However, there is general agreement on the list of features of these economies that contributed to success (Morrissey and Nelson, 1998; World Bank, 1993):

- high rates of savings and investment during a period of low capital flight so that there was rapid physical capital accumulation;
- investment in education and training to support human capital accumulation;
- capital accumulation and adoption of technology contributed to total factor productivity growth;
- careful fiscal and monetary policies to ensure macroeconomic stability;
- relatively open trade policy and high growth rate of manufactured exports;
- dynamic agricultural sector with increasing productivity;
- maintaining a relatively equitable income distribution so that there was some sharing of the benefits of growth;
- political credibility and a skilled bureaucracy.

Some of the HPAEs, such as Korea and Taiwan, tended to exhibit most of these features since at least the 1960s. Other countries lacked certain features – Malaysia was hardly noted for fiscal conservatism, while Indonesia was not exactly strong on redistribution and sharing the gains from growth widely. Nevertheless, strong performance seems to have been based on macroeconomic stability, high savings and investment, combining to promote rapid factor accumulation and productivity growth. There is a debate on the relative importance of accumulation and productivity growth (Rodrik, 1994) and of government intervention (Amsden, 1994; Wade, 1990). It is evident that HPAE governments intervened actively, notably in subsidising specific industries and/or encouraging exports of specific goods. However, the interventions have not been unambiguous successes; some of the subsidised industries have failed and often the cost of subsidies is a burden. The experience of HPAEs would not permit one to advocate public intervention as a general policy rule.

Morrissey and Nelson (1998) reviewed the experiences of six East Asian countries. Korea had the strongest overall performance based on high investment rates, largely financed by domestic savings (at least until the 1990s), and active export promotion to earn the foreign exchange required to finance imports of raw materials and, initially, capital goods. There is evidence that Korean growth was planned, notably with government intervention in promoting savings and exports. Taiwan's dramatic growth performance began in the 1950s, averaged annual growth rates over 5 per cent for some 30 years and GDP was still growing by about 7 per cent per annum in the early 1990s. Government intervention was to promote domestic savings to finance investment for industrialisation that provided the output to form the basis of an aggressive export strategy. Although the level of government spending was relatively high the budget deficit was kept under control. Taiwan promoted its economic independence and strength, with an eye always on mainland China.

Indonesia and Malaysia performed well, but less consistently. Malaysia's endowment of natural resources provided a solid basis for export-led growth: foreign exchange earnings financed capital imports and domestic savings supported investment. The government became an active promoter of investment financed by large budget deficits since the early 1980s, so Malaysia was not an example of fiscal rectitude. Indonesia, despite oil reserves, was less well endowed with natural resources relative to population, and export growth was moderate but sustained. The government was cautious in containing the balance of payments deficit, public investment and domestic savings rates were kept in line with each other and fiscal restraint was evident. The pervasiveness of corruption and non-productive investments was somewhat disguised until the 1990s.

Thailand exhibited relatively unstable growth patterns. Investment levels were consistently higher than could be supported by domestic savings while the trade and budgetary deficits were rarely under control. Consequently, net borrowing from abroad was high. Arguably, it was only after adopting International Monetary Fund (IMF) and World Bank adjustment programmes in the 1980s that Thailand established the macroeconomic stability to form a platform for sustained growth. The Philippines was one of the worst performing East Asian countries, although it was relatively rich with high growth rates in the 1950s. The underlying problem was a failure of government policy, notably stagnation of agriculture and industry and increasing inequality and political corruption.

The one feature common to all the successful economies is that their governments were able to implement effectively policies that encouraged enterprise, especially exporting, and that supported growth. The nature of the policies differed from country to country, but all represented active intervention. An interesting question is, why did some countries select and implement effective policies while others did not?

3.3   Politics and economic policy

Political and institutional factors are important determinants of the effectiveness of economic policy. There are gainers and losers from any economic policy, especially from reforms of economic policy. The ability of affected groups to represent their preferences regarding policy to the government will have an impact on the political commitment and ability to implement the policy. Commitment will be related to the ability of the government to convert preferences into policy proposals. Especially important is the government's ability to mobilise support for policy reform and to withstand, circumvent or compensate the opposition. Commitment itself is not enough: the policies must be implemented, which requires institutional and administrative capacity. A number of political features of the HPAEs can be identified as having contributed to their ability to implement effective economic policies:

- capacity to make and design economic policy; the presence of a technocracy (World Bank, 1993; Morrissey, 1999a);
- ability to withstand opposition, especially violent reactions (Frey and Eichenberger, 1994; Haggard *et al.*, 1995);
- establishing political support for policies (Frey and Eichenberger, 1994);
- regime not captured by specific sectoral interests (Olson, 1990);

- associate benefit to state with performance of the economy; principle of shared growth (Morrissey, 1999a; World Bank, 1993);
- implementation capacity (Morrissey, 1999b).

Successful regimes tend to exhibit authoritarian tendencies, at least during periods of intense (and contested) reforms. This allows them to resist opposition to their policies, although we can observe that force is more likely to be used against labour than business opposition (Korea and Indonesia are examples). This is not to suggest that authoritarian regimes will perform better than democracies in implementing successful economic policies. Rather, regimes wishing to implement specific policies in the face of strong opposition will find it easier to do so if they are able to act in an authoritarian manner. The ability to implement effective policies does not imply that the policies will be growth-promoting. In fact, the evidence from many authoritarian African regimes is that the policies implemented are those of kleptomaniacs and severely damaging to the economy and polity (the same can be said of the Philippines and, ultimately, Indonesia). The question is, what encourages regimes to choose policies that are conducive to growth? An important feature seems to be that the government associates state success (and a benefit to the government in terms of maintaining power) with the performance of the economy.

The East Asian economies considered in Morrissey and Nelson (1998) all exhibited some form of 'sharing the benefits' of growth, albeit in different ways and with different degrees of commitment. South Korea, Malaysia and Thailand had policies promoting relative equity in distribution, including rural sectors, often with an element of positive discrimination. All had implemented some degree of land reform and reduced biases against agriculture at an early stage. There is little evidence that Indonesia favoured equity; benefits were reserved for a small group (hence recent political and economic instability). The Philippines was also a case of sharing with a small group, as Marcos exhibited strong favouritism which gave rise to a greedy elite (Dohner and Haggard, 1994). There was little equity, a short political time horizon (as the regime may have lacked confidence in its ability to hold power as the 1980s progressed) and negligible growth.

A number of political considerations will influence governments in determining which policies to adopt (Morrissey, 1999b). Foremost of these, a government has to want to implement the policies in question. It may reach this decision because it believes that what is best for the economy is also best for the regime. Regimes tend to 'reward themselves' by extracting rents from the economy. The greater the rate of rent extraction, the greater the disincentives in the economic structure and the slower the growth rate of the economy (*ceteris paribus*). A regime with a short time horizon, anticipating it will lose power, tends to extract the maximum rents with an adverse effect on economic performance. So-called 'kleptocracies' do the same but over a longer period of time. Many African regimes fall into one of these categories (the dividing line is blurred), Zaire and Zambia are examples. On the other hand, regimes with a long time horizon may perceive the gain of extracting a relatively low rent (as a share of GDP) from a growing economy for a long period. This may reasonably apply to Korea, Malaysia and Taiwan. Since the late 1980s, this could apply to Ghana and Uganda. This does not guarantee economic growth, as it may also reasonably apply to Tanzania under Nyerere (such policies are conducive to stability).

The type of economic policies implemented, and the impact on growth, will also depend on whether the regime is essentially ideological, interest-based or technocratic. Ideological regimes will have priorities other than economic growth; Nyerere's, for example, was social equity. Mengistu's Ethiopia would also fall under this category. Some governments tend to represent specific interests, be they political (such as particular tribes or 'family') or economic (such as landowners); Marcos's Philippines and Suharto's Indonesia are East Asian examples, Moi's Kenya an African example. Such regimes will resist policies that weaken their vested interests or lose them rents, hence tend to promote a corrupt and inefficient economy. Other regimes are technocratic in nature, that is while vested interests exist they are at least balanced by a desire to maximise the performance of the economy, and the latter is guided by technical arguments (emphasising management and economic efficiency). Economies such as South Korea and Thailand seem to fit into this group. This highlights the importance of building institutional capacity as few African regimes could be called technocratic; although, in the 1990s, perhaps Ghana, South Africa and Uganda aspire to be (and thus require support for their administrative and technical policy-making and implementation capacity).

3.4 Deriving policy lessons

Before considering lessons that can be applied to SSA economies, it may be useful to consider briefly how SSA economies performed over the past few decades. There are wide differences in the performance of countries within SSA. Botswana, Gabon and Mauritius have all been successful, comparable to HPAEs. These are exceptions; Botswana has diamonds, Gabon has oil and Mauritius, while benefiting from the Sugar Protocol, was able to attract investment in textiles (benefiting from the Multi-fibre Agreement (MFA)). Many other countries have been ravaged by war for long periods – Uganda, Liberia, Angola and Mozambique, for example. Nevertheless, it is common to treat SSA as a region as the majority of countries have, over the long run, had an economic performance similar to the continental average. Thus, in Table 3.1 we present some data on average SSA performance since 1975; being large and atypical countries, we exclude South Africa and Nigeria from the averages.

The overall performance has been weak, especially in comparison to that of the HPAEs. As broad indicators, average annual GDP growth rates for SSA were 1.7 per cent over 1980–90 and 2.1 per cent over 1990–97, compared to figures of 7.8 per cent and 9.9 per cent respectively for East Asia (*World Bank*, 1999: 211). While much of the SSA growth was in agriculture, most East Asian growth was in industry; East Asia exhibited a far greater performance in terms of export and investment growth. In SSA, real GDP growth has seen a general decline from about 3 per cent in the late 1970s to about one per cent in the late 1980s, recovering only slightly in the 1990s. Public investment has remained fairly stable and low, at around 6 per cent of GDP (well below what would be required for

Table 3.1   Indicators of performance: SSA averages

	dGDP	I/GDP	S/GDP	T/GDP	G/GDP	X	M
Periods							
1975–84	2.9		12.4			5.7	6.2
1985–89	2.6	6.2	9.6	18.3	26.6	4.3	6.8
1990–94	1.1	5.9	7.7	18.3	26.3	–0.2	1.7
Years						X/GDP	M/GDP
1980	1.5		10.6			23.0	23.7
1985	1.5	5.8	10.5	18.7	26.6	21.3	19.2
1990	0.9	6.2	9.1	18.2	25.7	21.9	21.3
1994	1.6	6.5	6.6[a]	18.6	27.4	27.1	27.8

Notes: Figures are for SSA excluding South Africa and Nigeria. Year values as given ([a] is 1993); period values are period annual averages. Notation is evident: dGDP is average annual percentage growth; I/GDP is ratio of gross public investment to GDP; S/GDP is ratio of gross national savings to GDP; T/GDP is ratio of government revenue excluding grants to GDP; G/GDP is ratio of government spending and lending minus repayments to GDP; X and M are merchandise exports and imports, respectively; figures are period annual average growth; and years are shares of GDP.
Source: World Bank, *African Development Indicators 1996*.

Rostovian 'take-off'), despite national savings rates around 10 per cent of GDP. This suggests a problem of absorption. Public expenditure has generally been high, around 26 per cent of GDP, implying large budget deficits as revenue has been about 18 per cent of GDP on average. Merchandise trade appears to have been almost in balance although growth, of imports and exports, had stagnated by the 1990s. While trade shares of GDP rose, this probably reflects slow real income growth.

Although average figures hide the details, they reveal the lack of dynamism and point to some of the underlying problems. In particular, public spending has been high, relative to revenue and to other developing countries, although public investment has been low. Inefficiencies within and related to the public sector have been a major constraint on SSA performance. It is also clear that, on average, the region has been unable to attain any export dynamism. This will partly reflect dependence on primary commodity exports, but also reflects the tendency of these countries to adopt policies biased against agriculture in general and exports in particular (McKay *et al.*, 1997).

During the 1980s and 1990s, almost all SSA countries have adopted, to a greater or lesser extent, World Bank and IMF sponsored Structural Adjustment Programmes (SAPs). The types of economic policies contained in such programmes are indicative of the policies that the sponsors believe to be conducive to economic growth. Are similar policies evident in HPAEs? Table 3.2 details, in order of frequency, the principal policy areas where conditionality has been applied in SAPs (the numbers should be interpreted as indicative of rank importance). One of the most common policy reforms is trade liberalisation (removal of quantitative restrictions, reduction of tariffs and, less frequently, export promotion). The other important areas are tax reform (including fiscal policy); reducing public expenditure and the budget deficit; reform of parastatals (generally moves towards privatisation); agricultural price and marketing liberalisation (especially dismantling state marketing boards); financial sector liberalisation and industrial deregulation (removing price controls is prominent here). Reforms to monetary and exchange rate policy (devaluation and easing access to foreign exchange) feature less frequently because they are traditionally part of an IMF stabilisation loan which precedes the SAP.

The fact that a policy area is included in a SAP does not imply that it was actually implemented, although obviously the effectiveness of a SAP does depend on whether policies are implemented. There is a large literature evaluating SAPs, and it is not relevant to address that here (see McGillivray and Morrissey, 1999). The presence of a policy in Table 3.2 indicates that it

Table 3.2   Policy approaches present in HPAEs and SSA

	Incidence	HPAEs	SSA
1. Trade liberalisation	58	Partial	84
2. Tax reform (fiscal policy)	69	Yes	84
3. Privatisation/Public enterprise reform	58	?	71
4. Monetary policy	14	Yes	50
5. Agricultural liberalisation	62	Yes	75
6. Financial sector liberalisation	26	Partial	80
7. Industrial deregulation	30	?	96
8. Exchange rate liberalisation/devaluation	18	Yes	91
Other policy areas:			
Relative equity in income distribution	No	Yes	No
Land reform implemented	No	Yes	No
Directed credit policies	No	Yes	No

Key and Sources:
Incidence is the percentage of total SAP loans over FY1979–89 with conditions in the stated policy areas, from Webb and Shariff (1992: 71); HPAEs gives the author's view on whether the type of SAP policies proposed in this area were present in HPAEs where 'Yes' means similar policy present in HPAEs and SAPs. 'No' means HPAE policies are quite different to those proposed in SAPs. 'Partial' means some similarities, some differences, between HPAE and SAP policies, and '?' means intense debate over nature of HPAE policies; SSA gives the percentage of conditions in each policy area 'at least substantially implemented' by SSA adjusters over 1979–89, from Webb and Shariff (1992: 72); and Other policy areas are the issues identified in the text as important, but not typically incorporated into SAPs.

is seen as an important aspect of an economic growth strategy. We also indicate whether HPAEs exhibited similar policies. The third column gives an indication of the extent to which reforms associated with SAP conditionality in SSA economies were actually implemented. In general the figures are high, implying that most conditions were 'substantially' implemented. There are profound problems with using these measures of compliance, and it is beyond our scope to consider the problems here (see Milner and Morrissey, 1999). However, they do indicate that the policy areas were present in SAPs and were implemented to the satisfaction of the World Bank monitors.

There is a degree of congruence between HPAE policies and SAPs. Both emphasise macroeconomic stability, which appears to be fundamental for sustained growth. To a lesser extent, both support incentives for agricultural production, SAPs emphasising liberalisation but HPAEs having relied more on land reform, technology transfer and input subsidies (although the agricultural sectors in most HPAEs were relatively liberalised initially; see Hayami, 1997). The focus on trade policy is divergent but not incompatible: both approaches recognise the importance of exports; HPAEs place emphasis on import substitution at stages of trade strategy development and have not eschewed high levels of protection for specific sectors. The largest difference is regarding industrial policy: SAPs do not advocate one, whereas HPAEs have tended to be interventionist. There are also significant differences between what SAPs propose and what HPAEs implemented in regard to public enterprises.

Underlying these appearances of similarity are differences of interpretation. The 'SAP view' is that tax rates should be kept low and relatively non-distortionary, especially with respect to trade. The HPAEs did generally have low taxes, but were not averse to imposing discriminatory taxes or non-tariff barriers on imports of certain goods, especially if they wanted to protect particular sectors. The SAP view is strongly opposed to public enterprises and to regulation of industrial policy. Here again HPAEs have differed. While it may not be the case (as compared to SSA) that fully publicly owned companies control large parts of the economy, public intervention in the operation of firms and industrial policy was widespread. On macroeconomic policy and agricultural liberalisation, the SAPs and HPAEs were in almost complete agreement. On trade, taxation and fiscal policy they were in broad agreement. But on industrial policy and public intervention in the financial sector, they disagreed. It is pertinent to note, however, that problems to some extent associated with these industrial and financial sector interventions have contributed to the severity of the 1997–98 crises in East Asia (see below).

Often it is important to consider policies that were not implemented or proposed; certain policies featured in HPAEs that were not evident in SAPs (Morrissey, 1999a). One of the more important of these is relative equity in the distribution of income and wealth. As mentioned, this was a feature of most of the East Asian economies initially, in the 1960s, and was maintained in the 1970s and 1980s (World Bank, 1993). Few SSA countries could claim relative equity in income and wealth distribution, largely for political reasons (as indicated above). The relevant point is that equity has not featured as a policy issue in SAPs. Although poverty reduction is emphasised by the World Bank and other donors, and the poverty implications of adjustment programmes is an issue of concern, this has never been addressed in the context of equity.

A second issue absent from SAPs is equity regarding property rights for (agricultural) land use and appropriate incentives to farmers. The agricultural sector is a major component of the economy, especially in poor countries or those at early stages of economic growth. A prospering agricultural sector provides a solid basis for economic growth, and land reform (redistribution of land towards small holdings) is a foundation of such prosperity (Hayami, 1997). SAPs in SSA have emphasised removing price controls and liberalising marketing in agriculture, policies that do improve incentives to farmers, but have not addressed the issue of the distribution of land holdings. As land is an important source of collateral for access to credit, land reform can be a major component of agricultural development. In too many African countries, for too long, the agricultural sector, especially peasant farmers, was actively discriminated against. This bias against agriculture is gradually being eroded, but it will take some time for the sector to recover from past damage, and even longer for it to become the foundation of economic growth.

One of the areas of the most intense debate over the HPAE 'economic strategy' is regarding industrial policy. Economists recognise the existence of market failure and the associated case for appropriate government intervention, such as directed credit or targeted subsidies. However, economists rarely have trust in governments to identify the market failure correctly, to select the correct method of intervention and to terminate the intervention when it has served its purpose. Technocratic regimes will be better able to design a targeted intervention and resist rent-seekers, and this may explain why some East Asian economies were reasonably successful in industrial policy. The success was limited, and the root difficulty was in resisting rent-seekers and terminating interventions at the appropriate time.

For Indonesia the accumulation of non-performing debts, implicitly underwritten by the government, underlies the severity of the recent crisis. High borrowing for non-productive investments is not a sustainable policy, especially when corruption channels the funds into the pockets of a few members of the regime. When the bubble bursts, as it must, political and economic turmoil follow. Given the nature of many African political regimes, the Indonesian lesson is very salient. Directed credit may be an appropriate intervention to support specific (productive) activities, but in corrupt regimes this is manifested as subsidised credit allocated on non-market criteria and generating an unsustainable debt burden.

Trade protection has been the means used in SSA to support favoured industries. This fostered inefficient domestic industries, increased the bias against agriculture, and few, if any, of the so-called 'infant industries' managed to grow. As a result of adjustment policies in the late 1980s and 1990s, many SSA countries have implemented trade liberalisation and reduced protection considerably. One fear is that they may look at the East Asian experience to argue for replacing trade protection with directed credit. World Bank (1993) implicitly argued against such an inference and we concur. Market failure will give rise to specific cases for intervention, but great care must be taken in identifying and implementing the appropriate intervention. Care and caution are the salient lessons of the East Asian experience (of success and crisis).

Another fear of trade liberalisation in SSA is that import liberalisation, removal of import restrictions and reduction of tariffs, could expose inefficient domestic producers to increased competition from imports. Bennell (1998) examines the evidence on the impact of economic liberalisation on manufacturing in sub-Saharan Africa and finds that in some countries it appears to be associated with manufacturing decline but in others the sector responds well. This is to be expected as the response to liberalisation depends on how incentives facing different sectors are affected and what constraints are faced by each sector. The basic objective of trade reform is to remove the bias against exports and the anticipated beneficial effect is that exports will increase and, in turn, fuel economic growth. However, trade policy is not the only constraint on exports.

What lessons can we draw for policy in SSA? The basic principles of adjustment programmes are evident in the policies pursued by the HPAEs. Macroeconomic stability, with a liberalised exchange rate regime and control over budget deficits, is a generally recognised starting point, not least because it enhances business confidence. Noorbakhsh and Paloni (1998) argue that SSA countries that attained macroeconomic stabilisation achieved better economic performance than those that did not. Without going as far as to advocate free markets, it is important to let markets function. Government intervention to correct market failures should be appropriate (targeted, moderate and for a limited period). Increasing tax efficiency, both in terms of shifting the tax structure away from the most distortionary taxes (such as tariffs) and improving compliance and collection efficiency, is important to restore incentives. The government has a regulatory role, but this should be to address rather than create market distortions.

One of the most important policy issues is to provide price incentives to producers, especially in agriculture. Arguably, most HPAEs got their agricultural policy right at an early stage of development (Hayami, 1997). This has not been true in SSA, where historically there has been a strong bias against agriculture. Although considerable progress has been made in reducing this bias over the past ten years, farmers face many constraints that limit the export supply response to trade and agricultural liberalisation (McKay *et al.*, 1997). Transport costs can be quite high for many SSA countries and this can act as an important constraint on exports (see Milner *et al.*, 1999 for Uganda). Delays in implementing institutional reforms have constrained export supply response in Uganda (Belshaw *et al.*,

1999). In respect of agriculture, SSA countries have begun to implement the types of reforms that will restore incentives, but much more needs to be done to enable producers to respond to these incentives.

A similar argument relates to trade liberalisation in SSA more generally (i.e. beyond the implications for agriculture). Onafowora and Owoye (1998) find evidence that growth is higher in more outward-oriented economies, suggesting that trade liberalisation (represented as an index of outward orientation) offer potential for SSA countries to increase growth rates. The potential is very limited for some countries, especially given the commodity composition of exports and susceptibility to smuggling and volatile world prices (for Uganda see Belshaw *et al.*, 1999). Thus, while one should not expect an immediate or dramatic response of producers to changes in incentives, as other constraints remain (and may be binding), the general argument to provide incentives to producers is a valid basis on which to design economic policy.

3.5 Conclusions

The prevalence of market failures implies that governments will wish to intervene in the economy. The HPAEs, to a greater or lesser extent, had targeted interventions in agriculture (especially land reform), industry (directed credit and export promotion) and the financial sector (the success of which can now be questioned). African governments cannot replicate the economic and political or institutional environment of East Asian economies, and should not therefore aspire to copy HPAE policies. Nevertheless, they can learn from the successes and failures in East Asia.

Policies to support agriculture are important. These should be based on price incentives and market opportunities but should recognise equity concerns (land reform and support for small farmers) and relax constraints, such as access to credit and technology. Interventionist industrial policy in SSA may be ill-advised, not least because few, if any, SSA countries could identify a manufacturing sector in which they have or are likely to acquire a comparative advantage. Trade liberalisation, by removing domestic distortions, supports greater industrial efficiency and may be the first-best option for SSA; some sectors will suffer, but some should gain. It would be advisable to let market forces determine the distribution of gains and losses. This does not mean the government should do nothing: improved infrastructure (such as transport, power and telecommunications) and institutions (such as marketing support and information) may be the most effective means by which the government could intervene to support industry.

The underdeveloped financial sector is a major constraint in SSA, and one lesson from East Asia is that uncontrolled and excessive borrowing leads to the accumulation of non-performing private sector debts. In the SSA environment of non-performing public debt, this would be even more catastrophic than in the HPAEs. It will be necessary to develop viable financial and capital markets slowly, and government regulation to prevent market excess rather than distort capital flows and borrowing behaviour will be necessary. African governments and central banks would benefit from monitoring recent developments in East Asia in this regard (notably China and Korea).

There remains considerable debate regarding the appropriate role of government, but in East Asia interventionist government policies were used and contributed to growth. Government policy is essential to support a reasonably equitable distribution of income, and this appears to be conducive to growth. In this regard, donor policies towards poverty reduction may be better if framed in terms of reducing inequality than, as at present, in terms of social sector spending and good governance. There is no satisfactory definition of 'good governance' and too often it is interpreted in terms of processes rather than principles. A principle of 'shared growth' or an aspiration towards equity and ensuring that society works for and shares in the benefits of economic growth would provide a more solid foundation for good policy in SSA than would support for multi-party elections.

The weakness of the nation state, and frequent absence of any national identity, is a root political problem in SSA countries. Among the HPAEs, Korea, Hong Kong, Taiwan, Singapore and Malaysia all had strong national identities, the promotion of which motivated economic policy. The same, of course, also applies to Japan. Although Indonesia may have promoted a national identity, it is an artificial state held together by military repression (a reality that is very evident in the latter half of 1999). The principle of sharing, and equally a principle of sacrifice (often forced on some groups) emerges more easily when applied within a defined state (or national identify). This is lacking in many African states such that reformist regimes, Mandela in South Africa and Museveni in Uganda, have had to devote considerable political energy to creating such an identity. Once created, the possibility for growth with equity (or sharing) is enhanced.

National identity and political commitment are required initial conditions. They are also necessary conditions, although not sufficient. Technocratic capacity, the ability to make and implement policy based on analysis of the needs of the situation rather than weighing up conflicting interests and allocating rents, is invaluable. Support for building the administrative and institutional capacity in African countries will, in the long run, be an important factor in enabling them to identify and implement the policies that can achieve growth with equity. Before they can do this, however, politically they will have to desire equity. For too long in too many African countries that desire has been absent.

4
Should Africa Try to Learn from Asia? Lessons for and from Uganda

Peter Smith

4.1 Introduction

Post-colonial sub-Saharan Africa has languished. For many countries in the region, living standards are lower in the 1990s than they had been thirty years earlier. There is no shortage of possible scapegoats: drought, famine, civil war and unrest or the legacy of colonial oppression. However, it is too facile to argue that these factors alone led to stagnation on such an enormous scale.

Meanwhile, East Asia flourished. The so-called 'tiger' economies of Hong Kong, Singapore, South Korea and Taiwan entered the 1960s in poor conditions – South Korea at this time showed GDP per capita (in PPP$ terms) which was lower than the average for sub-Saharan Africa. And yet they boomed. Other countries in the Asian region have begun to experience rapid growth more recently – notably Malaysia, Thailand (before the crisis) and China. In the 1990s, it is difficult even to begin to compare living standards in sub-Saharan Africa with those in countries in East Asia (Smith, 1998) given the size of the rift between them.

In the light of the extreme divergence in the experience of the two regions, the question arises as to whether sub-Saharan Africa has anything to learn from East Asia, or whether there need to be remedies more closely tailored to suit African conditions. In very recent years, some countries in sub-Saharan Africa have begun to show some promise, seeming to open the possibility of development through structural adjustment.

Section 4.2 highlights the macroeconomic performance of Uganda under structural adjustment, reviewing its success and identifying short-comings. Section 4.3 explores the configuration of factors which aided the success of the tiger economies, distinguishing between replicable and

49

non-replicable conditions. In Section 4.4, the focus is on a recent study of Uganda to explore the desirability and feasibility of learning from the Asia experience. The final section summarises.

4.2 Uganda under structural adjustment

In common with many other countries in sub-Saharan Africa, Uganda experienced a decline in income levels in the 1970s. Political issues played a critical role in this period of decline, with the most marked decline in GDP per capita occurring during the regime of Idi Amin. The decline was slowed under Milton Obote in the early 1980s, but this was a period of economic stagnation rather than recovery, and inflation became a serious concern, reaching nearly 250 per cent at its peak. The present President, Yoweri Museveni, came to power in 1986 after five years of guerrilla warfare.

An Economic Recovery Programme (ERP) was launched in May 1987, supported by the World Bank, the IMF, the African Development Bank and the member countries of the Paris Club (Kikonyogo, 1996). The objectives of the ERP incorporated the conventional elements of structural adjustment – stabilisation through fiscal and monetary discipline, the liberalisation of prices and interest rates in the domestic economy, the removal of trade restrictions and the adoption of a realistic market-determined exchange rate, and an attempt to move away from import substitution towards export-oriented production, together with some degree of privatisation. This programme was set against the background of a country in which infrastructure had been devastated by an extended period of neglect and civil strife.

In the following years, GDP per capita grew steadily, until by 1996 it was almost back to the 1969 peak level. Inflation was brought down from its high of almost 250 per cent in 1986/87 to manageable levels. Indeed, Figure 4.1 reveals that growth rates in the early 1990s were comparable with those of Hong Kong and Singapore.

As far as trade is concerned, Uganda remains relatively closed. In 1996, exports comprised 12.2 per cent of GDP, a very similar proportion as had been evident a decade previously. Imports in the same year were 21.1 per cent of GDP. This export performance was disappointing, with only a modest expansion (relative to GDP) being apparent in the 1990s, part of which reflected the coffee boom of 1994/95 following the Brazilian frost. Coffee has always been a key crop in Uganda's exports. Indeed, in the early 1980s coffee made up more than 90 per cent of exports. The ERP period has seen the beginning of some diversification in exports with the encouragement of new crops.

Figure 4.1 Growth of real GDP

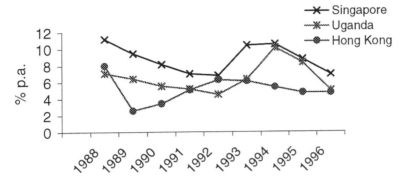

Sources: Department of Statistics, Singapore; MFEP, Uganda; IMF, International Financial Statistics.

Manufacturing activity continues to make up a small proportion of GDP (Figure 4.2). Much of manufacturing industry was dismantled during the Amin era, and it is only in very recent years that it has again begun to expand.

Nonetheless, in the context of the sub-Saharan African region, the economic growth and stability displayed by the Ugandan economy in the 1990s has been interpreted as a promising sign that appropriate structural adjustment policies can be effective. Closer inspection of the level of human development suggests that this optimism may need to be tempered with a careful awareness of the situation at the micro level. The United Nations Development Programme (UNDP, 1997b) has referred to 'two faces of Uganda', with outstanding macroeconomic performance being accompanied by lagging levels of human development.

Figure 4.2 Contribution of manufacturing to GDP 1970–96

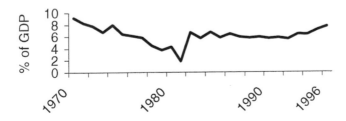

Source: World Bank and Government of Uganda, Background to the Budget 1997–98.

According to this analysis, the country continues to be characterised by substantial regional and gender disparities and a high incidence of absolute poverty in spite of the rapid expansion in real GDP. Indeed, structural adjustment may be perceived as being primarily concerned with short-run stabilisation rather than long-term development (Diabré, 1997).

This dichotomous view of the current state of development in the Ugandan economy is supported by a study carried out under the auspices of the Bank of Uganda in late 1997 (Smith, 1997; Musinguzi and Smith, 1998). In the study (the 'BOU survey'), more than 300 households in four regions of the country were interviewed in a benchmarking exercise intended to enable the monitoring of the effects of improved macro-economic conditions on people in rural areas of the country. The study catalogued dimensions of physical poverty and attempted to identify explanations for persistent poverty that could be interpreted in the framework of a market-friendly view of human development. In other words, it was hoped to explore the extent to which degrees of market integration can be seen to affect the incidence of physical poverty. Some results from this study will be discussed later in the paper.

4.3 Factors in the success of the tiger economies

The outstanding success of the so-called 'tiger' economies of East Asia has attracted much attention from analysts looking for the alchemical recipe that would turn poverty into development success. The consensus view appears to be that there was no single philosopher's stone that was the unique ingredient for success, but a configuration of qualities and circumstances that enabled the 'miracle' of rapid growth to take place. It has also been argued that it was the innate 'market-friendliness' of government policy that facilitated the miracle (World Bank, 1993). It has also been argued that much of the rapid growth of the East Asian economies can be explained by growth in inputs within a growth accounting framework (Young, 1995). However, this offers more of a description rather than an explanation, leaving unanswered key questions of why inputs (including investment in physical and human capital) were able to grow more rapidly in East Asia than elsewhere. It is thus helpful to look more closely at the configuration of factors that enabled growth to take place.

Two distinct classes of success factors can be distinguished. Some reflect serendipity; factors which were unique to the region and/or to the time at which development was taking place. Such factors cannot be simply replicated elsewhere by other countries looking to emulate the earlier experience of the newly industrialised countries (NICs). On the other hand, some of the ingredients are more general in nature, and may be both essential and replicable. It is these elements of East Asian success which may act as guides or targets for later developers. This may still leave the key issue of whether the replicable factors are *sufficient* factors to encourage development, or whether it was the particular configuration of replicable and serendipitous factors which led to success. If this is the case, the supplementary issue is whether there are *alternative* routes for sub-Saharan Africa to pursue in the quest for development success.

4.3.1 Human capital

Most analysts would agree that human capital has been a key factor for all of the tiger economies. All of them lack substantial natural resources, so human resources have been crucial. Education and the provision of healthcare are vital to the full exploitation of those human resources, and have been a high priority in each of the tiger economies (Mundle, 1998). The presence of a healthy, educated and well-trained pool of disciplined labour has contributed to economic development in various ways, not least in proving an attraction for foreign firms seeking to locate and invest. It is also expected that high levels of education in the population would increase the flexibility of the workforce – a potentially important factor when the economy is going through a period of rapid structural transformation. Mehrotra (1998) has pointed to the importance of the synergies between human capital formation and the process of economic growth in a range of high-performing economies.

In principle, this is a replicable factor. Governments can take action to promote and encourage education and the provision of good quality healthcare. A problem for sub-Saharan Africa is that existing levels of provision are so poor. Improving levels of education and health cannot be accomplished rapidly, but must be a priority in long-term planning. In practical terms, it is important that policies operate on the demand- as well as the supply-side. High drop-out rates in many African countries may be indicative of deficient demand, so that acting to supply education may be insufficient of itself. Bonnet (1993) argues that low rates of return to education and the poor quality of education are responsible for the high drop-out rates and low school participation in Africa.

4.3.2 Infrastructure

Public good arguments may justify government intervention in the provision of infrastructure – especially roads, communication networks, schools and other physical capital. The high dependence upon international trade in the tiger economies could not have evolved without infrastructure to enable trade to be carried out efficiently. There is an extent to which this is a replicable success factor, and may constitute another priority area for economic policy. However, within the context of sub-Saharan Africa, the deficiencies in provision combined with the dearth of resources make it difficult to see any but long-term improvements.

4.3.3   Stability

None of the tiger economies had very auspicious beginnings to their economic development, but all experienced periods of political stability during the key development years. The extreme example is perhaps that of Singapore, with a single prime minister in Lee Kuan Yew from 1959 until 1990. Such stability enables planning for development, and enables governments to avoid short-termism, but cannot easily be forced on a society.

Stability in the macroeconomy is also perceived to have been an important characteristic of the tiger economies. Such stability is essential if markets are to work effectively in guiding resource allocation and in engendering confidence of economic agents in the economy. In Singapore, inflation has been kept very strictly under control over long periods, averaging only 1.5 per cent per annum during the critical development years between 1965 and 1990. The same could not be said of South Korea or Hong Kong, where inflation has not always remained stable. Arguably, however, the macroeconomy of the tiger countries has never looked to be out of control, and perhaps it is the predictability of these economies that has been important in enabling markets to be effective.

Macroeconomic stability may be more of a replicable factor than political stability. However, the evidence from Uganda suggests that macroeconomic stability may be necessary, but is not *sufficient* to ensure that all members of a society benefit from economic development.

4.3.4   Savings and investment

The extraordinary performance of the tiger economies in generating a high flow of savings is well-known. This may in part depend upon there being political and economic stability, as well as upon the existence of effective financial markets and institutions that both provide the opportunities for individuals to save, and a mechanism for channelling those savings into productive investment. This is undoubtedly an area in which the tiger economies have had enormous success. In some cases (such as Singapore), this was accomplished through the medium of provident fund arrangements, in others by appropriate interest rate policies. In Singapore, the forced savings schemes (via the provident fund) were supplemented by a flow of voluntary savings through attractive terms offered by the Post Office Savings Bank (Huff, 1994; Stiglitz and Uy, 1996).

In the absence of political and economic stability, it may be difficult to conjure up voluntary savings. The extreme low income levels in much of sub-Saharan Africa may also make it difficult to encourage a flow of savings, but it must be recalled that South Korea in 1960 had similarly low income levels, but still managed to encourage a flow of savings – at least by the end of the 1960s by which time savings had increased to 15 per cent of GDP from virtually zero in 1960. Similarly, Singapore's domestic savings ratio went from being negative in 1960 to above 20 per cent in 1970 (and to 50 per cent in 1990). In the BOU survey, the lack of accessible financial institutions in the rural areas, combined with the lack of a savings culture was seen to have led to extremely low levels of household savings.

4.3.5 Export orientation

The relentless drive to export has been perhaps the most publicised feature of economic development in the tiger economies. The limited size of domestic markets makes exporting an attractive (even essential) proposition, especially if economies of scale in manufacturing activity are to be exploitable. The tiger economies turned to exporting relatively early in their development, realising the impossibility of relying on import substitution within domestic markets.

It was this early switch to exporting activity that made it so effective a strategy. The inward-looking attitudes that are often associated with an import substitution policy had not had time to become entrenched. Furthermore, the export drive coincided with a general increase in the volume of world trade. Expanding exports at a time of stagnant world trade is problematic, as it is more likely to induce retaliatory action from other countries. The *timing* of the export drive was thus of enormous importance, and implies that this factor may not be replicable – unless another period of substantial world trade expansion was to be launched. This does not look imminently likely, especially given the turmoil in Asian markets. This does not mean that countries should not be encouraged to be outward looking, and it is likely that export orientation will continue to be a key ingredient of structural adjustment programmes. However, it may well be that the expected returns to export promotion may be lower than that enjoyed by the tiger economies in earlier generations.

It is also well documented that the *composition* of exports was a vital part of export success in East Asia. The shift in the structure of exports towards appropriate manufactured goods (which was planned and encouraged by government interventions) may be less viable in today's international environment. There is a clear dilemma here, in that continued dependence upon primary products is equally undesirable in the context of price volatility and declining terms of trade. However, it is not clear whether the 'flying geese' pattern of industrialisation that worked so successfully in East Asia can be replicated under present conditions.

4.3.6   Entrepreneurship

Entrepreneurship is a relatively neglected factor of production, but is important in the successful translation of savings into growth (via investment). In the tiger economies, it was present, but from diverse sources. In some cases such as Hong Kong, it was indigenous innovators who provided the vision and risk-taking factor – this was crucial to Hong Kong's development, according to Yu (1998). Elsewhere it was provided by the State or through the encouragement of investment from multinational enterprises, as in Singapore. The latter route can be a dangerous one, as Singapore has been discovering during the 1990s, where over-dependence on the government/multinational nexus is said to have led to a dearth of local entrepreneurs, and the authorities have been looking for ways of encouraging more independent thought, at least within the education system, in the hope that this will encourage innovation. Indeed, the possibility that domestic entrepreneurship might be crowded out by foreign firms' involvement in the Singaporean economy was identified even earlier (Koh, 1987). This is another elusive factor for policy design, especially in an African perspective. Innovation requires imagination, which may be stifled by the culture of poverty that has afflicted sub-Saharan Africa for so long. Multinationals may be reluctant to invest in nations where human capital levels are low, or where political stability is suspect.

4.3.7   The cultural issue

Some writers have referred to Confucianism as a philosophy that has underlain the success of the East Asian economies (for example, Lim *et al.*, 1988). The respect for those in authority and the responsibility of the educated to rule benevolently have been cited as factors that enabled governments to rule and to plan economic development secure in the knowledge that the population would be compliant, accepting direction and regulation. The relative lack of corruption in the tiger economies has also been attributed to the Confucian philosophy combined with the heavy emphasis given to education within a meritocratic system. This view is probably more widespread in Singapore than elsewhere in the tiger economies, reflecting Lee Kuan Yew's preoccupation with Confucian philosophy and the need to inculcate 'Asian values'. The extent to which this has been important in practice is difficult to judge. For an economy to be run with heavy State direction, some degree of cooperation is essential, and better achieved by consensus than by force. Whether or not culture was a crucial factor, it is clearly not one which can be replicated, and any successful route towards development in sub-Saharan Africa must take into account the regional cultural values and attitudes.

4.3.8 The state and the market

For any society, there needs to be a balance between market forces and State guidance in the allocation of resources. The intrusiveness of intervention has varied in the tiger economies. In Singapore, South Korea and Taiwan, the authorities clearly had strong ideas about the desirable direction for their respective economies in terms of structural change, openness to international trade, human capital, savings – indeed, for many of the factors mentioned earlier in this section. Policies were introduced that would consciously guide resources in the wanted direction. Even in Hong Kong, often regarded as the very embodiment of *laissez faire*, there has been intervention in housing and land markets and in the promotion of trade and provision of necessary infrastructure.

A common factor has been the way that intervention has been in a form that has enabled markets to work effectively, rather than seeking to replace markets by substituting state control (Stiglitz, 1996). It may also be argued that the respective governments were sufficiently secure that they could form a vision for the future direction of the economy with a reasonable expectation of remaining in control long enough to see that vision turned into reality. In other words, there was sufficient political stability to enable long-term planning. There have been few countries in sub-Saharan Africa in recent decades that could claim such stability.

4.4 Lessons for Uganda?

The analysis of the previous section suggests that there is not likely to be a unique blueprint for successful development. The tiger economies were successful for a configuration of reasons, some of which were particular to the region or to the period in which they were undergoing rapid transformation. Other factors offer more hope for countries wishing to emulate the successful conditions, in the sense that appropriate policies may be able to encourage their replication. However, there may be good reasons for proceeding with caution.

First, there may be reinforcing interactions among the success factors, such that it is the *combination* of them which is critical. In these circumstances, the achievement of some but not all of the factors may not be a guarantee of development. Secondly, some of the factors may be in principle replicable, but yet out of reach of countries in sub-Saharan Africa in present circumstances. If some of the non-replicable (or replicable-but-unreachable) factors are essential, then the second-best solution may be to look for a *new* configuration of factors, rather than trying to capture just part of the East Asian pattern. The question also arises as to the balance of significance of the factors. Evaluating the relative importance of the various components is not a trivial exercise. It may indeed be argued that it is the underlying philosophy of market-friendliness that is more important than the individual elements. If this is the case, then the path to success may lie in finding ways of enhancing market effectiveness within the context of sub-Saharan African conditions, rather than attempting to recreate East Asia.

It was argued earlier that Uganda was showing signs of macroeconomic success, although it seemed that the benefits were not filtering down to the micro level. This being so, could this relative progress be enhanced and extended through the East Asian success factors? If this might be feasible in the Ugandan case, then perhaps there is hope for other countries in the region also. Consider first some potentially replicable factors.

4.4.1 Human capital

Human capital is in principle a replicable factor, in that it is possible for resources to be channelled into the provision of education and health care. In the context of Uganda (and many other sub-Saharan African countries), this strategy has to be seen as long term in nature, especially given the poverty of the existing provision. Figure 4.3 shows the educational attainment (in years of schooling) of heads of households in the BOU survey, in which a quarter of those interviewed indicated they had received three years schooling or less. Further probing about the reasons for adults having dropped out indicated that most had done so because of financial reasons. However, it was also clear that a number of women had dropped out of school because their parents saw no point in educating girls, and that many boys and girls had dropped out simply because they saw no value in education and their parents 'did not mind'.

Figure 4.3 Educational attainment

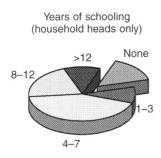

Years of schooling
(household heads only)

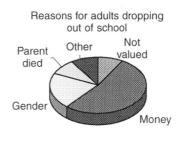

Reasons for adults dropping
out of school

For households which currently include children of school age, nearly 40 per cent had at least one such child not at school. This included a number of children of five, six and even seven-years old who were considered 'too young' to begin school.

In 1997, the Ugandan government (with financial assistance from the World Bank) introduced new measures to encourage higher participation in primary education, guaranteeing free primary education for four children in each family. This has increased enrolment, but also had some unusual effects. In some cases, children had been held back in anticipation of the new measures. In other cases, some older children have returned to school – there were several 13-year-olds in the first year of primary education, and 'children' of up to 19 years old still enrolled in primary education. Agricultural productivity was seen to be low, partly because of ignorance about good-practice farming techniques, suggesting that there is a key role for vocational training in the form of agricultural extension schemes. Improving the *quality* of education and its orientation may be as important as increasing the quantity.

In terms of healthcare provision, the survey again revealed flaws in provision. Few households indicated that they had no access to healthcare, but when pressed for comments, it was clear that effective healthcare facilities were accessible to less than 8 per cent of households. The causes of low accessibility were varied. Many indicated that healthcare was too expensive, or that the local clinics were poorly supplied with medicines.

Investment in improved education and healthcare provision is an important component of any development strategy. In these conditions, with existing levels at a low level, and with poor levels of infrastructure, substantial resources are required, and gestation lags will inevitably be long.

4.4.2   Infrastructure

Infrastructure provision in sub-Saharan Africa has been deficient. Even in the 1990s, access to social infrastructure (safe water, sanitation, healthcare) has been limited. In Uganda, for instance, only 38 per cent of the population have access to safe water, and only 64 per cent to sanitation. In the BOU survey, access to such facilities was even more restricted, although this may be misleading given that the survey was deliberately focused on relatively poor areas. In the survey, nearly one-tenth of households said that they relied on the 'bush' as a means of disposal of human waste, but this is probably an *under*-estimate. In some regions, this picture is made worse by cultural practice prohibiting many women from using the pit latrines.

In terms of transport and communication, the quality of roads was also seen to leave much to be desired. Uganda has workable trunk roads between the major cities, but feeder roads remain of poor quality, thus limiting the extent to which people living in the rural areas have access to national (or international) markets. This is a vital area for the conduct of international trade, as Uganda is land-locked, and thus relies on road transport.

A reliable source of energy is also crucial for the physical transformation of production. In the late 1990s, only 3 per cent of households in Uganda have access to electricity, although the country claims the second-largest hydro-electric dam in Africa. Households continue to rely heavily on firewood as fuel for cooking (and for light in some cases), with the concomitant demands on labour power for fuel-gathering.

4.4.3   Savings and investment

Uganda has one of the poorest savings records in the world (even by sub-Saharan African standards). The fact that the record is poor relative to some other countries in the region suggests that low savings cannot only be ascribed to low income levels. Respondents in the BOU survey were asked whether they had ever undertaken any savings. About 70 per cent indicated that they had never done so, most citing low income as the reason. Of those who had undertaken savings, relatively few had done so through formal financial institutions, which they indicated were either not accessible or not trusted. Much saving was in the form of physical assets (land or animals), or in the form of cash stashed in the house. One possibility for encouraging more positive savings behaviour might be via post office savings schemes. This route has been successful elsewhere, and is also supported by Cole and Slade (1997).

A similarly small proportion of households had undertaken borrowing. In classic fashion, much of the borrowing was from relatives, friends or local informal moneylenders, and at widely varying (and sometimes very high) interest rates. Borrowing was rarely for productive or innovative investment, but was more often for consumption, or for family funerals, and so on.

Knowing that the survey was being carried out by the Bank of Uganda, respondents were not slow to indicate that they would *like* to borrow. However, very few had any real idea about what they would do with credit if they were offered it. Microfinance schemes offer scope for mobilising savings and for channelling funds into investment, but an expansion of agricultural extension schemes and the provision of advice will be crucial if such schemes are to be successful in the sorts of areas covered by the survey.

4.4.4 Export orientation

When East Asia made its move to enter world markets, international trade was expanding, and the tiger countries made sure that they were producing goods for which there was a strong world demand. Conditions in the 1990s are very different. Trade is less buoyant overall, and the expansion and closer integration of the European market has had an impact on the pattern of directions in world trade.

There is a major dilemma here. It is difficult to imagine countries in sub-Saharan Africa being able to compete in world markets for manufactured goods, especially given the shortfalls in levels of human capital already highlighted. The shortage of a well-trained labour force accustomed to industrial working is a serious disadvantage which was not shared by the tiger economies in earlier years. On the other hand, continued reliance on primary goods for exporting has not served the region well in the past, and the prospects for the future look little better. Uganda has begun to diversify away from its dependence on coffee, but progress has been slow. In the survey, very few households had adopted new crops in order to diversify their activities, although there were instances of crops such as vanilla, sugar cane and others being grown. One enterprising household was cultivating silk worms, but such innovation was rare.

4.4.5 Non-replicable factors?

The remaining factors identified as having contributed to East Asia's success are even less promising for countries seeking to emulate the tiger economies. Indeed, in some instances, these rest on prior achievements in education, the construction of infrastructure or other ingredients of the East Asian success.

Political and macroeconomic stability have been elusive for countries at all stages of development. In the Uganda of the late 1990s there is evidence of both having been achieved, especially in comparison with the conditions of the previous years. However, this has not been sufficient to ensure that the benefits have pervaded the whole society. Insurgency remains a problem in some remote parts of the country, and previous regimes have left a legacy of high indebtedness. The relief package under the Highly Indebted Poor Country (HIPC) arrangement was implemented only in 1998, and may ease the situation.

Entrepreneurship and flexibility were seen to be important ingredients of the East Asian growth process, but replication may be problematic. The determinants of flexibility are difficult to isolate, although the importance of human capital in this respect should not be neglected (for example, Killick 1995; Smith and Ulph, 1995). Openness to new ideas or new production arrangements may be more likely in a society in which education levels are at least adequate, and in which the economy is exposed to international trade and communication. Cultural attitudes may also be critical in the willingness to adopt new ideas and ways of thinking, and also in shaping the perception and acceptance of leadership from the authorities.

Even more important than these factors is the need for adequate market arrangements. In East Asia, it was through the medium of the market that the state expressed and initiated its plans for growth and development. For example, individuals cannot be flexible in responding to changing trade or demand conditions unless they can identify new possibilities and potential initiatives. Without adequate markets in operation, signals of changing conditions cannot be identified.

Access to national markets in Uganda remains limited. In the BOU survey, only 58 per cent of households owned a radio, and 41 per cent a bicycle. With low levels of literacy, this suggests that access to market information is restricted. Marketing arrangements remain strongly traditional in character. For some crops such as coffee, local farmers in the rural areas rely on middlemen who purchase at the farm gate and sell on to the exporters. Prices are thus controlled by these traders. The privatisation of the former Marketing Board has led to increased competition among the traders, so that farmers in recent years have been getting a better price for their coffee. A possible concern here is that it may hamper the drive for diversification by reducing the incentives for adopting new crops. For other crops such as *matooke*, farmers must transport their crop to the nearest trading station or to strategic points on the trunk roads to the capital, where they can sell to passing trucks.

4.4.6 Interactions among the success factors

There are many complex interactions between the factors that underpinned the success of the tiger economies which cannot be ignored in any attempt to draw inferences for sub-Saharan Africa. The importance of human capital in facilitating the adoption of new activities has already been underlined. Savings and investment will not be effective without properly functioning financial markets and the confidence of individuals in them, which in turn requires political and macroeconomic stability. Markets cannot operate effectively without physical infrastructure to enable transport of goods and communication of market information. The fundamental dilemma seems to be that development requires simultaneous transformation across a broad front – but resources are in woefully short supply.

4.5 Summary: promoting market-friendly development?

Countries in sub-Saharan Africa such as Uganda cannot rely on the alchemy of East Asia's success to provide a blueprint for a miracle. The configuration of resources and circumstances cannot be replicated, but perhaps markets can be harnessed to create conditions more favourable to future development. The extent of the present shortfall in economic and human development suggests that a long-term perspective is required. East Asia's success was built on a platform of fundamentally sound characteristics, and sub-Saharan Africa may have to start by getting those fundamentals in place.

A prime prerequisite for effective operation of markets is macroeconomic stability. Countries like Uganda which have begun to build up a track record in this respect need to persist in order to establish the credibility of economic policies that will enhance the effectiveness of markets and policies.

Increased investment in infrastructure is needed to enable all regions of the country to participate in national success. Improved transport and communication will expand the scope of markets. Better market facilities at trading centres (storage facilities, for example) would improve the effectiveness of existing market arrangements. The extension of electrification would enable the establishment (and revitalisation) of manufacturing activity and improve labour productivity by reducing the need for collection of fuelwood. The fostering of financial institutions may enable the mobilisation of a flow of savings to enable investment.

Resources devoted to education and training will bring benefits, not only in terms of improved productivity, but also in terms of human development. Improved literacy and comprehension enables markets to be more effective, in the sense that participants in the market are better able to interpret market signals and to react to them.

None of these measures can be totally effective in the short run, but it is crucial to take steps that will lay the foundations for future long-term development to take place. Africa's problems are chronic and can only be solved gradually. This is not to say that steps are not also required to tackle immediate issues of poverty. According to the UNDP (1997b), half of Uganda's people live in absolute poverty on incomes of less than $1 per day (in PPP$). A higher proportion of households in the BOU survey were found to receive income below this level (Musinguzi and Smith, 1998). Efforts to alleviate poverty may be needed before the fruits of investment in the other success factors can be reaped. This may require increased cooperation from international agencies. South Korea and Taiwan enjoyed substantial flows of overseas assistance in their early years of development. Continued flows into sub-Saharan Africa are likely to be necessary for some time into the future, and may be effective if appropriately channelled into market-enhancing projects.

In summary, any successful strategy will need to allow resource allocation to be subject to market pressures, which in turn will require markets themselves to be effective. Strategic policy must also be tailored to local conditions, matching action to the individual configuration of problems, circumstances and opportunities of each individual country. Finally, international cooperation is needed if sub-Saharan Africa is to surmount the obstacles of indebtedness and inexperience in trade, and thus be able to participate fully in world markets.

Acknowledgements

I am grateful to Polycarp Musinguzi, Jackie Wahba, Maureen Smith, participants at the Reading conference and anonymous referees for helpful comments on this paper. I would also like to acknowledge the assistance and support of the Bank of Uganda in regard to the survey discussed in this paper. The views expressed in the paper are those of the author, and not of the Bank of Uganda. Errors remain those of the author.

5
Aid, Adjustment and Public Sector Fiscal Behaviour: Lessons from a Relatively Poor Performing East Asian Economy

Mark McGillivray

5.1 Lessons for Africa from Asia?

The outstanding pre-1997 economic performance of East Asia has attracted its fair share of attention. A number of factors have been offered as determinants of this performance, which has involved not only rapid and sustained economic growth but reduced income inequality and poverty. These factors include the achievement of macroeconomic stability, a strong export orientation, increased human and physical capital, high rates of saving, strategic interventions and flexible labour markets.[1] In these respects East Asia is, or at least was, held up as an example for other countries to follow, especially those in sub-Saharan Africa. Comparison of the underlying economic structures and conditions and economic policies between these two regions is not uncommon. While such pursuits have merit, the real benefit of looking at the experience of a particularly successful group of economies, and identifying factors which have caused their success, is that it conditions or informs questions about the performance of other countries, including the poor-performing countries of sub-Saharan Africa. This is especially so if relatively good empirical information is available for the former group of economies, as is generally the case in East Asia, as more questions about them can be answered with some confidence.

This chapter takes a slightly different approach. Its basic premise is that if we can derive lessons for Africa from the successful East Asian economies, then we can also learn from the experience of the poor performing economies of East Asia which offer reasonably good data sets, at least by developing country standards. Accordingly, it looks at the experience of the Philippines. While its income per capita and education and health status levels are higher, the experience of the Philippines is in many respects similar to that of sub-Saharan Africa. It has exhibited, for example, low GDP growth (one per cent during 1980–90), persistently high inflation (15 per cent during 1980–90 and 9.8 per cent during 1985–95), lasting current account deficits (5.9 and 2.7 per cent of GDP during 1980 and 1995, respectively), negative investment growth (–2.1 per cent during 1980–90) and ongoing public sector overall fiscal deficits (–1.4 and –1.5 per cent during 1980 and 1995, respectively) (World Bank, 1997b). The Philippines has, like most sub-Saharan African countries, received increased aid inflows (0.9 and 1.6 per cent of GNP in 1980 and 1994, respectively), and has in place a World Bank- and IMF-supported reform programme which has tended to focus more on stabilisation and less on adjustment (World Bank, 1990 and 1997, Mosley *et al.*, 1995).

The specific concern here relates an issue that has attracted considerable attention in the literature on development aid effectiveness, but little or no attention in the literature on structural adjustment and stabilisation. That issue is the impact of aid on public sector fiscal behaviour and how far the aid inflows to which structural reforms are tied are compatible with the aims of the adjustment programme. In other words, do these inflows, for example, reduce taxation effort or lead to larger fiscal deficits than would otherwise be the case? These questions would, on the surface, seem pertinent to sub-Saharan African countries given the amounts of policy-based aid inflows they have received and the fiscal problems they face.

We shall therefore examine whether the preceding concerns have been realised in the case of the Philippines. Among the aims of that country's adjustment and stabilisation programme are increasing the tax base, increasing public investment and reducing public sector deficits (Mosley *et al.*, 1991; World Bank, 1987). Building on recent advances in research on the public sector fiscal response to aid inflows, it looks at the impact of aid on public sector saving, taxation and borrowing. Given the motivation for the paper, it disaggregates aid into that from bilateral and multilateral sources. More significantly, however, it departs from previous fiscal response studies by developing a model which specifically caters for possible behavioural changes as a result of the introduction of an adjustment and stabilisation programme. This model is based on that originally proposed by Heller (1975), but which has been the subject of extensive modifications and refinements in recent years.

The rest of this chapter consists of four sections in addition to the introduction. A model of public sector fiscal behaviour in the presence of an adjustment programme is outlined in Section 5.2. Data and econometric estimation procedures are discussed in Section 5.3. Results are reported and analysed in Section 5.4. Conclusions and directions for future research, including that on Africa, are provided in Section 5.5. The main conclusion of the paper is that as much attention should be given to how structural adjustment lending, and aid funds in general, are allocated by the public sector of recipient countries, as is given to compliance with the conditions to which these funds are tied.

5.2 A model of public sector fiscal behaviour in the presence of an adjustment programme

Public sector decision-makers in all countries face the basic task of allocating revenue among various expenditure categories subject to budgetary constraints. For the purposes of this paper, expenditure is divided into two categories: recurrent expenditure or government consumption (G) and capital expenditure or public sector investment (I_g). Revenue is obtained from both domestic and foreign sources in the forms of taxation and other recurrent revenue (T), foreign aid from multilateral agencies (A_m), foreign aid from bilateral agencies (A_b) and borrowing from domestic sources (B). The environment in which these variables are determined changes according to the presence or otherwise of exogenously determined public sector reforms (R), especially those associated with a structural adjustment programme. The utility function of public sector decision-makers can therefore be written as follows:

$$U = f(I_g, G, T, A_b, A_m, B, R) \tag{5.1}$$

It is assumed that the public sector seeks to minimise the difference between actual revenues and expenditures and exogenously determined targets for each such variable. It is further assumed that the utility derived from a given level of expenditure or revenue, relative to its target, differs between reform and non-reform periods. Equation 5.1 can thus be represented by the following quadratic loss function:

$$U = \alpha_0 + \alpha_0 R - \frac{\alpha_1}{2}(I_g - I_g^*)^2 - \frac{\sigma_1}{2}R(I_g - I_g^*)^2 - \frac{\alpha_2}{2}(G - G^*)^2 - \frac{\sigma_2}{2}R(G - G^*)^2$$
$$- \frac{\alpha_3}{2}(T - T^*)^2 - \frac{\sigma_3}{2}R(T - T^*)^2 - \frac{\alpha_4}{2}(A_b - A_b^*) - \frac{\alpha_5}{2}(A_m - A_m^*)^2$$
$$- \frac{\sigma_6}{2}(B - B^*)^2 - \frac{\sigma_4}{2}R(B - B^*)^2 \tag{5.2}$$

where the asterisks denote the target values of the expenditure and revenue variables, $\alpha_i > 0$ and $\sigma_j > 0$ for $i = 1, \ldots, 6$ and $j = 1, \ldots, 4$, respectively. The utility function written in Equation 5.2 is symmetric, with undershooting a target by some amount yielding the same utility as overshooting it by that amount, and reaches a maximum at $\alpha_0 + \sigma_0 R$. All variables are for period t.

During an adjustment programme (when $R = 1$), Equation 5.2 becomes:

$$U = \alpha_0 + \sigma_0 - \frac{\alpha_1 + \sigma_1}{2}(I_g - I_g^*)^2 - \frac{\alpha_2 + \sigma_2}{2}(G - G^*)^2 - \frac{\alpha_3 + \sigma_3}{2}(T - T^*)^2$$
$$- \frac{\alpha_4}{2}(A_b - A_b^*)^2 - \frac{\alpha_5}{2}(A_m - A_m^*)^2 - \frac{\alpha_6 + \sigma_4}{2}(B - B^*)^2 \qquad (5.3)$$

and in the absence of a programme (when $R = 0$) reduces to

$$U = \alpha_0 - \frac{\alpha_1 + \sigma_1}{2}(I_g - I_g^*)^2 - \frac{\alpha_2}{2}(G - G^*)^2 - \frac{\alpha_3}{2}(T - T^*)^2 - \frac{\alpha_4}{2}(A_b - A_b^*)^2$$
$$- \frac{\alpha_5}{2}(A_m - A_m^*)^2 - \frac{\alpha_6}{2}(B - B^*)^2. \qquad (5.4)$$

Equation 5.4, or a variant thereof, is the specification used in previous fiscal response studies. The maximum unconstrained values of Equation 5.3 and 5.4 are α_0, σ_0, $+ \alpha_0$, respectively, which are obtained when each of the targets are met exactly. The difference between the two utility functions (for simple versions containing investment only) is depicted diagrammatically in Figure 5.1. The main difference between the two utility functions is that

Figure 5.1   Utility functions

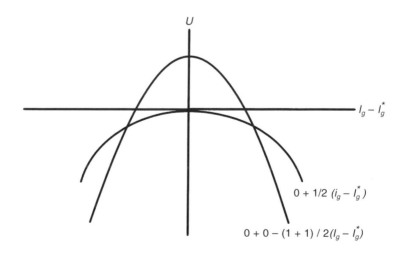

U

$I_g - I_g^*$

$0 + 1/2\,(i_g - I_g^*)$

$0 + 0 - (1 + 1)\,/\,2(I_g - I_g^*)$

5.3 results in greater utility reductions as the absolute gaps between actual and target variables increase. Moreover, provided $\sigma_0 > 0$, 5.3 provides more utility than 5.4 if all targets are exactly achieved.

Following Franco-Rodriguez *et al.* (1998), Equation 5.2 is maximised subject to:

$$I_g + G = T + A_b + A_m + B \tag{5.5}$$

$$G \leq \rho_1 T + \rho_2 A_b + \rho_3 A_m + \rho_4 B \tag{5.6}$$

Equation 5.5 is simply the government's overall budget constraint which must always hold. The rationale for the inequality written in Equation 5.6 is that there are *external* constraints which limit the manner in which the public sector in developing countries allocates revenues. The actions of donors or domestic interests cause the values of the ρs in 5.6 to be imposed on those involved in setting targets and allocating revenue, with there being no guarantee that targets can be met even though revenues may satisfy Equation 5.5. In other words, on the assumption that Equation 5.6 is binding (the possible value of G is upper bound), these external constraints prevent the attainment of $\alpha_0 + \sigma_0$ (because at least one expenditure target cannot be met).[2] Our analysis is premised on this assumption. If Equation 5.6 is not binding, the government is not prevented from reaching specific expenditure targets, utility is maximised subject to Equation 5.5 only and the government can attain $\alpha_0 + \sigma_0$ if revenues are sufficient.

Maximising Equation 5.2 with $R = 0$ subject to Equation 5.5 and 5.6 and re-arranging the first-order conditions yields the following simultaneous system of non- adjustment period structural equations:

$$
\begin{aligned}
I_g = {}& (1 - \rho_1)\beta_1 I_g^* + (1 - \rho_1)\beta_2 G^* + (1 - \rho_1)[1 - (1 - \rho_1)\beta_1 - \rho_1\beta_2]T^* \\
& + [(1 - \rho_2) - (1 - \rho_1)(1 - \rho_2)\beta_1 - (1 - \rho_1)\rho_2\beta_2]A_b \\
& + [(1 - \rho_3) - (1 - \rho_1)(1 - \rho_3)\beta_1 - (1 - \rho_1)\rho_3\beta_2]A_m \\
& + [(1 - \rho_4) - (1 - \rho_1)(1 - -\rho_4)\beta_1 - (1 - \rho_1)\rho_4\beta_2]B
\end{aligned} \tag{5.7}
$$

$$
\begin{aligned}
G = {}& \rho_1\beta_1 I_g^* + \rho_1\beta_2 G^* + \rho_1[1 - (1 - \rho_1)\beta_1 - \rho_1\beta_2]T^* \\
& + [\rho_2 - \rho_1(1 - \rho_2)\beta_1 - \rho_1\rho_2\beta_2]A_b + [\rho_3 - \rho_1(1 - \rho_3)\beta_1 - \rho_1\rho_3\beta_2]A_m \\
& + [\rho_4 - \rho_1(1 - \rho_4)\beta_1 - \rho_1\rho_4\beta_2]B
\end{aligned} \tag{5.8}
$$

$$
\begin{aligned}
T = {}& \beta_1 I_g^* +, \beta_2 G^* + [1 - (1 - \rho_1)\beta_1 - \rho_1\beta_2]T^* - [(1 - \rho_2)\beta_1 + \rho_2\beta_2]A_b \\
& - [(1 - \rho_3)\beta_1 + > \rho_3\beta_2]A_m - [(1 - \rho_4)\beta_1 + \rho_4\beta_2]B
\end{aligned} \tag{5.9}
$$

$$
\begin{aligned}
A_b = {}& \beta_3 I_g^* + \beta_4 G^* - [(1 - \rho_1)\beta_3 + \rho_1\beta_4]T + [1 - (1 - \rho_2)\beta_3 - \rho_2\beta_4]A_b^* \\
& - [(1 - \rho_3)\beta_3 + \rho_3\beta_4]A_m - [(1 - \rho_4)\beta_3 + \rho_4\beta_4]B
\end{aligned} \tag{5.10}
$$

$$A_m = \beta_5 I_g^* + \beta_6 G^* - [(1 - \rho_1)\beta_5 + \rho_1\beta_6]T - [(1 - \rho_2)\beta_5 + \rho_2\beta_6]A_b$$
$$+ [1 - (1 - \rho_3)\beta_5 - \rho_3\beta_6]A_m^* - [(1 - \rho_4)\beta_5 + \rho_4\beta_6]B \tag{5.11}$$

$$B = \beta_7 I_g^* + \beta_8 G^* - [(1 - \rho_1)\beta_7 + \rho_1\beta_8]T - [(1 - \rho_2)\beta_7 + \rho_2\beta_8]A_b$$
$$- [(1 - \rho_3)\beta_7 + \rho_3\beta_8]A_m \tag{5.12}$$

where

$$\beta_1 = \frac{\alpha_1(1 - \rho_1)}{\Phi_1}, \beta_2 = \frac{\alpha_2\rho_1}{\Phi_1}, \beta_3 = \frac{\alpha_1(1 - \sigma_2)}{\Phi_2}, \beta_4 = \frac{\alpha_2\rho_2}{\Phi_2}, \beta_5 = \frac{\alpha_1(1 - \rho_3)}{\Phi_3},$$

$$\beta_6 = \frac{\alpha_2\rho_3}{\Phi_3}, \beta_7 = \frac{\alpha_1(1 - -\rho_4)}{\Phi_4}, \beta_8 = \frac{\alpha_2\rho_4}{\Phi_4}$$

and

$$\Phi_1 = \alpha_1(1 - \rho_1)^2 + \alpha_2\rho_1^2 + \alpha_3, \Phi_2 = \alpha_1(1 - \rho_2)^2 + \alpha_2\rho_2^2 + \alpha_4,$$
$$\Phi_3 = \alpha_1(1 - \rho_3)^2 + \alpha_2\rho_3^2 + \alpha_5, \Phi_4 = \alpha_1(1 - \rho_4)^2 + \alpha_2\rho_4^2 + \alpha_6.$$

Like Heller (1975), Mosley *et al.* (1987), Gang and Khan (1991), Khan and Hoshino (1992) and Franco-Rodriguez *et al.* (1998) we have assumed *ex ante* that targeted domestic borrowing B^* is equal to zero.

Maximising Equation 5.3 with $R = 1$ and $B^* = 0$ subject to 'Equations 5.5 and 5.6 and re-arranging the first-order conditions yields the following system of simultaneous structural equations, which apply during the adjustment period:

$$I_g = (1 - \rho_1)(\beta_1 + \delta_1)I_g^* + (1 - \rho_1)(\beta_2 + \delta_2)G^* + (1 - \rho_1)$$
$$[1 - (1 - \rho_1)(\beta_1 + \delta_1)\rho_1(\beta_2 + \delta_2)]T^*[(1 - \rho_2) - (1 - \rho_1)$$
$$(1 - \rho_2)(\beta_1 + \delta_1) - (1 - \rho_1)\rho_2(\beta_2 + \delta_2)]A_b[(1 - \rho_3) - (1 - \rho_1)$$
$$(1 - \rho_3) + [(1 - \rho_4) - (1 - \rho_1)(1 - \rho_4)$$
$$(\beta_1 + \delta_1) - (1 - \rho_1)\rho_4(\beta_2 + \delta_2)]B \tag{5.13}$$

$$G = \rho_1(\beta_1 + > \delta_1)I_g^* + \rho_1(\beta_2 + \delta_2)G^* + \rho_1[1 - (1 - \rho_1)(\beta_1 + \delta_1)$$
$$- \rho_1(\beta_2 + \delta_2)]T^* + [(\rho_2 - \rho_1(1 - \rho_2)(\beta_1 + \delta_1) - \rho_1\rho_2(\beta_2 + > \delta_2)]A_b$$
$$+ [\rho_3 - \rho_1(1 - \rho_3)(\beta_1 + \delta_1) - \rho_1\rho_3(\beta_2 + \delta_2)A_m$$
$$+ [\rho_4 - \rho_1(1 - \rho_4)(\beta_1 + \delta_1) - \rho_1\rho_4(\beta_2 + \delta_2)]B \tag{5.14}$$

$$T = (\beta_1 + \delta_1)I_g^* + (\beta_2 + \delta_2)G^* + [1 - (1 - \rho_1)(\beta_1 + \delta_1) - \rho_1(\beta_2 + \delta_2)T^*$$
$$- [(1 - \rho_2)(\beta_1 + \delta_1) + \rho_2(\beta_2 + \delta_2)]A_b - [(1 - \rho_3)(\beta_3 + \delta_3) + \rho_3(\beta_4 + \delta_4)]A_m$$
$$- [(1 - \rho_4)(\beta_3 + \delta_3) + \rho_4\beta_4 + \delta_4)]B \tag{5.15}$$

$$A_b = (\beta_3 + \delta_3)I_g^* + (\beta_4 + \delta_4)G^* - [(1 - \rho_1)(\beta_3 + \delta_3) + \rho_1(\beta_4 + \delta_4)]T$$
$$+ [1 - (1 - \rho_2)(\beta_3 + \delta_3) - \rho_2(\beta_4 + \delta_4)]A_b^* - [(1 - \rho_3)(\beta_3 + \delta_3)$$
$$+ \rho_3(\beta_4 + \delta_4)]A_m - [1 - (1 - \rho_4)(\beta_3 + \delta_3) + \rho_4\beta_4 + \delta_4)]B \tag{5.16}$$

$$A_m = (\beta_5 + \delta_5)I_g^* + (\beta_6 + \delta_6)G^* - [(1 - \rho_1)(\beta_5 + \delta_5) + \rho_1(\beta_6 + \delta_6)]T$$
$$- [(1 - \rho_2)(\beta_5 + \delta_5) + \rho_2(\beta_6 + \delta_6)]A_b + [1 - (1 - \rho_3)(\beta_5 + \delta_5)$$
$$- \rho_3(\beta_6 + \delta_6)]A_m^* - [(1 - \rho_4)(\beta_5 + \delta_5) + \rho_4(\beta_6 + \delta_6)]B \qquad (5.17)$$

$$B = (\beta_7 + \delta_8)I_g^* + (\beta_8 + \delta_8)G^* - [(1 - \rho_1)(\beta_7 + \delta_7) + \rho_1(\beta_8 + \delta_8)]T$$
$$- [(1 - \rho_2)(\beta_7 + \delta_7) + \rho_2(\beta_8 + \delta_8)]A_b - [(1 - \rho_3)(\beta_7 + \delta_7)$$
$$- \rho_3(\beta_8 + \delta_8)]A_m \qquad (5.18)$$

where

$$\delta_1 = \frac{(\alpha_1 + \sigma_1)(1 - \rho_1)}{\Psi_1} - \beta_1, \ \delta_2 = \frac{(\alpha_2 + \sigma_2)\rho_1}{\Psi_1} - \beta_2, \ \delta_3 = \frac{(\alpha_1 + \sigma)(1 - \rho)}{\Psi_2} - \beta_3,$$

$$\delta_4 = \frac{(\alpha_2 + \sigma_2)\rho_2}{\Psi_2} - \beta_4, \ \delta_5 = \frac{(\alpha_1 + \sigma_1)(1 - \rho_3)}{\Psi_3} - \beta_5, \ \delta_6 = \frac{(\alpha_2 + \sigma_2)\rho_3}{\Psi_3} - \beta_6,$$

$$\delta_7 = \frac{(\alpha_1 + \sigma_2)(1 - \rho_4)}{\Psi_4} - \beta_7, \ \delta_8 = \frac{(\alpha_2 + \sigma_2)\rho_4}{\Psi_4} - \beta_8$$

and

$$\Psi_1 = (\alpha_1 + \sigma_1)(1 - \rho_1)^2 + (\alpha_2 + \sigma_2)\rho_1^2 + (\alpha_3 + \sigma_3), \ \Psi_2$$
$$= (\alpha_1 + \sigma_1)(1 - \rho_2)^2 + (\alpha_2 + \sigma_2)\rho_2^2 + \alpha_4,$$
$$\Psi_3 = (\alpha_1 + \sigma_1)(1 - \rho_3)^2 + (\alpha_2 + \sigma_2)\rho_3^2 + \alpha_5,$$
$$\Psi_4 = (\alpha_1 + \sigma_1)(1 - \rho_4)^2 + (\alpha_2 + \sigma_2)\rho_4^2 + (\alpha_6 + \sigma_4).$$

Reduced form equations corresponding to $R = 0$ are:

$$I_g = \pi_1 I_g^* + \pi_2 G^* + \pi_3 T^* + \pi_4 A_b^* + \pi_5 A_m^* \qquad (5.19)$$
$$G = \pi_6 I_g^* + \pi_7 G^* + \pi_8 T^* + \pi_9 A_b^* + \pi_{10} A_m^* \qquad (5.20)$$
$$T = \pi_{11} I_g^* + \pi_{12} G^* + \pi_{13} T^* + \pi_{14} A_b^* + \pi_{15} A_m^* \qquad (5.21)$$
$$A_b = \pi_{16} I_g^* + \pi_{17} G^* + \pi_{18} T^* + \pi_{19} A_b^* + \pi_{20} A_m^* \qquad (5.22)$$
$$A_m = \pi_{21} I_g^* + \pi_{22} G^* + \pi_{23} T^* + \pi_{24} A_b^* + \pi_{25} A_m^* \qquad (5.23)$$
$$B = \pi_{26} I_g^* + \pi_{27} G^* + \pi_{28} T^* + \pi_{29} A_b^* + \pi_{30} A_m^* \qquad (5.24)$$

and for $R = 1$ are

$$I_g = (\pi_1 + \eta_1)I_g^* + (\pi_2 + \eta_2)G^* + (\pi_3 + \eta_3)T^* + (\pi_4 + \eta_4)A_b^*$$
$$+ (\pi_5 + \eta_5)A_m^* \qquad (5.25)$$
$$G = (\pi_6 + \eta_6)I_g^* + (\pi_7 + \eta_7)G^* + (\pi_8 + \eta_8)T^* + (\pi_9 + \eta_9)A_b^*$$
$$+ (\pi_{10} + \eta_{10})A_m^* \qquad (5.26)$$
$$T = (\pi_{11} + \eta_{11})I_g^* + (\pi_{12} + \eta_{12})G^* + (\pi_{13} + \eta_{13})T^* + (\pi_{14} + \eta_{14})A_b^*$$
$$+ (\pi_{15} + \eta_{15})A_m^* \qquad (5.27)$$

$$A_b = (\pi_{16} + \eta_{16})I_g^* + (\pi_{17} + \eta_{17})G^* + (\pi_{18} + \eta_{18})T^* + (\pi_{19} + \eta_{19})A_b^*$$
$$+ (\pi_{20} + \eta_{20})A_m^* \tag{5.28}$$

$$A_m = (\pi_{21} + \eta_{21})I_g^* + (\pi_{22} + \eta_{22})G^* + (\pi_{23} + \eta_{23})T^* + (\pi_{24} + \eta_{24})A_b^*$$
$$+ (\pi_{25} + \eta_{25})A_m^* \tag{5.29}$$

$$B = (\pi_{26} + \eta_{26})I_g^* + (\pi_{27} + \eta_{27})G^* + (\pi_{28} + \eta_{28})T^* + (\pi_{29} + \eta_{29})A_b^*$$
$$+ (\pi_{30} + \eta_{30})A_m^* \tag{5.30}$$

5.3   Data and estimation procedure

The parameters of structural and reduced-form equations were estimated using 1960–92 time series data for the Philippines. Data were primarily obtained from Ahmed (1997), but supplemented by *Philippines Statistical Yearbook* (National Statistical Coordination Board, various years), *Statistical Yearbook* (Central Bank of the Philippines, various years) and the OECD's *Geographical Distribution of Financial Flows to Developing Countries* (OECD, various years). Following Franco-Rodriguez *et al.* (1998) we treat committed aid amounts as the aid targets. The maximisation problem, with respect to the aid variables, is thus to minimise the gap between committed and disbursed (actually spent) aid. All financial data are expressed in millions of Philippine pesos at constant 1987 prices.

Data for the target variables I_g^*, G^* and T^* could not be obtained directly. Estimates of the I_g^* and G^* were consequently derived from a cointegrating regression of vectors of exogenous regressors on each actual variable. The fitted values obtained from these regressions were taken as approximations of the target values. This is basically the approach used by Gang and Khan (1991), Khan and Hoshino (1992) and Franco-Rodriguez *et al.* (1998). Private investment, GDP and the PSBR were regressed on I_g. GDP, primary and secondary school enrolments and the PSBR were regressed on G. Each regressor was lagged one period in accordance with a naive expectations framework. A constant term was used in each regression. In a departure from previous studies, T^* was then obtained by subtracting the sum of A_m^* and A_b^* from the sum of I_g^* and G^* to ensure consistency with Equation 5.5.

The structural equations were estimated using the non-linear three-stage least squares method. This method is appropriate given that the system is simultaneous and that it contains cross-equation restrictions with respect to the ρ and β parameters. Estimates of the reduced form parameters were obtained via simulations of the estimated structural equations. All estimates of structural parameters which were judged to be insignificantly zero were set to zero in this exercise.

5.4   Results

Statistically satisfactory results were obtained from estimating the structural equations. In the final analysis, each equation has high functional fits and few estimation problems were encountered with convergence being achieved after relatively few iterations.[3] The adjustment programme variable R was initially set to zero for all years up to 1980 and one thereafter. This corresponds with the first policy-based (IMF) loan to the Philippines in 1980. After some experimentation R was subsequently set to zero for all years prior to 1986 and one thereafter. Results reported below correspond to this treatment. The conclusion one is tempted to draw from this is that economic reform was ineffective with respect to the public sector, either due to lagged impacts, policy defects, non-implementation or a combination of such factors until 1986.

Structural parameter estimates are shown in Table 5.1. Twelve of the twenty estimates are significantly different from zero. Summaries of the direct impacts of the aid and adjustment variables are shown in Table 5.2. In calculating these impacts parameters which are insignificantly different

Table 5.1   Econometric estimates of structural equation parameters

Parameter	Estimate	t-ratio
ρ_1	0.79*	68.32
ρ_2	1.00*	8.27
ρ_3	−0.08	−0.50
ρ_4	0.95*	19.94
β_1	8.03*	2.99
β_2	1.62*	3.71
β_3	0.002	0.51
β_4	0.05*	2.91
β_5	−0.005	−0.26
β_6	0.02*	2.17
β_7	2.87*	3.23
β_8	−0.19	−0.60
δ_1	−14.47*	−2.26
δ_2	1.93	1.59
δ_3	−0.15*	−1.86
δ_4	−0.04	−0.66
δ_5	−0.09	1.60
δ_6	0.01	0.19
δ_7	−6.93*	−2.71
δ_8	1.15*	3.21

Notes:
* Significantly different from zero at the 90% confidence level.

Table 5.2 Econometric estimates of direct impacts of aid variables

Impact		Mechanism	Estimate
A_b on I_g	$(R=1)$	$(1-\rho_2) - (1-\rho_1)(1-\rho_2)(\beta_1+\delta_1) - (1-\rho_1)\rho_2(\beta_2+\delta_2)$	-0.35
	$(R=0)$	$(1-\rho_2) - (1-\rho_1)(1-\rho_2)\beta_1 - (1-\rho_1)\rho_2\beta_2$	-0.35
A_b on G	$(R=1)$	$\rho_2 - \rho_1(1-\rho_2)(\beta_1+\delta_1) - \rho_1\rho_2(\beta_2+\delta_2)$	-0.25
	$(R=0)$	$\rho_2 - \rho_1(1-\rho_2)\beta_1 - \rho_1\rho_2\beta_2$	-0.25
A_b on T	$(R=1)$	$-[(1-\rho_3)(\beta_1+\delta_1)+\rho_3(\beta_2+\delta_2)]$	-1.60
	$(R=0)$	$-[(1-\rho_3)\beta_1+\rho_3\beta_2]$	-1.60
A_b on A_m	$(R=1)$	$-[(1-\rho_2)(\beta_5+\delta_5)+\rho_2(\beta_6+\beta_6)]$	-0.20
	$(R=0)$	$-[(1-\rho_2)(\beta_5+\delta_5)+\rho_2\beta_6]$	-0.20
A_b on B	$(R=1)$	$-[(1-\rho_2)(\beta_7+\delta_7)+\rho_2(\beta_8+\delta_8)]$	-1.15
	$(R=0)$	$-[(1-\rho_2)\beta_7+\rho_2\beta_8]$	0.00
A_m on I_g	$(R=1)$	$(1-\rho_3) - (1-\rho_1)(1-\rho_3)(\beta_1+\delta_1) - (1-\rho_1)\rho_3(\beta_2+\delta_2)$	2.42
	$(R=0)$	$(1-\rho_3) - (1-\rho_1)(1-\rho_3)\beta_1 - (1-\rho_1)\rho_3\beta_2$	-0.77
A_m on G	$(R=1)$	$\rho_3 - \rho_1(1-\rho_3)(\beta_1+\delta_1) - \rho_1\rho_3(\beta_2+\delta_2)$	5.02
	$(R=0)$	$\rho_3 - \rho_1(1-\rho_3)\beta_1 - \rho_1\rho_3\beta_2$	-6.26
A_m on T	$(R=1)$	$-[(1-\rho_2)(\beta_1+\delta_1)+\rho_2(\beta_2+\delta_2)]$	-8.03
	$(R=0)$	$-[(1-\rho_2)\beta_1+\rho_2\beta_2]$	-1.00
A_m on A_b	$(R=1)$	$-[(1-\rho_3)(\beta_3+\delta_3)+\rho_3(\beta_4+\delta_4)]$	0.15
	$(R=0)$	$-[(1-\rho_3)\beta_3+\rho_3\beta_4]$	0.00
A_m on B	$(R=1)$	$-[(1-\rho_3)(\beta_7+\delta_7)+\rho_3(\beta_8+\delta_8)]$	4.06
	$(R=0)$	$-[(1-\rho_3)\beta_7+\rho_3\beta_8]$	-2.87
R on I_g		$(1-\rho_1)\delta_1 + (1-\rho_1)\delta_2 + (1-\rho_1)[1-(1-\rho_1)\delta_1-\rho_3\delta_2] + [(1-\rho_2)-(1-\rho_1)(1-\rho_2)\delta_1-(1-\rho_1)\rho_2\delta_2]$ $+[(1-\rho_3)-(1-\rho_1)(1-\rho_3)\delta_1-(1-\rho_1)\rho_3\delta_2]+[(1-\rho_4)-(1-\rho_1)(1-\rho_4)\delta_1-(1-\rho_1)\rho_4\delta_2]$	1.27
R on G		$\rho_1+\delta_1\rho_1+\delta_2\rho_1[1-(1-\rho_1)\delta_1-\rho_3\delta_2]+[\rho_2-\rho_1(1-\rho_2)\delta_1-\rho_1\rho_2\delta_2]$ $+[\rho_3-\rho_1(1-\rho_3)\delta_1-\rho_1\rho_3\delta_2]+[\rho_4-\rho_1(1-\rho_4)\delta_1-\rho_1\rho_4\delta_2]$	2.73
R on T		$\delta_1+\delta_2+[1-(1-\rho_1)\delta_1-\rho_1\delta_2]T^* - [(1-\rho_2)\delta_1+\rho_2\delta_2] - [(1-\rho_3)\delta_1+\rho_3\delta_2]$ $-[(1-\rho_4)\delta_1+\rho_4\delta_2]$	1.00
R on A_b		$\delta_3+\delta_4-[(1-\rho_1)\delta_3+\rho_1\delta_4]+[1-(1-\rho_2)\delta_3-\rho_2\delta_4]-[(1-\rho_3)\delta_3+\rho_3\delta_4]$ $-[(1-\rho_4)\delta_3+\rho_4\delta_4]$	1.00
R on A_m		$\delta_5+\delta_6-[(1-\rho_1)\delta_5+\rho_1\delta_6]-[(1-\rho_2)\delta_5+\rho_2\delta_6]+[1-(1-\rho_3)\delta_5-\rho_3+\delta_6]$ $-[(1-\rho_4)\delta_5+\rho_4\delta_6]$	1.00
R on B		$\delta_8+\delta_8-[(1-\rho_1)\delta_7+\rho_1\delta_8]-[(1-\rho_3)\delta_7+\rho_3\delta_8]$	0.00

from zero are set to zero. Multilateral aid (including that tied to policy reform) is negatively associated with investment and consumption in the absence of a programme and positively associated with these variables in the presence of a programme. Multilateral aid has a negative impact on taxation and other recurrent revenue irrespective of whether a programme is present. Indeed, this impact is stronger in the presence of a programme. While multilateral aid is negatively associated with domestic borrowing in the absence of a programme, the reverse is true in the presence of a programme.

The preceding results are of course partial to the extent that they ignore indirect feedbacks. Moreover, most relate to changes in endogenous variables. Of greater policy relevance is the total (direct and indirect) impact of exogenously determined changes in revenues, especially the impact of multilateral aid on saving, taxation and investment. In the case of multilateral aid, these largely result from decisions by donors (including the World Bank and the IMF) to alter the level of aid commitments to the Philippines. Given Equations 5.5 and (26) to (30), it follows that multilateral aid causes a deterioration in public sector saving, a decline in taxes (and the tax base for a given level of GNP) and in public investment if, respectively, $\pi_{10} > \pi_{11}$, $\pi_{15} < 0$ and $\pi_5 < 0$.

Similarly, the presence of an adjustment programme further contributes to these respective outcomes if $\eta_6 + ... + \eta_{10} > \eta_{11} + ... + \eta_{15}$, $\eta_{11} + ... + \eta_{15} < 0$ and $\eta_1 + ... + \eta_5 < 0$.

Given the estimates reported in Table 5.3, multilateral aid has no net impact on saving given that $\pi_{10} = \pi_{11}$, and has negative although rather small incremental impacts on taxation and investment. The presence of a reform programme (at least from 1986 onwards), however, has a strongly negative impact on saving. Given the estimates of $\eta_6 + ... + \eta_{10} > \eta_{11} + ... + \eta_{15}$, such a programme has from 1986 reduced public sector saving in the Philippines by 177 million pesos per year in 1987 prices. The Philippines' reform programme has also caused reductions in taxation and public investment given the estimates of $\eta_1 + ... + \eta_5$ and $\eta_{11} + ... + \eta_{15}$. These outcomes are in contradiction to the stated aims of this programme, and are consistent with a stringent, 'big-bang' implementation of stabilisation measures.

5.5 Conclusion

This chapter attempted to analyse expenditure and revenue decisions of the public sector in the Philippines, taking special account of the impact of multilateral aid flows and the presence of a programme of economic

Table 5.3 Estimates of selected reduced form parameters

Parameter	Estimate
π_4	−0.003
π_5	−0.001
π_9	−0.0002
π_{10}	−0.01
π_{14}	−0.002
π_{15}	−0.01
π_{19}	0.95
π_{20}	0.00
π_{24}	−0.0002
π_{25}	1.00
π_{29}	0.00
π_{30}	−0.003
$\eta_1 + \ldots + \eta_5$	−177.74
$\eta_6 + \ldots + \eta_{10}$	−630.48
$\eta_{11} + \ldots + \eta_{15}$	−807.80
$\eta_{16} + \ldots + \eta_{20}$	−14.93
$\eta_{21} + \ldots + \eta_{25}$	0.21
$\eta_{26} + \ldots + \eta_{30}$	−404.21

reform on these decisions. Included in these flows are World Bank and IMF structural adjustment loans; the Philippines introduced an adjustment programme in late 1980 and received this sort of lending throughout the 1980s and early 1990s. A motive for the paper's analysis was to consider whether this aid promotes behaviour which is inconsistent with the aims of the Philippines' adjustment programme, which is typical of programmes worldwide. These aims include the expansion of the tax base, reductions in fiscal deficits and increases in public investment. Behaviour inconsistent with these aims are aid-induced reductions in taxation, aid-induced declines in public sector saving and aid-induced declines in public investment. Evidence of such behaviour was observed with respect to investment and taxation. Moreover, the presence of a programme actually seemed to worsen these outcomes, hence confirming the fears expressed at the outset of this paper.

The primary motive for this analysis, however, was to condition lines of enquiry for the structural adjustment experience of sub-Saharan African countries. Is it the case that adjustment has been less successful in these countries due to the sorts of problems that the Philippines has experienced? Is it the case that the aid inflows to which these programmes are tied induces behaviour which is consistent with the objectives of adjustment and stabilisation efforts? While this paper cannot answer this question, it certainly gives some validity to the question itself. The concerns underlying the question, given results here, seem to have been validated and there would appear to be no reason, *a priori*, to deny their validity with respect to sub-Saharan Africa, especially given their shared experiences (as outlined at the start of this paper). Given obvious data constraints, especially with respect to time series data, one will have difficulty replicating this analysis for these countries. This would require *inter alia* the application of a far more parsimonious fiscal response model, say with only one category of expenditure and one category of domestic revenue, or possibly even the use of cross- section or panel data.

Above all, however, the results of this analysis would suggest that there is a strong case for giving greater attention to monitoring how structural adjustment lending, and aid funds in general, are allocated by the public sector of recipient countries, in addition to continued monitoring of compliance with the conditions to which these funds are tied.

Acknowledgements

The author is grateful to the conference participants, especially Anne Booth, Susana Franco-Rodriguez and Oliver Morrissey, for useful comments. The usual disclaimer applies.

Notes

1. There still remains, of course, considerable disagreement regarding reasons for the outstanding pre-1997 performance of the high-performing East Asian countries. See, for example, World Bank (1993), Amsden (1994), Lall (1994) and Perkins (1994).
2. Franco-Rodriguez *et al.* (1998) provide a more detailed explanation of Equations 5.5 and 5.6.
3. Further details can be obtained from the author.

6
Population Ageing and Care of the Elderly: What Are the Lessons of Asia for Sub-Saharan Africa?

Mahmood Messkoub

6.1 Introduction

The population age structures of Sub-Saharan African (SSA) countries are among the youngest in the world. It is estimated that by the year 2000, 45 per cent of the SSA population would be below the age of 15, as compared with 33 per cent in South-East Asia, which has started its demographic transition much earlier. But fertility has started to decline in several SSA countries. Kenya, Rwanda, Zimbabwe, Botswana, South Africa and Côte d'Ivoire have experienced moderate to large declines in fertility with smaller declines occurring in Malawi, Tanzania, Zambia, Cameroon, Central African Republic, Burkina Faso, Gambia, Ghana, Mauritania, Senegal and Sierra Leone (Cohen, 1998). This trend is going to continue and will be repeated in other SSA countries, whose population by the middle of the twenty-first century will stabilise at replacement level. Other developing countries in Asia and Latin America have started their demographic transition earlier, and their population, particularly in South and South-East Asia, will reach replacement level by the first quarter of the twenty-first century (see Table 6.1).

Because of earlier high fertility, in particular since the 1920s, the absolute number of people entering old age has been on the increase in Africa. But it is the fertility decline which will lead to an older age structure of population increasing the old dependency ratio (see Table 6.2). In this respect the SSA countries lag behind Asian countries by about 30 years. In 2050 the age structure in SSA will be similar to that of South and South-East Asia in 2020. That in turn means that labour force is going to grow well into the next century in SSA (see Table 6.2).

Table 6.1 Period when fertility is assumed to reach replacement level: medium variant projections for African, and East and South-East Asian countries

Sub-Saharan Africa

2000–10	2010–20	2020–30	2030–40	2040–45
	Mauritius	Zimbabwe	Swaziland	Zambia, I ogo, Nigeria
		Botswana	Eritrea	Uganda, Ethiopia, Ghana
		S. Africa	Rwanda	Namibia, Malawi, Gambia
		Cape Verde	Burundi	Mozambique, Somalia
			Cameroon	Sudan, Chad, Congo
			Swaziland	Gabon, Zaire, Benin
			Kenya	Burkina Faso,
			(–)	Côte d'lvoire
			Lesotho	Guinea, Guinea-Bissau
				Mali, Niger, Sierra Leone
				C. African Republic
				Mauritania, Madagascar
				Djibouti,
				Equatorial Guinea

North Africa

1990–2010	2010–20	2020–30	2030–40	2040–45
	Algeria	Libya		
	Egypt			
	Morocco			
	Tunisia			

East and South-East Asia

1990–2010	2010–20	2020–30	2030–40	2040–45
China	Malaysia	East Timor	Cambodia	
Thailand	Bangladesh	Myanamar		
D.P.R. Korea	Vientnam	Lao's P.R.		
Sri Lanka	Mongolia	Maldives		
Brunei	Philippines	Nepal		
Indonesia		Pakistan		
	India			

Oceania

1990–2010	2010–20	2020–30	2030–40	2040–45
New Zealand	Fiji	Papua New		
New Caledonia	Guam	Guinea		

West and Central Asia

1990–2010	2010–20	2020–30	2030–40	2040–45
Georgia	Israel	Iran	Iraq	Saudi Arabia
Lebanon	Turkey	Qatar	Jordan	Oman
Azerbaijan	Kyrgyzstan	U.A. Emirates	Afghanistan	Yemen

Table 6.1   (continued)

Sub-Saharan Africa				
2000–10	2010–20	2020–30	2030–40	2040–45
Armenia	Turkmenistan	Tadjikistan	Bhutan	
Cyprus	Bahrain	Syria		
	Kuwait			

Note: Countries excluded from the above list have reached replacement level.
Source: Adapted from UN (1995), Tables 84–85, pp. 147–8.

As regards life expectancy at birth in SSA, it varies from a low of 40 years in Sierra Leone to a high of 68 years in Botswana, with the median being around 50 years. This compares with 65 years for East and South-East Asia, which shows a smaller variation than that in SSA. Much of these differences could be explained by the lower level of development, both in terms of per-capita income and national public health policies (World Bank, 1997b).

There is no prospect of the difference in life expectancy between Africa and Asia narrowing down in the near future because of the epidemic rise of HIV/AIDS in parts of SSA, which is going to experience a serious negative effect on life expectancy at birth. According to UN (1995) estimates, by the year 2005 life expectancy at birth in 15 severely affected countries will decline, on average, by 7.5 years (from 57.1 to 49.6). The average decline for the three highest seroprevalence countries (Uganda, Zambia and Zimbabwe) is 12.7 years. More devastating is the impact of HIV/AIDS on life expectancy in working years. For example, in Zimbabwe and Zambia, where life expectancy in working years (20–65) is projected to be around 33 years by 2005, 7.5 years (one fifth) would be lost because of the AIDS epidemic.

Notwithstanding the human tragedies of such losses, it is the impact on the productive capabilities in SSA that is of concern here. The loss of such a large section of the labour force is undoubtedly going to affect labour-intensive sectors of the economy, in particular small-scale farming. While high unemployment and a youthful age structure would in part compensate for the loss of the unskilled labour, the skilled labour would take longer to replace.

The other effect of the AIDS/HIV epidemic is on the availability of care within the household and family for both children and the elderly. The traditional care givers – women – are equally affected by HIV/AIDS in SSA. Their loss could increase the risk of malnutrition and infectious diseases among children. The elderly would not only lose an important source of

Table 6.2 Percentage distribution of population by age group, selected SSA and Asian countries, 1960, 1990, 2020, 2050

Country	Estimates (i) 1960			1990			Projections (ii) 2020			2050		
	0–15	15–60	60+	0–15	15–60	60+	0–15	15–60	60+	0–15	15–60	60+
Sub-Saharan Africa												
Angola	41.8	53.4	4.8	47.1	48.1	4.8	42.6	52.8	4.6	26.3	65.2	8.5
Cameroon	39.8	54.5	5.7	44.7	49.7	5.6	38.6	55.5	5.9	24.7	63.9	11.4
Botswana	47.4	47.8	4.8	45.0	51.4	3.6	32.8	60.2	7.0	22.6	61.6	15.8
South Africa	40.9	53.0	6.1	38.3	55.2	6.5	29.9	61.0	9.1	22.0	61.3	16.7
Ghana	45.6	50.2	4.2	45.4	50.1	4.5	38.3	55.9	5.8	24.3	64.2	11.5
Kenya	45.6	48.0	6.4	49.2	46.3	4.5	39.5	56.2	4.3	24.3	63.9	11.8
Malawi	45.7	50.1	4.2	47.0	48.7	4.3	41.2	54.2	4.6	25.2	64.9	9.9
Mozambique	41.4	53.7	4.9	44.3	50.5	5.2	40.2	54.7	5.1	25.6	68.1	6.3
Nigeria	45.4	50.7	3.9	45.4	50.2	4.4	39.2	55.3	5.5	24.4	65.1	10.5
Uganda	46.6	49.1	4.3	48.4	47.5	4.1	42.9	53.7	3.4	25.0	66.1	8.9
Tanzania	45.9	50.2	3.9	46.3	49.6	4.1	39.0	56.2	4.8	24.3	64.6	11.1
Zambia	45.2	50.8	4.0	47.9	48.3	3.8	38.8	57.3	3.9	24.1	64.3	11.6
North Africa												
Algeria	43.7	50.4	5.9	41.9	52.6	5.5	25.3	65.9	8.8	20.0	59.2	20.8
Egypt	42.5	52.0	5.5	39.7	54.0	6.3	25.3	64.1	10.6	20.2	59.6	20.2
East and South-East												
China	38.9	53.9	7.2	27.5	63.9	8.6	20.7	63.8	15.5	19.3	56.0	24.7
Thailand	44.7	50.8	4.5	31.8	61.5	6.7	22.2	63.9	13.9	19.4	55.8	24.8
Rep. of Korea	41.9	52.8	5.3	25.9	66.4	7.7	19.2	62.8	18.0	18.5	55.3	26.2
Philippines	44.7	50.4	4.9	39.7	55.2	5.1	26.8	63.7	9.5	20.6	66.1	13.3
Malaysia	45.3	49.4	5.3	38.2	56.0	5.8	27.7	61.5	10.8	19.8	59.1	21.1
Indonesia	40.1	54.2	5.7	35.7	58.0	6.3	23.6	65.3	11.1	21.1	57.3	21.6

Notes: (ii) Projections are based on the 'medium' fertility assumption (an average of high and low fertility changes). According to UN (1995: 143) the 'medium' fertility assumption has well predicted the path of population growth in the past.

Source: UN (1995)

Table 6.3   Dependency ratios per 100 working age population, selected African and Asian countries

Country	Estimates (i)				Projections (ii)			
	1960		1990		2020		2050	
	0–15	60+	0–15	60+	0–15	60+	0–15	60+
Sub-Saharan Africa								
Angola	78	9	98	10	81	9	40	13
Cameroon	73	10	90	11	70	11	39	18
Botswana	99	10	88	7	54	12	37	26
South Africa	77	12	69	12	49	15	36	27
Ghana	91	8	91	9	69	10	38	18
Kenya	95	13	106	10	70	8	38	18
Malawi	91	8	97	9	76	8	39	15
Mozambique	77	9	88	10	73	9	38	9
Nigeria	90	8	90	9	71	10	37	16
Uganda	95	9	102	9	80	6	38	13
Tanzania	91	8	93	8	69	9	38	17
Zambia	89	8	99	8	68	7	37	18
North Africa								
Algeria	87	12	80	10	38	13	34	35
Egypt	82	11	74	12	39	17	34	34
East and South-East Asia								
China	72	13	43	13	32	24	34	44
Thailand	88	9	52	11	35	22	35	44
Rep. of Korea	79	10	39	12	31	29	33	47
Philippines	89	10	72	9	42	15	31	20
Malaysia	92	11	68	10	45	18	34	36
Indonesia	74	11	62	11	36	17	37	38

Source: Calculated from Table 6.2.

support for their own needs, but have to take on the role of care givers for the orphans in their household.[1]

   This chapter focuses on the issue of population ageing and the question of care for the elderly. Section 6.2 compares informal systems of care in Africa and Asia. Section 6.3 compares policies regarding more formal systems of social security for the elderly in both continents. Section 6.4 specifically concentrates on a comparison of pension provisions. The final section draws some conclusions for future policy which emphasise the need to preserve the informal systems alongside the formal, particularly given public social security budget constraints.

6.2 A comparison of informal systems of care in Africa and Asia

The elderly are a differentiated population in terms of their ownership of assets and sources of income, that in turn determine the degree of their vulnerability over time. The elderly's income could be based on any combination of the following: ownership of assets, own work, social security, pensions, marital status, other family members, and so on. Available data on sources of income of the elderly in a selected number of developed and developing countries show that in general the richer the country the higher the percentage of those above the age of 60 relying on pensions/welfare for their livelihood (World Bank, 1994). In low income countries, except in urban areas of China, family and own work are the main sources of income. The data also suggests that as countries get richer the formal system gains importance in providing support to the elderly.

Table 6.4, limited as it is, shows that the family is a much more important source of income for the elderly in Africa than elsewhere in the developing world. Other sources of income, especially work in rural areas, would be important in Africa, but lack of information does not allow further comparison with Asia.

Empirical evidence also shows that 'the extent of intergenerational support is often dependent upon socio-economic status; the lower the status, the greater the degree of interdependence'.[2] The importance of family as a source of support is even stronger when we note that in most countries of Africa and Asia the elderly live with their children. Altruistic motives aside, in all cases it is the control of property and inheritance rights that act as the last sanction to ensure that children look after their elderly parents. In Asia the long and sustained economic growth of the 1960s through early 1990s has been a great help to families to care for their elderly. Higher income and growth have also helped the elderly to contribute to their old age through savings, values of which were protected by favourable economic conditions of macroeconomic stability and low inflation (World Bank, 1994).

In Africa the informal systems are based on broader familial links than in Asia. The extended family could contain adult brothers and sisters as well as children. Reliance on the younger generation is not limited to one's own blood children: adoption, fosterage, and raising grand children, all help to widen the support base (World Bank, 1994). The spread of AIDS would, most probably, strengthen rather than weaken such linkages between the younger and older generation.

Table 6.4 Sources of income in old age, selected less developed countries, 1980s

Percentage of persons over 60 receiving
income from:

Africa	Work	Family Welfare	Pension	Savings
Kenya	n.a.	88	n.a.	n.a.
Nigeria	n.a.	95	n.a.	n.a.
Median	n.a.	91	n.a.	n.a.
Asia				
China	45	34	13	n.a.
Urban	15	17	64	n.a.
Rural	51	38	5	n.a.
Indonesia	46	63	10	4
Philippines	63	45	13	2
Rep. of Korea	24	64	6	8
Singapore	18	85	16	37
Median	45	45	13	6
Latin America and Caribbean				
Argentina	26	8	74	6
Chile	20	9	73	n.a.
Costa Rica	21	23	46	n.a.
Trinidad and Tobago	15	26	77	n.a.
Median	20	16	73	n.a.

Notes: n.a. Means not available. Averages are unweighted.
Source: Adapted from World Bank (1994: 63).

Another source of informal support in Africa is the existence of kin, community and tribal support, though in this respect Asia also has a long tradition through village networks that like Africa have survived migration and urbanisation. This is particularly true in Asian countries, like China, where social security support is tied to place of residence. Development of 'villages' in urban areas of China reflects the strength and value of community and regional linkages.

Migration has played a complicated role in the development and maintenance of informal systems. On the one hand it has provided extra cash income that, as noted earlier, did alleviate poverty, and allowed the household to support its non-migrating members including the elderly. This is predicated on the maintenance of links between the migrating members and the family, that also allows the migrating members to come 'home' on retirement to be cared for by their family and the larger community. Such links are easier to maintain under circular patterns of migration, which have been common in parts of Africa.

The orthodox interpretation of the economics of the informal support system is based on the notion of risk sharing in extended multi-generational families and village groups. Given the family's size and the diversity of skills, risk pooling allows the realisation of economies of scale within a community be it a family, household or village. Informal arrangements do not have the costs and asymmetries of information that exist in formal systems (World Bank, 1994). The basic risks of ageing are ill health, disability and loss of income due to inability to work and lack of income-generating assets.

Informal systems, however, are not without costs, some of which are not monetised. Non-monetised costs are not spread equally across household members. For example, women bear the main burden of caring for the elderly. At times the health costs could be prohibitive and undermine the resource base of the family by forcing the sale of valuable assets. In some households the demographic balance could also shift so heavily against the younger generation putting the care of a rising number of elderly beyond the youngs' financial and physical capacity. The latter point is particularly important in Africa where AIDS is affecting those in the working age. The table is turned on the elderly who now have to care for their dying children and look after their grandchildren.

6.3   Social security and care of the elderly in Asia and Africa

The first objective of any old-age care and social security policy is to protect or to provide aged people with the entitlement to a basic standard of living in line with their life-time experience and expectations of the society concerned. The second objective is to reduce the gap between different sections of the elderly. While the first objective can be achieved under a variety of institutional arrangements, the second objective requires some degree of state intervention.

The literature identifies four main models of social policy and welfare delivery – residual, institutional, occupation-based and structural. The main difference between these models is the level of state intervention. At one end of the spectrum is the residual model in which basic means-tested benefits combined with remedial services would be made available to those in need. At the other end the state undertakes to provide a comprehensive service to all who require it (Phillips, 1992). Plans to set up pension schemes also follow a similar scheme. At the residual end means testing ensures that the state pension acts only as a safety net for those whose income and assets fall below a certain minimum level, while at the other end the state guarantees a minimum pension to all.

Parallel to the publicly provided care there exists the all important informal – household based – provisioning of care for the elderly. Family support systems generally make the least demand on state finances, and it is not surprising that in the debate on the role of the state, orthodox economic policies have increasingly looked to the family to fill the gaps wherever the state reduces its role in the provision of services including the care of the elderly.

In South and South-East Asia the family has been the main source of care for the elderly, and government support has at best played a residual role in welfare provision. Even in China where the state has set itself the goal of meeting the basic needs of the population, the care of the elderly is still seen as the prime responsibility of the family. Both culture and economic ideology have been important in giving family the primary caring role.

> Belief in the family as the prime source of care stems from, for example, the Chinese, especially Confucian, traditions of filial piety and respect, or from similar Malay cultural attitudes, or from the religious emphases of Islam which in the Koran and elsewhere, stress the need for children to accept responsibility for the care of their elderly relatives (Phillips, 1992: 15).

The role of economic ideology is not as transparent as that of the family, but given that ageing in Asia, as a public policy issue, emerged mainly in the 1980s,[3] when economic orthodoxy with its emphasis on the 'free market' and individual initiative and responsibility had become dominant, the official response to ageing has been to view the family as the primary provider of care with the social security as the secondary source of support. Countries like Taiwan and Singapore with a longer history of a social welfare system have had a more 'welfare state' approach to the question of ageing than countries like South Korea. Needless to say cultural attitudes have legitimised the 'family first' approach. Compare this with countries with a long tradition of a welfare state (e.g., the UK) where any move back to a family support system was rightly viewed with suspicion and hostility. Asian states, however, did not wash their hands of the care of the elderly and a variety of measures have been put in place either in direct support of the elderly or indirectly through the family. A brief survey of these measures would be useful for the planning of old-age care in SSA.

An obvious starting point in many of the East Asian countries has been the identification of the elderly's needs. Prioritising these allowed the state to meet them selectively and within its budgetary capacity. Table 6.5

Table 6.5 State support for the elderly, selected Asian countries, 1980s

Country[a]	Health insurance	tests	Income pension	assistant	Family tax relief	Community	Housing	work
Singapore	×	×	×	×	×	×	×	×
China[b]	×	×	×	×	–	×	×	–
Taiwan	×	×	×	–	–	×	×	–
S. Korea	×	×	×	×	–	×	–	×
Malaysia	×	×	×	×	–	×	–	–
Thailand	×	×	×	×	–	×	–	–

Legend:
×: available
—: not available or no information
Notes:
[a] In general these services and supports are available only on a selective and often means-tested basis. Pensions have the most limited cover and are usually available only to the employees of the government and formal sector.
[b] Most of these services are urban based.
Source: Compiled from Phillips (1992).

gives a summary of the main support provided by the state in several East Asian countries. Countries vary in the coverage and quality of support that they provide. In general the support is means tested and targeted towards the poor. All have some basic health and income maintenance support that works as a safety net to cover the most needy among the elderly; in addition, formal sector and state employees have entitlement to a secure contribution related pension.

The institutional organisation of the support system also varies across East Asian countries. While, in general, the Ministry of Health has the responsibility for health matters through its network of hospitals and dispensaries, the other welfare aspects are handled by different ministries. Non-medical support in some countries (e.g. Malaysia) is consolidated under a social welfare department, whereas in others like Taiwan the responsibility is divided between the government's insurance bureaux and social affairs department. Such divisions of labour in part reflect the history of institutional development for old-age care, and their usefulness as a model for African countries is rather limited. However, it is possible to draw some policy conclusions by looking at best practices.

One of the most fundamental and important rights that some of the East Asian countries have officially recognised is the constitutional right to a minimum standard of living. South Korea has had a Livelihood Protection Act since 1961, giving a constitutional right to a minimum but decent standard of living for all. For an elderly person to qualify for state support he or she must be poor (means tested against a minimum level of income and assets that is annually set by the government), must be at least 65 years old, and must not have anybody who would be legally responsible to care for them. Earlier, the Labour Standards Act of 1953 introduced the 'Retirement Benefit' system under which all workplaces with ten or more employees must reserve retirement benefits which are paid to workers in the form of a lump sum upon retirement. It should be emphasised that this is not a pension programme, but an income maintenance in the form of a one-off payment, that has been the principal income maintenance programme for most retirees in South Korea (Choi, 1992).

In South Korea work has been used as another measure to maintain the economic independence of the elderly and to alleviate the pressure on labour supply shortages. Job placement schemes were established for the retirees and elderly. For example, the elderly were helped to set up workshops and share the income, or would be given priority for setting up stalls in public places such as parks to sell basic necessities and government monopoly goods. A skill development fund was estrablished to retrain the older workers in order to improve their chances of re-employment (Cheung and Vasoo, 1992).

In China 'the Five Guarantee Household' system is expected to guarantee food, clothing, shelter, health care and burial expenses for the poor among the elderly. However, state support for the elderly varies greatly between rural and urban areas. Financial support for the state employees comes mainly from the enterprises where they work. A part of the enterprise's pre-tax income is set aside for payment to its retiree. Usually such level of support does not exist in rural areas where the great majority (about 80 per cent) of the elderly live. After the introduction of the household responsibility system in the early 1980s, when land of the rural collective farms were contracted out to households, the family became a much more important source of support than before, though the homeless and childless elderly are still cared for by the local government and the collectives. While the household responsibility system opened up great opportunities for some it also widened the income inequality in rural areas. This has had implications for the care of the elderly – the richer and bigger households have obviously had more resources at their disposal to care for their elderly who also provided some basic support in household duties for their families (Kwong and Gouxuan, 1992). Older parents have become an important source of support in families with migrating members.

Singapore is one of the countries with the most comprehensive and well-developed old age infrastructures in East Asia, in part because population ageing started earlier and was faster than others. From the early 1970s and through the adoption of successive policies that started with the provision of services to the elderly, initially as an extension of the existing social services, a national policy has emerged with important lessons for other countries.

To formulate a national policy the Singaporean government formed an Advisory Council on the Aged in 1988 which appointed four committees to report on: Community Based Programmes, Attitudes, Residential Care Programmes, and Employment with respect to the Aged. Members of these committees were drawn from government ministries, statutory boards and voluntary organisations concerned with the provision of services to the elderly people. An inter-sectoral approach to policy formulation has been an important feature of this national policy. That helped the committees to formulate implementable policies. Furthermore, the work of the committees was publicised to raise awareness in the country about the issue of ageing and to solicit public debate and feedback on the recommendations of the committees (Cheung and Vasoo, 1992).

In order to put the issue of ageing on the national policy-making agenda the Council recommended the setting up of a national council on ageing with the character and authority of a statutory body to plan and coordinate policies and programmes for the elderly people. Other policy recommendations were aimed at giving more financial independence to the elderly as well as reducing the financial burden on the state. These included the raising of the retirement age from 55 to 60, adjusting the seniority-based wage system in order to reduce the cost of hiring older people, and a reduced rate of provident fund contribution to employers so that they could retain their older employees.

On the advocacy and public awareness side, the strengthening of public education programmes on the aged was suggested. Some measures were also recommended in order to reduce the cost of caring for the elderly by voluntary organisations and families by making land available to set up homes for the elderly, lengthening the lease of such homes, and increasing the tax rebate for families who look after their elderly relatives.

What distinguishes the experience of Singapore is her giving the elderly the same statutory status as other sections of the society, and integrating the issue of ageing across different ministries and institutions. This is a model that can easily be followed in SSA and adapted according to the existing national practices and institutions. At the most general level SSA is quite similar to East Asia. In both regions family is the most important source of support for the elderly and the state plays a residual rule in the provision of care.

Drawing on these similarities, the issue of ageing in Africa could be addressed at various levels. At macro level and following the Singapore's model the ageing should be given a permanent and prominent presence at national level policy-making fora. This process could begin by setting up of an inter- departmental committee whose members would be drawn from, for example health, social security and welfare ministries, and voluntary organisations. Open and democratic debate is essential for the formulation of correct and legitimate policies. The legitimation issue is important for the public's acceptance and implementation of policies and for maximising donor's assistance.

Moving on to the informal and the household support system, as far as the family source of income is concerned there are no hard and fast rules, except the general principle of supporting the economic base of the informal system of care for the elderly. At the macro level, a stable economic environment as well as indexation of incomes to insure against inflation have been important features of the East Asian experience. In addition, supporting the rural economy, where the majority of the elderly live is important, in Africa. Another area of intervention is communication between rural and urban areas. Rural to urban migration of the younger people could weaken the link between the two generations within families, and increase the uncertainty for the elderly who rely on remittances. Improving the flow of information and communication between the two areas and offering incentives for remittances could help to maintain the economic and social links between the two areas and between generations.

At the micro level, Table 6.5 shows the range of state support available in East Asia. In general these services complement rather than substitute those provided by families and other voluntary sources of support. Some of them, like pension systems, would take longer to set up in Africa (see below), while others could be implemented quickly, such as tax relief to families caring for their elderly, and health support. Complementarity between formal and informal systems in the era of structural adjustment also means ensuring that the income of families caring for the elderly is protected when it comes to the charging of fees and cuts in public services. Since the late 1980s adjustment programmes have become sensitive to the needs of the elderly by treating them as part of the vulnerable groups in the society, and hence the object of targeted policies, such as exemptions from user charges (Cornia *et al.*, 1987). However, such policies should go further and offer practical help for maintaining the informal system of care. For example, cuts in health services usually entails early discharge from hospital. Elderly patients could be treated differently either by being hospitalised longer than others, or their families could be offered compensation and support after an early discharge.

The South Korean example of providing income earning opportunities for the elderly can easily be adopted in Africa, but to ensure that the benefits of the preferential treatment of the elderly would not go only to those who have the skill and the capital to set up a small business, this policy has to be complemented with the provision of small loans and training. Micro-credit institutions would help in this regard, and these could also be used to build up pension funds for the poorer sections of the population. As far as an employment policy for the elderly is concerned the Singaporean approach provides a useful agenda for SSA, but is of less immediate concern because of Africa's current young age structure. Yet, given the pressures of structural adjustment programmes and public sector retrenchment in SSA and the fact that the older workers are one of the first groups to be laid off (because of their higher wage costs, and that they can be paid by pension and provident funds), a targeted policy for the retraining of the poorer sections of the older workers and assisting them with income earning opportunities should be put on the agenda of retrenchment. Such a policy will increase the chance of their employment in the private sector and reduce the pressure on other poverty alleviation programmes and the social security system in general.

Moreover, the age structure of the population is also driven by the distribution of population across regions. The process of urbanisation and the development of urban based industries and services would have an asymmetric effect on the age structure of urban and rural areas through rural-urban migration, which has in general been selective of the younger people, and younger men in particular. Another major migratory flow has been towards mining areas in South Africa that has increased the number of female-headed households in the sending regions. Both these migratory flows have over time led to a weakening of rural household economy in many countries, that in turn had reduced the resources of the household to take care of their elderly. This implication of migration for the care of the aged in rural areas has been a recurring theme in the studies of rural ageing (Tout, 1989).[4]

As far as the management of changing age structure in rural areas is concerned, East Asia (except China) is not a good comparator for SSA, for the two regions have different population distributions between rural and urban areas. But we can draw on experience of other parts of Asia, like the

Indian sub-continent, which have a similar population distribution as SSA. As noted earlier, development of pension schemes for the self-employed in countries with inadequate financial institutions is fraught with difficulty. Some Asian countries, however, have come up with practical schemes to increase the productive capacity of the local economy which was then taxed to support the local old or provide income generating activities for the older people.

In India, for example, HelpAge India provided funds for the construction of fishing boats for a village in Andhra Pradesh whose stock of boats were destroyed by a cyclone, on the conditions that the boats would be collectively owned by a cooperative society of fisherfolk and that each boat crew would agree to contribute three kilograms of fish from each catch to the widows and elderly of the village who would then sell the fish in a nearby local market. Another project in Bangladesh, aimed at providing support for families whose younger males had migrated to cities, invested in the whole community by installing water pumps in a village, which in turn increased the number of annual harvests from one to three. In the same village groups of families were formed along the line of credit cooperatives in order to make very small savings every week that would provide the fund for future borrowing for members to purchase land, tools, seeds, etc. Retraining of older people to undertake new activities has been part of another project whereby the Bangladesh Rural Reconstruction Movement would train fishermen, whose source of livelihood was lost because of silting up of estuary rivers, to become farmers (Tout, 1989).

Similar schemes also exist in different SSA countries. Tout (1989) reports that in Zambia training of older farmers in new agricultural techniques was put on the agenda of the Ecumenical Centre of Makeni. Or in remote areas of Malawi where access to clean water was difficult for the elderly who used to walk long distances to fetch it, shallow wells were opened up with the support of locals who provided the labour.

Strengthening the link between migrants and their home villages could be of great help to the elderly. The stonger the link between the migrant and the origin, the more would be the pressure on the migrant to maintain his/her social obligations to the origin community, especially when it comes to the care of the elderly parents and relatives. Such links would also help the returning migrants to reintegrate into the community. There are several ways these links could be established and reinforced. Mobile postal offices and banks could be established in areas with a large number of out-migrants. In low migration areas government agriculture and development agencies should be encouraged to act as a courier for sending remittances. Remittances could also be channelled towards useful public projects like health and sanitation, access to which for families of migrants would be free.

For such schemes to be successful, it is essential that local communities should be involved in the planning and implementation stages of projects, in other words the locals should 'own' the projects. This requires some degree of decentralisation and local autonomy which may be lacking in many countries; however, it should not be difficult to organise initiatives with local support while planning for decentralisation of some key areas of social security like care of the elderly. Another advantage of decentralisation may be that it could encourage more donor involvement in old-age care projects.

Finally, it should be noted that fertility decline should be viewed as an opportunity by countries with a young age structure and by the next generation of working age people. Djuhari (1993) and Niehof (1995) commenting on Indonesia, which has been experiencing a steady decline in fertility since the late 1960s (see Table 6.2), have argued that population ageing is presenting a golden opportunity for improving the quality of education and employment, thus increasing the resource base needed to care for an elderly population. Another source of output growth, they suggest, is the increased labour force participation rate of women, which is associated with the decline in fertility and rising urbanisation.

6.4   Pension policies

So far we have touched on several macroeconomic issues that are important for the entitlement of the elderly. But the most important macro question in LDCs is the establishment of a formal system of pension and social security for the old, and where such systems exist the key policy question is how to ensure their financial viability. This section first provides a comparative view of the public pension systems in the two regions and then discusses various pension schemes for SSA.

An overview of the public pension systems in SSA and East Asia is presented in Table 6.6. In SSA it takes longer to qualify for public pensions (14 years) than in East Asia (9 years) and a far less proportion of people over 60 are covered – 5 per cent and 22.3 per cent respectively, which reflects the size of the public sector in the two regions, and also accounts for differences in the contributors/labour force ratio, which is 6.4 per cent in SSA and 35.1 per cent in East Asia. With the onset of population ageing in SSA there would be a need to increase the coverage, without necessarily increasing the size of the public sector employment, while ensuring the

Table 6.6 Public pension indicators in SSA and East Asian countries[a]

Indicator	SSA	East Asia
Normal retirement age:		
Female	56	60
Male	56	60
Covered years required for full pension	14	9
Percentage of salary contributed to payroll tax for pensions:		
Worker	3.6	5.4
Employer	5.6	9.4
Combined	9.2	13.8
Pension payroll tax/labour cost (%)	8.5	11.3
Benefit type	CR[b]	CR
Contributors/labour force (%)	6.4	35.1
Pensioners/persons over 60 (%)	5.0	22.3
Pensioners/contributors (%)	8.5	11.4
Pension spending indicators:		
Pension spending/GDP (%)	0.5	1.9
Pension spending/Govt spending (%)	1.8	9.6
Public employee pension spending/Govt pension spending (%)	67.1	67.7
Earmarked payroll tax less benefit spending/Benefit spending (%)	205	222
Financing of pension schemes:		
Receipts as a percentage of GDP	0.7	3.2
share of receipts from:		
Payroll tax	78.0	68.0
Investment income	20.0	30.0
General revenues	2.0	2.0
Year of survey	1989/90	1989/91

Notes:
[a] These are average figures for a selected number of countries for which data was available. To ensure that they are not affected too much by the outliers some countries have been excluded for certain indicators. The coverage of countries vary for each indicator.
[b] CR: Contribution related.

Indexation: There are no automatic indexation of pensions in progress to prices for the great majority of countries for which data are available.
Source: Compiled and calculated from World Bank (1994), Tables A.4–A.10.

financial viability of the public pension system and instituting pension schemes outside the public sector.

Financial viability of a public pension scheme is fundamentally about the balance between the number of beneficiaries (pensioners) and contributors, and more importantly the balance between benefits paid out and contributions. Other things being equal, the latter has to increase to cope with ageing, which in turn implies increasing the receipts from taxation and other sources. Currently the pensioners/contributors ratio in SSA and East Asia are comparable: 8.5 and 11.4 per cent respectively. Pension payroll tax/labour cost ratios are also not far apart and 8.5 per cent in SSA and 11.3 per cent in East Asia. However, SSA countries rely more on payroll taxes to finance their public pension schemes – these finance 78 per cent of the public pensions, compared with 68 per cent in East Asia. The position is reversed with investment income which accounts for 20 per cent of receipts in SSA and 30 per cent in East Asia. To ensure the viability of public pension systems in SSA there is a clear case for increasing the contribution of investment income to public pension fund, otherwise payroll taxes have to increase to unacceptable levels. In the early 1990s, 9.2 per cent of public sector salaries went to payroll taxes in SSA, compared with 13.8 per cent for East Asia. Keeping these figures low also contributes to the international competitiveness of SSA economies. The ratio of payroll tax to labour costs (defined as wages plus employer's share of payroll tax) is 8.5 per cent in SSA and compares favourably with similar ratios in East Asia (11.3 per cent), Latin America (7.1 per cent) and Middle East (9.4 per cent).

SSA is ageing more slowly, has a larger proportion of its population living in rural areas and has less developed financial and regulatory institutions than East Asia. For SSA the World Bank recommends (1) a small public pillar (covering urban areas – where the informal support system breaks down first – and big enterprises in order to keep the cost of operating the system low) and (2) direct support to the poor, including the old poor who are vulnerable because of their diminished ability to work. Governments should also try to maintain the informal support system by providing incentives for the families to continue taking care of their elderly. Other sets of policies involve the establishment of a legal and institutional framework for the development of personal saving and occupational plans.[5] In the 'young and rapidly ageing' countries of East Asia the World Bank proposes the establishment of a mandatory decentralised funded pillar, provided that governments have the regulatory capability, and the banking and financial infra-structures exist. In line with the World Bank overall multi-pillar scheme the public pillar is given a redistributive role in these countries (World Bank, 1994).

Fundamental to the establishment and efficient running of these different pillars in SSA, and for that matter elsewhere, is a well-functioning regulatory framework which would assure public trust in the system. Parallel to these developments, attempts should be made to enhance existing financial instruments like provident funds that are 'fully funded, defined contribution schemes in which funds are managed by the public sector' (World Bank, 1994: xxiiii).

A provident fund is fundamentally a compulsory savings scheme that primarily provides for old age, and contingencies of invalidity and death. As a defined contribution scheme in which the contribution determines the benefit accrued, the contributor usually receives a lump sum, or periodic payments based on the credit in his/her account with the fund and his/her actuarially calculated life expectancy. Because of the direct link between contribution and benefit the cost of the cover is not spread over all contributors, unlike social security systems. As a savings scheme provident funds help to accumulate capital at a much faster rate than the pay-as-you-go schemes since the former collects contributions at a higher rate than the latter, provided that the ratio of contributors to beneficiaries remains high, which is usually the case in countries with young age structures.

The establishment of provident funds in SSA dates back to early 1960s. They are generally limited to former British colonies, and their economic importance varies across countries – in 1980 the ratio of provident fund to GDP varied from a low of 8 per cent to a high of 49 per cent. These funds provide a useful vehicle for mobilising domestic savings and a clear and transparent link between contributions and benefit thus making them publicly acceptable and legitimate. Another advantage of provident funds is their use for contingency purposes allowing the contributors to draw on their savings before retirement.

In recent years there has been suggestion of converting provident funds to pension funds, but governments have been reluctant to do this because of provident funds' faster accumulation rates, and the fact that these funds have been mostly used to finance public projects (Gruat, 1990). Interestingly enough the contributors to provident funds have also had reservations about converting provident funds to pension funds. A provident fund provides a guaranteed interest and a lump sum, that despite the erosion of their values by inflation were considered more secure by the recipients than a regular pension whose real value could not be guaranteed in the unstable and vulnerable macroeconomic environment facing most African countries (Gruat, 1990). Another attraction of provident funds is their accessibility. They can be used for a variety of contingencies, depending on the terms and conditions, like marriage, debt payment, children's education. Obviously, provident funds are not a substitute for pensions, and the idea of conversion has to be put in the context of the strategic reform of the social security system, in which the contingency/insurance functions of provident funds is catered for and separated from their pension function.

Provident funds, however, share the problems of all funded pension schemes in which the return is dependent on where the money is invested. Governments have been criticised for misusing provident funds by treating them as a kind of tax income that could be used to finance government expenditure, or investing them in government bonds at very low interest rates (World Bank, 1994). Private management of these funds could improve the returns on them, but that requires strict regulation to prevent mis-investment by the private sector, hence the need to assess institutional and human capital capacities. In this respect constructive lessons could be learned from private management of pension funds in Chile and elsewhere.

The first condition for turning the management of a provident fund to the private sector is the existence of institutions and skills to monitor the activities of the private sector. In Chile, for example, funds are managed by pension funds administrators which are supervised by the Super-intendency of these funds, an autonomous agency linked to the Ministry of Labour and Social Security, that has, among others, 100 lawyers and auditors. It receives daily reports from the funds on investment transactions, and monthly reports on their financial positions and performance. It has the power to issue and revoke licences of fund administrators and can resort to on-site inspections to assure the accuracy of received reports. To minimise the investment risks of private-run pension funds ceilings are imposed on investment in particular areas. Until 1991 these funds were not allowed to invest in foreign securities and the lifting of restriction was gradual, starting at 1 per cent of the fund held, rising to 10 per cent by 1995.

Operating costs is another issue that should concern the authorities. By decentralising and privatising the management of funds the operating costs would inevitably increase. In Chile the ratio of operating costs to annual contributions was 15.4 per cent in 1990, that compares with 2 per cent in Malaysia and 0.53 per cent in Singapore and 51.7 per cent in Zambia for a similar year. The Chilean funds, on the other hand, had a higher return, as these funds were still in their early years, and their establishments were coordinated with large scale privatisation plans which offered investment opportunities in privatised public utilities. It is suggested that with increased competition and coverage operating costs would come down (World Bank, 1994).

6.5   Conclusion

The demographic transition is slowly changing the age structure of the SSA countries. By the year 2050 about 10–11 per cent of population will be over 60 in most SSA countries, compared with 4–5 per cent in 1990. Asian countries have experienced a much faster rate of fertility decline which started earlier than in Africa. It will take Asia 30 years (from 1990 to 2020) to double the proportion of its over 60 population compared with 60 years (from 1990 to 2060) in SSA which therefore has ample time to organise institutions, financial or otherwise, to care for a rising number of elderly.

Africa has time on its side, but has very few of the South and East Asian countries, economic advantages. From 1960 to the mid-1990s, the population of most of Asia has had a more diverse economic base and had been ageing in a stable, and growing macroeconomic environment, with reasonable political stability, albeit repressive in some countries, and within a growing international economic setting. For much of this period there also existed a consensus over the role of state in the economy enabling Asian governments to use public finance measures to organise social security systems. Most SSA countries do not enjoy the economic advantages of Asia. In addition they have to cope with an AIDS epidemic which could wipe out a large section of its working population in the next 20 years.

Not all is lost. The high mortality of the current working age population because of AIDS is in part would be compensated by the past high birth rate that would in turn increase working age population substantially by 2050, keeping the dependency rate of the elderly to a reasonable level. If the working age population of the next century is gainfully employed the economic base would be sufficiently strong to plan the necessary institutions for the care of the elderly.

Africa has a rich history of looking after its older generation. In designing policies due attention should be given to the existing institutional arrangement, both informal and formal, by trying to increase the complementarity between the two. The cost of running pay-as-you-go pension schemes would be lowered if household-based arrangements for the care of the elderly could be maintained. Providing financial incentives to households to care for their elderly should be part of this planning for population ageing. Strengthening the financial and other infrastructural links between rural and urban areas should also help the migrating members of the household to look after the rural-based older generation.

The establishment and reform of the formal system is a much more problematic policy area. The existing pension schemes have a very limited coverage in Africa and in the main are restricted to the wage earners. Expanding their coverage could be beyond the financial capacity of many African governments. Establishing private pension schemes, fashionable as it is, requires a strong regulatory infrastructure for the financial sector. As a first step such regulatory frameworks have to be put in place, while developing and strengthening the financial sector.

Within the formal financial sector provident funds have offered a certain degree of support to the elderly. Converting them to pension funds could be at the expense of the contingency function of these funds for the contributors. If people have to increase their savings for contingencies, their ability to contribute to a pension fund may well be eroded. The reform of provident funds has to take account of various functions of these funds by trying to establish different instruments for the main functions – such as pension funds, micro-savings/credit funds, and grant-based means-tested financial supporting.

Policies have to take account of the heterogeneity of the elderly in terms of social and economic background and their areas of residence (rural or urban). The formal pension schemes more often than not cater for the urban-based middle and upper strata of population. The rest are too poor to meet the requirements of the formal sector. The formal financial sector in most developing countries has not in general been a source of financial service and assistance to the poor. Development of micro-financial organisations with the aim of providing financial support to the elderly should be an integral part of government planning for the old age. Finally, a more general approach to the care of the elderly has to be established in which the needs of the aged are integrated in the support provided for the community which is expected to care for them. As the aforementioned example of the provision of boats to a fishing community in India shows, it is possible to combine income earning opportunities for the community with that of a pension in kind for the aged.

Acknowledgements

I am grateful to the participants of the conference and to Peter Lawrence and Colin Thirtle for their encouragement and comments. Alas, I am solely responsible for any remaining errors!

Notes

1. For further details on the demographic and social impact of AIDS see UN (1995: ch. IV).

2. See sources quoted in Sen (1995: 30).
3. Except in Singapore where decline in fertility occurred earlier, and ageing has become a public issue since 1970.
4. For a brief discussion of theoretical issues related to the interaction between migration, age structure and their effect on the elderly see Messkoub (1999).
5. For more details see World Bank: (1994: 19–22).

Part II

African and Asian Development Comparisons

7
Regionalism: Sub-Saharan Africa and East Asia Compared

Colin Kirkpatrick, Gareth Api Richards and Matsuo Watanabe

7.1 Introduction

This chapter is concerned with the remarkable revival of interest in academic and policy circles in regional trade and economic cooperation arrangements between developing countries. Having long been discounted by economists on the grounds that the costs of trade diversion were likely to far outweigh the efficiency gains from trade creation and dismissed by policy-makers for its failure in practice to accelerate the pace of economic development, regional integration in the developing world has now 'come in from the cold' and is being actively promoted as a vehicle for promoting economic growth and development.

In sub-Saharan Africa, despite the almost complete lack of success in the past, a second wave of regional cooperation initiatives is gaining momentum with the support and encouragement of various external agencies including the World Bank and the European Union (EU). In this chapter we examine the reasons for this apparent *volte-face* and try to identify the grounds for the current optimism and confidence that a new round of regional cooperation agreements in Africa will have more chance of success than in the past.

Our approach will be to provide an interpretative review of the history and evolution of regional integration in sub-Saharan Africa and East Asia. Our justification for doing so is straightforward. First, we argue that any assessment of the future prospects of regionalism in Africa must start from an analysis of the continent's past history. Secondly, we suggest that the perceived success of regional cooperation in East Asia has been an important factor in fostering the current optimism about the prospects for regional cooperation in Africa, but is based on an incomplete and in part mistaken interpretation of the Asian experience. Any assessment of the prospects for regional cooperation in Africa needs, therefore, to be based on an informed understanding both of past efforts to achieve African regionalism and of the Asian experience.

The chapter consists of five sections. This introduction is followed by a review of the rise of regionalism and of the various factors which have fostered the renewed interest in regional cooperation, particularly in Africa. Section 7.3 considers the history of regional integration in Africa and identifies the reasons why these past attempts have had, at best, only very limited success. Section 7.4 provides an interpretation of regionalism in Asia. The final section draws a number of conclusions for the future prospects of regionalism in Africa.

7.2   The rise of regionalism

While the international trading system has grown rapidly in recent years as a result of widespread unilateral trade liberalisation and the conclusion of the multilateral Uruguay Round of the General Agreement on Tariffs and Trade (GATT), regional trading arrangements have also assumed much greater prominence. New regional agreements have been concluded and existing agreements have been expanded to include new members. Indeed, one eminent observer has suggested that 'the rapid spread of regionalism is surely the most important recent development in the global trade system' (Baldwin, 1997: 865). More generally, the phenomenon of globalisation has been matched by the rise of regionalisation (Cook and Kirkpatrick, 1997).

The spread of regional trading arrangements has posed challenges for analysts at both the intellectual and policy level. It has stimulated a re-examination of the economic and other benefits and costs of regional arrangements. Do they foster growth and investment, facilitate technology transfer, exploit economies of scale and encourage greater trade specialisation or, on the other hand, do they divert trade in inefficient directions and undermine the multilateral trading system? It would be naive to seek for a definitive answer in the academic and research literature to what Baldwin calls 'the big question' – 'Is regionalism bad?'. It does appear, however, that the consensus of opinion has swung away from the earlier position that regional trading arrangements were almost always economically damaging and a second-best to multilateral trade liberalisation, towards the view that regionalism can be a move in the right direction, acting as a 'stepping stone' to wider trade liberalisation and economic expansion. The latter view, which sees regionalism as having a largely benign effect on the multilateral system (Summers, 1991) appears to have gained much more support than the school of thought that views regional arrangements as a serious threat to a WTO-centred world trading system (Bhagwati and Krueger, 1995).

There has also been a widening of the boundaries within which regionalism is analysed, with greater attention being given to the non-traditional gains from regional trading agreements (Fernandez, 1997) and '[i]t is increasingly recognised that regional integration goes beyond trade in goods, services and factors' (Melo and Panagariya, 1993). The static trade creation benefits can often be supplemented by other gains in policy credibility, signalling and policy coordination. Much of the new interest in regionalism has been focused on developing countries and, in this context, regionalism is seen as a means of progressing to a wider process of economic liberalisation and reform (Corden, 1996: 94).

Sub-Saharan Africa has a long history of regional cooperation schemes, stretching back to the immediate post-independence period when regionalism was actively promoted as a means of advancing industrial development and diversification. Following independence, many integration schemes were adopted, often between countries with former colonial ties of institutional structures, official language and currency (Foroutan, 1993: 240; Lyakurwa *et al.* 1997: 175). A distinctive feature of African regional cooperation and integration efforts is the large number of arrangements with many countries having membership of more than one agreement. These various agreements have had a variety of objectives, ranging from trade promotion to industrialisation and infrastructural development.

There is general agreement that African regional trading arrangements have failed to deliver any significant and positive benefits (Foroutan, 1992; Fine and Yeo, 1997). But despite this dismal record, there is renewed interest within Africa and among external parties in reviving regionalism in the sub-Saharan African region. The World Bank's 1989 study, *Sub-Saharan Africa: From Crisis to Sustainable Growth*, stated that 'progress towards market integration and increased cooperation in a whole range of areas ... is central to Africa's long term development strategy'. The EU's Green Paper which sets out the Union's proposals for the renegotiation of the Lomé Convention commends a regional approach with the EU concluding separate agreements with different regional groupings of the African, Caribbean and Pacific (ACP) countries. The World Bank was the leading sponsor of the Cross Border Initiative which brings together 14 countries who in 1995 adopted a programme for rapid tariff reductions and harmonisation. In 1998 the EU and the World Bank separately sponsored high level policy seminars in Southern Africa on regional trade cooperation.

There is a variety of reasons for the renewed enthusiasm for regional cooperation in sub-Saharan Africa. We have already drawn attention to the view that regional integration can act as a catalyst for more rapid trade liberalisation: 'a country's own liberalisation may be politically easier when it is part of a move to a FTA' (Corden, 1996: 94). The interest in regional groupings may also be a defensive response to the perceived marginalisation of Africa in the globalisation of the world economy. As Mistry (1995: 38) notes: 'a failure to overcome, or reduce, the costs of market fragmentation in regions whose countries have not yet begun to cooperate will mean that those regions, as a whole, will be less well placed in the future to attract the foreign investment, technology and know-how on which they will have to depend for their future growth'.

A third factor will be emulative in nature. A striking feature of the international economy over the past decade or more has been the growing economic strength and importance of the economies of East Asia. The remarkable growth performance of the region was accompanied by a growing interdependence among the regional economies, through regional trade and investment flows. This regionalisation of trade and investment served to focus attention on regional economic cooperation, and fostered the notion that East Asia's success was linked to institutionally organised cooperation. There is much interest among African policy-makers in the 'Asian model' of economic development, and regional cooperation is perceived as having played a key role in Asia's success.

Any assessment of the prospects and likely outcomes of extending the 'new regionalism' in Africa should be informed by a critical analysis of past experience. The following two sections of this chapter seek to provide such an interpretation by locating economic integration in both Africa and East Asia within the broader historical and political economy contexts of each region. The final section provides a summary of the implications of our analysis for future efforts to foster greater regional integration in Africa.

7.3   Regional integration in sub-Saharan Africa

From the late 1960s onwards, sub-Saharan Africa has experienced a number of concerted efforts to establish regional integration and cooperation schemes. As shown in Table 7.1, there are seven major integration schemes and some subregional groupings, such as the East African Community of Kenya, Tanzania and Uganda, have been pursued. These African regional integration efforts, however, have witnessed no significant success. As Langhammer and Hiemenz (cited in Aryeetey and

Table 7.1 Regional integration and cooperation arrangements in sub-Saharan Africa

Regional grouping	Members	Objectives	Instruments
ECOWAS: Economic Community of West African States (1975–)	Benin, Burkina Faso, Cape Verde, Côte d'Ivoire, Gambia, Guinea, Guinea Bissau, Liberia, Mali, Mauritania, Niger, Nigeria, Senegal, Sierra Leone, Togo	Promote cooperation and development, raise the living standard, maintain economic stability, eliminate tariffs and other barriers to trade, establish a common market by 1990	Elimination of tariffs and non-tariff barriers, adopt a common external tariff, fund for labour compensation and development, abolish obstacles to free movement of factors of production, harmonise monetary and fiscal policies
CEAO: West African Economic Community (1972–)	Benin, Burkina Faso, Côte d'Ivoire, Mali, Mauritania, Niger, Senegal	Promote cooperation and economic development through trade and community projects, establish a common external tariff	A single tax on intra-trade harmonisation of investment rules, a fund to finance regional projects
MRU: Mano River Union (1973–)	Guinea, Liberia, Sierra Leone	Promote economic cooperation through the establishment of customs union	Elimination of tariffs on intra-trade, common external tariff
CEPGL: Economic Community of the Great Lakes Countries (1976–)	Burundi, Rwanda, Congo (former Zaire)	Promote economic cooperation and development	Reduce tariff barriers and free factor mobility, joint industrial projects
UDEAC: Central African Customs and Economic Union (1964–)	Cameroon, Central African Republic, Chad, Congo, Equatorial Guinea, Gabon	Promote economic development to increase living standards, establish customs union	A single tax on intra-trade, elimination of non-tariff barriers, common investment rules, policy harmonisation and factor mobility

Table 7.1 *(continued)*

Regional grouping	Members	Objectives	Instruments
PTA: Eastern and Southern African Preferential Trade Area (1981–) (transformed into Common Market for Eastern and Southern Africa, COMESA, in 1993)	Angola, Burundi, Comoros, Djibouti, Egypt, Eritrea, Ethiopia, Kenya, Lesotho, Madagascar, Malawi, Mauritius, Mozambique, Namibia, Rwanda, Seychelles, Somalia, Sudan, Swaziland, Tanzania, Uganda, Zambia, Zimbabwe	Improve commercial and economic cooperation, transform the structure of production in national economies, promote intra-trade by removing tariff and non-tariff barriers, develop industry, cooperate in agriculture, improve transportation links, establish a common market by 1992	Multilateral clearing house, tariff reductions, a PTA Trade and Development Bank
SADC: Southern African Development Community (1992–) (formerly SADCC, 1980–)	Angola, Botswana, Lesotho, Malawi, Mauritius, Mozambique, Namibia, South Africa, Swaziland, Tanzania, Zambia, Zimbabwe	To promote cooperation and integration in the region, sectoral coordination and improve transport links	Sector coordination units in each member state

Source: Lyakurwa *et al.*, 1997: Table 4.2).

Oduro, 1996: 12) note, 'a dynamic initial phase, in which numerous programmes are launched' has been 'followed by a period of implementation difficulties or failures and ratification problems'. The following subsections will first review the motives and rationale for the establishment of regional integration arrangements in sub-Saharan Africa. After examining the low level of intraregional trade, the causes of the failure and impediments to African regionalism will be discussed.

7.3.1 Motives and rationale

Regional integration arrangements in Africa have been perceived primarily as a means of achieving self-reliant development. The Lagos Plan of Action, adopted by African Heads of Government in 1980, called for the development of intra-African cooperation and integration in order to attain collective self-reliance. The Plan stresses the role of domestic and intra-African production and facilitation of intra-African trade in enabling the continent to escape from the colonial pattern of trade characterised by the export of primary commodities and imported manufactures (Ndlela 1993: 303–10).

This emphasis on self-reliant development reflected a general sense of disillusionment with the international economy, which was viewed as being unfavourable to developing countries (Lyakurwa *et al.*, 1997: 175–6), and seen in declining commodity terms of trade for Africa's exports, export earnings instability, low trade elasticities and protectionism in developed economies. Regional integration was seen as a means of widening the market for infant industrial sectors and exploiting economies of scale. Politically, sub-Saharan Africa has promoted regional integration as a means of promoting closer political cooperation and building a common consensus on issues of mutual concern in areas beyond trade issues.

The fear of marginalisation from the process of globalisation has given sub-Saharan Africa an incentive to resurrect the regional integration strategy in the late 1980s. Onitiri (1997: 399–407), for example, argues that the changes in the international environment, which are 'generally of a nature requiring collective and co-ordinated action at the regional and continental levels', have pushed sub-Saharan Africa toward establishing regional blocs. The consequences of the GATT and its successor, the World Trade Organisation (WTO), have also had an impact on the motivations of African countries. There has been concern that the Uruguay Round Agreements (URA) might saddle sub-Saharan African countries with new obligations without compensatory gains in areas such as commodity market instability and market access for Africa's exports.

The Uruguay Round, therefore, heightened Africa's fears and anxieties on its trading position in the world (UNCTAD, 1997).

Traditionally, static trade creation and diversion issues have been identified as the major impact of economic integration. Regional integration generally increases the volume of intraregional trade by reducing trade barriers and tends to depress extra-regional trade. Through regional trade liberalisation, some domestic production in a member of the integration arrangement is replaced by lower-cost imports from another member, a process known as trade creation. This increases the welfare of member countries because it leads to greater specialisation in production based on comparative advantage. Trade diversion occurs when lower-cost imports from outside an integration arrangement are replaced by higher-cost imports from the members. Trade diversion reduces economic welfare because it shifts production from more efficient producers outside the arrangement to less efficient producers inside (Salvatore, 1994: 300–2).

Beside the static effects, the integrating countries are likely to benefit from several dynamic effects. These include the generation of economies of scale by the expansion of regional market, increased competition due to opening domestic market, stimulus to investment, and better utilisation of economic resources. International financial institutions have tended to stress these potential dynamic effects. The World Bank (1989: 148), for example, argues that 'regional co-operation and trade would assist Africa's long-term development'. The Bank notes four main reasons. First, regional champions in various fields would achieve top-quality training, research, business and economic management. Secondly, greater trade that stems from regional trade liberalisation would overcome imbalances in food supplies and hence reduce Africa's dependence on food imports from overseas. Thirdly, liberalising regional markets is regarded as a 'stepping stone' towards worldwide free trade where integrated regional markets would act as a 'shock absorber' for overprotected firms to become efficient through regional competition without immediately being exposed to international competition. And finally, regional cooperation would promote more efficient natural resource use within sub-Saharan Africa, with the exploration and development of oil, natural gas and hydropower being facilitated through interconnecting national power systems. The International Monetary Fund (IMF, 1993: 114–5) also points out the role of regional integration as a shock absorber. The Fund emphasises that regional integration should proceed in parallel with overall trade liberalisation outside regional integration arrangements.

Mansoor and Inotai (1991: 224–5, 229) also argue that regional integration would help sub-Saharan Africa to achieve economic development. They point out that further growth of single (and small) countries would be handicapped by lack of access to labour and raw materials in the absence of regional integration and rapid liberalisation with regional partners diminishing the costs of adjustment by forcing competition first with firms that are of comparable levels of (in)efficiency. They stress, however, that integration should be accompanied by outward orientation which will facilitate intraregional factor mobility (including capital, labour, goods and services) and competition. The liberalisation gives incentives to producers in sub-Saharan Africa for both domestic markets and exports.

7.3.2 Evaluation

Most studies conclude that past integration arrangements in sub-Saharan Africa have achieved very limited success (Aryeetey and Oduro, 1996; Foroutan, 1993; Lyakurwa *et al.*, 1997; Mansoor and Inotai, 1991). The major objective of integration arrangements in sub-Saharan Africa, to increase regional trade, has not accrued despite the conclusion of treaties and creation of multilateral institutions. The share of regional trade of most of the arrangements in sub-Saharan Africa remained less than 10 per cent and has even decreased in some arrangements in the last two decades (Table 7.2).

7.3.2.1 Low level of regional trade

One of the main explanations of the low intraregional trade is that Africa has limited trade potential. Since African countries are very similarly endowed and hence tend to import and export the same sets of goods, the formation of a preferential trade area or customs union is unlikely to generate the relevant incentives and competition required to induce entrepreneurs to export, which is a necessary

Table 7.2 Share of intraregional exports in total exports (%)

Regional grouping	1970	1975	1980	1985	1990
ECOWAS	2.9	4.0	3.5	5.3	5.7
CEAO	6.3	12.7	8.9	8.7	10.5
MRU	0.2	0.4	0.5	0.4	0.1
UDEAC	4.8	2.7	1.6	1.9	3.0
PTA	8.0	9.3	7.6	5.5	5.9
SADCC	2.6	3.7	2.1	3.9	4.8

Source: Foroutan (1993: Table 8.3).

condition for trade integration (Collier and Gunning, 1995: 392; Jebuni, 1997: 353–4).

Another reason for low regional trade is the failure to implement reductions in regional trade barriers. Mansoor and Inotai (1991: 218) contend that there has been little tariff reduction, due to the 'temporary' introduction of quantitative restrictions, slowdown of trade liberalisation schemes, implementation of 'administered trade' and increased tariffs on intraregional trade by individual member countries. Political pressure from the industries enjoying protected domestic markets has often been put on governments not to open the national market. Regional trade liberalisation involves the reduction of tax revenue imposed on extra-regional trade as well as intraregional trade (Foroutan, 1993: 254–5; Lipumba and Kasekende, 1991: 234), and governments therefore have disincentives to liberalise regional trade due to the revenue constraint. The IMF (1993: 114) indicates the importance of customs duties as the revenue base for member governments.

7.3.2.2 Distribution and equity issues

Efficient allocation of industries based on comparative advantage is essential to one of the benefits of economic integration. Bhagwati (1993: 28) and Mansoor and Inotai (1991: 222), however, argue that the distribution of industries has been based on political viability in sub-Saharan Africa, thus contributing to the economically inefficient location of investment. Instead of using trade liberalisation and hence prices to guide industrial allocation, sub-Saharan Africa's integration arrangements sought to allocate industries by bureaucratic negotiation that tied trade to such allocations. Salvatore (1994: 315) points out 'the greatest stumbling block is that the benefits are not evenly distributed'. In an integration arrangement, benefits accrue to the most advanced nations, so a foremost condition for successful integration is that a workable transfer mechanism be instituted whereby the net gainers compensate the net losers (Foroutan, 1993: 255). While African countries emphasise equity between members of integration arrangement as seen in the Lagos Plan of Action and the Abuja Treaty they have failed to address the issue of distribution of gains. This contradiction has contributed to the failure of regional integration in sub-Saharan Africa.

7.3.2.3 Lack of political commitment

Many studies point out that the failure of integration arrangements lies with the lack of political commitment. Haas (1968, cited in Kisanga, 1991: 6) defines integration as 'the process whereby actors ... are persuaded to shift their loyalties, expectations, and activities towards a new centre, whose institutions and processes demand jurisdiction over pre-existing states'. In other words, the readiness and willingness of each country to permit an encroachment on economic sovereignty by such an authority is essential to successful integration. Salvatore (1994: 315) and McCarthy (1996, cited in Aryeetey and Oduro, 1996: 32) suggest many sub-Saharan African countries have been unwilling to relinquish part of their sovereignty to a supranational community body. Kisanga (1991: 1–2) argues that although sub-Saharan African countries shared the view that economic integration would work as an instrument for facilitating development, there have been differences in conceptions of integration schemes arising from the different political and economic perceptions taken by the states. These different perceptions (on what and how an integration can achieve certain objectives and how the problems, e.g. methods to share the costs and benefits, should be solved) meant that governments have been reluctant to engage fully in the integration process (Ndlela, 1993).

7.3.2.4   Overlapping membership

Most countries in sub-Saharan Africa belong to more than one integration arrangement. For example, Aryeetey and Oduro (1996: 28) argue that parallel membership of several groupings with similar objectives such as establishing a preferential trade area or monetary union will cause some problems. The effectiveness of one grouping tends to be undermined by the existence of the other due to members' limited financial resources to meet all requirements of the schemes. Even if objectives are similar, the divergent priorities and pace in implementing integration schemes may conflict with each other in those countries with double or triple membership.

7.3.3   Summary

To summarise, the results of the various attempts at regional integration in sub-Saharan Africa have fallen far short of what was expected at their inception. The explanation for the failure of regional integration arrangements can be found partly in terms of absence of gains outside the tradition of economic efficiency and comparative advantage. The structural characteristics of the economies and the lack of political commitment to the regional integration project have been further contributory factors. There is little evidence to suggest, therefore, that the new wave of regional integration will be building on the achievements of earlier integration efforts.

7.4   Regionalisation and regionalism in East Asia

There has been a considerable increase in the interconnections of the peoples and institutions of East Asia, especially in the last decade. This has led to a heightened scholarly interest aimed at explaining both the causes of regional economic integration and the patterns of institutionalised regional cooperation. Most economists have addressed these interrelated phenomena fairly conventionally, by reference to ways in which the rapid expansion of gross domestic product (GDP) has induced the intensification of trade and investment flows among neighbouring countries. What the World Bank (1993) refers to as the high-performance Asian economies (HPAEs) experienced sustained real annual growth rates of up to 10 per cent over a period of two or three decades up to the mid-1990s, a fact that contributed to the phenomenal expansion of the productive capabilities of the region. This growth was accompanied by an expansion of the region's aggregate trade and investment – particularly intraregional trade – driven by the export-oriented nature of most of the commercial activity of the HPAEs, and supported by a range of factors including geographical proximity, the diversity of comparative advantages and entrepôt trade relations (Gangopadhyay, 1998; Singh, 1998).

In light of this, the diffusion of a region-wide 'model' of economic development and a growing sense of regional coherence have been identified. According to Stubbs (1998) it is the very distinctiveness of East Asian capitalism – based on a combination of a results-oriented approach to economic growth, selective state intervention in economic management and the ways in which firms are organised into networks – together with an increasingly self-confident 'Asian consciousness', that accounts for the emergence of greater regional economic integration. The characteristics of this particular form of capitalism and, until the onset of the Asian economic crises from mid-1997 onwards, its perceived successes are offered as the explanation for the formation of both intergovernmental and non-governmental 'second track' mechanisms to facilitate trade and investment flows and as the basis for enhanced economic dialogue across the region. This is evident in the proliferation of a range of multilayered, and often overlapping, regional agenda-setting networks that have emerged recently. The formation of the Asia-Pacific Economic Cooperation (APEC) forum, of the ASEAN Free Trade Area (AFTA) and ASEAN Regional Forum (ARF), of an informal 'Asia 10' and a putative East Asian Economic Council (EAEC), and the multiplication of natural economic territories or 'growth triangles' all attest to the efforts that have been made to enhance cooperation in a range of areas, particularly the reduction of barriers to intraregional trade (see Table 7.3). While these nascent arrangements, of varying institutional depth, reflect different (and sometimes contested) understandings of the region, taken together they are generally understood as confirmation of the benefits of progressive liberalisation of trade and capital movements (Garnaut and Drysdale, 1994; Kirkpatrick, 1994).

This section analyses the character of regionalisation in East Asia. It does so by first considering those attempts to theorise an East Asian *regional* 'model' of economic development, focusing initially on the dominant debate between neoliberal and statist-institutional perspectives, before discussing more recent conceptualisations of a regionalised political economy. The final part examines the contradictions that lie within the processes that have precipitated regionalisation in East Asia and it questions the claims that regionalisation in East Asia reflects a sustainable 'third form of capitalism' in contradistinction to the other leading regions of the global economy.

7.4.1   Theorising regionalisation in East Asia

There has been a vigorous and often inimical debate between competing perspectives on how best to portray the processes of regionalisation in East Asia.

7.4.1.1   *The orthodox debate: neoliberalism versus statist-institutionalism*

The conventional *neoliberal* view of regionalisation is that which characterises the East Asian region's political economy, and which distinguishes it from those of other regions of the world economy, is a policy orientation that is both 'open', that is, trade promoting, and market conforming. In this model, the state's role is relatively limited as a catalyst and corrector of market failures. This interpretation starts with a free trade regime, whereby national policy allocates resources in accordance with the country's existing comparative advantage: 'By "getting the price right" through trade liberalization and exchange rate reform, East Asian NIE states provide the optimal environment for the growth of private enterprise' (Chiu and Lui, 1998: 139). It conceives of the region in terms of the multiplication and density of transactions between private entrepreneurs of individual 'national economies'. To the extent that there is a regional commonality, it lies in the fact that a number of countries have pursued roughly the same constellation policies with regard to trade, foreign investment, interest rates, exchange rates and labour market regulation. The 'development' process proceeds in a parallel but largely segmented manner in country after country. The larger global

Table 7.3 Asia – Pacific: membership of regional groupings (1999)

Country	Association of South-East Asian Nations (ASEAN)	ASEAN Regional Forum (ARF)	Asia Pacific Ecomomic Cooperation (APEC)	'Asia 10'/Asia-Europe Meeting (ASEM)	Pacific Economic Cooperation Council (PECC)
Asia/Oceania					
Australia		✓	✓		✓
Brunei	✓	✓	✓	✓	✓
Burma/Myanmar	✓	✓			
Cambodia	✓	✓			
PRChina		✓	✓	✓	✓
Hong Kong, China			✓	✓	
Indonesia	✓	✓	✓	✓	✓
Japan		✓	✓	✓	✓
North Korea					
South Korea		✓	✓	✓	✓
Laos	✓	✓			
Malaysia	✓	✓	✓	✓	✓
Mongolia		✓			
New Zealand		✓	✓	✓	
Papua New Guinea		✓	✓		
Philippines	✓	✓	✓	✓	✓
Russian Federation		✓	✓		✓
Singapore	✓	✓	✓	✓	✓
Taiwan			✓		✓

Table 7.3 (continued)

Country	Association of South-East Asian Nations (ASEAN)	ASEAN Regional Forum (ARF)	Asia Pacific Ecomomic Cooperation (APEC)	'Asia 10'/Asia-Europe Meeting (ASEM)	Pacific Economic Cooperation Council (PECC)
Thailand	✓	✓	✓	✓	✓
Vietnam	✓	✓	✓	✓	✓
North/South America					
Canada		✓	✓		✓
Chile			✓		✓
Colombia					✓
Mexico			✓		✓
Peru			✓		✓
United States		✓	✓		✓
Others		EU India		EU	Pacific Islands

context is seen as exogenous with the world order conceived in terms of a collection of states that interact with one another through market-driven transactions, that is flows of commodities and capital, and (where possible) policy coordination (Yoshida and Akimune 1994). This transaction-centred approach has led to a preoccupation with inter-state, multilateral institutions and policy prescriptions that might deepen free exchange and investment.

What is often referred to as a revisionist view of the regional political economy has amounted to a *statist* challenge to neoliberal orthodoxy. Although not monolithic, this line of theorising has tended to focus on how the state – first in Japan, later in Taiwan, Korea and Singapore, and more recently in South-East Asia – intervened actively to promote the growth that orthodox economists had purported to explain. In short, states have had a strategic role to play in harnessing market forces to the goals of 'late industrialisation' and national development giving rise to what Castells (1992) identifies as the specificity of the East Asian 'developmental state'. The statist view rests on the virtues that allegedly derive from the political and organisational components of state strength. These include the assertion that strong states are relatively autonomous from powerful societal interests including rent-seeking groups, have forged bureaucratic unity, and thus have the capacity to extract resources, provide public goods, reconcile diverse needs, and encourage the most productive businesses. Organisationally, strong states are seen as internally cohesive, consistent and flexible, and able to accumulate and act on information necessary to reconcile diverse interests. Lacking its own autonomy and strength, business has been dependent on and loyal to the state. In the words of Wade (1992: 315), private firms have behaved liked subcontractors 'competing and cooperating under state supervision'. For Evans (1995) the combination of corporate coherence and close links to society – what he calls 'embedded autonomy' – provided the underlying basis for successful state involvement under the rubric of 'midwifery' and 'husbandry' of industrial transformation. The implications are that a regional model can be characterised by a common set of state institutions coupled with a similar developmentalist policy orientation in a succession of the region's countries (Johnson, 1987). Essentially, then, an account of regionalisation is extrapolated from the supposed macro-level similarities of a generic 'developmental state'.

While there are obviously different claims embodied in these accounts of region-wide convergence there is much in Bernard's (1996a) assertion that the 'tired wrangling' of the states versus markets debate camouflages more than it reveals. The theorists of East Asian growth and economic development have actually been drawn ever closer in promoting a narrow, apolitical account of the region's political economy which omits any systematic understanding of the structural imperatives of the international economy and their potential constraints on the domestic economy.

7.4.1.2 The product cycle model: regionalisation as a flock of 'flying geese'

An important attempt to overcome the difficulties in representing the regionalisation of East Asia's political economy is the product cycle view that intraregional similarity is related to the migration of industries from country to country, whereby latecomers replicate the development trajectory of countries preceding them. The result is the emergence of a homogenised industrialisation process in a succession of the region's countries. This view depicts the countries of the region as a flock of flying geese, with Japan in the lead, followed by South Korea, Taiwan, Hong Kong and Singapore, then Malaysia and Thailand, and next China and Vietnam. Each country, in the course of development, supposedly casts off specific industries as they progress up the developmental ladder. These industries are, in turn, picked up by less developed countries which replicate the state of the country ahead of it in the flock. The rationale behind the 'flying geese' pattern is the shifting competitiveness of an industry over time which is itself caused by changes in factor endowments of nations in the course of economic development. According to this view the process is further assisted by technology transfer from more developed to less developed nations (Gangopadhyay, 1998). In order to succeed in reaching (and maintaining) developed country status, each must fulfil two essential conditions. First, they must be able to generate industries whose leading companies can move beyond factor-led competitiveness (such as low labour costs) to a position where they can institutionalise innovation. And secondly, the value-added associated with innovation needs to be captured within the domestic economy if it is to have a significant effect on development. Whether this has actually taken place in most East Asian NIEs seems doubtful. As Henderson (1998: 376) notes in his critique of the 'flying geese' metaphor, 'it is not clear that decisive progress toward the economic first rank has been made ... or that it is likely to be in the foreseeable future'.

While the 'flying geese' portrayal of the region expands the narrow transaction focus of the neoliberal view by linking regionalisation to industrial production there are a number of critical shortcomings. In a devastating critique, Bernard and Ravenhill (1995) argue against the essentially state-centric notion that underscores the model (in ways analogous to both neoliberal and statist-institutionalist views) despite its recognition of an explicit regional dimension to industrialisation in any one country. The 'flying geese' representation, they contend, contains no account of the historical context of industrial change in the region nor of the specific processes and agents that have facilitated the migration of industries that it purports to explain. The unspoken assumption is that industries migrate naturally and that the result is the homogenisation of the various industrial structures of the region. Nor is there room in this kind of theorising for an account of the differences across societies that arise from local specificities of state–society relations and the organisation and social relations of – production. Beyond these methodological flaws, the empirical evidence for the 'flying geese' model is also weak. Bernard and Ravenhill point to the ways in which the evolution of a regional division of labour has effectively locked many of the East Asian economies into an 'intermediate role' from which they show little sign of escaping. The lead firms of South Korea, Taiwan and Malaysia, for example, remain overwhelmingly dependent on technological inputs and innovation from Japanese companies, on the one hand, and on access to international (especially the US) markets, on the other.

7.4.1.3   Regionalised networks

Recently an important and innovative strand of re-thinking regionalisation has adopted a network approach. Network approaches have incorporated the transnational linkages across East Asia into an analysis of a regionalised political economy. Regionalisation is, in turn, seen as an integral part of the broader process of the globalisation of production structures. Analyses that begin with a regional structure of production highlight how the regional political economy does not correspond to relations between states. The organisation of production across a range of industries from consumer electronics to machinery and vehicles reveal regionalised industries featuring interrelated manufacturing sectors in hierarchical networks of firms built around production and innovation concentrated in Japan and dependence on exports of finished products to the US and other extra-regional markets. There have been three variants on this kind of network approach: (1) *Japanese networks*: this identifies how Japanese networks have actually changed organisational shape over time, and are the core of what is seen as an increasingly regionalised (and globalised) strategy of Japanese manufacturers who mediate the activities of affiliates throughout the region (Hatch and Yamamura, 1996; Sum, 1997). (2) *'Greater China' networks*: this considers the commercial networks of ethnic Chinese capital that parallel the Japan-centred production structure. Originally centred in Hong Kong and Taiwan, and increasingly based in South-East Asia, they are now forging regional structures around different kinds of economic activity such as those related to property development, agri-business and services. They also increasingly encompass a proliferation of ties with state firms and party elites in coastal China. (3) *Commodity chains*: this focuses on a distribution structure that Gereffi (1996a, b) refers to as 'buyer driven commodity chains'. By this is meant a structure of circulation where large retailers, designers and trading companies play the pivotal role in setting up decentralised production networks. These networks highlight the central role that US distribution and consumption structures continue to have on regional production in a variety of labour-intensive consumer goods industries.

The salience of network approaches is fourfold (Bernard, 1996a: 654): they point to complex regional institutions that actually link various parts of the region together; they draw our attention to the way that the regional is juxtaposed to the global by locating regional production and distribution patterns in a broader global context; they offer the possibility for a more historicised rendering of region-formation by delineating changes in regional forms over time; and, they force a consideration of the manner in which each country is enmeshed in processes that are regional in scope. Nevertheless, there is still a major analytical problem at the heart of network approaches. They offer what is still fundamentally an apolitical understanding of regionalisation, one that in concentrating on the locational and management strategies of corporate elites does not delineate questions of power or considerations of social depth.

7.4.2   Region formation and intergovernmental collaboration

Any account of region formation and regional collaboration in East Asia needs to incorporate three vital levels of analysis: first, an awareness of the region's historicity; secondly, an understanding of how regions and regional projects are linked both to global processes and locally constituted social formations; and thirdly, the ways in which the region assumes particular identities and forms as a consequence of a particular configuration of power and through the agency of particular social forces.

The form that regionalisation has taken in East Asia is related to the specificities of its history. The regional form that emerged after 1945 did so in 'the crucible of the Cold War' and under the tutelage of Pax Americana, and built upon the legacy of Japanese and European imperialism in Asia (Bernard, 1996b: 342). Of the range of structures and practices that were put into place by the US in conjunction with the elites who came to control the newly independent states, three were crucial for the trajectory of economic development and the division of the region spatially. First, there were the Cold War bilateral military alliances designed to prevent the spread of communism which made Japan the centre of the US's broader regional operations. Secondly, there was the attempt by US elites to incorporate the non-communist countries as a regional sub-unit of the capitalist world order along the Pacific perimeters of Asia. Despite the importance of the political and military aspects of US hegemony 'it was the mode of integrating the world market under U.S. leadership that was central to creating regional formations in selected geographical arenas' (Palat, 1993: 11). And thirdly, there was the American desire to reintegrate neighbouring countries, especially South Korea and Taiwan, with a reconstructing Japan that was conceived as the industrial centre of a revivified version of the region. The regional and global dimensions of this project were not in any ways contradictory. As Bernard (1996a: 660) observes: 'The regional configuration that emerged was envisioned as a building block of a liberal world order'.

This led to a structure of flexible production that enabled Japanese companies to dominate global production in a range of assembly-intensive manufacturing industries. Paralleling this was a combination of localised networks of production, distribution and retailing, narrow importing channels controlled by general trading companies, and state protection, which cumulatively discouraged imports of manufactures from the rest of the region. This contrasted with the relative openness of the North American market and the US state's underwriting of investment by US capital in the region to replace domestic production with low-cost imports. It was in the use of the region as a low-wage assembly base by US capital and the response in kind by Japanese industry that regionalised production emerged (Bernard, 1994; 1996b).

Regionalisation of production was not merely about organising production in a regional vacuum. It confronted a range of post-colonial states, most of which featured coherent state apparatuses linked to different configurations of social forces and varying colonial legacies. In all the countries of the region the state preceded the emergence of an industrial bourgeoisie, resulting in capitalist industrialisation becoming incorporated into statist projects linked to regime legitimation and national identity formation. In Japan's former colonies – South Korea and Taiwan – the withdrawal of Japanese interests after 1945, along with export promotion and state-allocated credit, created respective indigenous capitalist classes that were protected by the state from the presence of foreign capital. The large-scale integrated conglomerates (*chaebol*) in South Korea and the smaller-scale firms in Taiwan became linked to

Japanese industry, often on the basis of personal relationships, in production networks tied to Japanese supplies of key components, machinery, materials, marketing channels and technological trajectory. By comparison, in South-East Asia post-colonial states, in most cases, co-existed with an ethnic Chinese commercial and financial bourgeoisie and the continued presence of capital from the former metropole. Indigenous industrialisation was weaker and state-imposed constraints on foreign capital, such as high tariffs, were intended more for the purpose of extracting rents than fostering local industry. Japanese manufacturing capital's initial forays into South-East Asia in the 1970s were designed to take advantage of this lack of an indigenous bourgeoisie and the protection afforded by undertaking locally oriented production behind high tariff walls. Linkages with local capital were commonly with the ethnic Chinese commercial bourgeoisie or with the state.

The regionalised production structure that emerged in North-East Asia in the 1970s incorporated parts of South-East Asia following the Plaza Agreement of 1985. It has fostered a much more powerful awareness of the regional nature of production, particularly through the crystallisation of a region-wide bloc of state and business elites and a cadre of technocrats who have been the prime beneficiaries of regionalised manufacturing. Thus the emergence of a sense of macro-regional coherence or what Higgott (1998a: 339–40) calls *de facto* regionalisation in East Asia is a relatively recent phenomenon. It has been largely driven by an integrated set of structural conditions. These have included the enhanced interactions deriving from dramatic technological and economic growth, the wave of Japanese FDI that swept through the region following the revaluation of the yen after 1985, and the establishment of production and distribution networks across a range of industries. Regionalised production was accompanied by a dramatic increase in Japanese official development assistance to enhance regional infrastructure and promote intra-regional bureaucratic ties (Bernard, 1996a,b; Hatch and Yamamura, 1996).

Related to the historicity of regional production structures and networks is the second feature of regionality, the way in which regions lie at the intersection of the local and the global. As Bernard (1996a: 657) rightly notes, 'regions must be seen as manifestations of global process *and* the way these processes assume concrete forms in a world where power emanates from within historically constituted national social formation'. While globalisation is often portrayed as bypassing the state, what we can actually witness in East Asia are highly active states and highly politicised capitalist classes and intellectual communities purposively forging the very conditions for macro-regional organisation and forma-tion. For example, the regionalisation of Japanese industrial production was shaped by the structure of domestic production and by the response of Japanese capital to the globalisation of US capital's low-wage assembly bases. But these processes of regionalisation did not take place in a vacuum. It was also shaped by the nature of the societies and state-society relations that Japanese business confronted. Thus in order to understand the actual pattern of the regional political economy, any account needs to take into consideration the timing of incorporation into this regional structure, differences in the class configurations and the linkages between local and transnational capital, and disparate state and financial institutions. In this way, we can witness divergent patterns of economic development that belie the proclamations of the models of economic replications.

Finally, the understanding of how the 'regional' is interconnected with the 'local' raises the question of the agency behind the forces and ideas that have forged the particular understandings and structures that the region(s) has assumed. It is a particular set of actors, the so-called 'tripartite' policy community of governments, corporations and advisers, that has overcome the longstanding institutional deficit – the absence of institutionalised regional intergovernmental collaboration – and encoded the practice of regional economic cooperation and institutionalised arrangements such as APEC and the various ASEAN affiliates (Ravenhill, 1998). The reasons for this growing trend toward multiple and over-lapping regionalism are not hard to discern. The end of the Cold War (which had restricted possibilities for region-wide arrangements) and the consolidation of regional groupings elsewhere, most notably with the advent of the post-Maastricht EU and signing of the NAFTA, provided the context for the new wave of collaboration. The new circumstances also encouraged regional elites in East Asia to elaborate a more self-conscious sense of identity and interests, one that exists both in contradistinction to Europe and North America but simultaneously allows them to participate more fully in the management of the world order both at inter-regional and global levels than previously (Stubbs, 1998).

7.4.3   Implications of the Asian crisis for regionalism

There is little doubt that the onset of the Asian economic crisis in mid-1997 has brought the problems and limitations inherent in region formation and attempts to consolidate regional collaboration to the surface. While most of the commentary and attention so far has focused on the problems in the region's financial sector, the crisis is also revealing more deep-seated problems in the real economy and in the ability to formulate coherent policy responses. It is the context of the crisis that enables us to consider the broader set of claims about the notion of East Asia as a region in the global economy that were outlined earlier.

The first claim focuses on the widespread enthusiasm for a distinctive East Asian 'model' of capitalism that has been seen to underpin both the processes of regionalisation described here and support for an 'Asian way' in regional economic collaboration. What the crisis has highlighted are the tensions between the capacity for sustaining national political legitimacy inscribed in the state, and the macroeconomic constraints of global capital mobility. In this context, the accelerated integration of East Asian economies with global financial structures calls into question the capacity of states and regions to develop alternate 'models' of capitalist development. Once global investors are able to pass direct judgement on the local practices of particular economies, these countries remain vulnerable to a rapid withdrawal of portfolio capital and related consequences in the form of exchange rate instability and financial crises. In short, integration with global financial markets increases the pressures on alternate models of economic development for convergence with neoliberal practices of the dominant economies. Crucially, financial integration also strengthens the hand of those sociopolitical constituencies which domestically and regionally have long argued for the introduction of more market-oriented neoliberal practices into distinct East Asian models of development (Underhill, 1998). The depth of East Asian economic problems would seem, at this juncture, to point to a grave weakening of the viability of 'Asian' domestic and regional alternatives to a global economic order defined mainly in neoliberal terms.

The crisis also calls into question the second claim, namely that a specifically 'Asian' conception of the regional order has been consolidated in such a way that provides leverage in the institutions of global economic governance. Higgott (1998b) has recently argued that the Asian crisis may provide an opportunity for East Asian 'bonding' and the deepening of 'multi-level' forms of regionalism. A much more probable scenario points to the insubstantiality of the 'Asian way' in regional diplomacy. This is evident in the three most important inter-regional summits that have taken place since the onset of the crisis. Both the Vancouver (November 1997) and Kuala Lumpur (November 1998) summits of APEC and the Asia–Europe Meeting (ASEM) in London, in April 1998, have demonstrated the collective weakness of its East Asian member states in face of calls by the US and the EU for them to conform to IMF adjustment packages and programmes of austerity. Both summits were used to advance an agenda which centred on the internalisation in the East Asian states of the disciplines associated with global neoliberalism (Cammack, 1999). In the longer run, the crisis has exposed the 'pragmatism' and 'consensuality' of East Asian diplomacy as unlikely to be an enduring or an effective basis for evolving regional cohesion.

The third claim made of East Asian regionalism – sometimes termed 'soft regionalism' – derives from its supposedly 'looser', more 'open' form of economic cooperation compared to the deeply institutionalised character of the European project or the contractual basis to the NAFTA treaty. The Asian model is said to have privileged the role of private-sector actors in the facilitation of collaborative networks. As we have seen, this understanding has always underestimated the role of state elites and the nature of state – business relations in fashioning the terms of intergovernmental engagement and fostering the regionalised business and industrial strategies of firms. The economic crisis is likely to enhance the process of 'state recomposition', in which political elites find their policy autonomy increasingly constrained by international regulatory agencies which enjoy powerful political support. The context for the ascendancy of neoliberalism is undoubtedly the globalisation of financial markets and the policy prescriptions and new regional financial architecture that has been put into place derive from the imperatives of the institutions of global economic governance. Nonetheless, the outcome of change in the development trajectories of East Asian societies will ultimately be decided in the realm of domestic politics.

7.5   Conclusions

The importance of regional trading arrangements in the world economy shows no sign of diminishing despite the strengthening of the multilateral trading system in recent years and there is an ongoing process in the industrialised and developing worlds to expand regional agreements and to deepen integration. The renewed interest in regional arrangements transcends the traditional concern with trade, and covers emerging issues such as services, investment and technology.

This chapter has been motivated by the mounting evidence of a renewed enthusiasm for regionalism in Africa. We have focused on two strands in the current dialogue. First, the fact that the new interest is occurring despite a long history of 'failure' for African integration. Secondly, that the East Asian regional model has influenced policy-makers' views on the contribution that regional integration agreements can make to economic growth and development.

Past attempts to achieve regional integration in Africa have been based on intraregional preferential trade agreements with a strong institutional structure for negotiating and coordinating preferential policies. The agreements that were established were inward-looking, maintaining high external tariffs and trade barriers. The current efforts at regional cooperation are more outward-looking, encouraging trade reduction and trade liberalisation both between members and with external trading partners, and are therefore seen by their proponents as being complementary to a more general process of multilateral trade liberalisation.

The current approach to regional cooperation in Africa is based, in part, on a particular interpretation and understanding of East Asian regionalism. This view characterises the East Asian regional model as being 'open', 'natural' (that is, being driven by economic forces rather than institutionally based decisions) and supportive of rapid economic growth. It is strongly implied that the East Asian model can be successfully transferred and applied in the African context. The chapter has challenged this simplistic view on two grounds. First, examining of the history of regional cooperation in Africa shows that the causes of 'failure' are much deeper and more complex than simply the adoption of an inappropriate 'inward-looking' integration model. Secondly, to characterise the East Asian model as being outward-looking, open and market-driven is to ignore the underlying interplay of economic, social and political forces that have shaped the Asian experience.

8
Explaining Differences in the Economic Performance of Micro-States in Africa and Asia

Harvey W. Armstrong and Robert Read

8.1 Introduction

The comparative economic performance of countries in Africa and Asia has attracted considerable attention from economists and policy-makers in recent years. In particular, significant contrasts have been made between the growth performances of the states in sub-Saharan African and the East and South-East Asian 'tiger' economies. From a different perspective, comparisons have also been drawn between sub-Saharan African states, South-Asia and China. Much less attention however, has been directed at the comparative economic performance of very small states or 'micro-states' in these two regions.

Although there is no universally accepted definition of what constitutes a micro-state, this chapter adopts a 'broad-brush' approach. It follows convention by defining size in terms of population and utilises an upper size threshold of three million. This threshold is higher than is normally used (the United Nations uses one million) but there is a distinct break point in the population size distribution of states at this point (Armstrong *et al.*, 1996, 1998). Also included in the micro-state definition are territories and sub-national regions which, while not politically sovereign according to UN criteria, possess a high degree of autonomy over domestic economic policy-making – an issue of critical importance here. The resulting global set of micro-state entities comprises 106 cases (see the Appendix). For statistical reasons, the large number of cases is better able to generate robust analytical results.

It is evident that both sub-Saharan Africa and Asia are well endowed with very small states, regardless of the definitions used. Within Asia, micro-states can be found in Central Asia, South Asia, the Middle East,

South-East Asia and East Asia. For the purposes of this chapter, the many micro-states in the Pacific region are also considered because the World Bank classifies them as a group with East Asia. Many of these Pacific island economies are now closely tied to East and South-East Asian markets. Moreover, as is shown in this chapter, the sets of micro-states in these two large regions show enormous diversity in terms of their economic performance. Both regions can point to extremely successful micro-states, such as Mauritius in sub-Saharan Africa and Singapore in Asia, and also extremely poorly performing micro-states, such as Bhutan in Asia and Equatorial Guinea in sub-Saharan Africa.

It is generally recognised that micro-states are a distinctive group of economies which face an array of unusual challenges (outlined in Section 8.2). As such, it has long been argued that it would be inappropriate to compare their economic performance directly with that of large states. The comparative analysis of the growth experience and performance of different micro-states, whether at the global level (see Milner and Westaway, 1993; Armstrong *et al.*, 1996, 1998), between global regions (as here) or within regions (see Armstrong and Read, 1995), has the potential to generate useful and more broadly applicable insights.

This chapter builds upon previous research by the authors on the determinants of growth in micro-states in an attempt to compare the performance of micro-states in Africa and Asia. It addresses the critical issue of whether African micro-states, almost all of which are in sub-Saharan Africa, differ fundamentally in their economic performance revealed by GNP per capita levels, from their Asian counterparts. This comparative analysis is undertaken within the context of an explanatory model developed and utilised successfully by the authors in earlier papers (Armstrong and Read, 1995, 1999; Armstrong *et al.*, 1996, 1999). The fundamental question is formulated as: do African micro-states respond to similar economic forces and in the same manner as their Asian/Pacific counterparts? The key findings are that the broader region in which a micro-state is located is a critical determining factor in its relative economic success and that there is no evidence, apart from this regional factor, of any specific 'Africa' effect. The relatively low levels of per capita incomes of African micro-states is strongly correlated with the low regional average level of per capita income although the micro-states are found to 'out-perform' the larger economies in the region.

Section 8.2 examines the theoretical background and evidence of earlier empirical research on the determinants of the economic performance of micro-states. This is followed in Section 8.3 by an examination of the restricted and highly partial data sets available for research on the economic performance of micro-states in different regions of the world. Section 8.4 examines the enormous variety of economic performance among different micro-states within each of the two regions in question as well as between the two regions. In Section 8.5, the approach pioneered by the authors elsewhere is adapted to address the key question of the extent to which micro-states in Africa and Asia can be said to be affected by similar economic forces. The concluding section considers the implications of the findings and points the way to future research.

8.2   Theoretical and empirical evidence on the determinants of micro-state economic performance

There is a large and long-standing literature on the economic performance of very small states which has been fully discussed elsewhere by the authors (Armstrong and Read, 1995; Armstrong *et al.*, 1996, 1998). This section confines itself to a brief summary of the key determinants of micro-state economic performance identified in the literature.

The research literature repeatedly stresses the highly unusual nature of the conditions under which the economies of micro-states must function and especially the distinctive difficulties facing micro-states seeking to grow rapidly, for example the difficulties faced by many micro-states which are also islands or archipelagos. More recently, however, the remarkable economic growth rates and prosperity levels of micro-states, such as Singapore and Luxembourg, has suggested that there are economic advantages that micro-states can enjoy in a rapidly globalising system of trade and factor mobility. The result is that a much more balanced picture is now beginning to emerge on the nature of the difficulties and advantages conferred on a state by virtue of its small size.

Taking the disadvantages of small size first, the problems facing micro-states arise not from size itself but relative openness. This makes micro-states extremely vulnerable to various external forces, whether of an economic, political, security or environmental nature. A focus on the economic aspects of vulnerability, which is the concern of this discussion, leads to the identification of a series of different challenges for micro-states. The first is of a small domestic market for manufactured products with production at levels well below the minimum efficient scale (MES) with steeply declining unit costs (Knox, 1967) together with high input prices, whether from small-scale local producers or via imports (Armstrong *et al.*, 1993). A small domestic market also hinders local research and development (R&D) and domestic innovation. This tends to weaken both the creation of indigenous technology (Briguglio, 1995) and also restricts the emergence of fast growth manufacturing sectors to serve foreign markets (Kuznets, 1960; Thomas, 1982). Further, most micro-states have a limited and undiversified natural resource base, a limited labour force, as well as a limited supply of physical and human capital (Bhaduri, *et al.*, 1982).

The archetypal response of micro-states has been to avoid diversification and focus instead on developing high value niche regional or world export markets. As a result, there is a high degree of concentration in the domestic economy on a limited number of niche products and a heavy reliance upon a limited number of export markets. This increases micro-states' vulnerability to exogenous shocks, leading to greater export earnings and balance-of-payments instability and the threat of 'Dutch disease' (MacBean and Nguyen, 1987; Corden and Neary, 1982).

Islandness is given great prominence in the literature. Islands have high transport costs, face monopoly transport provision difficulties and suffer transport reliability difficulties (Armstrong *et al.*, 1993). Typically a small island micro-state will have only a single key freight transport ferry link to an adjacent larger country further exacerbating vulnerability. Similar problems may also occur in land-locked micro-states (Pant, 1974) and are usually compounded in archipelagic states.

One of the advantages enjoyed by micro-states is that they are therefore more likely to be internationally competitive because they tend to be present in sectors in which they possess a comparative advantage. For other advantages one must look to a number of issues rarely considered in the traditional economics literature. One feature unique to micro-states is 'the importance of being unimportant' (Demas, 1965). This allows micro-states to develop distinctive and flexible financial, environmental and business regulations safe in the knowledge that their larger neighbours will not feel threatened by them. This distinctive regulatory regime enables micro-states to attract niche offshore finance and specialist business and shipping services of the kind which underpin some of the most successful of them, such as Jersey and Bermuda. Micro-states can also take advantage of their cultural distinctiveness, leading to the development of successful international tourist sectors. This is one of the few situations where being an island is a clear advantage.

Finally, there are the advantages to governments and societies of being small and enjoying close family, social, political and business networks (Putnam *et al.*, 1993). This closeness encourages the formation of social capital which can provide a more fertile environment for economic growth (Coleman, 1990) and facilitates a more rapid and effective response to change. Conversely, such close ties may promote nepotism and clientelism, so giving rise to socially-divisive rent-seeking. While comparative empirical evidence on social capital in micro-states is lacking, Briguglio notes the unusually strong performance of micro-state scores in the UN's Human Development index (Briguglio, 1995).

8.3   The micro-state data set

The collection and compilation of comparable data for micro-states is an extremely difficult task. The main international organisations, such as the UN, IMF and World Bank, produce data sets which systematically omit most micro-states, particularly the smallest ones. This is also true for large-scale international data sets produced by researchers such as Summers and Heston (1988). The principal reason for the inadequacy of data for economic variables for micro-states is that many of them lack fully developed statistical services and/or tend to collect statistics which are not harmonised according to international conventions. Even after selecting the size threshold of the micro-state set, a population of three million in this case, assembling data on variables such as GNP per capita presents a formidable problem.

The data sets utilised in this analysis have been assembled from a variety of sources. The focus of this chapter is economic performance as measured by GNP per capita, the indicator for which the most comprehensive harmonised data exist. A number of additional explanatory variables have also been drawn upon in order to standardise for various determinants of economic performance. These are considered in more detail later in the paper. The main data sets drawn upon here are: United Nations *Statistical Yearbook* data (available on CD-ROM), the World Bank *World Development Reports* (also available on CD-ROM), IMF *International Financial Statistics*, International Labour Organisation statistics and the Commonwealth Secretariat's *Small States: Economic Review and Basic Statistics*. Where necessary, data have also been collected directly from the governments and statistical services of many of the individual micro-states. It should be noted that, even with sustained effort, the data problems which arise when dealing with the smallest states means that the data is less reliable than is normally the case.

The results of the statistical collection process take the form of data sets of three levels of reliability. The first are data sets for which it was possible to construct continuous data series. The second are sets for which only ordinal measures of key variables are possible. The World Bank's annual four-fold classification of countries by GNP per capita is the best example of this type of data set and is utilised in this paper. Inadequacies in GNP statistics for micro-states and the lack of PPP adjustment has led to the World Bank producing GNP per capita statistics in the form of four very broad income classes. The third are ordinal data sets derived by the authors drawing upon data collected directly from very small micro-states. These data extend the existing ordinal data sets such as that of the World Bank. Since the published continuous data sets of the UN, IMF and World Bank systematically exclude most of the very smallest of the micro-states of interest in this paper, it is the second and third sets of data which have been utilised here.

Where ordinal data sets are used, many of the most common standard methods of analysis cannot be drawn upon. Here, therefore, we deliberately tailor the techniques of analysis to the ordinal nature of the data sets available. In particular, classificatory techniques suitable for ordinal data are employed as are censored regression approaches. In order to check for the robustness of the results obtained, different data sets are drawn upon where possible and the analysis undertaken is replicated.

8.4 Some initial comparisons of African and Asian/Pacific micro-states

It is possible to make some simple comparisons between the micro-states in Africa and Asia based upon the data presented in Table 8.1. First of all, it is evident that there is enormous diversity among the micro-states of Africa and Asia. In Africa, population sizes range from St Helena and its Dependencies with 6000, up to Liberia with 2.8 million. Land areas, too, vary enormously, from the 32 km^2 of the Spanish dependencies of Ceuta and Melilla up to the 1.03 million km^2 of Mauritania. Another feature of note in the table is the large number of island, archipelagic or land-locked entities which face a distinctive set of economic problems (see Section 8.3). Of the 22 African micro-states and dependencies, nine are island or archipelagic and a further three are land-locked. Turning to Asia (excluding the Pacific and Australasia), there are 14 micro-states, of which six are islands and two are land-locked. Considerable diversity is again revealed, with populations ranging from 1000 (Christmas Island and the Cocos Islands) to 2.79 million (Singapore). If the Pacific micro-states are grouped in with Asia, as is done by the World Bank, a further 21 entities join the list, all of them islands and almost all with extremely small populations and land areas.

With respect to levels of GNP per capita, the deficiencies in international statistics for continuous measures of GNP per capita for micro-states

Table 8.1   Authors' own set of micro-states and highly autonomous regions in Africa and Asia

Micro-state	Population, 1993 ('000s)	Land area (km²)
1. Sub-Saharan Africa and offshore islands		
Botswana	1 401	566 730
Cape Verde	370	4 030
Comoros	471	2 230
Congo	2 443	341 500
Djibouti	557	23 180
Equatorial Guinea	379	28 050
Gabon	1 012	257 670
Gambia	1 042	10 000
Guinea-Bissau	1 028	28 120
Lesotho	1 943	30 350
Liberia	2 845	96 750
Mauritania	2 161	1 025 220
Mauritius	1 091	2 030
Namibia	1 461	823 290
Sao Tome and Principe	122	960
Seychelles	72	450
Swaziland	880	17 200
Canary Islands (E)	1 526	7 273
Ceuta and Melilla (E)	126	32
Mayotte (F)	101	372
Reunion (F)	633	2 500
St Helena and Dependencies (UK)	6	319
2. Asia and Indian Ocean		
Bahrain	533	680
Bhutan	1 600	47 000
Brunei	273	5 270
Kuwait	1 762	17 820
Maldives	238	300
Mongolia	2 318	1 566 500
Oman	1 988	212 460
Qatar	524	11 000
Singapore	2 790	610
United Arab Emirates	1 807	83 600
British Indian Ocean Territories (UK)	2	59
Christmas Island (Aus)	1	135
Cocos Islands (Aus)	1	14
Macao (P)	381	17
3. Pacific		
Federated States of Micronesia	105	700
Fiji	762	18 270
Kiribati	76	730

Table 8.1   (*continued*)

Micro-state	Population, 1993 ('000s)	Land area (km^2)
Marshall Islands	51	181
Nauru	10	21
Palau	16	460
Samoa	167	2 830
Solomon Islands	354	27 990
Tonga	98	720
Tuvalu	9	24
Vanuatu	161	12 190
American Samoa (USA)	51	200
Cook Islands (NZ)	19	293
French Polynesia (F)	210	3 660
Guam (USA)	143	550
New Caledonia (F)	176	18 280
Niue (NZ)	2	258
Norfolk Island (Aus)	2	3
Northern Marianas (USA)	45	464
Tokelau (NZ)	2	1
Wallis and Futuna (F)	14	274

Source: See the Appendix.

and dependencies are very severe. Evidence from the World Bank data sets utilising World Bank regional definitions are set out in Table 8.2. Column 2 gives GNP per capita for 1994, the latest year for which data were available at the time of the study: there are many gaps and only some of the micro-states have adequate GNP per capita statistics. Column 3 gives the GNP per capita figures at PPP, where available. Column 4 represents the procedure adopted by the World Bank to circumvent some of the problems of inadequate statistics for micro-states. The World Bank utilises a fourfold GNP per capita income classification of states: low (less than $725), lower-middle ($725–$2895), and upper-middle ($2896–$8955) and upper (over $8955). The figure in Column 4 gives the World Bank GNP per capita category, running from 1 to 4 respectively, within which each micro-state lies and, as can be seen, most of the micro-states have an entry in this column. This ordinal or grouped data set is clearly far superior to the continuous variables of Columns 2 and 3 in terms of its coverage of the micro-states of interest here. The average values each are given at the head of each group.

It is evident from Table 8.2 that the African and Asian/Pacific micro-states have some interesting similarities as well as differences in their GNP

Table 8.2 A comparison of micro-state GNP per capita with regional averages, 1994

Micro-state	World Bank GNP p/c 1994		Group
	$US	$PPP	
1. Sub-Saharan Africa	546	1 478	1
Botswana	2 800	5 210	2
Cape Verde	930	1 920	2
Comoros	510	1 430	1
Congo	620	1 900	1
Djibouti			1
Equatorial Guinea	430		1
Gabon	3 880		3
Gambia	330	1 100	1
Guinea-Bissau	240	820	1
Lesotho	720	1 730	1
Liberia			1
Mauritania	480	1 570	1
Mauritius	3 150	12 720	3
Namibia	1 970	4 320	2
Sao Tome and Principe	250		1
Seychelles	6 680		3
Swaziland	1 100	3 010	2
Mayotte (F)			3
Reunion (F)			3
St Helena and Dependencies (UK)			
2. South Asia	325	1 401	1
Bhutan	400	1 270	1
Maldives	970		2
British Indian Ocean Territory (UK)			
3. Middle East and North Africa	1 995	5 562	2
Bahrain	7 460	13 220	3
Kuwait	19 400	24 730	4
Oman	5 140	8 590	4
Qatar	12 820	19 100	4
United Arab Emirates			
Canary Islands (E)			
Ceuta and Melilla (E)			
Madeira (P)			
4. Eastern Europe and Central Asia	2 145	4 210	2
Estonia	2 820	4 510	2
Latvia	2 320	3 220	2
Macedonia	820		2
Slovenia	7 040	6 230	3

Table 8.2 (*continued*)

Micro-state	World Bank GNP p/c 1994		
	$US	$PPP	Group
5. *Latin America and the Caribbean*	3 187	5 773	3
Antigua and Barbuda			
Bahamas	11 800	15 470	4
Barbados	6 560	11 210	3
Belize	2 630	5 600	2
Dominica	2 800		2
Grenada	2 630		2
Guyana	530	2 750	1
Jamaica	1 540	3 400	2
Panama	2 580	5 730	2
St Kitts and Nevis	4 760	9 310	3
St Lucia	3 130		3
St Vincent and Grenadines	2 140		2
Suriname	860	2 470	2
Trinidad and Tobago	3 740	8 670	3
Anguilla (UK)	6 770		3
Aruba (NL)			4
British Virgin Islands (UK)			
Cayman Islands (UK)			4
Falkland Islands (UK)			
Guiane (F)			3
Guadeloupe (F)			3
Martinique (F)			3
Montserrat (UK)			
Netherlands Antilles (NL)			4
Turks and Caicos Islands (UK)			
US Virgin Islands (USA)			4
6. *East Asia and Pacific*	3 525	4 660	3
Brunei	14 240		4
Fed States Micronesia			2
Fiji	2 250	5 940	2
Kiribati	740		2
Marshall Islands			2
Mongolia	300		1
Nauru			
Palau			
Samoa	1 000	2 060	2
Singapore	22 500	21 900	4
Solomon Islands	810	2 000	2
Tonga	1 590		2
Tuvalu			
Vanuatu	1 150	2 370	2
American Samoa (USA)			3

Table 8.2 (*continued*)

Micro-state	World Bank GNP p/c 1994 $US	$PPP	Group
Christmas Island (Aus)			
Cocos Islands (Aus)			
Cook Islands (NZ)			
French Polynesia (F)			3
Guam (USA)			3
Macao (P)			4
New Caledonia (F)			3
Niue (NZ)			
Norfolk Island (Aus)			
Northern Marianas (USA)			2
Tokelau (NZ)			
Wallis and Futuna (F)			
7. *Western Europe*	20 869	18 073	4
Andorra			4
Cyprus	10 260	14 800	4
Iceland	24 630	19 210	4
Liechtenstein			4
Luxembourg	39 600	35 860	4
Malta			3
Monaco			4
San Marino			
Azores (P)			
Faroe Islands (DK)			4
Gibraltar (UK)			
Guernsey (UK)			4
Isle of Man (UK)			3
Jersey (UK)			4
8. *North America*	25 240	25 286	4
Bermuda (UK)			4
Greenland (DK)			4
St Pierre and Miquelon (F)			

Notes:
1. Regional averages are calculated as the population-weighted values for GNP per capita for those countries for which World Bank statistics are available in 1994.
2. World Bank definitions of regions used throughout.
3. GNP per capita values are in US$ (World Bank Atlas method). PPP estimates are those of the World Bank and are expressed in international US$. Grouped GNP per capital values are: 1 = Below $725; 2 = $726–$2895; 3 = $2896–$8955; 4 = Over $8956 and are the groups defined in World Bank, *World Development Report 1996*, Table 1a.

Sources: Armstrong *et al.* (1996) utilising: World Bank, World Development Reports and CD-Roms, 1995 and 1996, Tables 1, 1a.

per capita performance levels when compared both to each other and also to the regional average values. In the case of sub-Saharan Africa, while most micro-states show very low levels indeed of GNP per capita – the region has the lowest average GNP per capita except for South Asia, in most cases, African micro-states have GNP per capita values in excess of their regional average. While they are poor states by world standards, there is no evidence that being small acts as a systematic impediment to their economic performance. There are, of course, some exceptions: Comoros, Equatorial Guinea, Gambia and Guinea-Bissau all have GNP per capita values below the sub-Saharan African regional average. The remaining micro-states however, are approximately equal to the regional average or better. In some cases, such as Mauritius, the Seychelles and Botswana, they are considerably better.

Turning to the Asian and Pacific micro-states, a similar picture of great diversity is revealed but with micro-states again usually outperforming the regional average per capita GNP values. In South Asia, all three micro-states and dependencies have GNP per capita values in excess of the (poor) regional average although they all have very low GNP per capita values by world standards. Some of the Middle Eastern micro-states have some of the highest GNP per capita values in the world (see Part 4 of Table 8.2) arising from their natural resource endowment, notably crude oil. The greatest degree of diversity in Asia, however, is found in East Asia and the Pacific. Micro-states such as Brunei and Singapore are among the richest states on earth. In contrast, many of the Pacific island micro-states are among the poorest states, even where they are closely tied in to the East Asian markets – for example Guam. Interestingly, it is among some of the Pacific island micro-states that it is possible to observe the highest concentration of cases where the micro-states have GNP per capita values *lower* than the regional average. The only other case where this occurs is in the Caribbean. In regions elsewhere, such as Europe and North America, the micro-states generally have GNP per capita values in excess of their regional averages. It should be borne in mind, nevertheless, that the regional average GNP per capita of the Pacific states is inflated by its inclusion with East Asia as a single World Bank region. This suggests that the results of this analysis are skewed by this regional definition. For the purposes of the later analysis, these two subregions are split into their separate components to ascertain whether this grouping actually affects the empirical results.

Several conclusions can be drawn from this initial comparison of micro-states in Africa and Asia/Pacific. It is evident that there is enormous diversity in the populations, areas and GNP per capita levels of different micro-states *within* each region. Both Africa and Asia each contain an array of highly successful *and* very poorly performing micro-states. In general, the lower the per capita income level of the region within which a micro-state is located, the lower will be the GNP per capita of the micro-state itself. Hence African and South Asian micro-states tend to be very poor indeed, whereas Middle Eastern and East Asian micro-states are much more prosperous. The economic success or otherwise of a micro-state in terms of levels of per capita GNP, therefore appears to depend, at least in part, upon the success or otherwise of the broader regional economy. Micro-states generally appear to have GNP per capita values greater than other countries in their region, with the exceptions of those in the Caribbean and Pacific. In this sense, they appear to be 'out-performing' larger countries in the same region, including more developed regions such as North America and Western Europe (Armstrong and Read, 1995). In the case of micro-states in the Pacific, their relatively poor performance may, however, be something of a statistical illusion since the regional GNP per capita average includes East Asia and its dynamic newly industrialising countries (NICs).

These particular features of micro-state performance in Africa and Asia are revealed more clearly in Table 8.3. In Part A of the table, the World Bank's four-fold classification of states by GNP per capita levels is used to compare African and Asian micro-states and, in Part B, the authors' own extension of the World Bank classification is examined. The latter classification is less accurate than that of the World Bank but has the advantage of incorporating all of the micro-states and dependent territories included in Table 8.1. The columns headed 'Asia/Pacific' in Table 8.3 aggregate all of the micro-states in South Asia, the Middle East, Central Asia, East Asia and the Pacific. In order to ascertain whether the Pacific micro-states are a special case and so ought not to be included in the East Asia group, their values are shown separately in parentheses in Columns 5 and 6 of the Table.

Table 8.3 illustrates the stark differences between micro-states in Africa and Asia. Using the World Bank's classification of GNP per capita classes (Part A), it can be seen that whereas 52.6 per cent of sub-Saharan African micro-states fall within the lowest GNP per capita class, the equivalent percentage for Asia/Pacific is 8.7 per cent. While none of the sub-Saharan micro-states fall within the highest GNP per capita class, the figure for Asia/Pacific is 26.1 per cent. Further, the unusual nature of the cohort of Pacific micro-states is clearly revealed. Most of the Pacific micro-states (69.2 per cent) lie within the lower-middle income group which suggests that the World Bank's practice of grouping them with East Asia may be misleading for the purposes of this analysis.

Table 8.3 Classification of micro-states in Africa and Asia/Pacific by GNP per capita income band, 1994

GDP per capita category, 1994	States for which data exists	Sub-Saharan Africa		Asia and Pacific[b]	
		Number	Percentage	Number	Percentage
(A) *World Bank Classification*[a]					
Below $725	12	10	52.6	2 (0)	8.7 (0.0)
$726–$2895	14	4	21.1	10 (9)	43.5 (69.2)
$2896–$8955	10	5	26.3	5 (4)	21.7 (30.8)
Over $8955	6	0	0.0	6 (0)	26.1 (0.0)
All categories	42	19	100.0	23 (13)	100.0 (100.0)
(B) *Extended World Bank data set, 'Best Guess' classification, with locally obtained and heterogeneous data sources*					
Below $725	21	18	62.1	3 (1)	8.6 (4.8)
$725–$2895	23	5	17.2	18 (15)	51.4 (71.4)
$2896–$8955	14	6	20.7	8 (5)	22.9 (23.8)
Over $8955	6	0	0.0	6 (0)	17.1 (0.0)
All categories	44	29	100.0	35 (21)	100.0 (100.0)

Notes:
[a] There are 10 micro-states in Sub-Saharan Africa and 12 micro-states in Asia/Pacific for which these data do not exist.
[b] Figures in parentheses in Columns 4 and 5 indicate values for Pacific micro-states alone.
Source: Part A – World Bank Indicators 1995, CD-ROM; Part B – World Bank Indicators 1995, CD-ROM and own calculations.

Part B of the table repeats the exercise using the authors' own more comprehensive classification of the GNP per capita of the micro-states. This shows that, even where the entities (mostly dependent territories) missing from the World Bank's data set are included, the overall picture remains much the same. African micro-states generally have lower GNP per capita values than their Asian/Pacific counterparts while the Pacific micro-states are generally at the lower per capita income end of the Asia/Pacific group.

8.5 The determinants of the differential economic performance of micro-states in Africa and Asia

The simple examination of crude GNP per capita levels and their rates of growth in Section 8.4 reveals wide variations between the economic performance of micro-states in Africa and Asia, particularly when the Pacific is treated separately from East Asia. This difference is also evident in the relative rates of growth between micro-states in these regions (see Armstrong *et al.*, 1998). This evidence would suggest, therefore, that

African micro-states perform very differently from their Asian counterparts. This is only partially true, however, since micro-states in South Asia as well as many of those in the Pacific have per capita GNP levels on a par with similar entities in Africa.

Of critical interest in this analysis is whether the determinants of the economic performance of micro-states in Africa differ systematically from those of their Asian/Pacific counterparts. This provides the basis for investigating whether the African micro-states have lower GNP per capita levels because of an unfortunate mix of factors, such as a lack of rich natural resource endowments, and geographical barriers to trade, such as islandness or being land-locked. Alternatively, their low levels of income may be the result of genuinely poor economic performance given their particular mix of characteristics.

8.5.1 The research methodology

Previous research by the authors has tackled the issue of how to account for the diversity observed in the economic performance of micro-states in different regions of the world by examining the characteristics of the micro-states concerned (Armstrong and Read, 1995, 1998; Armstrong *et al.*, 1996, 1998). In the absence of appropriate formal theoretical models, the approach adopted here draws upon the variables identified in the micro-states literature and in previous empirical work as likely to be of importance.

The approach used here utilises different data sets, each of which has its own deficiencies in terms of the numbers of micro-states included, in order to check for robustness of the research findings. It utilises statistical methods appropriate to the different types and quality of the data sets available. In particular, because the ordinal data sets are much more comprehensive than the continuous GNP per capita data, a combination of discriminant analysis and censored regression models is used. Discriminant analysis is a classificatory technique which is particularly appropriate for data sets in which the micro-states are grouped into GNP per capita classes, as is the case with both the World Bank's and the authors' own four GNP per capita income groups. Similarly, traditional regression models are inappropriate where the dependent variable (GNP per capita) is not a continuous variable. Here the grouped regression variant of the censored regression model utilising maximum likelihood estimation is chosen as being the most appropriate.

8.5.2 The explanatory variables

Previous research on micro-states, including that of the authors, suggests that those micro-states which tend to perform most strongly in economic terms are those with particular characteristics such as a valuable natural resource endowment or a less isolated geographical location. In addition, the best performing states tend, given the peculiarities of micro-states (for example small local markets), to be those which have adopted open trading regimes and niche market specialisation in some manufactures, international tourism and financial services. This argument suggests that there is a 'sectoral explanation' for micro-state success/failure (Armstrong and Read, 1995, 1998a; UNCTAD, 1997).

The discriminant and censored regression models utilised here incorporate eight explanatory variables. These are designed to measure the characteristics of micro-states and their sectoral structure.

REGION is an ordinal variable (coded from 1 to 9) which indicates the world region in which the micro-state is located according to World Bank regional definitions. As noted earlier, the World Bank groups East Asian and Pacific states together which is problematic given the nature of the analysis being undertaken here and in similar comparative research. For the purposes of this analysis, the Pacific and East Asian regions have therefore been separated. The REGION variable is coded according to the regional population-weighted average GNP per capita such that the poorest region (South Asia) is set as a '1' while the richest region (North America) is coded as a '9'. The underlying economic reasoning for the use of the REGION variable is that 'geography matters' and that the economic performance of a micro-state is intrinsically tied to that of the broader region within which it is located. In spite of increasing globalisation, the evidence of trade patterns and factor mobility suggests that micro-states remain very strongly linked to regional trading systems (Armstrong *et al.*, 1998). The *a priori* expectation with respect to the REGION variable is therefore that it will be positively related to the GNP per capita of micro-states.

ISLAND is a binary variable (coded '0' or '1'). The islandness characteristic of micro-states has been examined extensively in the literature and is argued to be an important adverse determinant of the economic performance of a micro-state. This is primarily because islands are more likely to be exposed to problems of remoteness, high unit transportation costs and adverse weather conditions. Islandness is incorporated in the vulnerability indices and small island developing states (SIDS) also have a special unit within UNCTAD. The empirical evidence on the impact of islandness, over and above that of being a micro-state, is less clear-cut (see Armstrong and Read, 1998b; Armstrong *et al.*, 1998; Read, 1998). In keeping with inferences of theory, the *a priori* expectation is of a negative relationship between islandness and GNP per capita.

TOURISM is the first of five 'sectoral' niche specialisation variables. While ideally, it would be appropriate to make use of variables which measure the underlying causes of comparative advantage in micro-states, the limited availability of data makes this objective impossible. Instead, the analysis makes use of proxy variables for the key niche sectors. The TOURISM variable is ordinal and based upon World Tourist Organisation data for 176 countries in 1993 combined with data collected directly from micro-states. It indicates whether a micro-state has fewer tourists per 1000 population than the median value (coded '0'), more than the median value up to the second quartile (coded '1') or within the upper quartile (coded '2'). Previous work suggests that a successful tourist sector has a positive impact on micro-state growth performance (Armstrong and Read, 1995; Armstrong *et al.*, 1998). The *a priori* expectation is therefore of a positive relationship with GNP per capita.

FINAN is a binary variable which indicates the absence (coded '0') or presence (coded '1') of a major financial services sector in a micro-state. This variable has been the most difficult of all to construct and relies on a more than usual degree of judgement by the authors. This is because good quality comparable data on the size of financial services in micro-states is extremely difficult to obtain. Moreover, the presence of institutions in large numbers does not necessarily guarantee the existence of a large and thriving financial services sector. Various sources have been used to construct this binary variable (including Tolley Publishing Co., 1993; Roberts, 1994). Again, the empirical evidence suggests that a successful financial services sector has a strongly positive impact on growth (Armstrong and Read, 1995; Armstrong *et al.*, 1998) such that the *a priori* expectation is again of a positive relationship with GNP per capita.

MANFG is another binary variable which again indicates the absence (coded '0') or presence (coded '1') of a significant manufacturing sector. The export of manufactures is regarded as a key element in the industrialisation of developing countries although this is less applicable to the case of micro-states because of their small size (see Section 8.2). Most previous research on micro-states links the export of manufactures to micro-state economic success, and states such as Mauritius and Singapore have based their recent success on manufacturing specialisation. Ideally, a measure designed to pick up high value-added niche sectors within manufacturing should be utilised. Data problems, however, mean that this is simply not possible. Instead, a binary variable is utilised based upon whether a micro-state has a greater or less than average share of manufacturing in GDP according to World Bank statistics supplemented by data from individual micro-states. The *a priori* expectation is of a positive relationship with GNP per capita.

AGRIC is also a binary variable based upon whether a micro-state has a higher (coded '1') or lower (coded '0') than average share of agriculture in GDP using World Bank GDP data for 119 countries in 1993. Many developing countries possess extensive agricultural sectors, producing some combination of subsistence output and commodity exports, which are regarded as being an obstacle to rapid growth. The generally small size of the agricultural sector in most micro-states might therefore be viewed as a distinct advantage although many micro-states remain specialised exporters of agricultural products, most notably of bananas in the Caribbean. Empirical research suggests that the possession of a sizeable agricultural sector will hamper the growth process such that the *a priori* expectation is of a negative relationship with GNP per capita.

RESOUR is another binary variable indicating the absence (coded '0') or presence (coded '1') of a major high value natural resource for export. The variable is hard to construct and has relied upon a high degree of judgement by the authors although it should be noted that the vast majority of micro-states have absolutely little in the way of natural resources apart from land. Those micro-states which do possess a valuable natural resource, tend to benefit greatly because even a small endowment can have a significant effect on GNP per capita, given a small population. The judgement exercised in developing RESOUR is not therefore as arbitrary as may appear at first sight. A variety of data sources are utilised, including the UN data on crude oil production and fisheries, together with data collected from the individual micro-states. The experience of the Middle Eastern crude oil exporting micro-states demonstrates the potential windfall benefits arising from a valuable natural resource and this also applies to micro-states with other resources, such as fish or phosphates. The *a priori* expectation is therefore of a positive relationship with GNP per capita.

SOVRT is a simple binary variable indicating whether a micro-state is a dependent territory (coded '0') or a sovereign state according to the UN definition (coded '1'). Sovereignty is included in this analysis as an explanatory variable because research by the authors indicates that politically sovereign micro-states tend to have significantly lower GNP per capita levels than the remaining dependent territories of the colonial powers (Armstrong and Read, 1998). The underlying reasons for this phenomenon are not fully clear but include the large per capita financial transfers and 'aid-in-kind' that dependent territories obtain from their metropolitan governments. This result is one of the reasons for the analysis of an extended data set which includes dependent territories in this study (see also the discussion in Section 8.2). In the light of this previous research result, the *a priori* expectation is of a negative relationship between sovereignty and GNP per capita.

NUMBERS represents the absolute number of micro-states in the broader region within which each micro-state is located. It is incorporated as an explanatory variable because, for many of the key explanatory sectoral variables (for example, offshore banking and finance or tourism), there is likely to be room in a given region for only one or two successful micro-states to occupy the niche market. This reflects a regional 'congestion' effect via the fallacy of composition. In a region such as the Caribbean therefore, with a large number of micro-states trying to occupy only one or two niches (such as cruise tourism), the majority may be doomed to failure. The *a priori* expectation is therefore of a negative relationship with GNP per capita.

8.5.3   Discriminant analysis of the determinants of micro-state growth

The results of the discriminant analysis for both the World Bank and the authors' own fourfold grouped data for GNP per capita are presented in Table 8.4. No attempt is made to fit the model to the World Bank continuous GNP per capita data set since the analysis is only appropriate for classificatory data. Column 2 gives the results using the World Bank 80-state data set while Column 3 gives the results for the authors' own full 105-state GNP per capita data set. In both cases, the grouping variable is GNP per capita using the four classes referred to in Section 8.4. The explanatory variables are listed in Column 1 of Table 8. 4 and are the variables described in the previous subsection.

A standard step-wise Wilks' lambda algorithm is used in which the independent variables are selected in order of importance as classificatory determinants in the final discriminant classification. This is shown in parentheses in the central section of each of Columns 2 and 3 of the Table. Where a variable fails to meet a minimum F-to-enter criterion, it is excluded from the analysis, shown by 'excluded' at appropriate points. It can be seen that the MANFG variable is consistently excluded, indicating that it plays very little role in distinguishing between high and low GNP per capita micro-states. Experiments with a further variable measuring the absolute size of each micro-state (using population as a measure of size) were also conducted but are not reported here. This is because the size variable is consistently excluded and it exhibits strong multicollinearity with the REGION, ISLAND and SOVRT variables. This result is interesting nevertheless, in that it reinforces the findings of earlier research that

Table 8.4 Discriminant analysis results for the determinants of micro-state GNP per capita 1994

Estimated characteristics	World Bank groups 1994	Authors' groups 1994
Standardised canonical discriminant coefficients		
REGION	0.37438	0.25834
ISLAND	0.05611	–0.00184
TOURISM	0.66152	0.62208
AGRIC	–0.56910	–0.53875
RESOUR	0.60064	0.54092
FINAN	0.18343	0.25946
MANFG	Excluded	Excluded
SOVRT	–0.39993	–0.42782
NUMBERS	–0.25178	–0.24722
Fit of model – Wilks' lambda		
REGION	0.31909 (3)	0.41091 (3)
ISLAND	0.14708 (8)	0.29484 (5)
TOURISM	0.56856 (1)	0.62081 (1)
AGRIC	0.42792 (2)	0.50470 (2)
RESOUR	0.25405 (4)	0.34859 (4)
FINAN	0.16442 (7)	0.22834 (7)
MANFG	Excluded	Excluded
SOVRT	0.21812 (5)	0.26159 (6)
NUMBERS	0.18641 (6)	0.21284 (8)
Eigenvalue	2.9404	1.9690
Canonical correlation	0.86	0.81
Chi-Square	39.821	44.980
	($p = 0.0003$)	($p = 0.0000$)
Wilks' lambda	0.5796	0.6319
Classification success:		
– Overall	77.5%	73.3%
– Low income group	81.8%	92.3%
– Lower-middle income group	76.9%	67.6%
– Upper-middle income group	73.9%	70.0%
– Upper income group	80.0%	75.0%
Number of micro-states	80	105

Notes:
1. The analysis is constructed using a stepwise Wilks' lambda method: to a maximum of three functions, results being shown for Function 1. Variables entering the function must satisfy tolerance level and F-to-enter criteria, where maximum tolerance level is 0.001 and minimum F-to-enter is 1.00. Selection rule is maximise Wilks' lambda. Variables not selected are shown as 'Excluded'.
2. Standardised canonical discriminant coefficients are similar, but not identical, to regression coefficients.
3. Eigenvalues measure the ratio of the between-group sums of squares to the total sum of squares. Large eigenvalues therefore imply a 'good' discriminant function.
4. In a two-group case, the canonical correlation is equivalent to the value of the Pearson correlation coefficient between the discriminant score and the binary group variable. A value close to 1.00 is therefore to be preferred.
5. The chi-square test is derived from Wilks' lambda and tests for the significance of differences between group means (shown in parentheses).
6. Variables and data sources are defined and discussed in the text.

absolute size has little effect on its economic performance (such as Milner and Westaway, 1993; Armstrong and Read, 1996, 1998).

The standardised canonical discriminant coefficients in the top part of Table 8.4 are similar to partial regression coefficients and can be interpreted in a similar way. The 'Fit of Model – Wilks' lambda' coefficients in the central part of the table show the significance of each variable in the discriminant function. The various diagnostic statistics in the bottom part of Table 8.4 show the overall degree of fit of the discriminant classification.

As in previous research by the authors, the explanatory variables used give excellent results. Overall canonical correlations are 0.86 for the 80-state data set and 0.81 for the authors' own 105-state data set. Eigenvalue, chi-square and Wilks' lambda diagnostics are also very good and suggest that the variables used allow a successful classification of micro-states into the four World Bank GNP per capita income classes. Overall, the model successfully classifies 77.5 per cent of micro-states into their actual GNP per capita group for the World Bank data set and 73.3 per cent in the authors' own data set. Interestingly, the model best classifies micro-states into the upper and low GNP per capita income groups with slightly poorer rates of success for the two middle-income groups.

The REGION variable has the expected positive relationship to GNP per capita, given by the standardised canonical discriminant coefficients (top panel of the table), which is also strong since it enters early at Stage 3 of the grouping algorithm. ISLAND has the expected negative sign only in the 105-state data set run but has only a weak effect. This confirms the mixed results discussed above but raises interesting questions, given the importance attached to island status in the literature (Section 8.2). The prosperity of the broad region within which a micro-state is located appears to be a rather more important influence than problems arising from islandness. Three of the sectoral variables, TOURISM, RESOUR and FINAN, have the expected positive signs and powerful effects. Unsurprisingly, however, given the earlier discussion, the MANFG variable performs poorly although this may just reflect the rather broad-brush nature of its specification. A variable designed to measure niche manufacturing more precisely would have been better. AGRIC has a powerful influence on the economic prosperity of micro-states with the expected negative sign. Both SOVRT and NUMBERS of other micro-states in the same region appear to have weaker influences but are negative as expected. While the sign of the SOVRT variable might be seen as surprising, its relationship with GNP per capita appears to be consistently negative in multivariate models of this kind (see the earlier discussion). This suggests that sovereign micro-states do not perform as well as dependent territories, allowing for their other key characteristics.

8.5.4 Discriminant analysis of differences between micro-states in Africa and Asia

The same model can be used to examine differences between micro-states in the African and Asian/Pacific regions. This is undertaken by comparing the actual GNP per capita group of each micro-state with that predicted by the discriminant function. In this way, it is possible to identify which micro-states have the expected GNP per capita levels for their particular characteristics, given the values of the independent variables used in the discriminant analysis. Similarly, those micro-states incorrectly classified by the discriminant analysis can be identified since they will over- or under- perform relative to the GNP per capita group predicted by the explanatory model.

Taking the World Bank 80-state data set first and concentrating solely on the African and Asian/Pacific states, the results of the discriminant analysis are shown in Table 8.5. It is evident from these results that remarkably few states are misclassified by the discriminant analysis. In the African group 14 micro-states are correctly classified, leaving only the five misclassified African states listed above. Similarly, in Asia, no fewer than seven states are correctly classified, leaving only the three cases misclassified. Finally, in the Pacific region, 12 states are correctly classified, leaving only the two misclassified cases. The implication of these results is that micro-states within both Africa and Asia/Pacific essentially respond to the same determinants of economic performance as all other world micro-states. There is virtually no evidence whatsoever here that, when a wide set of characteristics are allowed for, the economic performance of micro-states in Africa is out of line with that of micro-states in Asia/Pacific.

It should be recognised, however, that the model utilised here contains the REGION variable which is found to be a highly significant variable. There is therefore an issue of why the African region as a whole performs more poorly than parts of Asia, notably East Asia. What the results presented in Table 8.5 indicate is that per capita incomes in African micro-states are essentially dampened by the lower average levels of per capita incomes prevailing in the region. When this regional factor is allowed for, there is virtually no evidence of any systematic under-performance compared with micro-states in Asia and the Pacific. The same interpretation and comments therefore also apply to micro-states in the Asia and Pacific regions.

Table 8.5   Discriminant analysis summary results for differences between GNP per capita in African and Asian micro-states, World Bank data set

Africa	Asia	Pacific
(A) *Micro-states in GNP per capita group > predicted, 'over-performers'*		
Comoros	Kuwait	–
Gabon	Qatar	–
(B) *Micro-states in GNP per capita group < predicted, 'under-performers'*		
Djibouti	Bahrain	American Samoa
Lesotho	–	Northern Marianas
Namibia	–	–

Looking at the few micro-states which are misclassified, they seem to have very little in common with each other. There are some indications that the binary RESOUR variable may be too crudely specified to pick-up the full implications of the benefits derived from natural resource endowments (for example, for Kuwait and Gabon). This issue, however, is minor given that the overall classification performance is so good.

Turning to the authors' own larger 105-state GNP per capita data set, the misclassification cases in the discriminant analysis are shown in Table 8.6. Again, the numbers of misclassified states should be set in the context of those which are classified successfully by the model. Twenty African micro-states, eight Asian micro-states and 19 Pacific micro-states are correctly classified. Yet again, it can be seen that those micro-states

Table 8.6   Discriminant analysis summary results for differences between GNP per capita in African and Asian micro-states, authors' own data set

Africa	Asia	Pacific
(A) *Micro-states in GNP per capita group > predicted, 'over-performers'*		
Comoros	Kuwait	Nauru
Congo	British Indian Ocean Territory	–
Gabon	–	–
Canary Islands (E)	–	–
(B) *Micro-states in GNP per capita group < predicted, 'under-performers'*		
–	Bahrain	Tuvalu
–	–	American Samoa (USA)
–	–	Niue (NZ)
–	–	Norfolk Island (Aus)
–	–	Northern Marianas (USA)

which are misclassified form only a small minority of the data set. These results support those for the World Bank data set and suggest that, apart from having the misfortune to be located in a region dominated by low income markets, African micro-states essentially perform as expected, given their particular characteristics. No other special factors are revealed by the analysis. Moreover, as with the smaller World Bank data set, several of those states misclassified by the discriminant analysis appear to be so because of the broad-brush specification of the RESOUR variable utilised in the analysis. This would appear to be the case with Kuwait in Asia, the Congo and Gabon in Africa and Nauru in the Pacific, the latter having now exhausted most of its natural resource base of phosphates.

8.5.5 Censored regression analysis of the determinants of micro-state growth

Discriminant analysis is essentially a classification technique and does not purport to be an explanatory model of GNP per capita. The results of a censored (grouped) data analysis of the GNP per capita data sets are presented in Table 8.7. The censored regression analysis utilises the same explanatory variables that were used in the discriminant analysis. Columns 2, 3 and 4 of the table give the results using the 80-state World

Table 8.7 Censored (grouped) regression results for the determinants of micro-state GNP per capita, 1994

Independent variables	World Bank groups			Authors' own groups		
	Coefficient	t	Probability	Coefficient	t	Probability
Constant	4,401.2	2.89	0.00389	4,995.0	3.70	0.00021
REGION	511.2	3.01	0.00260	316.6	1.96	0.04950
ISLAND	−140.1	−0.17	0.86279	−679.6	−0.81	0.41785
TOURISM	2,063.1	4.23	0.00002	2,059.6	4.43	0.00001
AGRIC	−2,892.4	−3.64	0.00028	−2 825.6	−3.63	0.00028
RESOUR	3,462.2	3.97	0.00007	3,018.7	3.45	0.00056
FINAN	1,767.1	2.19	0.02824	2,517.6	3.00	0.00274
MANFG	−1,051.1	−1.27	0.20274	−977.1	−1.08	0.27935
SOVRT	−2,293.3	−2.57	0.01019	−2,052.8	−2.76	0.00583
NUMBERS	−134.2	−2.77	0.00567	−112.6	−2.43	0.01531
	$N = 80$			$N = 105$		
	Log-likelihood = 68.7222			Log-likelihood = 103.034		

Note: The results have been estimated using the LIMDEP7 software package, with grouped data regression being estimated using maximum likelihood procedures. Limits to the groups are those of the World Bank's GNP per capita classes (that is, below $725, $725–$2895, $2896–$8955 and over $8955).

Bank GNP per capita data set and Columns 5, 6 and 7 give the results using the authors' own 105-state data set. In each case, the GNP per capita groups are the dependent variable and the variables listed in the table are the independent variables.

The results presented in Table 8.7 bear out strongly those of the discriminant analysis and suggest that the findings in this chapter are robust to the technique adopted. The key variables REGION, TOURISM, RESOUR and FINAN are found to have a significantly positive effect on micro-state GNP per capita and AGRIC, SOVRT and NUMBERS have significantly negative effects, shown by the *t*-ratios and probability columns. The MANFG and ISLAND variables also have negative signs but the coefficients are generally not significant. It would be possible to set out the residuals of the model so as to pin-point those African and Asian/Pacific states with large negative or positive residuals, that is, those 'under-performing' or 'over-performing'. This has not been done here because the very close similarities between the results of the censored regression and discriminant analyses, together with the extremely small numbers of states misclassified, make such an exercise unnecessary. The results of the model again indicate that the real reasons for the poorer economic performance of micro-states in Africa (and South Asia) relative to Asia as a whole is a consequence of their particular characteristics and their misfortune in being within a low income region. There is no evidence of any other distinct adverse 'regional' effect that would suggest that the micro-states or their governments are in some sense 'inadequate'.

8.6   Summary and conclusions

This chapter is an attempt to throw some new light on the difficult issue of the comparative economic performance of Africa and Asia by analysing the distinctive case of micro-states in these regions. In so doing, it addresses the question as to whether there is a systematic explanation for the relatively poorer performance of the African micro-states relative to their Asian/Pacific counterparts. Any such analysis is hampered by a number of difficulties. The lack of a universally accepted definition of what constitutes a micro-state, the uniquely poor statistical sources for micro-states, including a lack of harmonised data for most critical variables, and the absence of a clear consensus as to appropriate measures of 'economic' performance.

The approach adopted in this chapter has been to adopt a clear, if controversial, definition of a micro-state in terms of both size and status. It utilises a population size threshold of three million derived from an earlier analysis of the size distribution of states by the authors and which is significantly above the one million convention established by the UN. Further, the analysis incorporates an unusually wide definition of status so as to incorporate dependent territories and a number of highly autonomous subnational regions with an unusual degree of self-determination. This wider definition permits the use of an extended data set within the analysis, leading to greater statistical robustness, but also incorporates inferences from earlier research concerning the role of economic, as opposed to political, sovereignty. The analysis has sought to make the best possible use of the limited data sets available at the global level, in terms of both the coverage of particular variables and the number of different variables, and has attempted to tailor the statistical techniques utilised to the types of data available.

The issue of whether the economic performance of African micro-states, as measured by GNP per capita, differs from their Asian/Pacific counter-parts is addressed within the context of explanatory models and an analytical methodology developed by the authors in earlier research. The, data provides strong evidence that African micro-states have significantly lower GNP per capita levels than almost all of their Asian/Pacific counterparts with the exception of those in South Asia. The analysis presented here suggests that the principal reason for this difference is that African micro-states have the disadvantage of being located within a broader region generally characterised by low income markets. As a consequence, their economic performance is 'dampened' by the widely acknowledged poor performance of the larger African countries. This conclusion is supported by the results of both discriminant analysis and censored group regression analysis. Further, the results suggest that micro-states in Africa respond to the same determinants of economic performance, and in the same manner, as Asian, Pacific and other world micro-states. This indicates that there is nothing unusual in the behaviour of their economies or their ability to manage them that would support the view that there is a 'unique' region-specific explanation of their economic performance. Apart from the 'dampening' impact of the larger economies in the region on the growth of African micro-states, there is little evidence of an 'Africa' effect.

The finding that the economic performance of the micro-states in Africa is generally superior to that of the larger African economies is an important subsidiary result since it is a recurrent feature in many global regions. Only in the Caribbean and the Pacific are micro-states as a group found to perform poorly vis-à-vis the larger adjacent economies in the same broad region.

These two findings, taken together, have important implications for the future prosperity of micro-states in Africa (as well as South Asia). In spite of the low levels of regional growth in Africa over the last two decades, the African micro-states continue to perform comparatively well although their GNP per capita incomes remain low by world standards. Any progress in stimulating renewed and sustained growth in many of the larger economies of Africa can therefore be expected to have very positive 'knock-on' effects for the region's micro-states. This would include the implementation of better quality economic policies – including the further liberalisation of trade, improved communication and transport links and greater political stability. The supposedly greater degree of social cohesion enjoyed by micro-states would suggest that most of them are well placed to take advantage of any new opportunities which arise from economic recovery in Africa as a whole. In addition, the tendency of micro-states to specialise in more human capital-intensive activities such as niche business and financial services may mean that, in the future, the African micro-states will be able to supply much-needed intermediate services to the larger developing economies in the region.

The results presented in this chapter should only be viewed as a first attempt to address the issue of the relative economic performance of micro-states in different regions of the world. The approach used here suggests that the differential performance of micro-states can be best understood within the context of *multivariate* analysis in which the explanatory variables are drawn from both theoretical analysis and previous empirical research on micro-states. Nevertheless, further progress still needs to be made on these models. In particular, the specifications of the variables utilised in this analysis and designed to measure the geographical isolation of micro-states, their access to key world markets such as the EU and the strengths of key sectors such as financial services and tourism, remain too broad-brush. Moreover, a number of key variables have had to be omitted. For example, it would be very useful to incorporate variables which reflect the strength, or otherwise, of social capital in individual micro-states, and the policy powers available to the local administrations in dependent territories. Issues such as these, however, must await future research.

Acknowledgements

The research reported in this chapter is based upon statistical material collected as part of a project funded by the Overseas Development Administration, now the Department for International Development

(DfID), ODA Grant R6622: *The Economic Performance of Micro-States*. The views and opinions expressed here do not reflect official policies or practices of ODA or DfID but are those of the authors alone. The authors would like to thank numerous conference participants and the editors of this volume for their helpful comments and suggestions. The authors are, of course, responsible for any errors and omissions.

Appendix: Authors' own set of micro-states and highly autonomous regions

Micro-state	Population, 1993 (thousands)	Land area (km^2)
1. Sub-Saharan Africa and offshore islands		
Botswana	1 401	566 and 730
Cape Verde	370	4 030
Comoros	471	2 230
Congo	2 443	341 500
Djibouti	557	23,180
Equatorial Guinea	379	28 050
Gabon	1 012	257 670
Gambia	1 042	10 000
Guinea-Bissau	1 028	28 120
Lesotho	1 943	30 350
Liberia	2 845	96 750
Mauritania	2 161	1 025 220
Mauritius	1 091	2 030
Namibia	1 461	823 290
Sao Tome and Principe	122	960
Seychelles	72	450
Swaziland	880	17 200
Canary Islands (E)	1 526	7 273
Ceuta and Melilla (E)	126	32
Mayotte (F)	101	372
Reunion (F)	633	2 500
St Helena and Dependencies (UK)	6	319
2. Asia and Indian Ocean		
Bahrain	533	680
Bhutan	1 600	47 000
Brunei	273	5 270
Kuwait	1 762	17 820
Maldives	238	300
Mongolia	2 318	1 566 500
Oman	1 988	212 460
Qatar	524	11 000
Singapore	2 790	610
United Arab Emirates	1 807	83 600
British Indian Ocean Territories (UK)	2	59

Appendix (*continued*)

Micro-state	Population, 1993 (thousands)	Land area (km²)
Christmas Island (Aus)	1	135
Cocos Islands (Aus)	1	14
Macao (P)	381	17
3. Pacific		
Federated States of Micronesia	105	700
Fiji	762	18 270
Kiribati	76	730
Marshall Islands	51	181
Nauru	10	21
Palau	16	460
Samoa	167	2 830
Solomon Islands	354	27 990
Tonga	98	720
Tuvalu	9	24
Vanuatu	161	12 190
American Samoa (USA)	51	200
Cook Islands (NZ)	19	293
French Polynesia (F)	210	3 660
Guam (USA)	143	550
New Caledonia (F)	176	18 280
Niue (NZ)	2	258
Norfolk Island (Aus)	2	3
Northern Marianas (USA)	45	464
Tokelau (NZ)	2	1
Wallis and Futuna (F)	14	274
4. Americas, including the Caribbean		
Antigua and Barbuda	65	440
Bahamas	268	10 010
Barbados	260	430
Belize	204	22 800
Dominica	71	750
Grenada	92	340
Guyana	816	196 850
Jamaica	2 472	10 830
Panama	2 538	74 430
St Kitts and Nevis	42	360
St Lucia	142	610
St Vincent and the Grenadines	110	390
Suriname	414	156
Trinidad and Tobago	1 278	5 130
Anguilla (UK)	9	91
Aruba (NL)	69	190
Bermuda (UK)	62	53
British Virgin Islands (UK)	18	153
Cayman Islands (UK)	29	259

Appendix (*continued*)

Micro-state	Population, 1993 (thousands)	Land area (km²)
Falkland Islands (UK)	2	12 172
Greenland (Dk)	57	341 700
Guadeloupe (F)	413	1 690
Guiane (F)	134	88 150
Martinique (F)	371	1 060
Montserrat (UK)	11	98
Netherlands Antilles (NL)	195	800
St Pierre and Miquelon (F)	6	242
Turks and Caicos Islands (UK)	13	430
US Virgin Islands (USA)	104	340
5. Europe		
Andorra	61	450
Cyprus	726	9 240
Estonia	1 552	42 270
Iceland	263	100 250
Latvia	2 611	42 050
Liechtenstein	30	160
Luxembourg	396	2 560
Macedonia	2 075	25 430
Malta	361	320
Monaco	31	2
San Marino	24	60
Slovenia	1 991	20 120
Azores (P)	239	2 247
Faroe Islands (Dk)	47	1 400
Gibraltar (UK)	28	10
Guernsey (UK)	59	63
Isle of Man (UK)	72	572
Jersey (UK)	84	116
Madeira (UK)	255	794

Sources: Armstrong *et al.* (1996) utilising:
(a) Population data: World Bank, World Data 1995: CD-ROM used as basis for table, 1996; *United Nations Statistical Yearbook 1994* (St Helena and Dependencies, British Indian Ocean Territories, Anguilla, British Virgin Islands, Liechtenstein, Nauru, Palau, Niue, Wallis and Futuna, Falkland Islands, Montserrat, Turks and Caicos Islands, St Pierre and Miquelon, Malta, Palau, Cook Islands and Tokelau); 1991 Australian census data (Christmas Island, Cocos Islands and Norfolk Islands); Eurostat data (Azores, Madeira, Canary Islands and Ceuta and Melilla).
(b) Land area data: World Bank World Data 1995: CD-ROM used as basis for table (land area *not* surface area); Hunter 1996 (Canary Islands, Ceuta and Melilla, Isle of Man, Azores, Macao, Liechtenstein, Marshall Islands, Nauru, Palau, Tuvalu, Cook Islands, Norfolk Island, Tokelau, Christmas Island, Cocos Islands); *Whitaker's Almanac 1996* (St Helena and Dependencies, British Indian Ocean Territories, Anguilla, Falkland Islands, Montserrat, Turks and Caicos Islands, Wallis and Futuna, St Pierre and Miquelon, Northern Marianas and Federated States of Micronesia); data collected directly from governments concerned (Monaco, Guernsey and Jersey).

9
Child Activities in South Asia and Sub-Saharan Africa: a Comparative Analysis

Sonia Bhalotra and Christopher Heady

9.1 Introduction

While South Asia has the largest number of working children, sub-Saharan Africa has the highest incidence of child labour. Child work participation rates are 41 per cent in Africa as compared with 21 per cent in Asia and 17 per cent in Latin America (Ashagrie, 1998). Comparative work is a first step in gaining an insight into the universality of the problem of child work. South Asia and sub-Saharan Africa are clearly very different environments, their common ground being that the average household, at least in rural areas, is poor. We compare the determinants of child labour in the two countries, including household living standards, household human capital and demographics, and community-level data on schools and infrastructure. The data describe prominent differences in the environment that children grow up in. We then present a summary of the determinants of the variation in child work across households within each country. Interesting contrasts across country and gender are highlighted.

There have been a number of empirical studies of child labour in recent years. However, as Basu (1999) points out, there remains considerable scope for good empirical work in this field. At this stage, patterns are only just beginning to emerge among the variety of results in the literature, corresponding to the vast variety of regions, types of child work, and empirical specifications. The main contribution of this chapter is that it uses comparable micro-data on two countries where child participation rates in work are currently very high, in an attempt to determine whether any patterns can be discerned amid the vast (observed and unobserved) heterogeneity in household conditions. Existing beliefs about the causes

158

and consequences of child labour have tended to be shaped by case studies. These typically interview working children. An advantage of using large-scale representative household surveys, as is done here, is that we have comparable information for children who do not work.

The chapter is organised as follows. Section 9.2 profiles child activities in the early 1990s in the rural areas of Ghana and Pakistan, and looks at the correlation of child labour with education. In Section 9.3 we discuss a range of variables that theory and existing evidence suggest have an impact on child labour. Section 9.4 compares the central tendencies of these potential explanatory variables across Ghana and Pakistan so as to describe the similarities and contrasts in the environments in which children live. In Section 9.5, we compare the means of the variables across the sub-samples of working and non-working children, for each country and each gender. This indicates the likely significance of the variables. In a natural extension of this analysis, Section 9.6 pools household-level data on working and non-working children and tobit models of hours of child work provide estimates of the size and significance of the range of variables considered, holding the others constant at their mean levels. The analysis of Sections 9.3–9.4 is restricted to child labour on the household farm, because this is the type of child work that is both more prevalent and more directly comparable across the two countries. Conclusions and policy implications are presented in Section 9.7.

9.2   A profile of child activities by gender and country

In this section we present empirical evidence on school attendance as well as on the prevalence, intensity and nature of child labour in rural areas. We discuss the extent to which school and work are combined by children, and we highlight the fact that a substantial proportion of children, especially girls, are neither in school nor at work (though they may well be engaged in domestic work). Interesting inter-country and gender differences in child activities emerge.

9.2.1   The data

The data are drawn from the Ghana Living Standards Survey (GLSS) for 1991/9.2 (wave 3) and the Pakistan Integrated Household Survey (PIHS) for 1991. The GLSS contains 4552 households, with an average household size of 4.5 members, giving a total of 20 403 individuals. Almost 50 per cent of males and 45 per cent of females are aged under 15. The PIHS for 1991 contains 4795 households. On account of a much larger mean household size of 7.5 members, we have a sample of 36 109 individuals.

About 43.5 per cent of males and 45.5 per cent of females in the sample are aged under 15.

The GLSS collects data on employment for persons 7 years or older whereas the cut-off age is 10 in the PIHS. While there are important differences in the two data sets, their structure and coverage are sufficiently similar to allow some interesting cross-national comparisons.

Participation rates of rural children in school and in different kinds of work are presented in Tables 9.1–9.2 for Ghana and 9.3–9.4 for Pakistan, for 7–17 year olds in three age groupings. Data on 15–17 year olds is of interest in so far as it illustrates how the school and work patterns of under-15s evolve with age. The discussion that follows refers to 10–14 year olds.

9.2.2   Participation rates in school

In rural Ghana, 79 per cent of boys and 72 per cent of girls aged 10–14 years are 'currently in school'. In contrast, school attendance in

Table 9.1   Rural boys in Ghana: participation rates in school and work by age group

Age in years:	7–9 N = 708 (%)	10–14 N = 1010 (%)	15–17 N = 491 (%)
School attendance	73.3	78.7	59.5
Outside employment	0.14	0.60	1.22
Work on the household enterprise	0.71	2.5	4.9
Work on the household farm	28.5	48.9	63.5
Domestic work	76.8	89.8	85.3

Note:
N: Number of observations

Table 9.2   Rural girls in Ghana: participation rates in school and work by age-group

Age in years:	7–9 N = 673 (%)	10–14 N = 869 (%)	15–17 N = 375 (%)
School attendance	65.4	71.6	45.9
Outside employment	0.0	0.11	1.10
Work on the household enterprise	1.9	3.6	9.1
Work on the household farm	22.0	44.1	57.0
Domestic work	82.8	96.2	94.2

Note:
N: number of observations

Table 9.3 Rural boys in Pakistan: participation rates in school and work by age group

Age in years:	7–9 N = 965 (%)	10–14 N = 1208 (%)	15–17 N = 577 (%)
School attendance	65.5	72.0	50.4
Outside employment		6.2	17.9
Work on the household enterprise		2.3	7.8
Work on the household farm		22.1	33.5
Domestic work	n.a.	n.a.	n.a.

Notes: Figures are percentages for the sample of *all rural households*. Data on work were not gathered for children under 10. The Pakistan survey did not address questions about domestic work to boys. N: Number of observations.

Table 9.4 Girls in Pakistan: participation rates in school and work by age group

Age in years:	7–9 N = 868 (%)	10–14 N = 1095 (%)	15–17 N = 490 (%)
School attendance	39.2	30.5	15.4
Outside employment		11.9	13.7
Work on the household enterprise		1.6	2.0
Work on the household farm		28.1	33.7
Domestic work		99.4	97.8

Notes: Figures are percentages for the sample of *all rural households*. Data on work were not gathered for children under 10. Participation includes participation in regular and seasonal activities. N: Number of observations.

Pakistan is remarkably larger for boys as compared to girls of all ages. Among 10–14 year olds, 72 per cent of boys and only 31 per cent of girls are in school. Except for girls in Pakistan who appear to withdraw into the household at an early age, school participation is lower in the 7–9 and 15–17 year ranges suggesting late entry and early exit (the latter, especially for girls). Consistent with this, participation in all sorts of work, for boys and girls, tends to increase steadily with age.

9.2.3 Participation rates in work

In Ghana, 49 per cent of boys and 44 per cent of girls undertake work on the household farm, about a further 3 per cent of each gender are engaged in household enterprises, while less than 1 per cent report any employment outside the household. In Pakistan, 22 per cent of boys and 28 per cent of girls work on the household farm, about 2 per cent of both genders work in a household enterprise, and 6 per cent of boys and 12 per cent of girls work outside the home.

The striking difference between the two countries is that children in Pakistan engage in wage work outside the household, which Ghanaian children do not. The data show that this is more or less full-time work[1] and that, for girls, it is predominantly seasonal agricultural work, whereas the large fraction of boys who work outside the home are engaged in non-agricultural work.

Data on domestic work, which includes fetching firewood or water, cooking, cleaning, laundry, shopping and child care, were collected for boys and girls in Ghana and for girls alone in Pakistan. Virtually all children participate in domestic work of some sort. In addition (not shown in the tables), about 5 per cent of Pakistani girls engage in home work for sales, an activity in which boys have no part. It appears unusual for children to be active in more than one type of work though a small fraction of Pakistani children do combine wage work and farm work (Tables 9.5 and 9.6).

Table 9.5   Rural Ghana: 7–14 year olds: how often are activities combined?

	Boys N = 1010 (%)	Girls N = 869 (%)
Total participation rates		
Farm work	48.9	44.1
Enterprise work	2.5	3.6
School	78.7	71.6
None of the above activities	8.0	13.7
Participation restricted to one activity		
Farm work only	13.1	12.7
Enterprise work only	0.2	2.1
School only	40.6	38.7
Combinations of types of work		
Farm and enterprise work	0.0	0.0
Combination of work and school		
Farm work and school	35.8	31.4
Enterprise work and school	2.3	1.5

Notes: Total participation rates are those in Tables 9.1 and 9.2, repeated here for reference.
N: Number of children.

Table 9.6   Rural Pakistan: 10–14 year olds: how often are activities combined?

	Boys N = 1208 (%)	Girls N = 1095 (%)
Total participation rates		
Household farm work	22.1	28.1
Household enterprise work	2.3	1.6
Wage work	6.2	11.9
School	71.5	30.5
None of the above activities	10.5	35.3
Participation restricted to one activity		
Household farm work only	9.2	21.4
Household enterprise work only	1.0	1.2
Wage work only	2.9	7.0
School only	60.3	27.3
Combinations of types of work		
Household farm and enterprise work	0.58	0.09
Household farm and wage work	1.7	3.8
Household enterprise and wage work	0.16	0.27
Combinations of work and school		
Household farm work and school	10.0	2.5
Household enterprise work and school	0.25	0.0
Wage work and school	0.50	0.0

Notes: The sample is of all rural households. Activities include seasonal and regular activities. Total participation rates are those in Tables 9.3 and 9.4 repeated here for reference. N: Number of observations.

9.2.4   Hours of work

How hard do working children work? Mean hours increase with age for all groups other than Pakistani girls working for the household (Table 9.7). Work intensity for the household is similar among girls and boys in Ghana. Pakistani girls exhibit lower intensity work, while boys in Pakistan work harder than the other sub-groups. The table shows wide dispersion around mean hours but, overall, household work would not appear to be full-time work. Indeed, as we shall see below, many children combine farm work with school attendance. On the other hand, wage work, which is restricted to children in Pakistan, is more or less full-time work. Boys work on average 45 hours a week while girls work about 30 hours a week.

9.2.4   Competition between work and schooling

Of Ghanaian children who work on the household farm, almost three in four boys and girls are at the same time in school (Table 9.5). Combining farm

Table 9.7   Hours of work: boys and girls in Ghana and Pakistan

Age in years	7–9	10–14	15–17
Household work			
Ghana boys	12.9 (sd = 12.9)	16.5 (sd = 13.4)	22.5 (sd = 15.2)
	N = 202	N = 494	N = 312
Ghana girls	14.8 (sd = 13.2)	15.6 (sd = 12.8)	20.1 (sd = 12.1)
	N = 148	N = 383	N = 214
Pakistan boys		23.3 (sd = 18.4)	27.7 (sd = 19.6)
		N = 258	N = 187
Pakistan girls	13.3 (sd = 13.0)	12.8 (sd = 11.8)	
		N = 278	N = 155
Wage work			
Pakistan boys	44.9 (sd = 22)	46.8 (sd = 20)	
		N = 61	N = 85
Pakistan girls	30.9 (sd = 16)	33.7 (sd = 15)	
		N = 73	N = 43

Notes: Figures are mean hours of work per week for the sample of rural children who work (number of whom is N) and standard deviations (sd) are in parentheses.

work and school would appear to be less easily done in Pakistan, where almost half the boys but only one in ten farm-working girls manage it (Table 9.6).[2] Similarly, in Ghana, virtually all boys and almost half of the girls combine working on the household enterprise with going to school while, in Pakistan, this is rare among the boys and unknown among girls. Child wage work is virtually absent in Ghana but in Pakistan, where it occupies about 6 per cent of boys and 12 per cent of girls, it clearly interferes with schooling: less than 1 per cent of children combine wage work and school. Overall, in all its forms, child work in Pakistan is much more evidently in competition with school attendance than is the case in Ghana.

A remarkable fact is that, in both countries, a substantial proportion of children neither work nor go to school. In Pakistan, this is 35 per cent of girls and 10 per cent of boys and in Ghana, it is 14 per cent of girls and 8 per cent of boys. These fractions are especially large among girls. Therefore, if the main concern is with low educational attainment (and the gender gap therein), then policies designed to discourage child labour may be rather less important than policies that directly promote school attendance.

9.3   Potential determinants of the variation in child work

In this section, we discuss the variables that both theory and existing evidence suggest have an impact on child labour. This underlies the empirical analysis in the remainder of the chapter.

Bhalotra and Heady (1999: Section 4) present a theoretical model of household choice relating to the supply of child labour. The key issue is the allocation of child time between work and school. This time allocation will depend on the relative advantages of work and school, both in the short term and in the long term.

The main quantifiable short-term advantage of work is the wage that is received. In the context of working for the household, which Section 2 showed to account for most of the child labour in Ghana and Pakistan, the wage will typically not be explicit. Instead, it is necessary to look for variables that determine the marginal product of child work. These include *child characteristics* such as age and sex, *household characteristics* such as land at the disposal of the household as well as household size and composition, and *community level characteristics* such as local infrastucture and indicators of local labour demand (for example, the region of the country or recent changes in local economic well-being). The main quantifiable measures of the short-term attractiveness of schooling is the access to schooling and quality of schooling, both of which are defined at the level of the community.

The long-term advantages of work and schooling depend on their ability to raise the child's future earnings. This is hard to measure in itself. However, there are observable variables that affect the relative weight that households put on the short-term and long-term advantages. In a perfect capital market, the relative weights will just depend on the rate of interest, but this is an extreme assumption. In reality, it is reasonable to think of households having differential access to credit and thus placing different weights on current and future benefits. As access to credit typically varies with income, this corresponds to the popular belief that children are more likely to work, the poorer the households they come from. We therefore include household income in the analysis, proxied by the natural logarithm of per capita food expenditure. In addition, household assets such as land and the availability of local risk-sharing institutions may influence households' access to credit, and thus their ability to keep their children out of work.

These economic considerations will be modified by household and community attitudes to the importance of education and the appropriate treatment of children. This might depend on the age and sex of the child and whether he or she is the child of the household head. There is also evidence of *birth order* effects on the distribution of household investments across children (for example, Das Gupta, 1987; Butcher and Case, 1994). Attitudes to education will depend on the education of the child's parents, although it is important to distinguish the effect of parental education on attitudes from its effects on household income. Attitudes will also depend on to which ethnic and religious groups the household belongs to.

Many of these variables have been shown to play a role in determining children's labour market participation by studies based on similar household surveys, such as Canagarajah and Coulombe (1998), Jensen and Nielsen (1996) and Patrinos and Psacharopoulos (1997).

9.4 Variation in explanatory variables between Ghana and Pakistan

9.4.1 Child work on the household farm

The following discussion will concentrate on farm work which employs by far the largest proportion of children in both countries and which is comparable across them. The vast majority of working children in developing countries, whether in Brazil or Pakistan or Ghana are engaged in agricultural work. Yet, this work is severely understudied as compared with the more visible forms of work in Latin America and Asia, which involve children in labour-intensive manufacturing.

9.4.2 Contrasting environments for children in Ghana and Pakistan

The discussion here is a summary of the broad magnitudes relating to some interesting contrasts between the rural regions of the two countries in the environments in which children work. Recall that children in Ghana are 7–14 and in Pakistan are 10–14 years old (Tables 9.8 and 9.9).

Approximately half the children in each sample are first-born children and something like three in four are children of the household head. However, cross country similarities stop at child characteristics. It is not uncommon in Ghana for a household to own more than one plot of *land*, but this is unusual in Pakistan. In Ghana, households appear to have access to freely available or village owned land, which is not the case in Pakistan. Sharecropping is much more prevalent in Pakistan than in Ghana, involving almost 40 per cent of households as compared with about 7 per cent.

The most remarkable contrasts between the countries appear with respect to household structure. Average household size is about seven in Ghana and is closer to ten in Pakistan. A striking difference between the countries is that almost 30 per cent of households in Ghana have a *female head* as compared with less than 3 per cent of households in Pakistan. Another difference of enormous magnitude is that approximately 35 per cent

Table 9.8 Variable means for workers and non-workers by gender – rural ghana: 7–14 year olds

| | Boys in Ghana | | Girls in Ghana | |
	Workers	Non-workers	Workers	Non-workers
No. of observations	687	884	523	884
Dependent variable				
Hours worked on farm	15.5	0	15.5	0
Child characteristics				
Age	10.9	9.8	10.9	9.7
First child	0.61	0.47	0.64	0.48
Child of head of household	0.77	0.84	0.72	0.81
Household resources				
In per capita food expenditure	–0.33	–0.40	–0.27	–0.39
Size of farm				
Acres of land	9.34	8.23	9.77	7.57
Number of farms	2.0	1.94	2.1	1.92
Rent land	0.086	0.055	0.071	0.083
Sharecrop land	0.070	0.067	0.067	0.066
Freely available land	0.23	0.15	0.21	0.15
Village-owned land	0.23	0.26	0.24	0.28
Household structure				
Household size	7.3	7.2	6.9	7.3
Proportion female	0.42	0.42	0.61	0.60
Female head	0.27	0.20	0.34	0.22
Age of household head	49.8	47.8	49.5	48.0
Mother absent	0.27	0.23	0.30	0.23
Father absent	0.41	0.30	0.47	0.32
Males under 7 years	0.10	0.11	0.091	0.11
Males 7–14 years	0.28	0.28	0.10	0.095
Males 15–19 years	0.059	0.049	0.059	0.049
Males 20–59 years	0.10	0.11	0.11	0.11
Males over 60 years	0.033	0.032	0.032	0.028
Females under 7 years	0.098	0.097	0.097	0.103
Females 7–14 years	0.085	0.088	0.27	0.26
Females 15–19 years	0.041	0.034	0.037	0.039
Females 20–59 years	0.16	0.18	0.18	0.18
Females over 60 years	0.033	0.020	0.037	0.019
Parents' education				
Mother none	0.68	0.66	0.66	0.69
Mother primary	0.15	0.11	0.13	0.14
Mother secondary	0.17	0.23	0.21	0.17
Father none	0.51	0.49	0.46	0.53

Table 9.8   (*continued*)

| | Boys in Ghana | | Girls in Ghana | |
	Workers	Non-workers	Workers	Non-workers
Father primary	0.086	0.088	0.079	0.085
Father secondary	0.40	0.42	0.46	0.38
Community variables				
Access to school				
Local primary school	0.85	0.89	0.87	0.88
Local middle school	0.61	0.64	0.70	0.63
Local secondary	0.14	0.11	0.11	0.10
Local public transport	0.52	0.50	0.52	0.47
Quality of school				
Age of primary school	33.5	32.1	35.1	32.6
Age of middle school	15.1	10.1	15.1	11.6
Age of sec/tech sch	16.1	17.1	15.9	18.0
Farming technology				
Co-operative society	0.29	0.31	0.36	0.27
Mutual aid for workers	0.87	0.88	0.86	0.88
Irrigation	0.038	0.041	0.026	0.039
Increased rain this year	0.64	0.77	0.60	0.75
Husking machine	0.074	0.060	0.072	0.058
Fertilizer	0.56	0.58	0.57	0.54
Economic infrastructure				
Electricity	0.12	0.14	0.15	0.17
Bank	0.094	0.084	0.14	0.076
Dynamism				
Life better than 1981	0.27	0.23	0.32	0.26
Easier to find work	0.27	0.31	0.32	0.29
Regions				
Central Region	0.14	0.08	0.15	0.10
Eastern Region	0.03	0.25	0.03	0.21
West	0.10	0.11	0.12	0.11
Volta Region	0.14	0.09	0.14	0.08
Ashanti Region	0.24	0.08	0.26	0.08
Brong Ahafo Region	0.13	0.13	0.15	0.14
North	0.08	0.11	0.05	0.12
Upper West	0.04	0.04	0.03	0.05
Upper East	0.08	0.10	0.08	0.11
Ethnic groups				
Akan	0.57	0.48	0.61	0.46
Ewe	0.038	0.058	0.056	0.059
Ga-adangbe	0.038	0.11	0.024	0.089
Dagbani	0.054	0.041	0.028	0.049

Table 9.8   *(continued)*

	Boys in Ghana		Girls in Ghana	
	Workers	Non-workers	Workers	Non-workers
Nzema	0.013	0.013	0.015	0.017
Other	0.29	0.30	0.26	0.32
Religion				
Christian	0.61	0.60	0.65	0.58
Animist/traditional	0.19	0.25	0.16	0.25
Muslim	0.20	0.15	0.19	0.17

Notes: The sample is now restricted to rural households that own or operate agricultural land. Workers are persons for whom farm hours are positive. Per capita expenditure for Ghana is expressed as a ratio to its mean, not so for Pakistan. The male/female age variables are the proportion of the household in that group.

of fathers and 25 per cent of mothers are absent from the home at the time of the survey in Ghana but in Pakistan only 1 or 2 per cent of households report at least one *parent absent*. This is also reflected in the household composition variables which show that the *proportion of males 20–59 years old in the home* is about 10 per cent in Ghana as compared with about 16 per cent in Pakistan. A further difference in household composition that may have a story to tell is that, while the proportions of elderly men in the two countries are similar, the *fraction of elderly women (over 60)* in Pakistani households is about half the corresponding fraction in Ghanaian households. This suggests that life expectancy for women is especially low in Pakistan.

Educational attainment of the adult generation in rural areas is considerably greater in Ghana as compared with Pakistan, and this is true for men and women. In Ghana about 65 per cent of mothers of our 7–14 year olds have no formal education and in Pakistan this fraction is about 96 per cent!. Close to 20 per cent of mothers in Ghana have completed secondary school as compared with less than 1 per cent in Pakistan. Less than 50 per cent of men in Ghana have no formal education as compared with about 65 per cent in Pakistan. This is reflected in levels of education too. The percentage of fathers that have completed secondary education is about 40 per cent in Ghana and less than 10 per cent in Pakistan. Turning to community-level infrastructure, the vast majority of communities in both countries have a primary school but while about 65 per cent of rural communities in Ghana have a middle school, in Pakistan only about 40 per cent have a boys' middle school and less than 30 per cent a girls' middle school.

Table 9.9 Variable means for workers and non-workers by gender – rural Pakistan: 10–14 year olds

| | Boys in Pakistan | | Girls in Pakistan | |
	Workers	Non-workers	Workers	Non-workers
No. of observations	191	427	200	365
Dependent variable				
Hours worked on farm	25.6	0	14.9	0
Child characteristics				
Age	12.2	11.6	12.0	11.8
First child	0.69	0.50	0.63	0.60
Child of head of household	0.85	0.78	0.87	0.79
Household resources				
In per capita food expenditure	5.28	5.36	5.36	5.34
Size of farm				
Acres of land	11.8	11.3	12.0	9.82
Rent land	0.13	0.15	0.16	0.16
Sharecrop land	0.48	0.33	0.43	0.30
Household structure				
Household size	9.6	11.2	9.8	10.9
Proportion female	0.43	0.43	0.53	0.55
Female head	0.03	0.01	0.045	0.014
Age of household head	47.0	48.4	48.6	47.6
Parents absent	0.021	0.012	0.0	0.025
Males under 5 years	0.051	0.056	0.062	0.060
Males 5–9 years	0.10	0.196	0.095	0.089
Males 10–14 years	0.18	0.16	0.072	0.052
Males 15–19 years	0.052	0.068	0.060	0.061
Males 20–59 years	0.16	0.16	0.15	0.17
Males over 60 years	0.027	0.028	0.033	0.026
Females under 5 yrs	0.059	0.064	0.070	0.063
Females 5–9 years	0.10	0.084	0.090	0.086
Females 10–14 years	0.060	0.051	0.16	0.17
Females 15–19 years	0.039	0.051	0.044	0.049
Females 20–59 years	0.16	0.16	0.15	0.16
Females over 60 years	0.014	0.021	0.0094	0.025
Parents' education				
Mother none	0.98	0.97	0.99	0.94
Mother primary or less	0.023	0.021	0.011	0.046
Mother mid/secondary	0.00	0.008	0.00	0.012
Father none	0.66	0.63	0.71	0.61
Father primary or less	0.22	0.21	0.20	0.19
Father middle	0.067	0.064	0.066	0.082
Father secondary	0.056	0.092	0.020	0.12

Table 9.9   (continued)

	Boys in Pakistan		Girls in Pakistan	
	Workers	Non-workers	Workers	Non-workers
Community variables				
Access to school				
Boy's primary school	0.88	0.91	0.93	0.90
Boy's middle school	0.44	0.44	0.38	0.41
Girl's primary school	0.85	0.86	0.87	0.82
Girl's middle school	0.28	0.28	0.25	0.26
Local public transport[a]	0.66	0.62	0.60	0.62
Farming technology				
Canal	0.69	0.53	0.63	0.61
Rent for a tractor	77.5	78.7	78.9	80.3
Economic infrastructure				
Shop	0.95	0.94	0.93	0.93
Market	0.021	0.026	0.015	0.036
Post office	0.63	0.60	0.63	0.61
Telephone	0.37	0.39	0.41	0.38
Regions				
Punjab	0.50	0.47	0.42	0.47
Baluchistan	0.031	0.054	0.020	0.082
Sindh	0.31	0.26	0.39	0.21
Northwest Frontier	0.16	0.22	0.17	0.24
Religion				
Muslim	0.91	0.96	0.89	0.98
Christian	0.031	0.007	0.030	0.008
Non-Muslim	0.058	0.033	0.080	0.017

Notes: The sample is restricted to rural households that own or operate agricultural land. Workers are persons for whom farm hours are positive. The male/female age variables are the proportion of the household in that group. [a]Corresponds to the presence of a bus route through the cluster.

9.5   Comparison of sample means for workers and non-workers

9.5.1   Ghana: working and non-working children

Table 9.8 shows that the average age among workers is about a year greater than among non-workers. Being the first child makes it more likely that the individual, girl or boy, will work; as does being a child who is not the child of the household head. It is of some interest to note that about three in four of 7–14 year olds are children of the head.

Households with working children are poorer (by 7 per cent for boys and by 12 per cent for girls), as measured by their per capita food expenditure.

This is *in spite of* the fact that child work will contribute to raising expenditures. In the analysis of Section 9.6, this feedback effect, running from child work to per capita expenditure is controlled for. What, at first glance, may seem contradictory to the expenditure effect, is that children are more likely to engage in household farm work if the household owns a larger acreage of land and has a larger number of farms. Land ownings would therefore appear to reflect the marginal productivity of family labour rather than wealth. In the regression analysis that follows, we will be able to look at the land effect holding constant food expenditure, which should reflect household wealth. Boys are more likely to work if the household rents land but the converse is the case for girls. Access to freely available land increases the probability of child labour while access to village-owned land decreases it. Whether the household sharecrops does not appear to have any impact on child work.

The effects of parents' education is complex. Mothers' primary education appears to increase boys' work and reduce girls' work, but their secondary education has the reverse effect for both boys and girls. Fathers' education has a smaller effect than mothers' education at the primary level, but a larger effect at the secondary level.

Household size does not appear to have much explanatory power, although working girls would appear to come from relatively small households, contrary to common perception. Children, and especially girls, are clearly more likely to work if they come from female-headed households. The regression analysis will confirm whether this is the result of the greater poverty of female-headed households or whether there is a further effect after controlling for poverty levels. Working children are more likely to be found in households where a parent is absent. This suggests that migration, for example, can be costly for children. Turning to the age and gender composition of the household, the female–male ratio is not correlated with child labour. The presence of elderly (over 60) women in the household appears to increase child work, especially for girls. The presence of elderly men also increases the likelihood that 7–14 year old girls work on the farm. The presence of a relatively large fraction of adults (20–59 year olds) has some beneficial effect on boys but does not display any tendency to reduce the work of girls.

The variables measuring access to school and the quality of local schools do not show the expected patterns. There does not seem, therefore, to be any overwhelming case, in looking at the data alone, to suggest that child labour on household farms in Ghana is primarily determined by weak school infrastructure. As indicators of availability of work, we have the response to subjective questions about whether life was better now and about whether it was easier to find work now than a decade ago. The latter has a weak positive relation with girls' work but, on average, children were seen to work more in communities where life was said to have improved. An indicator for the presence of a farmers' cooperative in the community may have been expected to reflect opportunities for consumption smoothing that would remove the need for child labour to operate as an insurance mechanism. However this variable appears to be associated with higher rates of girls' work. Similarly, there is a mild positive correlation of child labour with the existence of a bank and (for girls) with fertiliser use. More positive findings of some interest are that in village communities which have electricity, or irrigation facilities, or which report relatively good rainfall, children appear less likely to work.

There are dramatic variations in the rate of child work by region. Thus the Central, Volta and Ashanti regions exhibit high child labour participation while the East and West regions exhibit very low rates. Child workers are disproportionately from the Akan group while the Ga-adangbe ethnic group has low rates of child labour. Children from households following the animist religion appear to work less than other children.

9.5.2 Pakistan: working and non-working children

Table 9.9 shows that working children are only marginally older than non-workers. As observed for Ghana, working children are more likely to be first-born and less likely to be children of the household head.

The per capita food expenditure of households with working boys is smaller (by 8 per cent) than that of households without working boys, suggesting that they are poorer on average, in spite of the economic contribution of the child. This is not the case for girls, from which it would appear that the work of girls must be explained by factors other than household poverty. In households that own large plots of land, children appear more likely to be engaged in farm work and this effect is much larger for girls than for boys. An indicator for whether the household rents any land does not have a strong correlation with child work. However, in households that sharecrop land, the incidence of child farm work is considerably larger.

The illiteracy of parents ('mother none', 'father none') increases child work participation and the effects are larger on daughters than on sons. The effect of mothers' having completed between 1 and 5 years of education (primary or less but more than zero) on daughters' work participation is striking, reducing it fourfold; the effect on boys is much smaller. In no household where mothers have acquired more than primary (middle/secondary) education, do either their sons or daughters participate in work. The broad pattern is seen with fathers' educational levels as well but the differences, especially for fathers' secondary education, are less striking.

Working children come from households that are smaller by more than one individual (or by about 10 per cent). The female–male ratio of the household and the age of the head has no impact on child work participation. However, children are about three times as likely to work if they belong to female-headed households. There is a weak tendency for the absence of one or both parents to increase participation by boys and to decrease it for girls. An increase in the proportion of 20–59 year old males and females in the household would appear to have a small beneficial effect for girls but none for boys. In households with a relatively large fraction of 5–9 year old boys, the 10–14 year old boys that we consider are less likely to work. For a detailed comparison of the other age-gender composition variables, see Table 9.9.

Access, within the community, to a boys' primary school is associated with lower participation in work by boys but, interestingly enough, higher participation by girls. Inconsistent with expectation, we find that communities with a primary school for girls exhibit a higher participation rate of girls in work. The indicators for middle schools are uncorrelated with child work. The presence of local transport reduces the work rates of girls but increases those of boys. The presence of a canal is associated with considerably greater participation in work, especially for boys. Labour would, on average, appear to be a complement to irrigation water in the farming technology of these regions. Communities which have a market show lower child work participation rates but the presence of a post office has no such beneficial effect.

Compared with Punjab, the largest province in Pakistan, child participation is relatively low in Baluchistan and NWFP and it is relatively high in Sindh. As compared with Christians and other non-Muslims, Muslim children are less likely, on average, to be engaged in work.

9.6   Tobit estimates of influences on child work

This section is based upon Bhalotra and Heady (1999), who estimate tobit models to explain the weekly hours of child work on the household farm. The data on workers and non-workers are pooled within country and gender group, so as to determine the extent to which the variables considered above can explain the inter-household variation in child work. While comparison of summary statistics in Section 9.5 was restricted to looking at participation rates (by virtue of comparing the samples of workers and non-workers), this section generalises the discussion to look at the effects of different regressors on the participation and hours of work of children. As is clear from Table 9.7, child hours of work exhibit substantial variation. The analysis here also progresses from Section 9.5 in looking at the effects of every variable holding all other relevant variables constant, and controlling for any simultaneity. For theoretical under-pinnings and for details of the empirical specification, including a discussion of instrumentation of household income, refer to Bhalotra and Heady (1999).

9.6.1 Results for Ghana

Child characteristics have broadly similar effects for boys and girls (Table 9.10). Child work increases with age though this effect is quadratic. Dummies indicating highest birth order and relation to household head are insignificant.

Household poverty, as (inversely) represented by the natural logarithm of per capita food expenditure, appears to be orthogonal to boys' hours on the family farm. For girls, we observe the expected negative relation, significant at the 13 per cent level.

We find a strong positive effect of the number of farms operated on hours of work for boys and girls. Since this result obtains when controlling for acres of land operated by the household, it suggests not a size effect but an effect associated with the subdivision of land. This merits further micro-level research. Total acres of land utilised by the household has no impact on the farm labour of boys or girls. Household size is insignificant for boys and girls. Boys' work is uncorrelated with household composition but there is a weakly negative effect on girls' hours of the proportion of boys under seven in their households. The absence of the father from the home has a significant positive effect on girls' farm work but no effect for boys. The effect of a female household head is insignificant.

The finding that land size and household size are insignificant suggests that the hours of child work on the family farm are not very sensitive to the household-specific marginal product. This might be because while more land means more fruitful work opportunities for the household, it also signifies greater wealth and it may therefore be picking up the effect that we expect per capita expenditure to fully capture. It might also be a result of Ghanaian families being able to adjust the size of their landholdings to fit their desired labour supply.

Parents' education impacts on child work and since these effects are at given levels of household living standards they would appear to reflect

Table 9.10 Marginal effects for hours of child work on the household farm – rural Ghana

| | Boys | | Girls | |
	Conditional on working	Probability of working	Conditional on working	Probability of working
Child characteristics				
Age	2.28*	0.15*	2.14*	0.15*
Age squared	–0.66	–0.0042	–0.068	–0.0046
First child	0.74	0.048	0.78	0.053
Child of head of household	–0.47	–0.030	1.22	0.083
Household resources				
ln per capita food expenditure	0.46	0.030	–3.15	–0.22
Farm land				
Acres of land	–0.0092	–0.00060	0.043	0.0029
Acres squared	–0.00001	–8.93e–07	–0.000046	–3.14e–06
Number of farms	0.70*	0.045*	0.70*	0.048*
Rent land	2.13*	0.14*	1.96	0.13
Sharecrop land	–0.59	–0.038	0.33	0.022
Freely available land	2.23*	0.15*	2.32*	0.16*
Village-owned land	0.53	0.034	3.01*	0.21*
Household structure				
Household size	–0.054	–0.0035	–0.24	–0.016
Proportion female	–1.63	–0.11	0.30	0.021
Female head	–0.32	–0.021	–0.70	–0.048
Age of household head	0.018	0.0012	–0.0014	–0.000098
Mother absent	–0.28	–0.018	–0.41	–0.028
Father absent	1.17	0.076	2.53*	0.17*
Males under 7 years	–1.25	–0.081	–6.90*	–0.47*
Males 7–14 years	o.g.	o.g.	o.g.	o.g.
Males 15–19 years	–2.75	–0.18	–3.31	–0.23
Males 20–59 years	–0.81	–0.053	2.40	0.16
Males over 60 years	0.46	0.030	2.79	0.19
Females under 7 years	3.22	0.21	–5.67	–0.39
Females 7–14 years	o.g.	o.g.	o.g.	o.g.
Females 15–19 years	–1.83	–0.12	–2.38	–0.16
Females 20–59 years	–0.46	–0.030	–2.16	–0.15
Females over 60 years	0.85	0.055	2.93	0.20
Parents' education				
Mother none	o.g.	o.g.	o.g.	o.g.
Mother primary educ	0.68	0.044	–0.94	–0.064
Mother mid/sec educ.	–1.44*	–0.093*	–0.52	–0.035
Father none	o.g.	o.g.	o.g.	o.g.
Father primary educated	–0.24	–0.016	1.61	0.11
Father secondary educated	–0.50	–0.032	0.46	0.032
Community variables				
Access to school				
Local primary school	–0.64	–0.42	–0.96	–0.066
Local middle school	–1.43	–0.93	–0.92	–0.062

Table 9.10 (*continued*)

	Boys		Girls	
	Conditional on working	Probability of working	Conditional on working	Probability of working
Local secondary school	–1.69	–0.11	–1.69	–0.12
Local public transport	–0.42	–0.028	–1.72*	–0.12*
Quality of school				
Age of primary school	0.035	0.0023	0.052*	0.0035*
Age of middle school	0.017	0.0011	–0.027	–0.0018
Age of secondary school	–0.045	–0.0030	–0.044	–0.0030
Farming technology				
Co-operative society	–0.024	–0.016	1.49	0.10
Mutual aid for workers	–0.60	–0.039	–1.23	–0.84
Irrigation	1.64	0.11	–2.38	–0.16
Increased rain this year	–1.67*	–0.11*	–0.32	–0.022
Husking machine	–0.84	–0.055	–1.03	–0.070
Fertilizer	0.46	0.030	1.42	0.097
Economic infrastructure				
Electricity	–1.82*	–0.12*	–1.49	–0.10
Bank	–0.56	–0.037	–0.095	–0.065
Dynamism				
Life better than 1981	1.78*	0.12*	1.11	0.076
Easier to find work	0.36	0.023	1.73*	0.12*
Regions				
Centre	1.27	0.082	3.74*	0.25*
East	–8.06*	–0.53*	–5.07*	–0.35*
West	–1.18	–0.077	3.13	0.21
Volta	2.42	0.16	2.73*	0.19*
Ashanti	1.78	0.12	5.7*	0.39*
Brong Ahafo	–0.94	–0.061	2.44	0.17
North	o.g.	o.g.	o.g.	o.g.
Upper West	o.g.	o.g.	o.g.	o.g.
Upper East	o.g.	o.g.	o.g.	o.g.
Ethnic groups				
Akan	–0.76	–0.049	–0.071	–0.0048
Ewe	–5.98*	–0.39*	–1.00	–0.069
Ga-adangbe	–2.96	–0.19	–1.82	–0.12
Dagbani	1.02	0.067	–2.19	–0.15
Nzema	1.97	0.13	–0.43	–0.030
Other	o.g.	o.g.	o.g.	o.g.
Religion				
Christian	–1.95	–0.13	–3.31*	–0.23*
Animist/traditional	–1.54	–0.10	–2.59	–0.18
Muslim	o.g.	o.g.	o.g.	o.g.

Notes: Dependent variable = hours worked by 7–14 year old children on the household farm. Marginal effects are at the observed censoring rate. Asterisks denote significant effects at 7%. o.g. denotes omitted group. Groups were omitted to avoid exact multicollinearity. This required omitting several regions because they coincided with ethnic groups.

preference heterogeneity rather than resource constraints. The only clearly significant effect is that the sons of mothers with secondary-level education work less. There is a negative effect of mothers' primary education on girls' farm work, significant at 18 per cent. Fathers' primary education has a weakly significant (at 11 per cent) positive effect on girls' work. This does appear odd but might be explained by a chain of intra-household substitutions which the current analysis does not explore. The impact of fathers' education on boys' work is insignificant and has a negative sign.

Regional differences are significant and have larger effects for girls. Religion has no systematic effect on boys' work but Christian girls work significantly fewer hours on average than animist girls, who work less than Muslim girls. Ethnicity is insignificant for girls, but Ewe Boys are significantly less likely to work.

The effects of community variables are very different between boys and girls. The one variable that has a very similar and negative effect for boys and girls is the age of the secondary/technical college in the village. For both boys and girls, dummies for the presence of primary, middle and secondary schools in the cluster take the expected negative signs but their effects are poorly determined. Variables that have a significant negative effect on boys' work are indicators for electricity in the village, and for whether there was more rainfall in 1991–92 than in the preceding year. In households where the respondent judged life to be better than it was ten years before the survey, boys were found to be more likely to be in work. A positive effect for girls flows from a similar subjective question asking whether it was easier to find work in 1991–92 as compared with 1981. For reasons that are not evident, girls' work hours are positively correlated with the existence of a cooperative society and the age of the local primary school. A strong negative effect of the existence of public transport in the village on girls' work is consistent with the hypothesis that distance to school may deter the attendance of girls more than it does that of boys. Irrigation, tractors and fertilisers do not have significant effects on child work, nor does the presence of a village bank.

Overall, among a range of variables in the model, those that display a significant relation with hours of child work on the household farm are child age, the number of farms owned, mothers' education, region, ethnicity, religion, the age of the local primary school, availability of public transport, rainfall, electricity, and the dynamism of the region as reflected in subjective assessments of life and work opportunities having got better in the last ten years. Among variables directly manipulable by policy are maternal education, school quality (arising from age of local school), public transportation in the village, electricity and irrigation (arising via the significance of rainfall).

9.6.2   Results for Pakistan

The child's age has a positive effect on hours worked, which is much larger for boys than for girls (Table 9.11). There are no birth order effects. The 10–14 year olds who classify as children of the household head are more likely to be employed on the farm than other young people in the household including grandchildren, nephews, nieces and siblings of the household head. This effect is significant for girls but only marginally so for boys.

Household living standards have a highly significant negative effect on boys' hours of work. The corresponding effect for girls is also negative but about a fifth of the size and insignificant. The stronger effect for boys is consistent with the much greater participation of boys in school, as compared with girls in rural Pakistan (Section 9.2). In the cross section of households in the sample, those with relatively high incomes (expenditures) are better able to afford to send their children to school and, in this, boys have priority over girls. In contrast, variation in child farm work in Ghana appears to be independent of household income for boys and girls alike. This is consistent with the apparently greater facility for combining work and school in Ghana as compared with Pakistan (see Section 9.2).

In contrast with our findings for Ghana, farm size and household size are significant and take the expected signs in Pakistan. Acres of land operated by the household has a positive effect on girls' work, while it is insignificant in the boys' equation. For girls, it would seem that any (negative) wealth effect of acres is captured by household food expenditure and the observed (positive) effect is a 'wage' effect. Household size has a negative effect on child work which is significant for both genders but considerably larger for boys than for girls. Existing studies of child labour in other contexts tend to find positive effects of household size (for example, Patrinos and Psacharopoulos, 1997). However, where the discussion pertains exclusively to child work on household farms and farm sizes are relatively small, the negative effect of household size on child work is exactly what theory would predict. Our results therefore caution against hasty generalisations to the effect that the well-being of children is inversely related to the size of their households.

At given household size, there are some fairly complex effects of the age-gender composition of the household on child hours of work. Both girls and boys in the 10–14 year age group do significantly less farm work in households with a relatively large fraction of boys aged under 10. Boys are

Table 9.11 Marginal effects for hours of child work on the household farm – rural Pakistan

	Boys		Girls	
	Conditional on working	Probability of working	Conditional on working	Probability of working
Child characteristics				
Age	1.82*	0.081*	0.45	0.033
First child	0.21	0.0091	0.18	0.013
Child of head of household	3.02	0.13	2.14*	0.15*
Household resources				
In per capita food expenditure	–12.8*	–0.57*	–3.87	–0.28
Farm land				
Acres of land	0.017	0.00076	0.034*	0.0025*
Rent land	–0.087	–0.0038	2.03*	0.15*
Sharecrop land	2.57*	0.11*	0.53	0.038
Household structure				
Household size	–0.54*	–0.024*	–0.29*	–0.021*
Proportion female	–12.9	–0.57	–10.6	–0.76
Female head	9.76*	0.43*	3.99*	0.29*
Age of household head	0.047	0.0020	0.049	0.0035
Males under 5 years	–24.4*	–1.08*	–9.79	–0.70
Males 5–9 years	–19.3*	–0.86*	–18.3*	–1.31*
Males 10–14 years	o.g.	o.g.	o.g.	o.g.
Males 15–19 years	–18.2*	–0.81*	–11.8	–0.85
Males 20–59 years	–4.21	–0.19	–15.4*	–1.11*
Males over 60 years	–15.8	–0.70	0.36	0.026
Females under 5 years	–1.63	–0.072	5.79	0.42
Females 5–9 years	10.0	0.44	3.40	0.24
Females 10–14 years	o.g.	o.g.	o.g.	o.g.
Females 15–19 years	–22.3*	–0.99*	–3.43	–0.25
Females 20–59 years	12.4	0.55	6.29	0.45
Females over 60 years	–11.3	–0.50	–32.9*	–2.37*
Parents' education				
Mother none	o.g.	o.g.	o.g.	o.g.
Mother primary or less	1.07	0.047	–2.93	–0.21
Mother mid/secondary	–44.3*	–1.96*	–30.5*	–2.19*
Father none	o.g.	o.g.	o.g.	o.g.
Father primary	0.82	0.036	–0.37	–0.026
Father middle	1.27	0.056	0.25	0.018
Father secondary	3.45	0.15	–6.29*	–0.45*
Community variables				
Access to school				
Local primary sch, girls	1.62	0.072	–3.20*	–0.23*
Local middle sch, girls	–0.65	–0.029	–0.55	–0.39
Local primary sch, boys	2.09	0.092	7.03*	0.51*
Local middle sch, boys	0.92	0.041	0.053	0.0038

Table 9.11 (*continued*)

	Boys		Girls	
	Conditional on working	Probability of working	Conditional on working	Probability of working
Farming technology				
Canal	−2.50*	−0.11*	1.05	0.076
Tractor	0.021	0.00094	−0.0062	−0.00045
Economic infrastructure				
Shop	3.16	0.14	2.34	0.17
Market	9.78*	0.43*	−0.18	−0.013
Post office	1.17	0.052	−0.49	−0.035
Telephone	−2.99*	−0.13*	−0.31	−0.022
Bus	−1.51	−0.067	−1.69	−0.12
Regions				
Punjab	o.g.	o.g.	o.g.	o.g.
Baluchistan	−3.12	−0.14	−8.25*	−0.59*
Sindh	−0.12	−0.0053	2.11	0.15
NWFP	3.52	0.16	−0.39	−0.028
Religion				
Christian	7.32	0.32	−7.83	−0.56
Non-Muslim	−3.39	−0.15	12.3	0.89
Muslim	o.g.	o.g.	o.g.	o.g.

Notes: Dependent variable = hours worked by children on the household farm. In Pakistan, children are 10–14 year olds. Marginal effects are at the observed censoring rate. Asterisks denote significant effects at 7%. o.g. denotes omitted group. Groups were omitted to avoid exact multicollinearity.

also less likely to be in farm work, the larger the fraction of 15–19 year old boys or girls in the home. Girls, on the other hand, are significantly less likely to work on the farm in the presence of elderly females (over 60) or adult males (20–59 years) in the home. The overall proportion of females in the household has a negative effect on child work, significant at about 10 per cent, suggesting that child and female labour are substitutes. Children of both genders who come from female-headed households are more likely to be in farm work. This suggests that there are aspects of ill-being in female-headed households that a household income measure does not pick up. Work intensity for girls is, at the 15 per cent significance level, a positive function of age of the household head, possibly an indication that young adults (or parents) are better able to 'protect' their daughters from work than older adults.

Parents' education is represented by a set of dummies for up-to-primary, middle, and secondary education, with 'no education' being the benchmark (the omitted dummy). Since only 0.1 per cent of mothers have secondary-level education, this group is combined with middle-level education for mothers. There is a significant negative effect of fathers' secondary education on the work hours of their daughters, while fathers' education is not a significant predictor of boys' work. Mothers' education to the level of middle or secondary school has a strong negative effect on child work that is a bit bigger for boys than for girls. Comparing with Ghana, the broad tendency is for mothers' education to reduce child labour in both countries and for both genders, with fathers' education having no effect in Ghana and a benign effect restricted to girls in Pakistan.

The presence of a primary school for girls reduces the farm labour of 10–14 year old girls and, possibly because of sibling competition for resources, the presence of a primary school for boys increases girls' farm labour. These school access variables have no effect on boys' work. Dummies for the presence of middle schools are insignificant for boys and girls. Other cluster specific variables which have a significant effect on boys' work include positive effects from a market and negative effects from a telephone, a bus route and a canal. The presence of a post office and tractor do not have significant effect. For girls, community-level variables are altogether much less significant and the only effect to speak of is a negative one associated with a bus route. Might the bus-route effect, common to boys and girls, denote mobility away from the household farm, whether for outside work or for school?

Province and religion dummies affect girls though not boys. Among girls, those from Baluchistan work less. Christian girls work significantly less than Muslims, who work significantly less than other non-Muslims. Christians constitute 1.5 per cent of the population and other non-Muslims (mostly Hindus) account for another 3.6 per cent; the vast majority are Muslim.

9.7   Conclusions

This chapter has shown that there are substantial differences between Ghana and Pakistan in relation to child labour. It has shown that, although work on the family farm is the most common form of child labour in both countries, only Pakistan has significant child work outside the household. Also, the difference in both labour force participation and schooling is fairly similar for Ghanaian girls and boys, but very different for Pakistani boys and girls.

The chapter also shows that there are important differences between the countries in variables that might be expected to influence the incidence of child labour. The most important are the larger family sizes and lower parental education in Pakistan than in Ghana. However, the difference in child labour patterns between the two countries is not simply due to differences in these variables. The factors that determine child labour participation in the two countries are also different. For instance, any impact of household poverty or household size on child farm work is context-specific.

The one striking tendency that seems to hold across gender and country is that the children of relatively well-educated mothers are less likely to be engaged in work. Since this effect persists after controlling for household income, it would appear to reflect the impact of female education on preferences and the power of women in household decision-making.

In Pakistan, raising household income per capita appears to reduce boys' hours of work, the effect for girls being insignificant. The magnitude of the effect for Pakistani boys is rather large: an increase in food expenditure of 10 per cent, *ceteris paribus*, reduces the probability of work by 6 percentage points and, conditional on working, it reduces hours of work by 1.28 hours. However, there is no evidence for Ghana or for girls in Pakistan to suggest that increasing living standards will, on its own, reduce the incidence or severity of child labour on the household farm.

There is some evidence that both school quality and access to school affect child labour. The significant positive effect of female-headed households on child work in Pakistan, even after controlling for household income, is consistent with these families facing tighter capital market constraints than others and thus finding it harder to ensure survival without child work. The negative effect of a canal on boys' work in Pakistan and the negative effect of increased rainfall on boys' work in Ghana may indicate the importance for child labour of reducing income fluctuations.

The size of the household farm has no impact on child hours of work in Ghana, where land is relatively abundant. In Pakistan, it increases hours of girls' work, with no effect for boys. Household size has no effect on child labour in Ghana but it decreases hours of farm work performed by children in Pakistan. This is probably a reflection of the relative scarcity of land in Pakistan, the average household farm being smaller than in Ghana. There are some interesting effects of household composition in Pakistan: the greater child work in female-headed households has already been noted, and children tend to work *fewer* hours if they have male siblings younger than themselves. These effects are very large. There are no household composition effects for Ghanaian children. Our results contradict evidence from other regions (see Lloyd, 1993 and Jomo, 1992, who find that children – and especially girls – with more siblings work longer hours on average). Existing work has tended implicitly to think of large size as creating large consumption needs and therefore greater labour supply to meet needs. This neglects the fact that household assets are often constrained, at least in South Asia, and that this may drive the marginal productivity of family labour to levels that are too low to compensate withdrawal from school, leisure or other alternative uses of time.

Fathers' secondary education significantly reduces girls' work in Pakistan but has no effect on the labour of the other three groups. Mothers' education tends to reduce boys' hours of work in Ghana and the hours of work of both boys and girls in Pakistan. The magnitude of these effects is so large that policy aimed at eliminating child work is best targeted here.

Acknowledgements

We are grateful to Fiona Coulter and Catherine Porter for excellent research assistance. This work was funded by the Economic and Social Research Council (grant number R000237121) and the Department for International Development as part of its Employment and Labour Markets Programme.

Notes

1. The wage economy is better developed in Pakistan, possibly on account of the relative scarcity of land in South Asia as compared with sub-Saharan Africa. Therefore, for adults and children alike, wage employment presents productive opportunities where the returns to self-employment are relatively limited. Child work outside the home in Pakistan is analysed in Bhalotra (1999).
2. The correlation of school attendance (a binary variable for the individual) with work-participation and hours of work was examined for 7–17 year olds, holding constant age, household size, current household expenditure per capita, and all cluster-specific effects. The conditional correlation of work participation with school participation in Ghana is positive but increasing hours of work did appear to reduce the probability of school attendance. In Pakistan, both participation and hours of child work are negatively correlated with school attendance (results available from the authors on request).

10
The Comparative Performance of African and Latin American Agriculture

Raul Hopkins and Bilge Nomer

10.1 Introduction

The dominant perception about African agriculture is that of a declining output performance (World Bank, 1994). This is also reflected in falling growth rates of agricultural exports and declining market shares. In contrast, agricultural output and exports performed well in Latin America and the Caribbean (Twomey and Helwege, 1991), and there was a significant diversification in agricultural exports. Such a diversification did not materialise in Sub Saharan Africa (Akiyama and Larson, 1993), where the composition of agricultural exports became increasingly dependent on a few products.

This chapter examines these contrasting patterns of growth. Section 10.2 outlines the literature on the subject and Section 10.3 presents a consistent set of data for the period 1961–97. Section 10.4 looks at the sources of growth, including an econometric exercise on the determinants of agricultural output expansion. Section 10.5 concludes.

The analysis is based on a panel data set for 42 countries: 19 from sub-Saharan Africa and 23 from Latin America and the Caribbean (although in some topics the number of countries is smaller, due to the unavailability of data).

10.2 An overview of the literature

There has not been, until now, a systematic comparison between the performance of agriculture in sub-Saharan Africa (SSA) and Latin America and the Caribbean (LAC), although there are a large number of studies at a country level (for example, the collection of papers in Twomey and

Helwege, 1991; Weeks, 1995; Thirtle, 1998), and an increasing number of cross-country comparisons (Jaeger, 1992; Hopkins, 1995; Meerman, 1997). An exception is Commander (1989), which compares the agricultural performance of several African and Latin American countries, but the emphasis is on the effects of structural adjustment, without looking at differences in the long-term performance.

A leading theme regarding the performance of the agricultural sector in SSA has been the importance of price incentives. The prevalent view in the World Bank (World Bank, 1994) has emphasised the correction of relative prices (mainly real exchange rates) as a precondition for achieving better output and export performance. Following this diagnosis, one of the targets of Agricultural Sector Adjustment Programmes (AGSECALs) has been to reduce government regulation on pricing, marketing and trading of agricultural products through Export Crop Marketing Boards.[1] The Bank holds that the linking of producer prices to the world levels is a necessary step towards the adjustment of the agricultural sector. It argues that for the private sector to operate successfully in the marketing of crops, public agencies should be reduced to merely buyers and sellers of last resort. Deregulation of food marketing boards was therefore given priority in African AGSECALs.[2]

The opposing view contends that agricultural output is price inelastic and therefore responds sluggishly to price incentives (Binswanger, 1989; De Janvry, 1986). Other authors point out that distortions in relative prices are less important than other factors such as the levels of profitability relative to other on- and off-farm activities. It is argued that the most important factor with regard to on-farm profitability is productivity and other factors such as payment on time, as opposed to actual price levels.

With regard to the responsiveness of agricultural supply, Schiff and Montenegro (1995) have pointed out that the influence of other factors such as the credibility of reforms, world market conditions and the provision of public goods should be taken into account when measuring the responsiveness of agriculture to price incentives. They argue that under unfavourable policy environments the speed of adjustment will be low. Hence, the estimates of the impact of policy change obtained from time series data may be biased downwards.

In a recent study on the effects of structural adjustment in agriculture Alain De Janvry (1994: 100–2) observes that, in comparison with Asia, African agriculture is heavily dependent on public goods due to a number of related factors: (1) poor infrastructure in irrigation and transport; (2) unfavourable agro-climatic conditions; (3) a shortage of new technological options; and

(4) the weakness of the private sector in providing agricultural inputs. In addition, the reduction in the size of the state was more extensive in Africa than in Asia because state intervention in Africa was more pervasive than in Asia. Furthermore, the economic crisis in Africa has been more prolonged and deeper than in Asia and has had a more disruptive impact on the capacity of the African states to manage the economy. De Janvry indicates that in Asia private marketing networks and indigenous rural institutions were never weakened to the extent that they were in Africa.

Research on agricultural performance in Latin America has been related to the effects of stabilisation and structural adjustment on agricultural growth. Twomey and Helwege (1991:4) highlight the influence of the broader macroeconomic environment on agricultural production noting that, unfortunately, the links between agriculture and the macro economy were getting stronger precisely when the performance of the national economy was weakening. Other major themes in the Latin American debate have been the diversification of production, the restructuring of land tenure and the process of economic liberalisation, among others.

Exogenous shocks have been another significant factor with an impact on agricultural performance, particularly in Africa. Countries in sub-Saharan Africa are typically dependent on a few primary commodities for a large share of their export earnings. Their poor output performance may therefore be related, at least in part, to the trends in the international price of these commodities. It has been argued that since the demand for these commodities is price inelastic, export expansion can depress world price, reducing the marginal export revenue – a phenomenon known as the *fallacy of composition* or the adding up problem (Akiyama and Larson, 1993). It is a documented fact that growth rates in agricultural output and exports deteriorated in the aftermath of the commodity price shocks in the 1970s. The main arguments highlight the importance of relative price distortions, which were higher in Africa compared to Latin America.

9.2.1 The long-run determinants of agricultural performance

Various theories have been developed in the past few decades in an attempt to explain differences in agricultural performance. Hayami and Ruttan (1985: Chapter 3) present a useful outline, which we have summarised, in a schematic way, in Table 10.1. We will make use of some of these variables below, in our empirical analysis of African and Latin American agriculture.

The resource exploitation approach and particularly the vent-for-surplus model (which can be regarded as a subset of the former) emphasises the importance of the stock of agricultural resources, population pressure and

Table 10.1   Theories of agricultural development

Approaches	Factors affecting agricultural output growth
Resource exploitation	Stock of agricultural resources, population pressure, transport costs.
Conservation	Farming practices that maintain the organic content of the soil. Unit costs of extractive output.
Location	Urban industrial development; transport costs.
Diffusion	Diffusion of better husbandry practices and of crop and livestock varieties. Management and extension.
High payoff	Expected profits. The model is general enough to embrace the concepts of the conservation, location and diffusion models.

Source: Hayami and Ruttan (1985: Chapter 3).

transport costs. Scholars who developed these models were interested in exploring the conditions by which under-utilised natural resources could be exploited to generate growth in the economy. Currently the main limitation of this model to explain current differences in the patterns of growth is that there are only a few countries where new land is still available.

The conservation model stresses that any sustainable system of agriculture must provide for a complete restoration of all the elements removed by a crop. It asserts that natural resources are scarce and that scarcity affects the pace of economic growth. In order to test the resource-scarcity doctrine two versions of the scarcity hypothesis were developed: (1) the 'strong' scarcity test, which takes as a reference the unit costs of extractive output; and (2) the 'weak' scarcity test based on changes in the relative price of extractive resources. One of the main criticisms of this model is its oversimplified view about the role of land in agricultural development. Historical evidence suggests that the use of land has been much more elastic than implied by the model.

In the conservation model, locational differences in agricultural development are explained by environmental factors within the agricultural sector. In the location model, it is the urban-industrial growth that plays the key role: (1) increasing the demand for agricultural commodities; (2) providing new and more productive inputs; and (3) promoting a more efficient functioning of factor and product markets. The diffusion model, as its name indicates, emphasises the role of the dissemination of technical knowledge and a narrowing in the productivity differences among individual farmers. Its popularity led, particularly in the 1950s and

1960s to the strengthening of extension services as one of the core elements in the strategies for agricultural development.

According to the high payoff model, farmers, and peasant producers in particular, are rational and efficient. They, like any other private firm, try to maximise profits. As Schultz emphasised, they are, 'efficient but poor'. The main constraints they face are the limited technical and economic opportunities due to the lack of access to modern factors of production. The high payoff model emphasised the importance of agricultural experiment stations producing new technical knowledge; as well as the capacity of the industrial sector to develop, produce and market these new technical inputs, and the ability of farmers to use them effectively.

A more general model (not included in Table 10.1) which incorporates the high payoff model, together with the resource exploitation, conservation, location, and diffusion models is the model of induced technological and institutional innovation developed by Hayami and Ruttan (1985). In such a model both technical and institutional changes are treated as endogenous.

10.3   How different is Africa from Latin America?

10.3.1   Overall trends 1961–97

Table 10.2 summarises the agricultural performance in sub-Saharan Africa (SSA) and Latin America and the Caribbean (LAC) between 1961 and 1997. Overall, the performance of agriculture has been better in LAC than in SSA: an annual average rate of growth of 2.7 per cent in the former and 2.2 per cent in the latter. It is interesting to note, however, that the performance of Latin America and the Caribbean is quite uneven among different countries, being particularly low in the Caribbean (see Table 10.4 below). Agricultural output in South America had an annual average rate of growth of around 3.0 per cent.

The contrast between Latin America and Africa is greater if we look at the per capita annual average rate of growth (0.5 per cent in Latin America versus *minus* 0.7 per cent in sub-Saharan Africa), highlighting the fact that demographic issues are one of the key differences between these two regions. The contrast is even sharper if we look at the performance of agricultural exports: 3.4 per cent in Latin America versus *minus* 0.6 per cent in Africa.[3]

10.3.2   Is African agriculture recovering?

In the 1960s, and until the mid-1970s, the rate of growth of agricultural output in Africa and Latin America was remarkably similar (see Table 10.3

Table 10.2   The performance of agriculture in sub-Saharan Africa and Latin America and the Caribbean (annual average rate of growth, 1961–97)

	(1) Sub-Saharan Africa	(2) Latin America and the Caribbean
Total agricultural output	2.16	2.71
Output per capita	–0.65	0.48
Total food production	2.20	2.97
Food production per capita	–0.60	0.73
Total agricultural exports	–0.55*	3.36**

Notes:
* Period 1961–94. This figure refers to Africa as a whole (and not only sub-Saharan Africa). A weighted average of the export performance of the countries in our sample gave a lower figure: –1.87% (period 1961–95).
** Period 1961–96.
Source: FAOSTAT.

Table 10.3   Agricultural output growth by decade

	1961–70	1970–80	1980–90	1990–97
(a) *Africa*				
Total agricultural output	2.92	1.14	2.79	2.90
Output per capita	0.29	–1.60	–0.14	0.03
Total agricultural exports*	1.32	–1.35	–0.68	2.74
(b) *Latin America*				
Total agricultural output	2.97	3.34	2.25	2.76
Output per capita	0.29	0.92	0.25	1.07
Total agricultural exports	4.22	4.40	1.51	3.47**

Notes:
* Africa as a whole (including North Africa and South Africa).
** Period 1990–96.
Source: FAOSTAT.

and Figures 10.1 and 10.2). Since then, however, a substantial gap has appeared between the two regions. This gap became particularly acute in the 1970s when output growth in Africa experienced a substantial decline. In the 1980s and early 1990s there was a partial recovery in African agriculture and the rate of growth was slightly above the Latin American average. In the 1980s, for example, total agricultural output in Africa grew at an annual average of 2.8 per cent against a more modest 2.3 per cent in Latin America. This picture repeated itself in the 1990s although the difference between the two regions was smaller than in the previous decade.

Figure 10.1   Total agricultural output

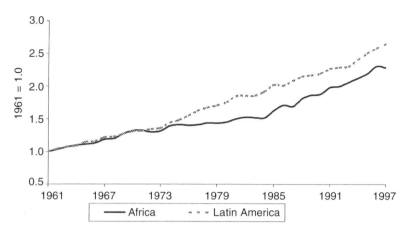

Figure 10.2   Agricultural output per capita

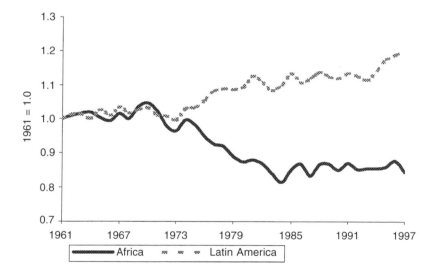

The image of a recovery in African agriculture vanishes, however, if we look at its performance in per capita terms, where Latin America has always outperformed Africa. The most striking contrast between the two regions is in agricultural exports, where Latin America has had growth rates several times higher than in Africa (although the gap has diminished through time). The growth rate of agricultural exports in Africa in the period 1990–97 was 2.7 per cent, which is substantially higher than – in the previous periods (though lower than the figure for Latin America). It is important to note, however, that the figure in Table 10.3 refers to Africa as a whole. As the table in the Appendix shows, the export performance of most SSA countries was substantially lower.

10.4   Sources of growth

An intermediate step towards an understanding of the causes of agricultural expansion is to examine the sources of growth in the sample of countries under study. To what extent are differences in growth rates explained by differences in the growth of agricultural land, labour inputs, capital accumulation, and technological change? What is the specific contribution of each of these factors to the overall figures?

Under specific assumptions (constant returns to scale and factors of production being paid their respective marginal productivities) output growth rate, g, can be decomposed into its main components, such as:

$$g = a + \alpha \Delta L/L + \beta \Delta N/N + \gamma \Delta K/K$$

where a is the rate of technological change; $\Delta L/L$, $\Delta N/N$, $\Delta K/K$ are the rates of growth of the three main factors of production in agriculture (land, labour and capital) and α, β and γ are their respective shares in agricultural GDP. Table 10.4 gives useful information regarding the performance of some of the key factors of production: land, labour and capital, and an indicator for the technical change which occurred during the period 1970–94.

Column 1 is the rate of growth of value added generated in agriculture. Columns 2 and 3 give an indication of the expansion of agricultural land during the period. The former refers to the total area used as cropland and permanent pasture, and the latter to the irrigated area. The measurement of the change in the use of capital inputs is more difficult. The use of fertilisers gives an idea regarding one of its components but it is certainly incomplete (an important omission being capital equipment). The last column provides information related to changes in land productivity.

The data in Table 10.4 suggest that the availability of land played a far more important role in Latin America than in Africa. In several Latin American countries the stock of agricultural land grew at a rate above 2 per cent per annum (Paraguay, Ecuador, Costa Rica Guatemala). In all African countries the rate of expansion of agricultural land was below 1 per cent per annum. Table 10.4 also shows that there was an important

Table 10.4 Sources of growth (average growth rate 1970–94)

	(1) Agriculture GDP	(2) Agriculture land	(3) Irrigated land	(4) Agriculture labour force	(5) Fertilisers (total)	(6) Fertilisers (total per ha)	(7) Value added (per ha)
Sub-Saharan Africa							
Benin	3.60	0.44	4.95	1.26	7.38	6.66	3.15
Kenya	3.35	0.1	2.73	3.12	4.85	4.21	3.25
Cameroon	3.04	0.52	5.48	1.47	2.50	2.05	2.51
Burkina Faso	2.45	0.67	6.65	1.95	16.67	14.27	1.76
Burundi	2.41	0.62	6.12	2.11	7.93	8.24	1.77
Botswana	2.32	0	2.65	0.64	-4.14	-4.32	2.32
Malawi	2.04	0.73	5.80	2.67	7.17	5.44	1.30
Côte d'Ivoire	1.71	0.35	5.18	2.16	2.30	0.09	1.36
Madagascar	1.44	0.12	5.38	2.12	-0.49	-1.44	1.32
Zimbabwe	1.41	0.11	3.19	2.69	1.07	0.35	1.29
Senegal	1.19	0.01	0.34	2.18	-1.02	-1.00	1.18
Sudan	1.01	0.58	0.86	2.49	1.75	1.34	n.a.
Nigeria	0.94	0.18	0.57	0.37	17.59	17.08	0.76
Ghana	0.71	0.42	-0.41	2.70	1.28	-1.27	0.29
Mauritius	-0.49	0.01	0.81	-0.90	0.72	0.72	-0.51
Latin America and the Caribbean							
Paraguay	4.58	2.21	1.71	2.08	10.71	5.61	2.32
Chile	4.33	0.59	0.19	1.44	5.61	5.34	3.72
Brazil	3.50	1.10	5.87	0.23	4.55	1.96	2.37
Ecuador	3.46	2.42	-3.24	1.39	4.54	4.91	1.02
Colombia	3.29	0.14	5.36	1.31	5.27	6.70	3.15
Costa Rica	2.78	2.00	8.07	1.43	3.66	3.64	0.77
Guatemala	2.75	2.46	3.39	2.52	5.91	5.12	n.a.

Table 10.4 (*continued*)

	(1) Agriculture GDP	(2) Agriculture land	(3) Irrigated land	(4) Agriculture labour force	(5) Fertilisers (total)	(6) Fertilisers (total per ha)	(7) Value added (per ha)
Honduras	2.68	0.50	0.36	1.71	2.77	2.01	2.17
Venezuela	2.58	0.48	4.79	0.68	7.97	7.92	2.10
Bolivia	2.45	-0.04	0.47	1.73	4.85	3.35	n.a.
Panama	2.24	1.05	2.13	0.98	1.86	1.09	n.a.
Mexico	2.09	0.25	1.82	1.48	4.46	4.18	1.83
Dominican Republic	1.86	0.62	3.17	0.25	1.59	0.24	1.23
Argentina	1.54	-0.04	1.11	0.25	6.08	5.96	1.59
Uruguay	1.25	-0.09	4.83	-0.17	0.42	0.99	1.35
Guyana	1.04	1.15	0.51	0.67	0.79	-0.62	-0.11
Jamaica	0.72	-0.36	0.68	0.94	1.05	2.30	1.08
El Salvador	-0.05	0.34	8.29	0.23	-0.84	-1.70	-0.39
Nicaragua	-1.12	1.23	2.61	0.64	0.91	-2.82	-2.33
Barbados	-1.24	0	0	-2.63	-3.06	-3.06	-1.24
Trinidad and Tobago	-3.21	0.55	1.34	-0.11	-1.72	-2.50	-3.74

Source: World Bank (1998). Definition of variables: *Value added:* Agriculture, value added (constant 1987 LCU). *Agriculture land:* land used as cropland and land used for permanent crops. *Irrigated land:* areas purposely provided with water, including land irrigated by controlled flooding. *Agricultural labour force:* is the result of multiplying the labour force in agriculture (% of total) and total labour force. *Fertiliser:* total fertiliser consumption (metric tons) and per hectare of arable land. The following countries were excluded because of lack of data: Central African Republic, Congo Democratic Republic and Congo Republic, Ethiopia, Haiti, Mauritania, Peru, Rwanda, Tanzania and Uganda.

transformation in African agriculture. Several countries had rapid increases in labour productivity (such as Benin, Kenya and Cameroon), similar to the top Latin American performers.[4]

The fact that LAC performed better than SSA is reflected in the ranking of countries in terms of agricultural output growth (see the Appendix). From the list of top ten countries (in terms of the annual average rate of growth 1961–97) six are from Latin America and four from Africa.[5] All of them show growth rates above 2.5 per cent. However, the participation of Africa in the top ten falls to three countries when we look at the per capita rate of growth.

It is interesting to note that the level of dispersion in growth rates is much higher in agricultural exports, ranging from 10 per cent (Bolivia 12 per cent, Paraguay 11.1 per cent and Chile 9.7 per cent) to around –4 per cent (Haiti –3.9 per cent, Peru –4.2 per cent and Nigeria –5.2 per cent). The only African country in the top ten, in terms of agricultural export growth, is Côte d'Ivoire. All the others are from Latin America.

The bottom ten countries in terms of agricultural output growth (in per capita terms) are the Republic of Congo, Haiti, Uganda, Ethiopia (PDR), Madagascar, Mauritania, Trinidad and Tobago, Senegal, Botswana and Nicaragua. All of them had a negative rate of growth below *minus* 1 per cent. This implies a cumulative fall of 30 per cent (or more) in the volume of agricultural output per capita from 1961 to 1997.[6]

There is a positive association between the rate of growth of agricultural exports and food production. That is, most countries with good export performance also experienced a positive expansion in food production (see the Appendix). Côte d'Ivoire had, for example, a substantial expansion in agricultural exports (4.8 per cent) and also experienced a noticeable expansion in the production of foodstuffs (4.4 per cent). Something similar happened in other countries like Venezuela, Colombia and Benin. There are, however, important exceptions: Nigeria had the lowest rate of growth of agricultural exports (–5.2 per cent) but a fairly good expansion in food production (2.8 per cent).

The correlation coefficient between the rate of growth of agricultural exports and food production is 0.62. It is interesting to observe that this coefficient was higher in Latin America (0.75) than in Africa (0.41).

As a final exercise we examined the relationship between the rate of growth of agricultural output, Q_t and a number of economic and non-economic factors. Four sets of variables were considered:

- The population rate of growth, N;
- Natural resources: the stock of agricultural land, L; forest area (as proportion of arable land), F, and the share of irrigated land as a

proportion of agricultural land, I. While L and F give an indication of the *volume* of agricultural resources, I provides an approximation of the *quality* of these resources.

- The rate of growth of non-agricultural activities, Yn.
- Initial conditions: per capita agricultural income, Ya_{1961}. This variable is included to test the convergence hypothesis.

The regression equation was,

$$Q_t = a_0 + a_1 N + a_3 F + a_4 + a_5 Yn + a_6 Ya_{1961} + \varepsilon$$

where Q_t is the rate of growth of agricultural output. As an additional complementary exercise, a similar regression equation was run, taking as the dependent variable the rate of growth of agricultural exports, Q_x. Table 10.5 summarises the results.

The elasticity of agricultural output with respect to population turns out to be between 0.52 and 0.56. This implies that population growth increases output but less than proportionally. Hence, an increase in the rate of growth of population causes a fall in the per capita rate of growth.[7]

In all the estimations the stock of agricultural land has the expected positive sign, highlighting the relevance of the resource model outlined in

Table 10.5 Regression results: cross section

Dependent variable	(1)	(2)	(3)	(4)	(5)
	Agricultural output growth, Q_t				Q_x
Population growth	0.53	0.56	0.56	0.52	
	(2.57)	(2.81)	(2.85)	(2.83)	
Agricultural land	0.15	0.16	0.14	0.34	0.50
	(2.06)	(1.58)	(1.44)	(3.81)	(1.55)
Forest area	4.64	2.71	2.3		
	(1.90)	(1.74)	(1.54)		
Irrigated land (%)	−0.01				
	(−0.56)				
Non-agricultural activites				0.22	0.33
				(3.79)	(1.53)
Dummy Africa			−0.63	−1.18	−3.32
			(−1.64)	(−3.11)	(−2.45)
Dummy Nicaragua			−1.59	−2.16	−2.06
			(−1.55)	(−2.31)	(−0.61)
Ya61	0.00015	0.00015	−0.0001	−0.0002	0.0010
	(0.49)	(0.48)	(−0.31)	(−0.70)	(0.978)
R^2	0.36	0.33	0.41	0.70	0.36
F	3.32	3.97	3.55	10.56	3.15
Observations	35	36	36	33	33

Section 10.2 above. Columns 3 to 5 include dummies for Africa and for Nicaragua. The extent of the conflict in Nicaragua during a substantial part of this period fully justifies this dummy, which, as expected, turns out to be negative. The dummy for Africa is consistently negative and in most cases significant.

Column 4 includes the rate of growth of non-agricultural activities. This variable has the expected positive sign, which is consistent with the location model outlined in Section 10.2. The level of agricultural per capita income at the beginning of the period is not statistically significant in most equations, thus rejecting the hypothesis of convergence in the levels of agricultural income per capita (that is, countries with the lowest agriculture income per capita at the beginning of the period were not catching up with those with higher levels of income per capita).

The last column of Table 10.5 shows a preliminary estimation of the determinants of agricultural exports. The stock of agricultural resources has the expected positive sign but the convergence hypothesis is once again rejected. The dummy for Africa has a very high negative value suggesting that the poor performance of agricultural exports in Africa cannot be explained by any of the variables considered in the analysis.

10.5 Conclusions

There are substantial differences in the performance of African and Latin American agriculture over the period 1961–97. Agriculture grew faster in LAC compared to SSA but the figures suggest a catching up process in the 1980s and 1990s, when the growth rates in Africa were higher than in Latin America. The perception of a recovery in African agriculture vanishes, however, when we look at their performance in per capita terms, where Latin America has always outperformed Africa. The most striking contrast between the two regions is in agricultural exports, where Latin America has achieved a substantially better performance (although the gap between the two regions has diminished through time).

The data examined in Section 10.3 suggest that the availability of land played a far more important role in Latin America than in Africa. In several Latin American countries the stock of agricultural land grew at a rate above 2 per cent per annum. In all African countries the rate of expansion of agricultural land was below 1 per cent per annum. Section 10.3 also shows that there was an important transformation in African agriculture. Several countries had rapid increases in labour productivity, similar to the top Latin American performers.

The final part of the chapter attempted to examine, in a systematic way, the main determinants of agricultural output growth. The choice of variables is related to the theories of agricultural development surveyed in Section 10.2. The analysis included as explanatory variables population growth, the stock of agricultural land, the expansion of non-agricultural activities and the initial level of agricultural income per capita.

The analysis shows that a population expansion increases agricultural output but less than proportionally, hence *reducing* agricultural output per capita. The estimated elasticity *ranges* from 0.4 to 0.6. The econometric exercises also suggest a positive correlation between the stock of natural resources (measured in terms of agricultural land and forest area) and agricultural output growth. There is not a clear relationship between agricultural output growth and the level of agricultural income per capita at the beginning of the period. On the other hand there is a strong positive relationship between the performance of agricultural and non-agricultural activities.

Finally, it is interesting to note that the dummy for Africa has a very high negative value suggesting that the poor performance of agriculture in Africa cannot be fully explained by the set of variables considered in the analysis. This is consistent with the view that the problems of African agriculture cannot be limited to the standard demographic and economic factors. Variables related to human capital and to the strength of public and private institutions, for example, were not included in the analysis, which may explain, at least partially, the robustness of the dummy variable for Africa.

Notes

1. The World Bank's approach to African agriculture has gone through a series of phases: from large scale projects seeking to introduce modern technologies in the 1960s, to rural integrated development projects in the 1970s; and to structural adjustment in the 1980s and 1990s. The main elements of the structural adjustment approach were set in the World Bank's major 1981 study *Accelerated Development in Sub-Saharan Africa: An Agenda for Action* (Gibbon *et al.*, 1993: 7–8).
2. By late 1992, among the SSA countries that initiated reforms in the second half of the 1980s all except 2 out of 28 had eliminated restrictions on purchases and sales of a variety of food crops (World Bank, 1994: 84–85).
3. For the period 1970–85 Akiyama reports the following growth rates of agricultural commodity exports (agricultural raw materials): –4.0 per cent for Africa, –0.7 per cent for Latin America and 0.6 per cent for Asia.
4. A regression of agricultural GDP, Y_a, on agricultural land, L_a, agricultural labour, N_a, and fertilisers, K_f gave the following results (t-statistics in brackets),

$$Y_a = 0.41\,L_a + 0.51\,N_a + 0.11\,K_f$$
$$(1.26) \qquad (2.55) \qquad (2.23)$$

$F(4,\ 31) = 7.30.\ R^2 = 0.39$. In a similar regression for sub-Saharan Africa fertilizers turned out to be very small and not statistically significant. In the regression for Latin America the parameter related to fertilisers had a very high value ($0.40,\ t = 3.68$). Another interesting contrast between these two regions was related to land. In Latin America the most significant land variable was 'total land' (cropland plus permanent pasture) while in Africa the most significant one was irrigated land.

5. The top Latin American countries are Paraguay, Costa Rica, Brazil, Bolivia, Venezuela and Mexico. Those from Africa are Benin, Côte d'Ivoire, Burkina Faso and Kenya.

6. In the case of Senegal, Botswana and Nicaragua (the countries with the worst output performance) the cumulative fall was between 50 per cent and 60 per cent respectively.

7. The implied elasticity of output per capita with respect to population growth is equal to $(a_1 - 1) = -0.47$ (using the values from column 1 in Table 10.5). Thus, a 1 per cent fall in the population rate of growth would increase the per capita agricultural output growth rate by about 0.47 per cent.

Appendix: Output ranking (annual average rates of growth, %, 1961–97)

Rank	Total agriculture		Agricultural output per capita		Agricultural exports		Food production	
1	Benin	4.1	Brazil	1.5	Bolivia	12.0	Côte d'Ivoire	4.4
2	Paraguay	4.0	Benin	1.4	Paraguay	11.1	Brazil	4.2
3	Côte d'Ivoire	3.9	Bolivia	1.4	Chile	9.7	Costa Rica	4.0
4	Costa Rica	3.8	Paraguay	1.1	Brazil	6.1	Paraguay	3.8
5	Brazil	3.8	Chile	0.9	Uruguay	5.2	Bolivia	3.8
6	Bolivia	3.7	Costa Rica	0.9	Venezuela	5.0	Benin	3.5
7	Burkina Faso	3.3	Burkina Faso	0.7	Costa Rica	5.0	Guatemala	3.4
8	Kenya	3.2	Uruguay	0.5	Guatemala	5.0	Venezuela	3.3
9	Venezuela	3.2	Colombia	0.5	Côte d'Ivoire	4.8	Mexico	3.1
10	Mexico	2.8	Central African Rep.	0.3	Colombia	4.0	Colombia	3.0
11	Guatemala	2.8	Mexico	0.2	Argentina	3.7	Kenya	3.0
12	Nigeria	2.7	Venezuela	0.2	Zimbabwe	2.8	Burkina Faso	2.9
13	Colombia	2.7	Côte d'Ivoire	0.2	Panama	2.8	Central African Rep.	2.8
14	Malawi	2.7	Argentina	0.1	Malawi	2.5	Nigeria	2.8
15	Chile	2.6	Rwanda	0.0	Ecuador	2.4	Chile	2.8
16	Central African Rep.	2.6	Guatemala	-0.1	Kenya	2.4	Tanzania	2.8
17	Tanzania	2.5	Nigeria	-0.1	Benin	2.4	Sudan	2.5
18	Honduras	2.5	Panama	-0.2	Central African Rep.	1.9	Congo, Dem. Rep.	2.4
19	Rwanda	2.3	Jamaica	-0.2	Mexico	1.7	Cameroon	2.3
20	Cameroon	2.3	Kenya	-0.3	Cameroon	1.5	Honduras	2.3
21	Ecuador	2.3	Cameroon	-0.4	Honduras	1.2	El Salvador	2.2
22	Zimbabwe	2.3	Sudan	-0.4	Burundi	1.1	Ecuador	2.2
23	Congo, Den. Rep.	2.3	Mauritius	-0.4	Sudan	0.8	Panama	2.2
24	Sudan	2.2	Ecuador	-0.4	Mauritius	0.3	Rwanda	2.2
25	Panama	2.2	Malawi	-0.5	Rwanda	0.2	Uganda	2.1
26	Ghana	1.8	Guyana	-0.5	El Salvador	-0.3	Peru	2.1

Appendix: (*continued*)

Rank	Total agriculture		Agricultural output per capita		Agricultural exports		Food production	
27	Dominican Rep.	1.8	Dominican Rep.	-0.6	Nicaragua	-0.3	Dominican Rep.	2.0
28	Congo, Rep.	1.8	Tanzania	-0.6	Botswana	-0.7	Malawi	1.9
29	Peru	1.8	Honduras	-0.7	Burkina Faso	-1.0	Zimbabwe	1.9
30	Uganda	1.7	Peru	-0.7	Guyana	-1.0	Congo, Rep.	1.9
31	Madagascar	1.7	Burundi	-0.7	Dominican Rep.	-1.0	Ghana	1.8
32	Argentina	1.6	Barbados	-0.8	Uganda	-1.7	Madagascar	1.8
33	Burundi	1.4	Ghana	-0.8	Ghana	-1.7	Argentina	1.7
34	Ethiopia PDR	1.2	Zimbabwe	-0.8	Ethiopia PDR	-1.7	Burundi	1.3
35	El Salvador	1.2	El Salvador	-0.9	Mauritania	-2.1	Nicaragua	1.3
36	Uruguay	1.0	Congo, Dem. Rep.	-1.0	Trinidad and Tobago	-2.4	Ethiopia PDR	1.2
37	Botswana	1.0	Congo, Rep.	-1.0	Tanzania	-2.6	Uruguay	1.2
38	Mauritania	1.0	Haiti	-1.1	Madagascar	-2.7	Botswana	1.0
39	Jamaica	1.0	Uganda	-1.3	Jamaica	-3.1	Mauritania	1.0
40	Mauritius	0.9	Ethiopia PDR	-1.3	Senegal	-3.2	Jamaica	0.9
41	Senegal	0.9	Madagascar	-1.3	Congo, Rep.	-3.3	Mauritius	0.8
42	Haiti	0.7	Mauritania	-1.5	Congo, Dem. Rep.	-3.5	Senegal	0.8
43	Nicaragua	0.4	Trinidad and Tobago	-1.8	Barbados	-3.9	Haiti	0.8
44	Guyana	0.3	Senegal	-1.9	Haiti	-3.9	Guyana	0.3
45	Barbados	-0.4	Botswana	-2.2	Peru	-4.2	Barbados	-0.4
46	Trinidad and Tobago	-0.6	Nicaragua	-2.4	Nigeria	-5.2	Trinidad and Tobago	-0.5

11
The Demand for Money in Selected SADC Countries: Structure, Policy and a Comparison with the ASEAN Countries

Raghbendra Jha and Mridul Saggar

11.1   Introduction

The choice of nominal anchors has confounded policy makers the world over. Yet, conventional money demand functions have offered the easiest and the surest route for conducting monetary policy in pursuit of their central objective of inflation control. While considerable literature exists on the money demand functions in developed countries, the issue is still under-researched in relation to developing countries (see Arrau *et al.*, 1995). In the case of African countries, monetary institutions are still maturing and several enabling legislative initiatives have recently been taken in this direction. Most countries have preferred to adopt the traditional route of monetary targeting which makes it necessary that we improve our understanding of the factors determining money demand.

This chapter estimates conventional money demand functions, using robust procedures for four members of the South African Development Community (SADC) – Malawi, Mauritius, South Africa and Tanzania. The choice of these four countries has been, in the main, influenced by considerations of data availability. The results from these estimates are then compared with the available evidence for major ASEAN (Association of South-East Asian Nations) countries to consider if the monetary policy framework in the SADC countries needs to be different from that in these ASEAN countries.

It is now well recognised that the estimation of money demand functions of the Goldfeld (1973) type or its variants, with income and interest rates as arguments, can lead to spurious results, if the variables are non-stationary. Goldfeld's equation, however, made an important contribution in that it established stability of money demand, although real money balances since 1974[1] were biased upwards. This spurred new empirical research, but with the exception of Canada, money demand was found to be sufficiently stable. More recent developments show that incorrect specification of demand for money functions and non-stationarity of log-level or log-differenced equations might be producing spurious regression results. In particular, Phillips (1986) and Phillips and Perron (1988) pointed out that the usual t- and F-statistics in least square regressions do not have exact limiting distributions in cases of absence of stationarity.

Following the works of Johansen (1988) and Johansen and Juselius (1990) it became possible to test for an underlying equilibrium relationship between real money balances and a given set of explanatory variables. Studies using the cointegration error correction model (ECM) framework came up with several interesting results: for example, the proposition that the broad money aggregate is more stable than narrow money was confirmed for the United States (see Hafer and Jansen, 1991 and Miller, 1991).

Our work on the SADC countries has been, in part, motivated by the paucity of empirical evidence on this issue for developing countries in general and SADC countries in particular. Money demand functions have been virtually unexamined in the case of Mauritius and Malawi. In the case of Tanzania, the only notable contribution has been from Gerdes (1993). The major evidence for South Africa is confined to Tavlas (1989) and Nyong (1993). However, the few studies available for the region have not used the Johansen cointegration error correction framework. They, therefore, do not permit the possibility of more than one cointegrating vector even when more than two variables are present in the money demand function. Also, the growing interdependence among SADC countries and the possibility of currency substitution makes it important to study demand for money in these countries. To the best of our knowledge this is the first study of money demand in the SADC countries from a comparative perspective.

The rest of the chapter is organised as follows: Section 11.2 discusses the monetary policies in the four selected countries in the SADC region. Section 11.3 contrasts the monetary policy framework in SADC countries with that for selected ASEAN countries. Section 11.4 gives a description of the experimental design and the estimates for the long-run and the short-run forms of the money demand function, including the evidence from the impulse response functions. Section 11.5 compares the results of the study with the available empirical evidence on money demand in selected ASEAN countries. Against the backdrop of the cross-country evidence, Section 11.6 provides some conclusions relevant for the conduct of monetary policy in the region.

11.2   Monetary policy in selected SADC countries

In each of the four selected SADC countries some monetary aggregate is targeted in one form or another. Formal targeting is done in the case of Malawi and Tanzania, whereas this targeting is pursued in somewhat broader terms in the case of Mauritius and South Africa through a policy mix based on monetary aggregates and interest rates. In Mauritius the monetary authorities influence monetary aggregates through refinancing activity. South Africa has a broad band of money supply growth as its target, the efficacy of which appears to be declining with interest rate deregulation and growing inter-linkages of money and foreign exchange markets. The exchange rate can have important implications for money demand as has been demonstrated by Bahmani-Oskooee and Pourhey-darian (1990) in the case of United Kingdom and some other countries. The main features of the conduct of monetary and exchange rate policies in these countries are explained below.

11.2.1   Mauritius

The financial system comprises the Bank of Mauritius (BOM) as the central bank, ten commercial banks (five incorporated in Mauritius and five branches of foreign banks), seven offshore banks, several non-bank financial institutions (FIs), and a stock exchange. In 1996 BOM closed two banks – the Mauritius Cooperative Central Bank Limited (MCCB) and Union International Bank (UIB) which were facing financial problems – due to poor recovery in the case of the former and fraud in the case of the latter.

BOM had traditionally relied on affecting the monetary conditions through changes in refinancing policy and the quantitative limits prescribed for refinancing. But since 1995, BOM has in addition to using limits on refinance imparted increased flexibility to the bank rate. The bank rate has been linked to the average Treasury bill (T-bill) rate and refinance above limits is charged at twice the bank rate. Banks are required to satisfy minimum reserve requirement and liquid asset ratio. In 1996 the Cash Reserve Ratio (CRR) was reduced from 10 per cent to 8 per cent and the liquid asset ratio (LAR) was cut from 23 per cent to 20 per cent. In September 1996, BOM introduced repos. Since the reduction in lending rates in mid-1992, growth of credit to the private sector has accelerated. Instruments used for the conduct of monetary policy include CRR, LAR, limits to commercial banks' access to BOM credit facilities, auctions of T-bills and BOM bills and variations in interest rates, including bank rate and prescriptions for the ratio of credit to deposits. The Mauritian rupee was pegged to an undisclosed basket of currencies between February 1983 and July 1994. Over this period the nominal effective exchange rate (NEER) depreciated by over 30 per cent. The rate of nominal depreciation has somewhat slowed down in the 1990s. In recent years the rate of nominal depreciation has exceeded that of real depreciation. The Mauritian rupee is now fully convertible on current account and in September 1993 Mauritius formally accepted Article VIII obligations of the IMF.

11.2.2   Malawi

Monetary policy in Malawi has been based on targeting monetary aggregates keeping in view the pace of real activity, the objective being to keep inflation low and to maintain equilibrium in the overall balance of payments. For instance, in 1996, the monetary programme targeted the increase in broad money to be 30 per cent. It assumed a large reduction in the inflation rate and increased autonomy for the central bank, the Reserve Bank of Malawi (RBM), in the form of limiting the monetisation of government deficits through the route of automatic access to ways and means advances. RBM maintains a high CRR of 35 per cent, which is planned to be brought down in a phased manner with the development of open market operations. In fact, the government and the RBM pushed reforms during 1989–92 with the objective of replacing direct instruments of monetary control by indirect instruments. In June 1989, statutory reserve requirements were introduced and increased progressively. This provided RBM the flexibility to focus on shifting its reliance from credit ceilings to the control of base money. Credit ceilings on commercial banks were completely eliminated by early 1991. RBM also established a discount and lending facility and introduced a bank rate in 1990. The bank rate was linked to the auction rate for bills. RBM had moved to auctions since November 1990. The bills were first issued by RBM but were later replaced by government T-bills of varying maturities.[2] The liquidity needs are higher in the tobacco auction season (April–September) and the RBM generally takes into account this seasonality in its conduct of monetary operations. Malawi's financial sector is small, though it is growing in size.

Traditionally, the financial system of Malawi comprised of the RBM, two commercial banks, post office saving banks, a building society, various insurance and development financial institutions, and a number of credit societies. The Investment and Development Bank of Malawi (Indebank) was licensed to accept corporate deposits a few years ago. Two new banks were established in 1995, namely the First Merchant Bank and the Finance Bank.

Malawi had an administered exchange rate system throughout the 1980s with stringent controls over the use of foreign exchange, including quantitative restrictions. Allocations were generally approved by the Exchange Control Department of the RBM. However, quantitative restrictions were by and large removed (in phases) by early 1991. The Malawi kwacha was pegged to a basket of currencies reflecting the composition of Malawi's external trade and the importance of invoicing currencies in the country's foreign exchange transactions. The exchange rate arrangement was one of managed float designed to retain the competitiveness of tobacco exports. However, the exchange rate regime has now switched from a managed to a free float. The introduction of market- determined exchange rate system in 1994, resulted in the Malawi kwacha depreciating sharply by nearly 50 per cent in real effective terms in the span of a single year. Though much of these gains have been eroded, labour cost increases still lag behind general price increases, giving a competitive edge to its products. Malawi accepted Article VIII status of the IMF on 7 December 1995 and is a participant of the Cross-Border Initiative (CBI) to promote regional trade and investment integration in SADC, Southern and East Africa (COMESA) and Indian Ocean Commission (IOC) regions. Foreign currency deposits were introduced in February 1994, but have not yet grown in size sufficiently to derail monetary targets.

11.2.3   Tanzania

Tanzania targets its broad money aggregate. For instance, broad money was targeted to grow at 10 per cent during 1997/98, less than the projected nominal growth of economy. The central bank, the Bank of Tanzania, (BOT) is presently aiming to improve its credibility by seeking a sharp reduction in its inflation rate. Of late there is increased coordination between monetary and fiscal policies. BOT is developing open market operations, rather than transactions in the foreign exchange market, as its key instrument for monetary policy.[3] With the proposed restructuring and privatisation of the National Bank of Commerce (NBC) – one of the two main commercial banks, the other being the National Microfinance Bank (NMB), the BOT hopes to have a wider and deeper financial market to conduct its operations for monetary control through indirect instruments. Also, bank credit to government is being decelerated and a monetary target of 13 per cent broad money growth being sought on a long-term basis.

11.2.4 South Africa

South Africa acts as a central economy in the region, transmitting monetary policy impulses to other countries in the periphery. It is one of the important emerging markets attracting large direct investment and portfolio flows. Surges in capital inflows to South Africa have imposed the biggest constraint on maintaining sound monetary policies. They have caused real appreciation of the rand and derailed monetary targets. The central bank, the South African Reserve Bank (SARB), was forced to contain the consequent inflationary pressures by sterilisation. SARB also resorted to raising the bank rate by three-percentage points in 1995 to 15 per cent, but upward pressure on interest rates had a deleterious impact on monetary prudence as it attracted further capital inflows. Monetary control has also attenuated because demand for rand-denominated financial assets has risen not just from within the SADC region, but also from outside.[4]

Monetary authorities have targeted at an annual M3 growth of 6–10 per cent since 1995. This is considered as an informal band for monetary targeting. Strong monetary pressures since mid-1994, depreciation of the rand in 1996 and the current speculative pressures on the rand have heightened inflationary pressures. The authorities have been intervening both in the spot and the forward markets. They have established a cap on forward sales on a net basis. The bank rate was raised twice in 1996 to re-establish monetary control.

More recently, the medium-term Growth, Employment and Redistribution Strategy (GEAR) introduced in June 1996 has placed societal pressure on monetary policy to reduce inflation and prevent real exchange rate appreciation. GEAR targets to reduce the inflation rate (based on CPI) on an average basis from 8.0 per cent in 1996 to 7.6 per cent by the turn of the century, even while stepping up the real GDP growth from 3.5 per cent to 6.1 per cent over the same period. The transition envisaged also includes lowering the fiscal deficit, accelerating tariff reductions, exchange rate liberalisation and regulated flexibility in the labour markets.

11.3 The monetary policy framework in SADC and ASEAN: a comparison

A particularly interesting comparison would be that between the monetary policy frameworks in SADC countries and countries of the

Association of South East Asian Nations (ASEAN). Both the SADC and the ASEAN operate as important trade blocs in their respective continents, with some loose form of macroeconomic coordination without a formal institutional mechanism for the same. The size of these trade blocs in terms of the number of countries is also the same, though the size of these economies and the levels of development and financial sophistication differ in the following respects.

First, several of the ASEAN economies have depended on exchange rates as nominal anchors. These include Thailand, Singapore and Hong Kong.[5] In contrast, most SADC countries have relied on a managed or freely floating exchange rate regime and depended on monetary targeting to anchor their price levels. While some SADC countries in some periods have chosen to peg to the South African rand, the general disposition has been to avoid the currency getting misaligned. In hindsight, the currency crisis in East Asia in 1997–98 has demonstrated that the operating framework of the SADC countries has been useful in averting the long-run problems associated with importing credibility in the short and medium run through fixed exchange rates. Secondly, while some ASEAN countries have relied on monetary targeting, the chosen operating framework may not be particularly suitable for these countries. For instance, recent estimates by Dekle and Pradhan (1997) suggest that narrow or broad money growth in Indonesia cannot be explained by changes in real income and interest rates. This is primarily because a stable and predictable demand for money function does not hold for several ASEAN countries, particularly Indonesia, as a result of financial innovations and financial deepening. Money growth is found to be a poor predictor of future inflation and output trends as a result and monetary authorities cannot repose a reasonable degree of confidence in monetary targeting.[6] Thirdly, financial innovations have been a major consideration in the conduct of monetary policies in the ASEAN countries. Interest rate liberalisation, banking sector deregulation and competition, deregulation and new instruments, new institutions and new practices in the money market and stock markets and increased capital account liberalisation played an important role in influencing the operating framework for the monetary policies in these countries. Improved governance and regulation including banking supervision also affected monetary conditions and policy.[7]

Fourthly, most ASEAN countries are in transition, increasing their reliance on indirect instruments of monetary control with greater focus on money market liquidity and interest rates. For instance, Bank Negara Malaysia (BNM), which had been relying, until very recently, primarily on

Statutory Reserve Requirements (SRR) has begun to influence interest rates through trading in government securities and BNM bills. Efforts are being made to develop an effective system of open market operations. The principal dealers system is being restructured and a fully automated system of tendering (FAST) has been introduced. The quantum of securities being placed in the market has been increased particularly since 1996. This has somewhat relieved the dependence on SRR which is unremunerated and had to be increased 9 times from 4.5 per cent of eligible liabilities in 1989 to a whopping 13.5 per cent in 1996.[8]

However, Malaysian monetary authorities still need to depend on some direct instruments of monetary control, such as direct borrowing or lending to the banking system and transfer of government and employees pension fund deposits to the central bank. The Bank of Indonesia is also switching from the current system in which interest rates on central bank paper (SBIs) are administratively set to essentially an auction based system. Similarly, the Thai central bank is also attempting to change its operating framework to interest rate targeting. However, the acute paucity of high-grade securities and a generally shallow government securities market due largely to a series of budget surpluses since 1988 has thwarted its attempt to develop open market operations as a major tool of monetary policy. BOT attempted to overcome this constraint by introducing Bank of Thailand bonds in August 1995. These bonds are now auctioned every week for a wide variety of maturities and the authorised amount for them has been increased to a sizeable limit of 80 billion baht. Yet, the Thai monetary authorities have not been able to reduce substantially their reliance on control of monetary and credit aggregates. Instead, BOT has had more success with its occasional use of currency swaps to influence money market liquidity. The swap market has become reasonably liquid and deep. Also, the BOT has been forced to rely on a credit monitoring system in which financial institutions are required to submit credit plans for central bank approval and the central bank has used these plans to influence the quantum as well as direction of credit through moral suasion. The use of moral suasion has been far more effective in many ASEAN countries including Thailand, Indonesia and, in particular, Malaysia than in SADC countries.

11.4   The model and its results

We employ the Johansen multivariate cointegration technique to model money demand in the selected countries. With the Engle–Granger approach, we may run into problems when more than two $I(1)$ variables are involved and the possibility of more than one cointegrating vector cannot be ruled out *a priori*. In such cases the Johansen method may be preferred.

The Johansen method defines an unrestricted vector autoregression (VAR) of the vector of variables z_t as involving up to k lags of z_t.

$$Z_t = A_t Z_{t-1} + \ldots + A_k Z_{t-k} + U_t \qquad U_t \sim IN(0, \Sigma) \qquad (11.1)$$

where z_t is $(n \times 1)$ and each of the A_l is an $(n \times n)$ matrix of parameters.

Now consider an $(n \times r)$ matrix β such that

$$\beta' z_{t-k} \sim I(0) \qquad (11.2)$$

If all elements of z_i are $I(1)$, then the columns of β must form cointegrating parameter vectors for z_{t-k} and hence z_t. Since there can be only $(n - 1)$ cointegrating vectors, β must have r less than n. If, however, z_t is $I(1)$ but the elements are not cointegrated, β must be a null matrix. Now define another $(n \times r)$ matrix α such that:

$$-A_k = \alpha\beta' \qquad (11.3)$$

The Johansen technique is based upon the factorization of Equation 11.3. This technique involves reducing Equation 11.3 to solving an eigenvalue problem. The eigenvectors associated with these eigenvalues are the cointegrating vectors.

The Vector Error Correction Mechanism (ECM) of the system in Equation 11.1 can be written (in one form) as:

$$\Delta Z_t = \Gamma_1 \Delta Z_{t-1} + \Gamma_2 \Delta Z_{t-2} + \ldots + \Gamma_{k-t} \Delta Z_{t-k+t}$$
$$+ \xi_1(EC_1(-1)) + \xi_2(EC_2(-1)) + \ldots + \xi_r(EC_f(-1)) \qquad (11.4)$$

where $(\Gamma_l = -I + A_1 + \ldots + A_l$ $(i = 1,\ldots, k)$ and EC_j (-1) is the one period lagged error term when we use the jth. cointegrating vector and there are r such error terms – one for each cointegrating vector. ξ_j is the coefficient on the lagged error term from the jth. cointegrating vector. In case there are some pertinent $I(0)$ variables, they will be part of the ECM but not the cointegrating equation.

Dynamics of the model can be further investigated by considering the response of the cointegrating equation to shocks in the various variables. In our case this set would include the log of real cash balances, log of real GDP and, in some cases, the interest rate and the exchange rate. The orthogonalised impulse response records the behaviour of the variables in the cointegrating equation over time. Another way of tracing the dynamics of the system is to shock one variable at a time and see its effect on the cointegrating relation. In either case, the response is orthogonalised, that is, we consider the VAR(1) format:

$$Z_t = A_1 Z_{t-1} + \varepsilon_t = \sum_{i=0}^{\infty} A_1^i + \varepsilon_{t-i}$$

This is often called a vector moving average (VMA) representation. This can then be orthogonalised so that the error terms are not correlated and written as

$$Z_t = \sum_{i=0}^{\infty} \phi_i e_{t-i}$$

where the residuals e_{t-i} are orthogonal. The matrices ϕ_i are the impulse response functions since they represent the behaviour of the modelled series in response to shocks (innovations) and the vector e_t is the vector of innovations: the vector of impacts induced for particular variables when these impacts are independent from each other. The data used here comes from the World Bank data base and covers the period 1961–1994.

A number of variables were tried in the cointegrating equations separately for M1 and M2. These included log of real GDP, the lending rate (data on deposit rates are not available), and the exchange rate with respect to the dollar. The South African lending rate turned out to be $I(0)$ whereas the exchange rate needed to be included only for the M2 equation for Tanzania and both the M1 and the M2 equations for South Africa on the basis of the likelihood ratio test.[9] Results in Table 11.1 indicate the variables chosen for the demand functions for M1 and M2 in the case of each country as well as any $I(0)$ variables chosen for the ECMs. In the case of each country income elasticities of demand for M1 and M2 are positive and significant. In the case of Mauritius the demand for M1 carries a higher elasticity than that for M2 and both are high. In the case of Malawi the own rate of interest is not significant and best results are obtained with the South African lending rate taken as an $I(0)$ variable. Income elasticities of money demand are high with the demand for M2 being more elastic than that for M1. In the Tanzanian case income elasticities are low with that for M1 higher than that for M2. In the case of South Africa income elasticity of money demand is high and sharply higher for M1 than M2.

The short-run dynamics of money demand are also very interesting. We estimated ECMs for all variables for all countries as well as the orthogonalised impulse responses.[10] Results for M1 for the four countries are shown in Table 11.2 and for M2 in Table 11.3. Tables 11.2 and 11.3 are

Table 11.1   Characteristics of long-run relations

Country	$l(1)$ variables in Cointegrating Equation	$l(0)$ Variables used in ECM
Mauritius	For log of real M1: log of real GDP and lending rate. Cointegrating vector: $-1^* \log(M1/P) + 2.95^* \text{Log RGDP} - 0.6035^* i = 0$ For log of real M2: log of real GDP and lending rate. Cointegrating vector: $-1^* \log(M2/P) + 2.7165^* \text{Log RGDP} - 0.2496^* i = 0$	None
Malawi	For log of real M1: log of real GDP. Cointegrating vector: $-1^* \log(M1/P) + 1.2700^* \text{LogRGDP} = 0$ For log of real M2: log of real GDP. Cointegrating vector: $-1^* \log(M2/P) + 1.3975^* \text{LogRGDP} = 0$	(i) South African lending rate. (ii) South African lending rate.
Tanzania	For log of real M1: log of real GDP. Cointegrating vector: $-1^* \log(M2/P) + 0.33269^* \text{LogRGDP} = 0$ For log of real M2: log of real GDP. Cointegrating vector: $-1^* \log(M2/P) + 0.2929^* \text{Log RGDP} + 0.011036^* \text{ter} = 0$	(i) South African lending rate. (ii) South African lending rate.
South Africa	For log of real M1: log of real GDP and nominal exchange rate. Cointegrating vector: $-1^* \log(M1/p) + 2.8707^* \text{logRGDP} + 0.59136^* \text{ser} = 0$ For log of real M2: log of real GDP and nominal exchange rate. Cointegrating vector: $-1^* \text{Log}(M2/P) + 1.2882^* \text{LogRGDP} + 0.16159^* \text{ser} = 0$	(i) South African lending rate. (ii) South African lending rate.

Notes: RGDP = real GDP; i = lending rate; ter = nominal exchange rate (domestic currency/US dollar) or Tanzania; ser = nominal exchange rate (domestic currency/US dollar) or South Africa.

to be read as follows. The first column indicates the first difference of the variable in question, for example log of real M1. Thus in Table 11.2 the

Table 11.2 Error correction equations model for log of real M1

Country	Mauritius	Malawi	Tanzania	South Africa
Log of RM 1	Coefficient on interest weakly significant; sign on lagged ECM positive and insignificant.	No variable Significant; sign on lagged ECM positive but not significant.	Coefficient on South African lending rate significant and negative, sign on lagged ECM positive but not significant.	Only GDP significant. Sign on lagged ECM negative but not significant.
Log of RGDP	Coefficient on M1 significant, positive. Sign on lagged ECM negative but Insignificant.	Sign on lagged on ECM negative and significant.	Coefficient on South African lending rate significant, sign on lagged ECM positive but not significant.	Trend and lagged GDP significant. Sign on lagged ECM positive and significant.
Own lending rate	Coefficient on interest positive and significant. Sign on lagged ECM negative and significant.	Not applicable.	Not applicable.	
South African lending rate	Not applicable.	Not variable significant.	No variable Significant.	Only lagged value significant. Sign on ECM positive and significant.
South African nominal exchange rate	Not applicable.	Not applicable.	Not applicable.	Sign on lending rate significant; sign on lagged ECM positive and significant.

first difference of the log of real M1 in Mauritius is affected by the first difference of the Mauritius interest rate. Furthermore, the dependent variable is weakly exogenous since the coefficient on lagged error correction term is insignificant.[11] In the case of the first difference of the log of real M1 of Tanzania, the South African lending rate is significant and negative but the Tanzanian interest rate does not belong to the ECM. Once again, the dependent variable is exogenous. Similar interpretations apply to other entries in Tables 11.2 and 11.3. The ECMs show a varied

Table 11.3   Error correction equations model for log of real M2

Country	Mauritius	Malawi	Tanzania	South Africa
Log of RM2	Coefficient on lagged ECM positive but not significant. No other variable significant.	Coefficient on lagged ECM negative and insignificant. No other variable significant.	No variable is significant, coefficient on lagged ECM positive but not significant	Coefficient on exchange rate significant, coefficient on lagged ECM negative, significant.
Log of RGDP	Coefficient on lagged ECM positive but not significant. No other variable significant	Sign on lagged on ECM positive and significant. No other variable significant.	Coefficient on South African lending rate negative and significant, endogenous, sign on lagged ECM positive but not significant.	Coefficient on lagged ECM positive and significant. Lagged M2 significant.
Lending rate	Coefficients on interest rate and M2 significant. Sign on lagged ECM negative and significant.	Not applicable.	Not applicable.	
South African lending rate	Not applicable.	No variable significant.	Not applicable.	No variable significant.
South African nominal exchange rate	Not applicable.	Not applicable.		Coefficients on M2 and lending rate significant; endogenous; coefficient on lagged ECM positive but not significant.
Tanzanian nominal exchange rate	Not applicable.	Not applicable.	No variable significant. Sign on lagged ECM positive and insignificant.	Not applicable.

picture. In the case of Mauritius, Malawi and Tanzania both M1 and M2 are exogenous. Hence monetary targeting may be pursued in these cases provided, of course, that the money demand functions are stable. A negative sign on the (insignificant) lagged value of the ECM would be more conducive to monetary targeting. This was found to be true only in case of Malawi for broad money and for South Africa for narrow money.

South Africa had been targeting broad money until very recently and has now changed its operating procedure. SARB has now opted to rely on a set of intermediate targets that include change in bank credit, level and maturity structure of interest rates, change in foreign exchange reserves, movements in nominal and real exchange rates and current and expected inflation rates rather than monetary targeting. Financial innovation, deregulation and exchange control liberalisation in South Africa in recent years has made strict Bundesbank-type monetary targeting a profitless tool. Whether a shift to inflation targeting would be more useful remains an unsettled issue but there are several grounds on which such a move can be argued for.[12] However, it is important to note that there is a lack of political consensus on keeping inflation very low. The SARB has been strongly criticised by the African National Congress (ANC) and the main labour union federation, COSATU, for practising an excessively restrictive monetary policy which, while allowing acceleration in real activity, has nevertheless allowed unemployment to rise. While the possibility of changing the operating procedure in favour of inflation targeting is being considered on the grounds of money demand instability, our results show that at least for now, it may be possible for the SARB to target narrow instead of broad money. Any operating procedure based on a set of eclectic indicators or on final target that is not quite predictable could be less efficient from a policy point of view.

The general short-run instability in the case of Tanzania, for example, is well mirrored in the impulse response functions. In general, even orthogonalised shocks take some considerable time to die out.[13] As a matter of fact, almost all impulse response functions show that shocks take a long time to dampen.

11.5   How different is empirical evidence for SADC from that for ASEAN?

Empirical evidence of money demand for ASEAN countries suggests money demand instability in the case of many of these countries. Estimating a conventional real money demand function with real GDP as a scale variable and time deposit rate as an opportunity cost variable, Dekle and Pradhan (1997) fail to obtain a stable relationship for the time period spanning mid-1970s to mid 1990s. This was the case for both narrow and broad money in the case of Indonesia, Thailand and

Singapore. The results were based on trace eigenvalue and maximal eigenvalue tests following the Johansen procedure.[14] These findings are perhaps not all that surprising, as in contrast to the SADC countries, the Asian counterparts had experienced substantial financial sector reforms and financial innovations since 1980s. Singapore had freed interest rates in the mid-1970s itself, but other ASEAN countries underwent this process in early 1980s. Money demand stability in all major ASEAN countries, including Singapore, could have been affected by the introduction of electronic fund transfer (EFT) facilities, credit cards, mutual funds with checking accounts, and so on which picked up considerably in the first half of the 1980s. These changes had a profound impact on the velocity of money demand. Interestingly, attempts to find a stable long-run relationship fail in the case of Singapore, even when foreign interest rate along with return on broad money is introduced in the equation to account for openness of its capital markets. The introduction of foreign returns is important in many cases as emphatically demonstrated by Agenor and Khan (1996). They show that the foreign rate of interest and the expected rate of depreciation of the parallel market exchange rate could be important factors in explaining the choice between domestic money or foreign currency deposits abroad, once capital accounts are open. Of the countries impacted by money demand instability, the null of no cointegration could not be rejected for any of the money demand specifications, even when foreign returns and domestic returns on broad money were used as opportunity cost variables. Even inclusion of dummy variables to capture the impact of the well known 1983 and 1988 financial liberalisation episodes failed to result in a stable relationship, though the dummy variables themselves were significant.

Malaysia, where these reforms were less extensive than other major ASEAN countries and started only in 1990s, continued to enjoy a stable real narrow money demand function. In fact, the null hypothesis of no-cointegration for real narrow, nominal broad and real broad money could be rejected only in case of Malaysia. For real narrow money, the coefficient on log of GDP was significant and indicated that a 1 per cent increase in GDP raised the demand for real narrow money by 1.18 per cent.[15] The obtained magnitudes for the selected SADC countries, except Tanzania are much higher, perhaps indicating that these economies are still under-going monetisation and also that innovations to support economy in transactions may not have caught on. In the case of real broad money the income elasticity of 1.56 is higher than that for Malawi, Tanzania and South Africa, though lower than that of Mauritius. The magnitude of interest semi- elasticity of real money demand for Malaysia obtained by

Dekle and Pradhan (1997) is very low and is around –0.07 in case of both the narrow and broad money. The interest semi-elasticity of comparable magnitude is obtained only in the case of Tanzania among the four SADC countries. For Malawi interest rate is not found to be cointegrated with money.[16] For Mauritius and South Africa, the interest semi-elasticities are found to range between –0.2 to –0.6 in magnitude. The low interest elasticities are hardly surprising and are in line with the general empirical findings for developing countries.

Interestingly, in both narrow and broad money equations for Malaysia income and interest rate variables are not weakly exogenous. It is, therefore, possible that a bi-directional relationship exists between money demand and its conventional explanatory variables. Similarly, endogeneity is a serious problem more in the case of South Africa for the broad money case, though for some SADC countries the short-run dynamics turn out to be unstable, indicating that in the short run, it may not be easy for monetary authorities to correct for monetary overshooting or undershooting.

It is important to note that despite deregulation of interest rates in ASEAN countries, broad real money demand fails to provide a stable relationship with output and the term deposit rate. Ordinarily, one would expect the freeing of interest rates to result in a portfolio switch from narrow to broad money components. Perhaps in ASEAN countries other competing asset opportunities existed in stock markets and real estate markets that resulted in broad money demand remaining unstable. However, the fact is that among the four SADC countries only South Africa has competing asset opportunities that almost match that of the ASEAN countries.

11.6 Conclusions

In this chapter we estimated money demand functions for selected SADC countries and investigated the long-run and short-run properties of such demand functions. The evidence presented in this chapter on long-run and short-run determinants of the demand for narrow (M1) and broad money (M2) has important policy implications in terms of the appropriateness of the monetary policy framework being adopted in these countries. The monetary policy experience and the empirical evidence on money demand for these selected SADC countries were compared with the experience and evidence for selected ASEAN countries. These countries are partners in a trade bloc similar in characteristics to that of SADC, though they have economies and financial sectors which are more developed than those of the SADC countries. Comparisons drawn show similarities and differences, and also indicate the likely changes which the SADC countries may have to encounter as they move up the growth path and reach financial sector development comparable to that of the ASEAN countries today.

The evidence presented in this chapter indicates that targeting narrow money still appears to be feasible in all SADC countries. However, targeting of broad money should not be done in South Africa but can be practised especially in Malawi and, to a lesser extent, in Tanzania and Mauritius. Nevertheless, except for Malawi and South Africa, the instability of short-run dynamics of monetary aggregates throws a challenge for the effective conduct of monetary policy in these countries. Experience of some of the ASEAN countries, particularly Indonesia, shows that with financial innovations and financial deepening, these instabilities could increase and the policy-makers could be confronted with not only unstable short-run dynamics, but also the instability of the long-run money demand. A change in operating procedure may become necessary when the SADC countries reach similar levels in terms of financial sophistication.

Major ASEAN countries, except Malaysia, may have to contemplate a change in their operating targets and procedures. Since monetary aggregates are not a good leading indicator of future inflation, they need to move away from conventional monetary targeting and base their policies on a range of indicators. Inflation targeting could be considered in these circumstances, but its success and credibility will crucially hinge on the predictability of inflation. Further research would be necessary to find forecasting equations which have good in- sample and out-of-sample tracking. Money, exchange rate and lags of inflation could form an integral part of such an inflation forecasting exercise, but given the nature of these economies, it is unlikely that inflation could be successfully predicted in the absence of structural parameters that determine food prices. The high variability of inflation makes this exercise particularly difficult. In most SADC countries it is a little too early to consider a change in the operating framework for monetary policy. It appears that monetary targeting is still useful.

Clearly, SADC countries face the challenge in the conduct of their monetary policy in face of their short-run dynamic instabilities and the possibility that the long-run money demand function may in future become unstable as has been the case in South Africa and in ASEAN countries. Further research in this area would be necessary and this should focus on the way the adjustments in short-run dynamics take place.

Future research, among other things, should attempt to develop better notions of the openness of these economies and of financial innovations in order to understand the importance of increasing globalisation and the financial reforms process for the conduct of monetary policy in these countries.

Acknowledgements

We are grateful to Peter Lawrence for helpful comments on an earlier draft. Responsibility for all opinions and any errors is ours alone.

Notes

1. For a good survey on this issue see Judd and Scadding (1982) and Hoffman and Rasche (1997).
2. These include 30-day, 61-day, 91-day, 180-day and 271-day T-bills.
3. Open market operations take place through 91-day BOT-bills as well as government's T-bills. T-bill auction was introduced in August 1993 as a key instrument for liquidity control. T-bills of 91-day, 182-day and 364-day are traded.
4. For instance, during 1995–96, nearly USD 2.0 billion value of rand-denominated bonds were issued in European markets by non-South African entities, including Merrill Lynch, EBRD, and Government of Sweden.
5. Of these, Hong Kong operates a currency board system under which the Hong Kong Monetary Authority (HKMA) remains ready to freely convert Hong Kong dollars to US dollars or vice-versa, by providing a 100 per cent backing for domestic currency through maintenance of equal US dollar foreign exchange reserves.
6. Not surprisingly, over the last four years, money supply growth in Indonesia exceeded its pre-announced targets testifying that monetary targeting may not be viable any longer.
7. For instance, Indonesia introduced legislative changes to support central bank independence and has also invested heavily in re-capitalisation of weak banks. It also introduced new rules on capital adequacy and placed restrictions on bank's exposures to equity and commercial paper markets. Malaysia has been particularly proactive in updating regulations through the Banking and Financial Institutions Act (BAFIA) of 1989. Singapore too has set minimal capital and licensing standards for banks. Thailand introduced several measures for asset quality and capital adequacy that go even beyond the BIS guidelines.
8. While this constituted a tax, the commercial banks benefited immensely from a sharp drop in their non-performing loans from 20 per cent of outstanding loans in the 1990s to 3.9 per cent in 1996, due largely to sustained economic growth and a substantial rise in property prices. The trend, however, has got markedly reversed since the onset of the East Asian financial crisis following the Thai- baht devaluation in mid-1997.
9. The likelihood ratio test calculates the value of λ, where $\lambda = 2$ (log likelihood ratio of unrestricted equation – log likelihood of restricted equation). Under

the null hypothesis that the restrictions hold this has a χ^2 distribution with r degrees of freedom where r is the number of restrictions imposed. See Davidson and MacKinnon (1993).

10. The graphs of the orthogonalised impulse response functions are available from the authors on request.

11. Whenever a lagged ECM term is insignificant we will label the dependent variable weakly exogenous. The sign on the coefficient of lagged ECM denotes stability. Thus with this coefficient being negative and significant, the short-run dynamics are stable, if this coefficient is positive and significant the dynamics are unstable. If this coefficient is insignificant then the short-run dynamics are random. In this case, a negative sign would be consistent with stability.

12. The Reserve Bank Act 1989 with its subsequent amendments has granted SARB a reasonable degree of legal independence. Though transparency and accountability had suffered on account of the lack of clear statements on what level of inflation is desired, such targeting has become feasible in principle with the publication of 'Core Inflation Rates' stripping volatile food prices and administered prices by the country's Central Statistical Services. SARB now has very little direct control on the broad money aggregate. However, its predictability still remains to be established. Also, the SARB runs a two-tier system of demand determined accommodation for commercial banks with its window linked to bank rate or bank rate plus a small spread depending upon the kind of collateral offered by the banks.

13. We carried out several diagnostic tests to ensure that each ECM is well specified. These included Lagrange multiplier tests for serial correlation, and ARCH up to two lags, normality of residuals and RESET tests. In each case the performance of the ECMs was satisfactory. These results are not reported here to conserve space.

14. The results obtained for recent estimations are in contrast with some earlier studies, especially Tseng and Corker (1991), Arize (1994) and Price and Insukindro (1994) which do find stable money demand functions for ASEAN countries. However, these results were based on less recent and shorter sample periods and were different in their estimation procedures.

15. In another study, Arrau *et al.* (1995) obtain an extremely low elasticity for Malaysia for the scale variable and an high elasticity for the opportunity cost measure, when a stochastic trend is introduced in the money demand equation as a proxy for financial innovation.

16. For instance, Johansen and Juselius (1990) incorporate the inflation rate as an opportunity cost variable when interest rates were regulated. Joshi and Saggar (1995) find that both term deposit rate and inflation rate fail to enter a cointegrating relationship, specifying an otherwise stable money demand system for India.

12
Credit to the Government: Central Bank Operation and its Relation to Growth

Shaikh S. Ahmed

12.1 Introduction

How systematically do central banks operate in developing countries? What is the relation between central bank credit creation to government financial demand and economic growth? Answers to these two questions form the subject matter of this chapter.

In general, it is argued that a central bank is an important institution for managing various aspects of the economy. Romer and Romer (1998), for example, claim that there are important links between monetary policy and the economic well-being of the poor. Instead of exploiting such a relation, however, it is observed that developing countries jeopardise the systematic operation of their central banks by, among other things, causing the bank to be the prime source of financing government deficit (Fry *et al.*, 1996).

In this chapter I attempt to evaluate how effectively central banks have neutralised the monetisation of government's demand for finance. I use data for 30 developing countries across Africa, Asia and Latin America. Concomitantly, I evaluate whether monetisation by central banks impacts on the growth of the economy.

It is discovered that neutralising operations by the sample of central banks are not substantial. It is observed that central bank financing of government deficits is detrimental to economic growth. There are operational differences among central banks when grouped on the basis of geographical regions. However, central bank provision of credit for governments has a negative impact on the groups irrespective of groupings.

This chapter contains six sections. Section 12.2 looks at the theoretical models of central bank operation and economic growth. In Section 12.3

the data and the sample are described. Section 12.4 discusses the methodology to be employed to answer over the key questions. Empirical results of the estimations are presented in Section 12.5. Concluding observations are contained in the final section.

12.2   The model

To put these two key questions in perspective a theoretical overview of the issues involved is presented. In the first part of this section I discuss the central banking theory and practice and in the second part, I focus on neoclassical growth theory.

12.2.1   The operation of central banks

To draw briefly on the theoretical modelling of the operation of a central bank, following Blinder (1998), we assume a Tinbergen (1952) – Theil (1961) framework for a macroeconomy of this structural form:

$$Y = F(y, x, z) + \varepsilon \qquad (12.1)$$

where y is a vector of macroeconomic endogenous variables including central bank objectives, x is a vector of policy instruments and z is a vector of non-policy exogenous variables. Stochastic shocks are contained in the vector ε. The reduced form of Equation 12.1 can be written as:

$$y = G(z, x) + \varepsilon \qquad (12.2)$$

When $F(.)$ is linear and the quadratic objective function of monetary policy is

$$W = H(y, y^*) \qquad (12.3)$$

where y^* is the bank's target. The vector of disturbances ε vanishes leaving the optimal policy rule:

$$x^* = H(z, y^*) \qquad (12.4)$$

where central bank maximises the expected value of Equation 12.3 subject to the policy constraint in Equation 12.2.

A reaction function can be easily configured on the basis of the foregoing theory to understand central banking in practice. Technically a central bank reaction function is an estimation procedure of central bank's operation that maximises different objectives with respect to a given set of instruments. A further analysis of a general monetary policy reaction function can be found in Henderson and Kim (1998).

12.2.2 Economic growth

This study employs a neoclassical growth theoretic approach to investigate the relation between credit creation for the government and economic growth. Temple (1999), Durlauf and Quah (1998) and Levine (1996) present surveys on the economic growth literature. It is observed that the neoclassical growth model has been widely used in an endeavour to understand monetary factors.

We first discuss the neoclassical growth theory. In an equation form, following Barro (1997), such a growth relation can be represented as:

$$Dy = f(y, y^*) \qquad (12.5)$$

where Dy is the per capita output growth rate, y is the per capita current level of output, and y^* is the steady-state level of per capita output over the transition period. Dy is increasing in y^* for given y. As y^* increases, Romer (1990) type R&D dependent Dy is achieved due to diminishing returns to capital. This growth process remains persistent as the transition path from y to y^* is prolonged. Dy is also diminishing in y for given y^*. Here, a higher y capitalises lower Dy representing convergence. Now, y may or may not be equal for all economies. If it is, then there will be convergence of poor countries to rich countries in an absolute sense; if it is not, then such convergence is achieved in a conditional sense. Since economies are prone to random shocks, economies differ in their attributes. So, target value y^* depends on condition.

The concept of capital in the fundamental neoclassical model, with a Cobb–Douglas production system, can be extended to capture other issues that are possibly related to the development process. Therefore conditions are considered to control for discrepancies in steady-state income levels among countries. Various conditions, both economic and non-economic, have been used as conditioning parameters. For instance, Table 2 of Durlauf and Quah (1998) provides a summary of 36 different categories of variables used as conditions in 87 specific examples. Levine and Renelt (1992) in their data appendix also list some 50 possible control variables.

Taking this concept at the outset, we directly introduce credit created for the government in the growth equation to test if there is any impact of such operation by the central bank on classical economic growth. The literature suggests that credit to the government would either have a negative or neutral effect on economic growth.

12.3 Data

We study a group of developing countries. The sample countries are chosen on the following criteria. First, population must be at least ten million in 1987. Secondly, countries that are labelled industrialised by the IMF are excluded. The Eastern European and Former Soviet Republics as classified in the World Development Indicators along with centrally planned economies, China, Cuba and North Korea are also excluded. This results in 42 countries in the initial sample, some of which had to be removed because of lack of data. The final sample consists of 30 countries.

The countries are, by regional group, Indonesia, Korea, Malaysia, Philippines, and Thailand forming the Pacific Basin; Argentina, Chile, Colombia, Mexico, Peru and Venezuela forming Latin America; and the African group consists of Algeria, Côte d'Ivoire, Cameroon, Ghana, Kenya, Morocco, Madagascar, Nigeria, South Africa and Zaire. Nine other countries of the sample are not included in any regional group: Bangladesh, Egypt, India, Sri Lanka, Mayanmar, Nepal, Pakistan, Syria and Turkey. Zaire is dropped from the growth regression since there are no data available on its investment and education.

The time period covered is based on the *World Development Indicators 1998*, database which covers a period from 1960 to 1996. However, many of our sample countries have missing data for that period. This significantly hinders the application of sophisticated econometric techniques. Table 12.1 provides precise definitions of the variables and their sources. As there is no readily available and comparable data on unemployment, output is used as a proxy when transformed by the widely used Hodrick–Prescott Filter (HPF). Since unemployment data is computed, the method of estimation of the unemployment variable is of particular attention – the rest of the section discusses this method.

Hodrick and Prescott (1980) propose a simple transformation technique for macroeconomic time series. To put HPF simply, let

$$y_{(t)} = g_{(t)} + c_{(t)} \tag{12.6}$$

where, $y_{(t)}$ is a stochastic time series expressed in natural logarithm, $g_{(t)}$ is the growth component, and $c_{(t)}$ is the cyclical component.

HPF decomposes this series into two components by minimising the variance of the $c_{(t)}$ subject to a penalty for variation in the second difference of the $g_{(t)}$ as:

Table 12.1 Data definitions and sources

Variable	Definitions and sources
DDCY	Net domestic credit scaled by GDP (first differences) *World Development Indicators 1998*, World Bank.
DDCGY	Claims on governments and other public entities scaled by GDP (first differences) *World Development Indicators 1998*, World Bank.
DNFAY	Net foreign assets scaled by GDP (first differences) *World Development Indicators 1998*, World Bank.
INFGAP	Difference between a countries consumer price index and the US wholesale price index *World Development Indicators 1998*, World Bank and *International Financial Statistics*, June 1998 CD-Rom, IMF.
DOILINF	World petroleum average crude price index (first differences) *International Financial Statistics*, June 1998 CD-Rom. IMF.
BC	Real GDP based output gap computer by the Hodrick–Prescott Filter method *World Development Indicators 1998*, World Bank.
DGDP	Real per capita GDP between the first year and the last year of each five year sub-sample period
EGDP	One period lagged value of the DGDP
DCGA	Sub-sample period average of the DCGY
SNA	Sub-sample period average gross domestic savings *World Development Indicators 1998*, World Bank.
EDULA	Product of gross enrolment ratio of the second level in the school and working age population for each sub-sample period UNESCO and *World Development Indicators 1998*, World Bank.
GDIFA	Sub-sample gross domestic fixed investment scaled by GDP *World Development Indicators 1998*, World Bank.
USINF	US wholesale price index *International Financial Statistics*, June 1998 CD-Rom, IMF.
RW	World real interest rate based on World Economic Outlook Method *International Financial Statistics*, June 1998 CD-Rom, IMF.
GW	OECD real growth rate *International Financial Statistics*, June 1998 CD-Rom, IMF.
GDP	GDP at market prices *World Development Indicators 1998*, World Bank.
GDPK	GDP at constant prices *World Development Indicators 1998*, World Bank.

$$\min_{g_{(t)}} \left\{ \sum_{t=-\infty}^{\infty} [y_{(t)} - g_{(t)}]^2 + \lambda \sum_{t=-\infty}^{\infty} [g_{(t+1)} - 2g_{(t)} + g_{(t-1)}]^2 \right\} \qquad (12.7)$$

In HPF the parameter λ = variance of $c_{(t)}$/variance of $g_{(t)}$. The Lagrange multiplier λ controls the smoothness of $g_{(t)}$. 'The larger the value of λ, the smoother is the solution series' (Hodrick and Prescott, 1997). The first order conditions of this problem are linear in $y_{(t)}$ and $g_{(t)}$ (Prescott, 1986). Hodrick and Prescott (1980) prove that change in $g_{(t)}$ and $c_{(t)}$ are orthogonal white noise process. They use a 'prior view that a five percent cyclical component is moderately large as is a one-eight of one percent change in the rate of growth in a quarter. This leads us to select $\lambda^{1/2} = {}^5/_{1/8}$ or $\lambda = 1600$ as a value for the smoothing parameter.' Similarly, λ has a standard value of 100 for annual data, which has been used in the case of this chapter.

12.4   Methodology

This section explains the methodology on which the empirical tests of the issues raised will be implemented. Once again, in the first part, central banking is discussed and the section concludes explaining issues of growth regression. In each case, applied econometric issues have also been discussed.

12.4.1   Reaction function of the central bank

A reaction function is developed to address our first question on how systematically the central banks are operating. Performance is assessed here by comparing theoretical expectations with estimated performances on the grounds that there is no exact yardstick to judge the subtle matter of system-orientation by a central bank. In the following paragraphs construction of this reaction function is described. In each case theoretical expectations of the relation between instrument and objectives are also mentioned. Definitions of these variables and their data sources are listed in Table 12.1.

The *World Development Indicators 1998* states that 'Domestic credit is the main vehicle through which changes in the money supply are regulated, with central bank lending to the government often playing the most important role.' Even though Aghevli *et al.* (1979) in their analysis of various instruments and targets conclude that developing countries have institutional constraints on the flexibility of instruments, Tseng and Corker (1991) state that in the wake of liberalisation and reforms, indirect monetary policy instruments have enhanced the effectiveness of monetary policy in the developing economy. Alexander *et al.* (1995) also emphasise the transition towards indirect controls. Their study provides evidence of better monetary control by indirect instruments, for example domestic credit, in some non-industrial countries. Guitian (1973) proposed that control over credit is the main instrument of monetary policy in developing countries. Kaskarelis and Varelas (1996) also emphasise that credit is the only degree of freedom in an open developing economy which has budget deficits to control money supply when the private holding of government securities is small in band and width. More importantly, developing countries have been typified as classical rather than Keynesian. Hence the role of domestic credit is dominant in reflecting monetary policy. This inspires the use of domestic credit as the instrument in the central bank reaction function.

Emphasis is placed on the neutralisation function of a central bank, especially given its possible relation to the concept of central bank independence. Central bank independence is widely considered as a means to macroeconomic stability and growth (see for a survey, Eijffinger, 1997). But the models are developed from the perspective of industrialised economies and adherence to these models is less relevant to the developing world. Moreover, recently Forder (1998) and Posen (1998) cast doubt on the relationship between commonly available indices of independence and low inflation. In overcoming some of these drawbacks, Fry (1998) proposes an executable definition of central bank independence with reference to developing countries:

> There is one degree of freedom or independence in their balance sheets that all central banks can exploit, at least to some extent. To pursue a monetary target, the central bank in any open economy acts to control domestic credit expansion. If the government's demands would otherwise produce inflationary domestic credit expansion, the central bank can react by reducing credit to the private sector.

A further explanation of the importance of the central bank neutralisation function is provided since it is the core factor analysed here. A central bank has a natural monopoly in producing money for the government in the real world. Governments of developing countries exploit this excessively. Generally it is the case also that in a fiscal versus monetary policy game, fiscal needs dominate. This causes an outward shift in the LM curve when a government deficit is financed by monetary expansion. On the other hand, a deficit does not add to net wealth since 'Ricardian Equivalence' does not hold (Masson *et al.*, 1995; Haque and Montiel, 1989). Therefore, if a central bank is compelled to finance the government in addition to or instead of financing the private sector, a monetary policy cannot be beneficial to economic development owing to its resultant impacts. This leads a central bank, for systematic operation and effective independence, to neutralise government demand for credit by reducing credit to the private sector. This objective is manifested in the neutralisation coefficient DCGY in our reaction function. A neutralising central bank reduces domestic credit in response to a government demand for credit. The higher a central bank can neutralise, the more credible will be its operation. The magnitude of neutralisation also depends on the extent of central bank independence. A complete neutralisation is represented in the zero value of the coefficient and partial neutralisation is represented in a positive, but less than unity, value of the coefficient.

It is evident that a developing country central bank is generally engaged with a wide spectrum of objectives emanating from various domestic and foreign causes and consequences (Maxfield, 1997; Fry, 1995; Ghatak, 1995). Hence, additional variables are included in the reaction function to allow for a range of possible objectives that a central bank actually pursues. The following paragraphs explain such objectives.

Capital inflow, as well as outflow, may cause money market disequilibrium. Being a non-reserve country this may also cause loss of some monetary independence. Furthermore, Obstfeld (1983) noted that

> The conflict between internal and external equilibrium ... arises when the domestic credit measures appropriate for attaining a domestic policy target move the economy away from an important external target. Central banks have often attempted to resolve such dilemmas by sterilising the monetary effects of foreign reserve flows in the hope of temporarily divorcing their domestic policies from balance-of-payments considerations.

It is observed that substantial flows of foreign assets are a feature of developing countries particularly since the collapse of the Bretton Woods era. Sterilisation is hence considered an objective of central banks. Sterilisation is represented by the DNFAY coefficient in the reaction function. This coefficient is expected to have an inverse relationship to the growth of domestic credit and complete sterilisation is represented by a coefficient of -1 (Pasula, 1994).

Developing economies largely adopt monetisation to finance a fiscal deficit. This results in the increase of inflation and inflation uncertainty. Since domestic sources are insufficient to support massive resources demand, for reasons including the 'Olivera (1967) – Tanzi (1978) effect', these trapped countries resort to external financing. But getting external resources from the international market is limited by creditworthiness (Haque *et al.* 1996, Edwards, 1986) for which these economies have a poor standing. When foreign inflation is taken into consideration these consequences aggravate other factors such as 'capital flight' (Cuddington, 1986; Rojas-Suarez, 1990) and deterioration of the condition of international trade. In this scenario, controlling the widening gap between domestic inflation and foreign inflation, measured by INFGAP, is an important objective of the central bank. A prudent central bank is supposed to tighten domestic credit in response to increases in that gap. This strategy by a central bank is supposed to operate both for export promotion and import substitution and to prevent the development of parallel markets.

A central bank also considers the impact of exogenous shocks in the performance of its systematic operations. The oil price is a predominant factor in that class of shocks. This is because the price of energy affects the supply side of the goods and services market on the one hand and on the other, affects the demand for countries' output (Ferderer, 1996; Tatom, 1991). Here, DOILPL is included in the reaction function to take account of this exogenous shock. A central bank is expected to reduce credit creation activities to counter such a shock.

The exchange rate plays a key role in the process of internationalisation of an economy. Typically a central bank of a developing country manages the foreign exchange rate and foreign exchange reserves. Lizondo (1993) proposes that real exchange rate targeting is useful for developing countries in the presence of high domestic inflation to preserve international competitiveness and a satisfactory external trade performance. Similarly, it is argued that government spending requires adjustment in the real exchange rate (Koray and Chang, 1991). Ellis (1996) also mentions, 'real exchange rate movements related to the generation of international transfers can be important not only for the inflation process and the burden of financing external debt, but also for the design of an anti-inflation program.' Therefore, maintaining the stability of the real exchange rate is an objective of central banks. In practice, this is a dilemma whereby effective devaluation needs restrictive credit creation policy but such restriction increases the service cost of foreign debt leading to further increase in the demand for credit by the government. Inclusion of the lagged real exchange rate REXL(-1) can assess this complex attribute. This variable expresses restriction if the coefficient is positive; otherwise, central bank accommodation is manifested.

It is also argued that monetary policy affects real activity. In an overheating economy restrictive monetary policies prevent output from over- expanding and in recession, expansionary monetary policy can be pursued since in the short run the Phillips curve trade off between inflation and unemployment is plausible. Hence, Fischer (1996) advocates that stabilisation of real output in terms of cyclical unemployment is an appropriate goal of monetary policy. This leads to consideration of unemployment in the reaction function of the central bank. The variable BC in the reaction function considers the real output gap, as a proxy for unemployment since unemployment data for the sample countries are inadequate. The procedure for estimating this proxy variable is explained in the following section.

Given the above discussion, the specification of the central bank reaction function to be estimated is:

$$DDCY = \beta_1 DDCGY + \beta_2 DNFAY + \beta_3 INFGAP + \beta_4 DOILINF$$
$$+ \beta_5 REXL + \beta_6 BC \tag{12.8}$$

However, it can be easily expected that all of these countries do not perform monetary policy uniformly. It is also generally observed that the group of Pacific Basin countries is performing economically better than other groups of economies. This calls for a closer look at the difference in regional patterns which we attempt by utilising a shift parameter. Specifically, the following methodology has been applied.

At first a dummy $k = 1$ has been assigned for each country in a particular regional group and $k = 0$ for the rest of the cross-sections. Then, an additional set of all variables is regressed for countries of this group upon multiplying by dummies representing the region. Finally, a regression of the following configuration is run for the panel:

$$DCY = \beta_1 DDCGY + \beta_2 DNFAY + \beta_3 INFGAP + \beta_4 DOILINF + \beta_5 REXL$$
$$+ \beta_6 BC + \beta_7 (k^* DDCGY) + \beta_7 (K^* DNFAY) + \beta_9 (k^* INFGAP)$$
$$+ \beta_{10} (k^* DOILINF) + \beta_{11} (k^* REXL) + \beta_{12} (k^* BC) \tag{12.9}$$

Three Stage Least Squares (3SLS) is employed to estimate Equations 12.8 and 12.9. A common equation structure for the 30 countries of the sample is estimated as a system of equations. In the system, cross-equation restrictions are imposed for all slope coefficients excluding the intercept terms that are allowed to vary. Parameters estimated by this system represent a typical cross-section of the sample. The 3SLS method is asymptotically efficient in the class of instrumental variable techniques and also asymptotically full-information maximum likelihood (Greene, 1997). Instruments used, following Fair (1970), are the lagged endogenous variables in the equation and exogenous variables along with US inflation rate, world real interest rate and world economic growth rate. First order serial correlation is tested by the Breusch (1978)–Godfrey (1978) Lagrange multiplier test. Any remaining autocorrelation is corrected by including a common AR(1) term in the equation.

12.4.2 Economic growth

Temple (1999) mentions some advantages in applying panel techniques over the cross-section estimates in the case of growth equations. First, such an approach tracks omitted variables by controlling for unobserved heterogeneity in the initial level of efficiency. Secondly, lagged regressors can be used as instruments, and such use can control measurement error and endogeneity biases.

In the growth estimates, a fixed effect specification similar to Islam (1995) is employed. The data used in the system equation is rearranged for reaction function estimation in a panel format. In this framework, first the initial sample is divided into seven sub-samples with five-year periods for each. This produces seven non-overlapping data points in the time horizon for each cross-section. Such an arrangement for yielding a panel data framework allows policy to come in to affect the economy which yearly data points cannot properly track down. It helps reduce influences from the business cycle and serial correlation. Similar to reaction function estimates, growth estimates also consider regional sub-panels to find any regional differences.

Under this methodology, to test the issue two sets of conditions have been tested. In the first set, only credit created for the government is added exclusively as a condition in Equation 12.10:

$$DGDP_{i,f-l} = \beta_l + \beta_2\,EGDP_{l,f} + \beta_3\,DCGA_f \qquad (12.10)$$

where i = cross-section, f = first year of each five-year sub-period, l = last year of each five-year sub-period. Definitions of these variables and their sources are mentioned in Table 12.1.

Equation 12.10 is not sufficient to explain economic growth since it does not contain other basic conditions. Therefore a second test is required with other factors of economic growth as imposed in the restriction implied by the Cobb–Douglas production function. This second set of conditions is jointly considered along with central bank credit creation for the government. Other conditions are education representing human capital and investment similar to Knight *et al.* (1993). So, we now write:

$$DGDP_{i,f-l} = \beta_1 + \beta_2\,EGDP_{i,f} + \beta_3\,DCGA_f + \beta_3\,EDULA_f \\ + \beta_4\,GDIFA_f \qquad (12.11)$$

12.5   Empirical results

In this section empirical estimates are analysed. Reaction function estimates are followed by economic growth estimates. In each case, the relevant sensitivity analyses are also included.

12.5.1   Central bank reaction function

Table 12.2 reports the results of reaction function estimates. The first observation is that this group of countries does have an active central bank responding systematically to some objectives. Secondly, there are significant differences in the way each of the sub-groups is performing. The sub-group regressions are statistically different as reflected in the χ^2 tests presented in the table. The third observation is that the monetary policy stance in the Pacific Basin countries is relatively better than the rest of the groups. In the following paragraphs these results are further elaborated.

Table 12.2 also depicts these differences in the behaviour of monetary policy pursued among different regions. In interpreting this table, the general economic expectations of variables remain the same. Here, coefficients for these calculations for a region are to be interpreted adding the regional shift parameter along with the standard parameter, for example, $(\beta_1 + \beta_7)$ and comparing with the standard parameter, for example, β_1.

Central banks do neutralise government credit requirements as reflected in the coefficient of the variable *DDCGY*. In the all-country estimate, 29 per cent $(1 - 0.71)$ neutralisation is observed. The African group of countries do neutralise 27 per cent $(1 - 0.73)$ in a year and 19 per cent $(1 - 0.81)$ over a two-year period. Latin American countries however neutralise merely 13 per cent $(1 - 0.87)$ in a year. Among these three types of countries, Pacific Basin countries appear to have performed relatively better. This group of countries neutralise 71 per cent $(1 - 0.29)$ in a year and about 82 per cent $(1 - 0.18)$ of the government credit demand.

The sterilisation of foreign asset flows is captured by the variable *DNFAY*. In the full sample estimate, about 11 per cent of the increase in the net foreign assets have been sterilised. A mere 4 per cent sterilisation occurs in the African countries and 27 per cent of sterilisation is found from Latin American countries. Pacific Basin central banks sterilised 52 per cent. This is a significantly different performance from all other sub-groups.

Reaction to the gap between domestic inflation and US inflation (*INFGAP*) is not substantially accommodative in any of these estimates.

Table 12.2 Reaction function by region

Variable	Dependent variable *DDCY*			
	All countries	Africa	Latin America	Pacific Basin
	(a)	(b)	(c)	(d)
DDCGY	0.714601	0.598216	0.593048	0.765603
	(56.17698)	(46.3548)	(45.34575)	(62.78189)
DDCGY(-1)	0.063412	0.118186		0.051404
	(4.992612)	(9.92752)		(4.080074)
DNFAY	-0.105974	-0.424824	-0.09177	-0.080413
	(-15.98696)	(-33.85586)	(-16.09231)	(-15.26342)
INFGAP	0.014127	0.016632	0.012989	0.012337
	(9.35663)	(14.26054)	(11.6081)	(9.22316)
DOILINF(-1)	0.007056	0.005427	0.008768	0.009244
	(6.983979)	(3.725081)	(8.316226)	(9.211615)
REXL(-1)	-0.007432	-0.010811	-0.00754	-0.008412
	(-4.356376)	(-7.302008)	(-4.347922)	(-5.237982)
BC	0.074274	0.053927	0.10219	0.046661
	(8.050559)	(6.25464)	(10.54356)	(5.242247)
AR(1)	0.3749	0.376746	0.392422	0.380002
	(11.89628)	(12.15412)	(12.37356)	(12.05327)
*DDCGY		0.127723	0.279799	-0.4746
		(5.676163)	(10.01745)	(-9.962171)
*DDCGY(-1)		-0.199257		-0.16635
		(-8.703823)		(-3.533432)
*DNFAY		0.382827	-0.182383	-0.441135
		(28.66147)	(-8.551327)	(-10.81654)
*DOILINF(-1)		0.004737	-0.008809	-0.012091
		(1.992299)	(-3.693258)	(-3.119024)
*BC			-0.158723	0.247648
			(-8.031114)	(5.783886)
Adjusted R^2	0.690547	0.712791	0.699309	0.705533
Standard error	0.033936	0.032694	0.033374	0.033104
Probability	0.000000	0.000000	0.000000	0.000000
Number of observations	849	849	854	849
Number of countries	30	30	30	30
χ^2 against panel (a)		68.4386	163.5623	52.9075

Notes:
1. Sample period 1960–96.
2. Method of estimations is three stage least squares.
3. *t*-statistics are in parentheses.
4. An asterisk represents shift parameter.

The coefficient is regularly about 1 per cent for each of these equations. A similar finding is observed when oil price inflation (*DOILINF*) is considered: this has a flat rate of less than one percentage point. When the lagged value of the real exchange rate ($REXL(-1)$) is taken into account it possesses a negative sign but its absolute value is again small for each of these equations.

There emerges a differential performance among these groups of countries in relation to the output gap (BC). In the control group estimates, such a gap is accommodated by an increase in domestic credit of about 7 per cent representing a pro-cyclical monetary policy. Africa is also accommodative with a 5 per cent increase in credit. In contrast, in Latin American countries there is a 6 per cent reduction in credit when there is an output gap representing a counter-cyclical monetary policy stance. Once again, the behaviour of Pacific Basin central banks is substantially different from that of the control group. They increase domestic credit substantially.

Further analysis is required on the relevance of credit creation for the government and a central bank's ability to neutralise government credit demand. To this end, a set of additional regressions was run and the results are reported in Table 12.3. Here, countries are ranked on the basis of period average domestic credit to the government. Out of 30 countries, the ten countries with the lowest average values and the ten countries with highest average values of the discriminating variable are included in the regression. This method permits understanding of the impact of credit creation in the low ranking cases within the sample. In the control group regression these 20 countries are estimated with the similar 3SLS methodology of system equations as explained earlier. In the second regression countries with low values of average credit to the government are represented by a shift parameter.

It can be further inferred from panel (a) of Table 12.3 that those countries that produce less credit to the government operate more systematically. This is because compared to a 53 per cent increase in domestic credit creation by all 20 countries, which means 47 per cent ($1 - 0.53$) neutralisation, lower domestic credit creating countries do neutralise 92 per cent ($1 - 0.079$) of any government credit demand. In the second year, the low ranked countries neutralise more when other control group countries create domestic credit by around 7 per cent. As a whole the low group countries over the two-year period of time neutralise more than they create credit to the government.

This study points out that developing central banking operations is significantly influenced by government credit requirements. and supports the view that there should be controls on government access to finance channels so that the monetary policy can work towards economic

Table 12.3 Reaction function by disciriminatory variable

Variable	Dependent variable: *DDCY* Control group (a)	Shift parameter included (b)
DDCGY	0.460091	0.527288
	(15.37963)	(15.77621)
DDCGY(-1)	0.058982	0.073136
	(2.505097)	(2.951430)
DNFAY	–0.439900	–0.431212
	(–18.11278)	(–16.38335)
INFGAP	0.030851	0.038209
	(8.006017)	(8.413161)
DOILINF(-1)	0.012875	0.015307
	(5.885462)	(6.502953)
REXL(-1)	–0.019148	–0.022997
	(–6.083704)	(–6.528836)
BC	0.057762	0.049221
	(3.156581)	(2.504491)
AR(1)	0.337132	0.313813
	(8.218749)	(7.682582)
*DDCGY		–0.447475
		(–6.973166)
*DDCGY(-1)		–0.221273
		(–4.529627)
Adjusted R^2	0.690367	0.693838
Standard error	0.036053	0.035850
Probability	0.000000	0.000000
Number of observations	615	615
Number of countries	20	20

Notes:
1. Sample Period 1960–96.
2. Method of estimations is three stage least squares.
3. *t*-statistics are in parentheses.
4. An asterisk represents shift parameter.

development (Rajapatirana, 1995). These findings are largely similar to those of Fry (1995). However, Kamas (1986) finds, in a different set up, a counteracting central bank reaction to inflation in Mexico and Venezuela. The present estimation for Latin American central banks reaction to inflation accords with Porzecanski's (1979) estimation for Argentina and Chile that these banks accommodated inflationary pressure. But this study produces results for reaction to unemployment and net asset flow which conflict with those of Porzecanski. The findings of this paper re-emphasise the view of Folkers-Landau and Ito (1995) who observe that to insulate the banking system from capital surge and to resist the consequential nominal appreciation, most of the developing countries adopt sterilisation. Most of all, the current study contradicts the Connolly and Taylor (1979) view since it is observed that central banks in developing countries can operate reasonably systematically.

12.5.2   Economic growth

Table 12.4 reports the results of estimation of the growth equations. In both Equations 12.10 and 12.11, when all countries are estimated together, growth of credit created by the central bank to finance government, exerted a significantly negative impact on economic growth.

Estimates for the African countries suggest that credit creation for the government produces no significant impact on economic growth. However, in the estimates of panels (c) and (d), the coefficients are negative. Latin American countries reveal a significantly negative impact on economic growth of any credit created for the government as estimated by Equation 12.11 in panels (e) and (f). In the Pacific Basin countries, an increase in such credit provision has a significant negative impact on growth as shown in panels (g) and (h).

It is evident from the estimates in Table 12.4 that credit creation by the central banks for demand of the government has a significant negative influence to economic growth. Therefore, according to current estimates, systematic operation of central banks may foster economic growth.

Further tests were undertaken to draw more conclusive findings on the effect on economic growth of credit created for the government. The resultant regressions are presented in Table 12.5. Here the methodology of fixed-effect estimation used earlier is retained. Similarly to Table 12.3, first, the countries are ranked on the basis of period average domestic credit to the government. Out of 30 countries, the ten countries with lowest average values and the ten countries with highest average values of the discriminating variable are included in the regression. Three regressions are run on the specification of Equation 12.11. Such estimates help to understand within the sample the differences among groups with different levels of credit creation.

It is observed that credit created for the government has a significant negative impact when all 20 countries are considered and as well in the case where ten countries with the high values for the discriminatory variable are considered. In the regression based only on the lowest values for the discriminatory variable, creation of credit does not exert any significant impact on economic growth. These estimates satisfy the

Table 12.4 Relation of credit creation for the government to growth by region

| | All countries | | Africa | | | Latin America | | Pacific Basin | |
	(a)	(b)	(c)	(d)	(e)	(f)	(g)	(h)
				Dependent variable: *DGDP*				
EGDP	-0.037409	-0.177422	-0.258323	-0.327104	-0.097491	-0.473381	0.039715	-0.112186
	(-1.679548)	(-3.902932)	(-3.829992)	(-2.867819)	(-1.521182)	(-3.528304)	(2.055308)	(-1.481736)
DCGA	-0.226653	-0.398487	-0.210691	-0.337250	-0.538619	-0.559076	-0.639095	-0.945732
	(-2.553094)	(-3.463487)	(-1.574134)	(-1.606307)	(-2.154416)	(-1.884453)	(-2.337048)	(-2.328891)
EDULA		0.015387		-0.006428		0.067942		0.034298
		(0.848352)		(-0.246246)		(1.851165)		(0.537802)
GDIFA		0.200955		0.145020		0.330835		0.167777
		(5.207402)		(2.883561)		(1.859405)		(1.345004)
Adjusted R²	0.256209	0.433115	0.251501	0.267655	0.194830	0.307171	0.460455	0.444144
Standard error of regression	0.097925	0.092820	0.107856	0.103613	0.091330	0.098810	0.075174	0.088580
Probability	0.000000	0.000000	0.000000	0.000043	0.000054	0.000789	0.000000	0.000389
No. of Cross-section	29	29	9	9	6	6	5	5
Total panel observations	252	163	81	52	54	34	42	28

Notes:
1. Sample period 1960–96.
2. Fixed-effect methods of estimation.
3. *t*-statistics are in parentheses.
4. Standard errors are White-heteroscedasticity consistent.

Table 12.5 Relation of credit creation to growth by discriminatory variable

Variables	Dependent variable: *DGDP*		
	ALL20 (a)	HIGH10 (b)	LOW10 (c)
EGDP	−0.146053	−0.192568	−0.128824
	(−2.933543)	(−2.049805)	(−1.596726)
DCGA	−0.414187	−0.411466	−0.624949
	(−3.203175)	(−2.727148)	(−1.869381)
EDULA	0.010059	0.042248	−0.013720
	(0.447154)	(1.081095)	(−0.415734)
GDIFA	0.201150	0.168275	0.213148
	(4.362378)	(4.262736)	(1.866936)
Adjusted R^2	0.464357	0.354654	0.501820
Standard error of regression	0.093274	0.078874	0.107209
Probability	0.000000	0.000001	0.000000
No. of Cross-section	20	10	10
Total panel observations	115	58	57

Notes:
1. Sample 1960–96.
2. Fixed-effect method of estimation.
3. *t*-statistics are in parentheses.
4. Standard errors are White-heteroscedasticity consistent.

expectation that credit creation for the government is not conducive to economic growth.

12.6 Conclusion

In this chapter, it has been argued that the creation credit for the government by the central bank has implications for the operation of a central bank. It has also been argued that such credit creation exerts a negative impact on economic growth. This study supposes that such credit is created due to a government's financing demand which a central bank is called to follow other than its own rule, thus forgoing its probable systematic operation that could possibly lead to economic development.

According to the estimates presented here, these considerations are found to be important. It is observed that central banks in the Pacific Basin countries neutralise more than all other groups of countries. The findings support the view that central banks of low credit generating countries, perform more systematically than the other central banks. By the same token, creating credit for the government is detrimental to economic growth; but a low level of credit creation for the government does not cause any significant negative effect on the economic growth.

The policy implication here is that, in the interests of economic growth, a central bank should be allowed to operate systematically towards its own objectives. Using the central bank to supply credit to the government remains detrimental to both the central bank and the economy as a whole.

Acknowledgements

I am grateful to Maxwell J. Fry, Jim Ford, John Cadle, Peter Burridge, the ESRC-DESG 1998 Annual Conference participants and the editors of the book.

Part III
Convergence or Divergence?

13
Convergence or Divergence in and between Developing Regions?

Harald V. Proff

13.1 Introduction

Convergence or divergence in and between developing regions in Africa, Asia and Latin America is an important issue in the present convergence debate.[1] This paper analyses the intra- and inter-regional similarities and differences among developing countries in the main integration arenas AFTA, SADC and MERCOSUR, to evaluate the question whether regional integration will lead to strong inequality in and between these regions and to prove the relevance of comparing aggregated geographical units like 'Africa' or 'Asia'. Convergence is understood as a faster per capita growth of poor economies than of richer ones according to the neoclassical assumption of diminishing returns to capital (cf. Barro and Sala-i-Martin, 1992: 226). The divergence assumption rejects the inverse relationship of per capita growth and the starting level of output due to the availability of technological progress.

This paper looks for theoretical and empirical evidence for either convergence or divergence in and between developing regions. The literature for this topic can be grouped into two ideal types of comparative research of developing regions (see Chapter 1):

1 cross-national multiple regressions with the introduction of SADC or AFTA as dummy variables beside the traditional (growth theory) variables and,
2 comparative case studies with comparison of pairs and smaller groups in different regions for a specific field situation to explain differences or similarities.

Both types of comparative research face severe limitations. In economics, it is only necessary to introduce 'space' if it has an impact on the performance of markets (cf. Giersch 1995: 8). It is not the location of an economy in the SADC or AFTA as such that affects the market performance, so that dummy variables in the first ideal type of comparative research do not possess a high explanatory power. Comparative case studies lack the theoretical grounding of the multiple regression approach and are hardly able to draw any far-reaching conclusion.

In spite of these theoretical problems multinational enterprises are looking for criteria to reduce the complexity of their environment in the process of designing and implementing global strategies for the 'non-triad' markets.[2] The formation of regional integrations between countries provides a popular framework for this kind of complexity reduction (cf. Proff and Proff, 1996), so that there is a demand for comparative research which this paper wants to address.

The plan of the paper is as follows. In Section 13.2 the impacts of regional integration among developing countries is theoretically analysed. Section 13.3 then empirically examines the interregional homogeneity and heterogeneity of developing regions with the help of a multivariate cluster analysis. Section 13.4 concludes.

13.2   The impact of regional integration on developing countries

Since the beginning of the 1990s there has been an increased trend in the world economy towards regional trade agreements. Of particular importance for development policy are SADC, MERCOSUR and AFTA. In addition to these there are a large number of other regional integration agreements in all parts of the globe in which industrialising countries participate.

Generally regional integration concentrates on the creation of trade. The trade creation effect is one of the non-monetary effects of regional integration and leads to increased trade between the participating countries, due to the reduction of customs duties. As a result the economies of these countries will be stimulated and hence increase their economic growth rates. This positive integration effect, which is based on the most efficient utilisation of the resources available in the participating countries, stands in contrast to the trade diversion effect. This arises because competitive products from third countries, which are not party to the regional integration, are replaced by less competitive products (meaning the *same* products at higher prices) from the participating countries, which are cheaper because of the reduction in tariffs. From a purely theoretical point of view, therefore the whole theory of regional integration belongs to the theory of *second best*. Thus, a movement towards one condition for Pareto optimality by reducing tariffs on imports from one source *may* not be welfare-improving unless other conditions are fulfilled, which they are not when tariffs remain on non-preferred (third-countries') imports (Lipsey and Lancaster, 1956/57). This is the reason why generalisations on welfare gains from regional integration are hard to make thus opening up the field on non-economic motivation for or against regional integration (Pomfret, 1986).

The traditional argumentation indicates that the liberalisation of trade tends to polarise regional development in the more advanced partner countries. Initial regional disparities are thus perpetuated by a cumulative process and industrial growth tends to gravitate towards the economically more advanced countries (cf. McCarthy, 1994: 10).

As Krugman has noted, a full analysis of the costs and benefits of regional trade agreements requires not only a strong theoretical base but also an analysis of the bargaining process in the trade negotiations (Krugman, 1991: 10). A decision tree of a bargaining process in trade negotiation contains four steps (cf. Figure 13.1).

The first decision is centred around the political will towards substantial regional integration. If this hurdle is taken, the question then arises of the overall gains from trade through regional integration. After a positive answer the distribution of the gains among the partner countries is the next issue to negotiate. Here lobbyism occurs, as the potential gains may vary among different subgroups of the partner countries. Influential pressure groups try to raise their welfare during the negotiation process (cf. Becker, 1983: 373–4). Designing an optimal strategy from the theoretical point of view, even if it is *only* second best, does not mean at all that the implemented policy will be optimal due to lobbyistic influences (cf. Oberender and Daumann, 1995: 95). As there is, for example, no ambiguity in the economic assessment of regional free trade 'policy oriented economists must deal with a world that does not understand or accept that case' (Krugman, 1997: 114). Introducing pressure groups in the bargaining process explains the large exclusion lists in regional trade agreements. Exclusion generally improves the chances to reach an agreement due to a bargain of special treatment of a mighty pressure group for their support of the agreement (cf. Grossman and Helpman, 1995: 684). Government assessments of discounted welfare effects of exclusions and concessions under incomplete information are relevant in this third step. Incomplete information generally leads to a long negotiation process because better understanding of the negotiation partners gives higher security in assessing the partners' reactions (cf. Bac and Raff, 1997: 500).

Figure 13.1   The bargaining process in trade negotiations for regional integration

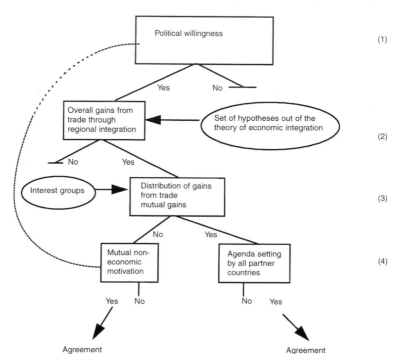

If mutual gains can be expected the agenda setting is the last decision to take in a fourth step. Without these mutual gains only a non-economic motivation will lead to an agreement.

The distribution of gains from trade is in the centre of the theoretical convergence/divergence discussion in the bargaining process for regional integration. Therefore this paper concentrates on step (3) in Figure 13.1, looking for theoretical evidence of either convergence or divergence among partner countries of regional integration.

The analysis of the distribution of the gains from trade is easiest done in a simple trade model (Figure 13.2). The starting point is the equilibrium E in isolation. As nation 1 specialises in the production of commodity A and moves down its production frontier, it incurs increasing opportunity costs in the production of A as is reflected in the increasing slope of its production frontier. For nation 2 the same effect will take place with commodity B. The process of specialisation in production continues until relative commodity prices become equal in the two nations.

Figure 13.2   Gains from trade in the traditional static model

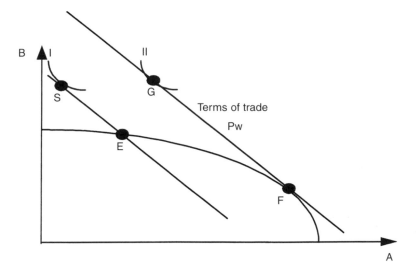

Source: Salvatore, 1995: 67.

The gains from trade can be broken down into two components: the gains from exchange and the gains from specialisation, which is shown for nation 1 in Figure 13.2. On the assumption that nation 1 could not specialise in the production of A with the opening of trade but continues to produce at point E, nation 1 could export commodity A and import commodity B at the prevailing relative world price of Pw, which leads to a consumption at point S on indifference curve I. The movement from point E to point S in consumption measures the *gains from exchange*. If subsequently nation 1 also specialises in the production of A and produces at point F, it could then trade and consume at point G on indifference curve II. The movement from S to G in consumption measures the *gains from specialisation* in production. The common price Pw (line G-F) defines the *terms of trade* between the two economies. They indicate the terms on which each economy can acquire imports from the other. In Figure 13.2, an increase in the relative price of commodity A, making GF steeper, would improve the terms of trade of nation 1 and worsen the terms of trade of nation 2. As the terms of trade determine the distribution of the gains from trade (Kenen, 1989: 28), the consumer in both nations would still gain from trade, but the consumer of nation 1 would gain more than the consumer of nation 2. This leads to the conclusion that the gains from trade are divided according to the relation of the terms of trade. Assuming a persistence of a negative terms of trade evolution for developing countries according to the Prebisch–Singer thesis and extending this thesis to all unequal economic environments, a bias of the gains from trade towards the more developed countries can be expected.

However, a statistical indicator – only appropriate to characterise comparative static situations – does not seem to be methodologically adequate to assess a dynamic development process. Another way to analyse the distribution of gains from trade is the more dynamically oriented cumulative causation model. The argumentation is mainly based on core-periphery models, which were developed to explain the economic transactions between the northern hemisphere as the core and the southern hemisphere as the periphery (Myrdal, 1957: Chapter 3). The mechanism of differences in size between economies and level of development can also be used within a region as well as within a country. These models suggest that within a region the growth-inducing trickle-down effects of trade are small compared with the negative 'backwash effects' for the less developed countries. The economically more developed countries will attract industry because of increasing returns to scale, the better availability of a trained workforce and the existence of necessary industrial services like finance, transport and lawyers (McCarthy, 1994: 9). As a consequence, labour-intensive craft industries in the less developed countries decline due to the inability to compete with cheap imported mass produced goods from economically more developed countries within the region. As an extension of Myrdal's thoughts Kaldor (1970) and Dixon and Thirlwall (1975) developed a formal model of cumulative causation which consists of four equations based on four assumptions:

1. The higher the returns to scale, the higher growth rates in productivity (p) leading to a higher growth rate of output (g)
   $p = f1\ (g)$, where $f1$ is rising and > 0.
2. The higher the productivity the lower the efficiency wages (we) (money wage index wm divided by a productivity index)
   $we = f2\ (p)$, where $f2$ is falling and < 0.
3. The higher the growth rate of output, the lower the efficiency wages
   $g = f3\ (we)$, where $f3$ is falling and < 0.
4. The money wages and their rate of increase will be similar in all countries $wm = W$.

If the four equations are put together (Figure 13.3) the cumulative causation becomes evident. Rising growth rates in output induce higher productivity which reduces efficiency wages, and in turn the fall in efficiency wages leads to a higher growth rate in output and so on.

The economically more developed countries at a starting point g_0 will benefit from higher output and productivity growth so that this cumulative causation model supports the argumentation that a regional integration between unequal partners tends to bias the distribution of gains towards the more advanced partner because the benefits vary according to the type of productive activity in which a region specialises.

Some sectors are more susceptible to productivity gains than others. In particular, the manufacturing sector is able to reap substantially greater benefits from growth than are land-based activities such as mining and agriculture. The consequence of this bias in the potential for exploiting the benefits from greater specialisation due to regional integration leads to

Figure 13.3   Gains from trade in the theoretical cumulative causation model for a more advanced country

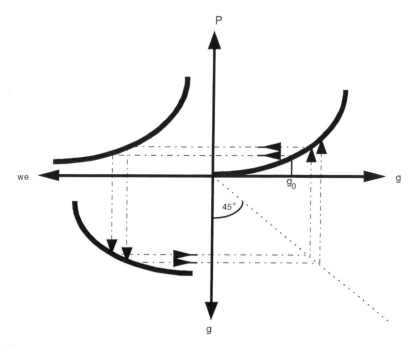

Source: Kaldor, 1970.

the prediction that countries specialising in land-based activities are likely to grow slower than those specialising in manufacturing activities.

Krugman and Venables (1995) deduce a similar cumulative causation process by analysing regional differentiation (core-periphery) driven by the interaction of scale economies and transport costs.

The Kaldor model leads to two main hypotheses: (a) the money wages and their rates of increase are approximately the same in all countries and (b) a region's rate of productivity growth is an increasing function of its rate of growth of output. A look at the AFTA, MERCOSUR or SADC rapidly indicates that there is no similar money wage in the respective regions, for example because of restrictions in labour mobility or different economic institutions in the countries. The hypotheses might be true in a *very* distant future but this is not the problem today and tomorrow. The remaining money wage gap between different countries involved in a regional integration will nevertheless aggravate the problems of (illegal) migration in the short run. The illegal inflow of labour to the more developed countries generates social and political pressure within the countries but also between them. The experiences of the border region between the United States and Mexico, where there is a worldwide unique situation of a 3000 km common border between an industrialized and a developing country, show that even with the extremely resource intensive US border patrol system, the illegal inflow of Mexicans cannot be stopped. This insight was one main reason for the wish of the US to establish a NAFTA. The integration in North America is leading to strong economic interdependence. The positive economic development of Mexico must therefore be in the interests of the US because the migration of Mexico's poor can only be effectively reduced by improving living conditions in Mexico itself (Proff, 1993: 280).

The second hypotheses is not that easy to reject. It is basically true for the developed countries in the EU. For the Asian economies there is an intensive debate around the future sustainability of the tremendous growth rates these countries have been experiencing for at least ten years. Kaldor assumed a high correlation between productivity growth and growth of output. A look at the contribution to growth for the high-growth countries Singapore, South Korea or Taiwan shows a different picture. In growth theory the GDP growth rate is explained by:

$$\Delta \, GDP = \Delta \, \text{Contribution} + \Delta \, \text{Labour Contribution} + \Delta \, \text{Total Factor Productivity}$$

Because of a strongly rising investment rate and labour-force participation rate the 'residual' total factor productivity accounts for only 10–15 per cent of growth in the three high-growth Asian countries (Behravesh, 1996: 11). So, in the case of these developing countries factor accumulation and not productivity progress is the explanation for growth, with the consequence that the second hypothesis of Kaldor is not relevant either.

Neither the traditional static model explaining the distribution of gains from trade according to the terms of trade nor the cumulative causation model of Myrdal and Kaldor are able to prove a bias in the distribution of gains from trade for regional integration among developing countries. This result contrasts on a first glance the results of Krugman and Venables (1995). Their model predicts a first stage of growing inequality (in real wages) due to falling transport cost leading to a core periphery situation. Assuming transportation cost keeps falling the lower wage rates in the periphery will offset the agglomeration advantages of the core in a second stage (Krugman and Venables, 1995: 861). This will lead to a reduction of the inequality. Transport costs in many developing countries are extremely high due to the poor infrastructure with the consequence that an uneven distribution of gains from trade might be expected. The impact of regional integration on infrastructure, however, is certainly positive. Infrastructure needs a critical mass like any public or semi-public good. Infrastructural improvements will reduce transaction costs, which are prohibitively high in many developing countries. Infrastructural improvements are very sensitive to regional integration if a multispeed approach through cooperation among different infrastructure providers is possible (cf. Odén 1996: 34). Looking at the restrictive assumptions of the Krugman and Venables model (such as no labour and capital mobility) it also becomes evident that this model is not able to prove an uneven distribution of gains from trade.

Summing up this theoretical consideration of the impact of regional integration on developing countries' mutual gains can be expected so that the bargaining process out of Figure 13.1 can be finished without a non-economic motivation. Furthermore it became evident that theoretical considerations do not indicate a clear convergence or divergence pattern explaining the results of comparative research of developing regions.

The next section will now examine inter- and intra-regional homogeneity and heterogeneity of developing regions. Due to the fact that the theoretical consideration focusing only on GDP terms could not give a satisfying result the empirical analysis will introduce more variables than only per capita income. This is in line with the aforementioned need for comparative research by the multinational enterprises which does not focus on GDP growth alone.

13.3   Interregional homogeneity and heterogeneity of developing regions

A trend towards convergence or divergence can be supported by testing the hypotheses of an intraregional heterogeneity and some interregional homogeneity of the most important new regional integrations (AFTA, MERCOSUR and SADC) with the help of a cluster analysis.

The objective of clustering is to minimise the within-group variance and maximise the between-group variance. The cases to be clustered are all 27 member countries of the three new important regional integrations. The variables used as criteria for clustering these countries were obtained from the analysis of the immediate business environment for multinational enterprises, namely those determinants of the sales, procurement and investment conditions that are affected by regional integration (cf. Proff and Proff, 1996). Multinational enterprises are looking for criteria to reduce the complexity of their environment to decide where to allocate their resources in the process of designing and implementing global strategies for the non-triad markets, so that there is a demand for comparative research which should be addressed with this cluster analysis.

Relevant determinants of the sales conditions used as variables are:

1   per capita income in US$ as a three-year average of the latest existing data for all 27 countries (mainly 1993–95);
2   annual growth in per capita income (predominantly 1996–2000);
3   income distribution shown by the latest available Gini coefficients, and
4   tariffs which can be seen by the post-Uruguay Round (WTO) applied rate.

In addition relevant determinants of the procurement conditions used as further variables are:

5   wages in US$ which are the latest available for 1991;
6   the state of education shown by an education index, and
7   infrastructure operationalised by electricity consumption per capita in 1994.

For the investment conditions only one relevant determinant is used as a last variable, namely:

8   the investment risk shown by the Institutional Investors Ranking 1995 (for sources and further explanation of the variables see the Appendix to this chapter).

In a first step of clustering a standardisation through z-transformation was necessary to ensure complementarity between data of different scales (cf. Backhaus *et al.*, 1996: 314), while in a second step the Euclidean distance process of minimum squared error was chosen as a distance measure, for it tends to produce more 'spherical' (and, hence, different but usually more interpretable) clusters than other algorithms (cf. Harrigan, 1985: 60). In a next step of the clustering process, Singapore was identified as an outlier with the single linkage technique (cf. Backhaus *et al.*, 1996: 315) and was eliminated from the analysis.

Then in the fourth step it came to the choice of a clustering algorithm. Usually the Ward technique is recommended, for it is the only technique that simultaneously finds a very good partition and signals the right number of clusters and was therefore also chosen in this analysis. According to a comparison of the sum of error squares a five-cluster solution seems to be suitable. The elbow-criteria (cf. Raffée *et al.*, 1994: 385–386; Backhaus *et al.*, 1996: 307) that chooses the cluster solution which characterises the sharp bend in the curve of the sum of error squares, is decisive. With the transition from five clusters to a four-cluster solution a significant increase in the sum of error squares can be seen. In addition a comparison of the explained variance of the two canonical discriminant functions within the discriminant analysis shows the highest result (95.5 per cent) for the five-cluster solution compared with all other solutions, for example the six-cluster solution (90.8 per cent).

When interpreting the clustering output, the hypothesis of intraregional heterogeneity and some interregional homogeneities can be confirmed. The five clusters can be characterised as:

1 'emerging markets', comprising all MERCOSUR members, Zimbabwe, Indonesia and Thailand;
2 'poor SADC', comprising all SADC member countries besides South Africa, Namibia and Zimbabwe;
3 'advanced SADC', comprising South Africa and Namibia;
4 'advanced AFTA', comprising Malaysia and Brunei as well as
5 'poor AFTA', comprising Vietnam, the Philippines, Cambodia, Laos and Myanmar.

Table 13.1 shows the five cluster-averages for all eight variables. Looking at Table 13.1 it becomes evident that Malaysia and Brunei forming cluster 4 ('advanced AFTA') are very attractive markets and production locations due to high market potential and growth, low tariffs, a high standard of education and good infrastructure. In spite of high wages they

Table 13.1   Five cluster averages for all eight variables

Variables	Clusters 1 'Emerging markets'	2 'Poor SADC'	3 'Advanced SADC'	4 'Advanced AFTA'	5 'Poor AFTA'
Per capita income (US$)	3.067	967	2.495	**6.772**	**493**
Annual growth in per capita income (%)	4.86	3.46	2.65	6.75	6.10
Income distribution (Gini coefficient)	50.31	46.97	52.65	43.65	36.92
Tariffs (%)	**31.03**	19.40	19.40	15.15	21.18
Wages (US$)	3.197	**1.423**	**8.685**	7.159	1.213
Education Index	0.82	0.60	0.68	0.79	0.67
Electricity consumption per capita (kw/h)	1.319	492	2.707	3.364	144
Institutional investors Ranking	43.40	25.40	45.20	**69.10**	**23.64**

Source: Own compilation based on clustering results.

have the highest average Institutional Investors Ranking of all clusters. The 'emerging markets' cluster (1) has a lower institutional investors ranking because especially in the MERCOSUR countries there is still a high inflation risk. Therefore production bases should be full-fledged with the greatest possible independence from the local environment or should be relinquished. The average per capita income in this cluster is lower than that in the two low populated 'advanced AFTA' countries Malaysia and Brunei. However, due to high purchasing power in a sufficiently extended upper class market segment as a consequence of the unequal income distribution (high Gini coefficient) and a high broad education, cluster 1 can be evaluated as quite attractive for multi-national companies. 'Advanced SADC' on the other hand has the problem of high wages and political uncertainty but good infrastructure, low tariffs but high purchasing power especially among the white population due to a very unequal income distribution. 'Poor SADC' and 'poor AFTA', the latter despite high GDP growth rates, have very bad environmental conditions. Especially 'poor AFTA' with the quite equal income distribution has no effective demand and the lowest Institutional Investors Ranking of all five clusters.

Concerning the 26 countries' relation, an interregional homogeneity can reversely be proved because member countries of all three integrations belong to cluster 1. This result can be seen as a support for the club convergence hypothesis of countries that are similar in their structural characteristics (cf. Galor, 1996: 1056). The clustering results also show intraregional homogeneity only between the MERCOSUR countries, that all belong to cluster 1, while AFTA and SADC members are in both cases split up in three clusters. This confirms the hypothesis of intraregional heterogeneities. The heterogeneity of AFTA would have been even higher if Singapore, which constitutes its own cluster, had not been eliminated from the analysis.

13.4   Outlook and policy recommendations

The traditional notion in the technical papers dealing with the convergence/divergence debate, that a backward economy will accumulate human capital and later knowledge capital more rapidly than a technologically advanced country, is a difficult assumption. Why should the technologically advanced country stop investing in human and knowledge capital? These questions indicate that it might be better not to continue focusing only on the statistical robustness of the convergence/ divergence finding than to the economic interpretability. Summing up, it became clear that it does not provide too many insights to compare aggregated geographical areas like 'Africa' or 'Asia' *en bloc*. Economic convergence may take place in a form of convergence clubs with members out of all developing regions. This increases interregional homogeneity which can be taken as indicative of a transition to multilateralism instead of an aggressive stabilisation of regional trading blocks.

Appendix: The variables of the cluster analysis

The variables of cluster analysis were operationalised as follows:
A.   Determinants of the sales conditions:

1   *Per capita income* in US$ as a three-year average of the latest existing data sets of all 27 countries to avoid deviations, for example according to exchange rate fluctuations (in most cases 1993–95, cf. World Bank, 1997: 214–5 and 222–3; Weltbank, 1996: 214–5; and Weltbank, 1995: 188–9) for Swaziland and Brunei only data for 1996 (cf. United Nations Development Programme, 1997: 158–60) was available. Although per capita income in US$ tends to underestimate the economic power compared to purchasing power parity, it is more important for multinational companies which usually calculate in US$.
2   *Annual growth in per capita income.* Data for some of the AFTA countries have been taken from the DRI/McGraw-Hill Asian automotive industry forecast report 1996–2000 (DRI/McGraw-Hill 1996a) and for Argentina and Brazil from

the world car industry forecast 1996–2000 (cf. DRI/McGraw-Hill 1996b). Because of a lack of data for the other AFTA and MERCOSUR countries, for Brunei, Vietnam, Cambodia, Laos and Myanmar the average of the other AFTA countries (6.1 per cent annual growth rate) was taken and for the other MERCOSUR countries the annual growth rate of Brazil (5.0 per cent), which was recommended by country experts. For SADC countries, growth forecasts for South Africa, Namibia, Botswana have been taken from the Centre for Proactive Marketing Research (1996) while for the other SADC countries only an average growth forecast for sub-Saharan Africa of 3.5 per cent was available.

3 *Income distribution* shown by the latest available Gini-coefficients (cf. World Bank, 1997: 222–3 and Deininger and Squire, 1996). For countries which are lacking data the average actual Gini coefficient for the respective region was used (cf. Deininger and Squire, 1996: 548).

4 *Tariffs* (post-Uruguay applied rate) taken from the statistics on tariff concessions in the Uruguay Round (cf. World Bank, 1996), because these tariffs will be compulsory after 1999. Some data are missing and had to be estimated as average tariff rates, that is for Paraguay the average tariffs of Latin America; for Brunei, Cambodia, Lao, Vietnam and Myanmar the average tariffs of East Asia and Pacific and for all SADC countries except South Africa the average tariffs of sub-Saharan Africa.

B   Determinants of the procurement conditions:

5 *Wages*, which are the last available for 1991 (cf. International Labour Office, 1996). The wages were taken as an average of different industries (ISIC 2 categories 2–9) and had to be converted in US$ with the help of International Monetary Fund (1997). The lack of wage data was supplemented for the SADC countries by multiplying the quotient of wages and per capita income for Zimbabwe and Malawi (which are both poor countries) with the per capita income of the countries for which the data are not available. For Brunei this quotient of Singapore (as a city state) was multiplied with its per capita income and for Vietnam, Laos and Cambodia this quotient of Myanmar and Indonesia was multiplied by each of the three countries' per capita income.

6 *State of education* operationalised by the education index (cf. UNDP, 1997: 146–8), as measured by a combination of adult literacy (two-thirds weight) and combined primary, secondary and tertiary enrolment ratios (one-third weight).

7 *Infrastructure* measured by electricity consumption per capita in 1994 (cf. UNDP, 1997: 196–7). The unavailable data for Botswana, Namibia, Lesotho, Swaziland and Cambodia were estimated by country experts.

C   Determinants of the investment conditions:

8 *Investment risk* shown by the Institutional Investors Ranking 1995 (cf. O.V., 1996). Unavailable data for Laos and Cambodia were supplemented by the index for Myanmar and the unavailable data for Brunei were supplemented by the index of Malaysia.

These eight variables have not been weighted to avoid distortion. However, an empirical investigation of the effects of environmental changes for multinational enterprises (cf. Proff, 1994) showed the outstanding importance of sales conditions for the assessment of the business environment followed by the procurement conditions. To correspond to the importance of these environmental conditions from the companies' perspective, four variables were chosen concerning the sales conditions, only three variables concerning the procurement conditions and just one variable concerning the investment climate.

Notes

1. For an overview of this debate see, for example, the controversy on the convergence and divergence of growth rates in the *Economic Journal* Vol. 106, 1996: 1016–69, (cf. Durlauf, 1996).
2. The expression 'non-triad' refers to markets outside the 'triad', that is, Europe, North America and Japan.

14
Productivity Growth and Convergence in Asian and African Agriculture

Kecuk Suhariyanto, Angela Lusigi and Colin Thirtle

14.1 Introduction

A number of studies have been done to compare economic performance in Asia and Africa. These include the works of Stein (1994) on
industrialisation, Chibber and Leechor (1995) on overall development
experience and Harrold *et al.* (1996) on trade and industrialisation.
Given the outstanding success in the economic growth of East and
South-East Asian countries such as Japan, Taiwan, South Korea, Hong
Kong, Singapore, Malaysia, Thailand and Indonesia, there has been a
widespread belief that Asia has achieved much better economic
development than Africa, and therefore Africa should try to learn from
Asia's experience. Most of the previous studies have focused extensively on the performance of aggregate economies. The question arises
as to whether Asia has also achieved better performance at the sectoral
level. This study fills this gap by comparing productivity in the
agricultural sector: first, measuring and comparing total factor
productivity (TFP) growth in Asian and African agriculture over the
last three decades; and secondly investigating the behaviour of
the agricultural productivity growth rate over time, focusing on the
question of convergence.

Cross-country comparisons of agricultural productivity in Asian
agriculture have been undertaken in a number of studies (see Hayami
and Ruttan, 1979; Yamada, 1987; Hayami and Kawagoe, 1987; Vyas and
James,1988). For African agriculture, such studies have been done by
Frisvold and Ingram (1995), Thirtle *et al.* (1995), Lusigi and Thirtle (1997),
Lusigi (1998) and Lusigi *et al.* (1998). Two important features appear from
surveying the literature.

First, compared to Africa, studies in Asian agriculture are quite limited in number. African agriculture has naturally received a great deal of attention in the literature since there is a conventional wisdom that Africa has been undergoing an agrarian crisis marked by falling food production per capita and rising imports of cereals (Jahnke *et al.*, 1987). This, however, has overshadowed the current state of Asian agriculture, which despite its apparent success due to the Green Revolution since the 1960s still experiences many problems. Some of the Asian countries whose economies depend heavily on agriculture are still considered as the poorest in the world. Chen *et al.* (1994) noted that in terms of numbers of people, the magnitude of poverty in South Asia far exceeds that of sub-Saharan Africa and Latin America combined (quoted in Quibria and Dowling, 1996). Furthermore, the increase in agricultural land area in many Asian countries has not kept pace with the growth of agricultural labour, which continues to rise at a higher speed because of the faster rate of population growth and lack of absorption of agricultural labour into the manufacturing and service sectors. As a result, the population pressure on agricultural land continues to increase in all Asian countries except Japan, South Korea, Mongolia and Malaysia. This may add to the already enormous problems of rural poverty and hunger, especially in South Asian countries.

Secondly, studies in Asian agriculture are out of date in terms of period studied and methodology used. They have applied either partial productivity or total factor productivity using index number approaches such as the Tornqvist index or traditional econometric approaches. The estimation is based on average practice production functions rather than the best practice technology, implying that the studies have applied methods which assume that producers are efficient, which might be unreasonable. In this case, the technical change growth rate is then identified as synonymous with productivity growth rate. In contrast, studies of African agriculture have measured agricultural productivity using recently developed methods which explicitly account for inefficiency. As a result, productivity change can be decomposed into two component measures: technical efficiency change and technical change.

The purpose of this study is to measure and compare total factor productivity (TFP) growth in Asian and African agriculture over the last three decades using a method which accounts for inefficiency. It is also intended to observe the behaviour of agricultural TFP growth rate over time, focusing on the question of whether convergence in agricultural TFP is occurring in Asian and African countries. The evidence of convergence indicates that the gap in agricultural TFP differences among countries tends to narrow and will vanish in the long run. Since most empirical studies on convergence have focused extensively on the convergence of aggregate economies, this paper may add to the few studies in the literature that have investigated the convergence process at the sectoral level. The remainder of this chapter is organised as follows. Section 14.2 briefly describes the method used to measure TFP and statistical test for convergence. Section 14.3 presents a description of sources and definitions of the data used. Section 14.4 contains empirical results, followed by a conclusion in the last section.

14.2   Methodology

14.2.1   The Malmquist productivity index

To measure agricultural TFP, the Malmquist productivity index is used in this study because of its desirable features, as listed in Fare *et al.* (1994b), Thirtle *et al.* (1995), Grifell-Tatje and Lovell (1996, 1997) and others. First, the index is non-parametric, therefore it does not require a specification of the functional form of the production technology. Secondly, it does not require an economic behaviour assumption of production units such as cost minimisation or revenue maximisation, which is useful if the objectives of producers differ or are unknown. Thirdly, the index does not require any data on prices. Fourthly, the index decomposes productivity change into two components, namely technical efficiency change and technical change. Since the economic behaviour of the production units in agriculture is uncertain, and since price information is unavailable, the choice of the Malmquist index for this study is well justified.

The basic idea of the Malmquist productivity index is to construct the *best practice* or the *frontier production function* and then measure the distance functions of each country in the sample from the frontier by applying a linear programming method known as data envelopment analysis (DEA). The production frontier, which is constructed from the data on inputs and outputs from all of the countries included in the sample, represents the maximum attainable level of output given a level of inputs, or the minimum level of inputs required to produce a given level of output. The frontier production function distinguishes the method fundamentally from the traditional econometric or index number approaches to productivity growth analysis. It should be noted, however, that the Malmquist productivity index assumes a deterministic production frontier and interprets every deviation from the frontier as inefficiency. Therefore, this approach does not account for noise in the data and does not allow statistical inference.

Following Fare *et al.* (1994a, b), the input-orientated Malmquist productivity index, *M*, for country *i* between period *t* and *t* + 1 is defined as

$$M_i^{t,t+1} = \left[\frac{D_i^t(y^t, x^t)}{D_i^{t+1}(y^{t+1}, x^{t+1})} \right] \left[\frac{D_i^{t+1}(y^{t+1}, x^{t+1})}{D_i^t(y^{t+1}, x^{t+1})} \frac{D_i^{t+1}(y^t, x^t)}{D_i^t(y^t, x^t)} \right]^{1/2} \quad (14.1)$$

where *D* denotes a distance function, *y* an output level and *x* an input level. This expression provides the decomposition of the Malmquist productivity index into its two components: technical efficiency change (catching-up) and technical change (innovation). The change in technical efficiency between period *t* and *t* + 1 is captured by the ratio in the first bracket, which measures the proximity of the observation to the best-practice isoquant. The ratio in the second bracket provides a measure of technical change between two periods. It represents the shift in the best-practice isoquant. The technical efficiency change (TEC) component is greater than, equal to, or less than unity according to whether technical efficiency improves, remains unchanged, or declines between periods *t* and *t* + 1. The technical change (TC) component is also greater than, equal to, or less than unity, according to whether the frontier is improving, stagnant or deteriorating. The improvement in the technical change component is considered to be evidence of innovation. The value of the Malmquist productivity index is also greater than, equal to, or less than unity. If the value of the index is greater than unity, it reveals improved productivity, and if the value is less than unity, a decrease in productivity occurs. Using this decomposition we will be able to identify which component drives productivity growth in Asian and African agriculture. For detailed explanations of the methodology and the calculation see Fare *et al.* (1994a, b) and Grosskopf (1993). In terms of rates of growth, Equation 14.1 can be written as

$$TFP(t) = TEC(t) + TC(t) + [TEC(T).TC(t)] \quad (14.2)$$

The value in the bracket, which is the cross-product of both rates of growth, is rather small for current rates of growth and may be neglected.

14.2.2 Test of convergence

In recent years there have been a number of studies using a time series approach for testing convergence, arguing that the cross-section approach has many weaknesses. Evans and Karras (1996), for instance, show that cross-section results are valid only under incredible assumptions; specifically, the economies must have identical first-order autoregressive dynamic structures and all permanent cross-economy differences must be completely controlled for. Using the time series approach, productivity is viewed as a non-stationary variable and convergence implies that productivity differences should vanish in the long run (Bernard and Durlauf, 1996). This study applies the time series approach for testing convergence in agricultural TFPs. It is assumed that countries are at different levels of technology and that the diffusion of technology from advanced to backward countries is the main driving force towards convergence.[1] The basic theoretical framework of the method is provided by Bernard and Jones (1996), which can be described as follows.

Let A_{ijt} represent TFP in country i, $i = 1,2, \ldots n$, sector j, at time t. It may vary across economies. At any one point in time t, one of the economies has the highest level of TFP than the others and let this most productive economy be termed as the frontier economy f. TFP is assumed to evolve according to

$$\ln A_{ijt} = \gamma_{ij} + \lambda \ln \left[\frac{A_{ijt-1}}{A_{ijt-1}} \right] + \ln A_{ijt-1} + \varepsilon_{ijt} \qquad (14.3)$$

where γ_{ij} is the asymptotic rate of growth of sector j in country i, the parameter λ characterises the speed of catch up, which is a function of the productivity differential in country i from that in country f, and ε_{ijt} is the error term. Equation 14.3 implies that TFP in sector j of each economy i may potentially grow either as a result of sector-specific growth rate or as a result of technology transfer from the frontier country. If country i is the most productive country, there is no technology transfer and Equation 14.3 becomes

$$\ln A_{ijt} = \gamma_{ij} + \ln A_{fjt-1} + \varepsilon_{fjt} \qquad (14.4)$$

Combining Equations 14.3 and 14.4, one obtains an equation for the evolution of relative TFP,

$$\ln \left[\frac{A_{fjt}}{A_f jt} \right] = (\gamma_{fj} - \gamma_{fj}) + (1 - \lambda) \ln \left[\frac{A_{fjt-1}}{A_{fjt-1}} \right] + \hat{\varepsilon}_{fjt} \qquad (14.5)$$

Equation 14.5 can be used to test for convergence in the time series. This equation can be estimated directly using the augmented Dickey–Fuller (ADF) test, with a drift. If there is no catching up ($\lambda = 0$), the difference between TFP in country i and that in country f will contain a unit root (non-stationary). This means that productivity levels will grow at different rates permanently and there is no evidence of convergence. In contrast, if $\lambda > 0$, the difference between the technology levels in the two countries will be stationary, indicating the evidence of convergence which implies that productivity differences between the two countries should vanish in the long run. The work of Levin and Lin (1993) develops a technique for testing for unit roots in panel data, which can be used to test for convergence in a panel. For a detailed explanation of the methodology and the calculation, see Evans and Karras (1996) and Bernard and Jones (1996).

14.3   Scope of the study and data sources

The analysis covers 18 Asian countries, over the period 1961–96 and 47 African countries over the period 1961–91. The menu of countries included in the analysis can be seen later in this chapter in Table 14.2. Agricultural TFP is measured using a one output, five input technology. The inputs are land, labour, livestock, fertiliser and machinery. The data of output is from the USDA Watiview database, while input data are from the FAO Agrostat database. The definitions of the variables used are as follows.

Aggregate agricultural output is the total value of agricultural production which is expressed in 1979–81 international dollars and includes food and non-food output (fibres, hides and skins, rubber and tobacco). Agricultural land is the total area of arable and permanent crop land, measured in 1000 ha. Agricultural labour is in thousands of economically active participants in agriculture. Livestock is the aggregate of the various kinds of animals in livestock units irrespective of their age and the place or purpose of their breeding. It includes cattle, sheep, goats, pigs, mules, horses, asses, buffaloes, camels, ducks, chicken and turkeys. The weights used for aggregation are those used by Hayami and Ruttan (1985: 450). Fertiliser is the sum of the Nitrogen (N), Potassium (P_2O_5) and Phosphate (K_2O) content of fertiliser used which is measured in thousands of metric tons in nutrient units. The machinery variable covers the total number of wheeled and crawler tractors (excluding garden tractors) used in agriculture.

14.4   Empirical results

14.4.1   Agricultural productivity growth

Agricultural TFP and its components are measured for each country and continent using the Malmquist productivity index, which is computed under the assumption of CRS, using the input-orientated approach, with one output and five inputs. One of the critical issues in measuring productivity using the DEA model is how many outputs and inputs should be included in the model. This is important since computed technical efficiencies appear to be dependent upon the dimensionality of the input/output space relative to the number of countries (Leibenstein and Maital, 1992). Given enough inputs, the dimensionality problem causes all or most of the countries to be efficient and furthermore, production technologies move back and forth, producing a large number of intersections, which makes the results difficult to interpret.

Preliminary results suggested that dimensionality was not a problem for the larger African sample, but affects the Asian results, since the number of countries in the sample is only 18, which is relatively low compared with the number of outputs and inputs used. To solve this problem, for the Asian countries the Malmquist productivity index is calculated with respect to the sequential frontier. That is, the frontier is constructed for each year on the basis of all observations from the first year up until the year considered (see Tulkens and van den Eeckaut, 1995; Grifell-Tatje and Lopez Sintas, 1995; Suhariyanto, 1999). In order to guarantee that the dimensionality problem does not exist at the beginning of the period of the study, estimation begins at 1965, using the pooled samples for the period 1961–65. This is not costly since it is reasonable to assume that the green revolution did not have much effect in most Asian countries until the later 1960s. It should be noted, however, that using the sequential frontier, technology knowledge is not lost and instead accumulates over time. In other words, the possibility of technological regress is excluded.

14.4.1.1 Asian agriculture

Agricultural productivity in Asian countries increased slightly over the 1965–96 period at an annual growth rate of 0.30 per cent, as Table 14.1 shows. During this period, positive technical change dominated the negative technical efficiency changes, giving a net increase in productivity.

Table 14.1 Annual growth rates of TFP, TEC and TC in Asia and Africa by period

Region	Period	TFP (%)	TEC (%)	TC (%)
Asia	1965–80	–0.70	–1.80	1.10
	1981–96	1.40	0.70	0.70
	1965–96	0.30	–0.65	0.95
Africa	1961–70	0.55	–0.29	0.84
	1971–80	–1.54	0.67	–2.21
	1981–91	1.77	–0.52	2.29
	1961–91	–0.86	0.10	–0.96

Note: The average growth rates are weighted by the country shares in total change.

The rate of change in technical efficiency was –0.65 per cent per annum, while technical progress had an average growth rate of 0.95 per cent per year. This means that the production frontier shifted inwards, while the gap between standard practice and best practice widened. Thus, innovation or technical change appears to be the source of agricultural productivity growth among Asian countries, suggesting that they have benefited modestly from the introduction of new agricultural technology.

This result is clearly shown in Figure 14.1, which illustrates the annual averages of the TFP, TEC and TC over time. If the sample period is split into two sub-periods, 1965–80 and 1981–96, the behaviour of productivity exhibits a different pattern. In the first sub-period, from 1965 to 1980, technical change grew at an annual rate of 1.10 per cent. In contrast, technical efficiency declined at an annual rate of 1.80 per cent. The sum of these two components causes TFP to decrease at annual rate of 0.70 per cent. In the next sub-period, from 1981–96, agricultural productivity increased at an average growth rate of 1.40 per cent per year due to both innovation and technical efficiency improvements, which each increased at an annual growth rate of 0.70 per cent.

The high rate of technical progress in the first period can be attributed to the green revolution varieties, but the decline in average efficiencies is also to be expected, as the diffusion of the green revolution varieties was uneven, both between poor and rich farmers and between countries. These results are also not surprising when we consider the economic situation and weather conditions in Asia during the 1970s, as reported by the Asian Development Bank, (1984). During this period, the Asian economies were shaken by a number of major external shocks. It began with the 1971 collapse of the fixed exchange rate system. Two years later, between 1973 and 1975, Asia experienced a food crisis because of drought and pest attacks, which led to harvest failure in many parts. During 1973–74, oil prices quadrupled, resulting in the inflation of fertiliser prices, which made the promotion of crop intensification more difficult. This was then followed by the 1975–76 recession. The 1970s closed with a further doubling of oil prices during 1979–80. As a result of this sequence of external shocks, demand for agricultural exports reduced and the more developed Asian countries resorted to increased agricultural protectionism.

Thus, although the rate of technical change in Asian countries slowed down from the first to the second sub-period, falling from 1.10 per cent to 0.70 per cent, the productivity gains were actually greater, as efficiency also improved. This would happen as the technologies, and the required inputs, spread to the less advantaged farmers and more backward regions and countries, although the ADB warned that the rates of adoption of

266

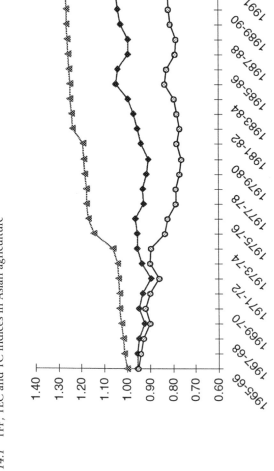

Figure 14.1 TFP, TEC and TC indices in Asian agriculture

high-yielding seed varieties and chemical fertilisers were slowing down (Vyas and James, 1988). Our results suggest that it was the rate of technical progress that slowed down during the 1981–96 period, while continued adoption improved efficiency levels.

Agricultural productivity growth for the individual Asian countries is reported in Table 14.2. The results show that only nine out of 18 Asian countries have positive productivity growth during the 1965–96 period. Four countries (China, Mongolia, Indonesia, Sri Lanka) have less than 1 per cent positive growth, two (Lao PDR and Philippines) are between 1 and 2 per cent and only three countries (Malaysia, South Korea and Japan) grow at more than 2 per cent per annum. The productivity growth in these three countries is totally attributable to innovation since their agricultural sectors are efficient for most of the period of study.

Using a translog total cost function, Kuroda (1997) also found that on average, 90 per cent of the TFP growth in Japanese agriculture is explained by the effect of technological change for the period 1960–90. For the other six countries with positive growth, the agricultural productivity increases are mainly due to improvement in innovation (technical progress). All of them, except Philippines, experienced falling technical efficiency. The other nine Asian countries have experienced declining productivity. They are North Korea, Cambodia, Myanmar, Thailand, Vietnam and all South Asian countries, except Sri Lanka. Technical efficiency in all these countries has declined and at the same time there is no significant technological progress, except in Cambodia. In general, these results are in agreement with the results from the previous studies. Using the Malmquist productivity index with respect to a contemporaneous frontier, Fulginiti and Perrin (1997, 1998) and Arnade (1998) found that on average, agricultural productivity seems to have declined in many developing countries. Using a different technique, Frisvold and Lomax (1991) also concluded that the developing countries experienced negative productivity growth be-tween 1970 and 1980, with the notable exception of the Philippines. Note, however, that in the previous studies the declines in productivity are mainly attributed to technological regression, since the method they used allows technological regression. This study suggests a different explanation, since the method used, which is a sequential frontier, excludes the possibility of technological decline. It can be concluded that agricultural productivity in Asian countries has declined because many countries have experienced a loss in technical efficiency and technological progress has not been sufficient to compensate.

Table 14.2   Annual growth rates of TFP, TEC and TC in Asian and African agriculture

Country	Africa (1961–91) TFP (%)	TEC (%)	TC (%)	Country	Asia* (1965–96) TFP (%)	TEC (%)	TC (%)
Burundi	0.54	−0.04	0.58				
Kenya	1.87	1.36	0.52	China	0.47	−0.41	0.88
Rwanda	1.45	0.70	0.75	Japan	2.70	0.00	2.70
Somalia	0.51	0.98	−0.48	Korea, DPR	−0.30	−0.70	0.40
Tanzania	0.50	0.92	−0.41	Korea, Rep.	3.30	0.00	3.30
Uganda	0.79	0.00	0.79	Mongolia	0.51	−0.31	0.82
East Africa	**0.96**	**0.71**	**0.25**	**East Asia**	**0.73**	**−0.51**	**1.23**
Algeria	0.77	−0.65	1.44				
Chad	−1.42	−0.12	−1.31	Cambodia	−1.86	−3.02	1.19
Egypt	−0.38	0.00	−0.38	Indonesia	0.17	−0.45	0.63
Ethiopia	−3.85	0.02	−3.86	Lao, PDR	1.75	−0.26	2.02
Libya	4.88	2.70	2.18	Malaysia	3.55	0.00	3.55
Mauritania	−4.93	−6.02	1.08	Myanmar	−0.02	−0.09	0.07
Morocco	0.52	−0.10	0.62	Philippines	1.33	0.07	1.26
Sudan	−0.08	−0.05	−0.03	Thailand	−1.00	−1.32	0.33
Tunisia	1.93	0.23	1.70	Vietnam	−0.18	−0.71	0.54
North Africa	**−0.57**	**−0.08**	**−0.49**	**S-E Asia**	**0.32**	**−0.43**	**0.74**
Cameroon	1.72	1.45	0.28	Bangladesh	−0.42	−0.77	0.35
Central African Rep.	1.92	2.77	−0.87	India	−0.50	−1.05	0.55
Congo	−1.46	−1.47	0.01	Nepal	−0.70	−0.89	0.20
Gabon	−1.58	−1.06	−0.51	Pakistan	−0.48	−1.29	0.82
Zaire	0.61	0.00	0.61	Sri Lanka	0.67	−0.62	1.29
Central Africa	**0.91**	**0.55**	**0.35**	**South Asia**	**−0.40**	**−0.98**	**0.58**
Benin	0.92	1.14	−0.22				
Burkina Faso	−0.83	1.22	−2.06				
Côte d'Ivoire	0.63	0.00	0.63				
Gambia	−2.12	−0.75	−1.38				
Ghana	−1.42	−0.22	−1.20				
Guinea	0.66	1.72	−1.08				
Guinea Bissau	−0.78	−0.90	0.13				
Liberia	−0.74	−0.43	−0.31				
Mali	0.84	1.00	−0.18				
Niger	−0.69	−0.65	−0.04				
Nigeria	−7.98	0.00	−7.98				
Senegal	−0.93	−0.16	−0.78				
Sierra Leone	0.62	−0.41	1.03				
Togo	−0.92	−1.70	0.78				
West Africa	**−4.04**	**0.07**	**−4.12**				
Angola	−2.57	−2.75	0.17				
Botswana	0.22	0.45	−0.23				

Table 14.2 (continued)

Country	Africa (1961–91) TFP (%)	TEC (%)	TC (%)	Country	Asia* (1965–96) TFP (%)	TEC (%)	TC (%)
Lesotho	–1.99	–2.34	0.34				
Madagascar	0.19	0.55	–0.37				
Malawi	0.20	–0.42	0.62				
Mauritius	0.51	0.00	0.51				
Mozambique	–0.16	–1.32	1.17				
Namibia	0.13	0.00	0.13				
Reunion	1.58	0.88	0.69				
South Africa	1.48	0.00	1.48				
Swaziland	3.25	1.65	1.61				
Zambia	0.82	–0.95	1.78				
Zimbabwe	1.10	0.73	0.36				
Southern Africa	**0.79**	**–0.16**	**0.95**				
AFRICA	**–0.86**	**0.10**	**–0.96**	**ASIA**	**0.30**	**–0.65**	**0.95**

* The data used is 1961–96. However, the Asian data for 1961–65 is pooled to ensure an adequate sample size at the beginning of the period of study.

14.4.1.2 African agriculture

In contrast with Asia, agricultural productivity in the African countries decreased at an annual rate of 0.86 per cent over the 1961–91 period, as Table 14.1 shows. Productivity decreased because there was no significant improvement in technical efficiency and at the same time, African agriculture has experienced technological regression at 0.96 per cent per year. Figure 14.2 illustrates the annual averages of the TFP, TEC and TC indices over time, showing that the behaviour of agricultural productivity has been fairly uneven with several breaks.

Different patterns appear when the period of study is broken down into three decades. In the first decade, 1961 to 1970, productivity increased slightly at an annual growth rate of 0.55 per cent due to technical progress, which was sufficient to outweigh the loss in technical efficiency over this period. In the next decade, 1971 to 1980, productivity decreased at an annual rate of 1.54 per cent. This was due to technical regress, which was greater than the improvement in technical efficiency. However, in the last decade African agriculture recovers. Agricultural productivity grew at an annual rate of 1.77 per cent, due to technological progress at the rate of 2.29 per cent, which was sufficient to outweigh the decrease in technical efficiency of 0.52 per cent. Technical progress, especially in East and Southern Africa, seems to coincide with the dissemination of maize

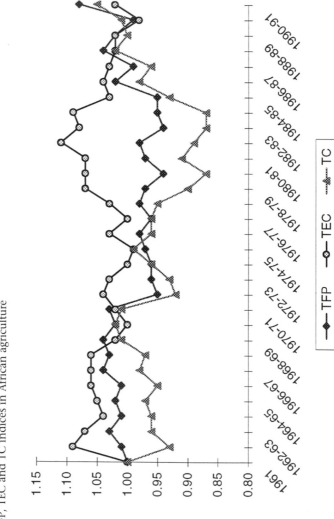

Figure 14.2 TFP, TEC and TC indices in African agriculture

technology developed by the international agencies in conjunction with the national agricultural research systems. This result shows that the pessimism in much of the literature about the African agricultural crisis does not appear to be well founded. However, the results support recent research that suggests African agriculture is recovering. Block (1994) measured agricultural productivity using wheat units, showed that after 15 years of stagnation, African agricultural productivity increased substantially during the mid 1980s, growing roughly at 2 per cent per year from 1983 to 1988 and 0.8 per cent per year between 1978 and 1988. The Malmquist index results reported by Thirtle *et al.* (1995) and Lusigi and Thirtle (1997) also found evidence of a recovery in the 1980s and the extent of the crisis was questioned in ODI-IDS (1995).

Agricultural productivity growth for the individual African countries is reported in Table 14.2. It appears that 19 of the 47 African countries experienced negative productivity growth during the 1961–91 period. Compare with Asian agriculture, the percentage of African countries with a negative growth rate is smaller. Of the 19 countries with negative productivity growth, five are North African, two are in Central Africa, nine in West Africa and three in Southern Africa. All of the East African countries have experienced positive growth in TFP, which is mainly due to increased technical efficiency, as well as technical progress. Note that two of the three Southern African countries having negative productivity growth are Angola and Mozambique, which have experienced civil wars, that disrupted the agricultural sectors by moving populations and making areas unsuitable for agriculture. The highest growth rates of productivity in Africa are found in Libya (4.88 per cent), followed by Swaziland (3.25 per cent) and Tunisia (1.93 per cent). Libya, starting from a relatively low level of productivity, appears as the most productive country because of improvements in both technical progress and technical efficiency. The greatest loss of productivity has been found in Nigeria, which is one of the most populous countries in Africa, followed by Mauritania and Ethiopia. Indeed, it is the heavy weight put on Nigeria that dominates the results for the continent and leads to the pessimism that has prevailed regarding Africa's prospects.

14.4.1.3 *Africa and Asia compared*

The results reported in Table 14.2 show that both continents are made up of sufficiently disparate countries and regions that the variations within Africa and Asia outweigh the similarities. Thus, we find that although the continent averages show that over the full period, Africa had negative TFP growth, while the Asian TFP shows modest growth, the regional groupings tell a more interesting story. The simple aggregates disguise the fact that East, Central and Southern Africa all had faster TFP growth than East Asia, which had the highest growth in Asia. Next in the ranking is South-East Asia, which is the last region with positive TFP growth, followed by South Asia, North Africa and finally West Africa, which all had negative growth. So, the Asian regions are bracketed by the African regions, which have the greatest successes and the greatest failures. In West Africa, 9 of the 14 countries had negative TFP growth, including Nigeria. Thus, it is West African agriculture that is in crisis and because of the size of the region, it dominates the results for the African continent.

14.4.2   Convergence in agricultural productivity

In order to test the convergence hypothesis in Asian and African agriculture, Equation 14.5 is estimated using the procedures outlined in Evans and Karras (1996) and Bernard and Jones (1996). To correct for possible serial correlation, a lag is included in the equation. Since the lag length usually increases with the sample size at the rate $T^{\frac{1}{3}}$, the lag used is between 0 and 3. The most appropriate lag length is then chosen according to the Schwarz information criterion. The results from using different lag lengths, however, are very similar. Table 14.3 reports the results from the panel unit root test, presenting the values of the estimated coefficients $(1 - \lambda)$ with their corresponding *t*-statistics. For Asian agriculture, the coefficient on the lagged agricultural TFP is 0.99925, which is very close to one. It indicates that the value of λ is very close to zero. The *t*-statistic fails to reject the null hypothesis of unit root. Therefore, the dispersion of productivity is non-stationary, providing strong evidence that these countries do not exhibit long-run convergence. It can be concluded that there is no evidence of convergence in agricultural TFP in the Asian countries during the last three decades. The poorer countries of Asia show no signs of catching up with the leaders.

In contrast, evidence of convergence is found in African agriculture. The null hypothesis of unit root is rejected since the coefficient of the lagged agricultural TFP is 0.49961, which is significantly less than one at the 5 per cent level. Thus, the less productive countries do appear to be

Table 14.3   Panel-based unit root tests

Continent	Variable	Coefficient	*t*-statistics
Asia	$(\gamma_{ij}-\gamma_{fj})$	–0.00962	–0.116
	$(1 - \lambda)$	0.99925	–0.394
Africa	$(\gamma_{ij}-\gamma_{fj})$	0.59601	20.99*
	$(1 - \lambda)$	0.49961	–3.87*

* indicates significance at the 5% level.

closing the gap, but this is not an entirely positive outcome. It is caused as much by the agricultural failure of some of the richer countries, such as Nigeria, as it is by the relative success of many of the Eastern, Central and Southern countries.

14.5   Conclusion

This study measures and compares agricultural TFP in Asian and African agriculture over the last three decades using the Malmquist productivity index. The index is computed using input orientation and a one output–five input technology, under the assumption of constant returns to scale. The issue of convergence in agricultural TFP is also investigated. The important findings here are as follows. First, Asian agriculture does not uniformly perform better than African, despite its apparent success due to the Green Revolution, which began in the 1960s. Agricultural productivity has declined in 9 of the 18 Asian countries, mainly due to a loss in technical efficiency and stagnation in technological progress. In Africa, 19 of the 47 countries have also experienced a decline in productivity, mainly due to technological regression.

The regional results show that East, Central and Southern Africa have had faster productivity growth than any of the Asian regions, while North and West Africa have had negative growth. This suggests that Asian agriculture still faces as many problems as African agriculture, high-lighting the need to intensify research, since the rate of technical change in Asian agriculture has slowed down. The evidence of declining productivity for so many countries also suggests that agricultural output growth in the two regions has been driven by input growth rather than improved productivity.

Also, African agriculture has shown a marked recovery since 1980, indicating that the future is not as bleak as has often been predicted. Finally, there is evidence of convergence of productivity in African agriculture, but not in Asian agriculture. Thus, there is no evidence that productivity differences among Asian countries are decreasing.

Notes

1. Some economists such as Hansson and Henrekson (1994) and Targetti and Foti (1997) prefer to use the term 'catching up' instead of 'convergence'. They used the latter to refer to a model, which assumes that all countries have the same knowledge of technology. Here, the term convergence is used since most of the literature does not distinguish between the two terms.

Bibliography

Agenor, P. and M.S. Khan (1996), 'Foreign currency deposits and the demand for money in developing countries', *Journal of Development Economics*, 50, 101–18.

Aghevli, B.B., M.S., Khan, P.R. Narvekar *et al.*, (1979), 'Monetary policy in selected Asian countries', *IMF Staff Papers*, 26, 775–824.

Ahmad, E., J. Dreze, J. Hills and A.K.S. Sen (eds.) (1991), *Social Security Systems in Developing Countries*, Oxford: Clarendon Press.

Ahmed, A. (1997), *The Macroeconomic Impact of Foreign Aid to Developing Countries*, unpublished PhD thesis, Geelong: Deakin University.

Ahuja, V., B. Bidani, F. Ferreira and M. Walton (1997), *Everybody's Miracle? Revisiting Poverty and Inequality in East Asia*, Washington DC: World Bank.

Akita, T. and R. A. Lukman (1995), 'Inter-regional inequalities in Indonesia: a sectoral decomposition analysis for 1975–92', *Bulletin of Indonesian Economic Studies*, 31(2), 61–82.

Akiyama, T. and D. Larson (1989), 'Recent trends and prospects for agricultural commodity exports in Sub-Saharan Africa', World Bank, *Policy Planning and Research Working Paper, International Commodity Markets*.

Akiyama, T. and D. Larson (1993), 'Adding up problem: strategies for primary commodity exports in Sub-Saharan Africa', World Bank (unpublished manuscript).

Alesina, A. and D. Rodrik (1994), 'Distributive politics and economic growth', *Quarterly Journal of Economics*, 109, 465–85.

Alexander, W.E., T.J.T. Balino and C. Enoch (1995), *The Adoption of Indirect Instruments of Monetary Policy*, Washington DC: International Monetary Fund.

Amsden, A. (1989), *Asia's Next Giant: South Korea and Late Industrialization*, New York: Oxford University Press.

Amsden, A. (1994), 'Why isn't the whole world experimenting with the East Asian model to develop? Review of the East Asian miracle', *World Development*, 22(4), 627–34.

Amsden, A. (1995), 'Like the rest, South-East Asia's "late" industrialization', *Journal of International Development'*, 7(5), 791–9.

Arize, A.C. (1994), 'A re-examination of money demand in small developing economies', *Applied Economics*, 26, 217–28.

Armstrong, H.W. and R. Read (1994), 'Micro-states, autonomous regions and the European Union', *European Urban and Regional Studies*, 1(1), 71–8.

Armstrong, H.W. and R. Read (1995), 'Western European Micro-States and EU autonomous regions: the advantages of size and sovereignty', *World Development*, 23(8), 1229–45.

Armstrong, H.W. and R. Read (1998a), 'Trade and growth in small states: the impact of global trade liberalisation', *World Economy*, 21(7), 563–85.

Armstrong, H.W. and R. Read (1998b), 'The phantom of liberty?: Economic growth and the vulnerability of micro-states', *mimeo*.

Armstrong, H.W. and R. Read (1999), 'Comparing the economic performance of dependent territories and sovereign micro-states', *Economic Development and Cultural Change*, 48(2), 285–306.

Armstrong, H.W., G. Johnes, J. Johnes and A.I. MacBean (1993), 'The role of transport costs as a determinant of price level variations between the Isle of Man and the United Kingdom', *World Development*, 21(2), 311–8.

Armstrong, H.W., R.J. de Kervenoael, X. Li and R. Read (1996), *The Economic Performance of Micro-States: Report for the UK Overseas Development Administration*, London: Overseas Development Administration.

Armstrong, H.W., R.J. de Kervenoael, X. Li and R. Read (1998), 'A comparison of the economic performance of different micro-states and between micro-states and larger countries', *World Development*, 26(4), 639–56.

Arnade, C. (1998), 'Using a programming approach to measure international agricultural efficiency and productivity', *Journal of Agricultural Economics*, 49(1), 67–84.

Arrau, P., J.D. Gregorio, C.M. Reinhart and P. Wickman (1995), 'The demand for money in developing countries: assessing the role of financial innovations', *Journal of Development Economics*, 46(2), 317–40.

Aryeetey, E. and Oduro, A. (1996), 'Regional integration efforts in Africa: an overview', in J. Teunissen (ed.), *Regionalism and the Global Economy, the Case of Africa*, The Hague Forum on Debt and Development, 11–49.

Ashagrie, K., (1998), *Statistics on Working Children and Hazardous Child Labour in Brief, Mimeo*, International Labour Office, Geneva.

Asian Development Bank (1984), 'Agriculture in Asia: its performance and prospects, the role of ADB in its development', *Staff Working Paper*, Manila.

Bac, M. and Raff, H. (1997), 'A theory of trade concessions', *Journal of International Economics*, 42, 483–504.

Backhaus, K., B., Erichson, W. Plinke, R. Weiber (1996), *Multivariate Analysemethoden, Eine anwendungsorientierte Einführung*. 8. verb. Aufl. Berlin u.a.

Bahmani-Oskooee, M. and M. Pourheydarian (1990), 'Effects of exchange rate sensitivity of demand for money in an open economy: the United Kingdom', *Applied Economics*, 22: 917–25.

Baldwin, R. (1997), 'The causes of regionalism', *World Economy*, 20(7), 865–88.

Barnett, W.A. (1997), 'Which road leads to stable money demand?', *Economic Journal*, 107(443), 1171–85.

Barro, R.J. (1991), 'Economic growth across a cross-section of countries', *Quarterly Journal of Economics*, 196, 407–33.

Barro, R. J. (1997), *Determinants of Economic Growth: A Cross-country Empirical Study*, Cambridge/London: MIT Press.

Barro, R.J. and X. Sala-i-Martin (1992), 'Convergence', *Journal of Political Economy*, 100(2), 223–51.

Barro, R.J. and X. Sala-i-Martin (1991), 'Convergence across states and regions', *Brookings Institute Papers*, 1, 107–82.

Bartlett, C.A. and S. Ghoshal (1989), *Managing Across Borders* Boston, MA: Harvard Business School Press.

Basu, K. (1999), 'Child labor: cause, consequence and cure, with remarks on international labor standards', *Journal of Economic Literature*, 37(3), 1083–119.

Becker, G.S. (1983), 'A theory of competition among pressure groups for political influence', *Quarterly Journal of Economics*, 98(3), 371–400.

Behravesh, N. (1996), 'Asia: can the miracle be sustained?', *DRI – World Markets Executive Overview*, New York: McGraw-Hill, 7–14.

Belshaw, D., P. Lawrence and M. Hubbard (1999), 'Agricultural tradables and economic recovery in Uganda: the limitations of structural adjustment in practice', *World Development*, 27(4), 673–90.

Bennell, P. (1998), 'Fighting for survival: manufacturing industry and adjustment in sub-Saharan Africa', *Journal of International Development*, 10(5), 621–37.

Bernard, M. (1994), 'The pattern and implications of trans-national production in Eastern Asia', *East Asia Policy Papers no. 2*, Toronto: York University, Joint Centre for Asia–Pacific Studies.

Bernard, M. (1996a), 'States, social forces, and regions in historical time: toward a critical political economy of Eastern Asia', *Third World Quarterly*, 17(4), 649–65.

Bernard, M. (1996b), 'Regions in the global political economy: beyond the local-global divide in the formation of the Eastern Asian region', *New Political Economy*, 1(3), 335–53.

Bernard, A.B. and S.N. Durlauf (1996), 'Interpreting tests of the convergence hypothesis', *Journal of Econometrics*, 71, 161–73.

Bernard, A.B. and C.I. Jones (1996), 'Productivity across industries and countries: time series theory and evidence', *Review of Economics and Statistics*, 78, 135–46.

Bernard, M. and J. Ravenhill (1995), 'Beyond product cycles and flying geese: regionalisation, hierarchy and industrialisation in East Asia', *World Politics*, 47(2), 171–209.

Berry, A. (1978), 'A positive interpretation of the expansion of urban services in Latin America, with some Columbian evidence', *Journal of Development Studies*, 14(2), 210–31.

Bhaduri, A.A., Mukherji and R. Sengupta (1982), 'Problems of long term growth in small economies: a theoretical analysis', in B. Jalan (ed.), *Problems and Policies in Small Economies*, London: Croom Helm, 49–68.

Bhagwati, J. (1993), 'Regionalism and multilateralism: an overview', in J. De Melo and A. Panagariya (eds.), *New Dimensions in Regional Integration*, Cambridge: Cambridge University Press, 22–50.

Bhagwati, J. and Krueger, A. (1995), *The Dangerous Drift to Preferential Trade Agreements*, Washington DC: American Enterprise Institute.

Bhalotra, S.R. (1999), 'Is Child Work Necessary?', *mimeo*, University of Bristol.

Bhalotra, S.R. and C.J. Heady (1999), '*Working for the Family: an Investigation of Child Labour on Household Farms in Rural Ghana and Pakistan*', *mimeo*, University of Cambridge.

Binh, T. and M. McGillivray (1993), 'Foreign aid, taxes and public investment: a comment', *Journal of Development Economics*, 41, 173–176.

Binswanger, H. (1989), 'The policy response of agriculture', *Proceedings of the World Bank Annual Conference on Development Economics*. Supplement to the *World Bank Economic Review* and the *World Bank Research Observer*, Washington DC.

Birdsall, N., D. Ross and R. Sabot (1995), 'Inequality and growth reconsidered: lessons from East Asia', *World Bank Economic Review*, 9(3), 477–508.

Blinder, A.S. (1998), *Central Banking in Theory and Practice*, Cambridge, MA: Massachusetts Institute of Technology.

Block, S.A. (1994), 'A new view of agricultural productivity in sub- Saharan Africa', *American Journal of Agricultural Economics*, 76, 619–24.

Bonnet, M. (1993), 'Child Labour in Africa', *International Labour Review*, 132(3), 371–89.

Booth, A. (1980), 'The economic impact of export taxes in ASEAN', *Malayan Economic Review*, 25(1), 36–61.

Booth, A. (1992), 'Income distribution and poverty' in A. Booth (ed.), *The Oil Boom and After: Indonesian Economic Policy and Performance in the Soeharto Era*, Kuala Lumpur: Oxford University Press.

Booth, A. (1996), 'Intergovernmental relations and fiscal policy in Indonesia', in C. Fletcher (ed.), *Equity and Development Across Nations*, St Leonards: Allen and Unwin.

Booth, A. (1997), 'Rapid economic growth and poverty decline a comparison of Indonesia and Thailand, 1981–1990', *Journal of International Development*, 9(2), 169–87.

Booth, A. (1998), 'Rural development, income distribution and poverty decline in South East Asia', Paper prepared for the African Economic Research Consortium, Nairobi.

Booth, A. (1999), 'Initial conditions and miraculous growth: why is South East Asia different from Taiwan and South Korea?', *World Development*, 27(2), 301–21.

Bowles, P. (1997), 'ASEAN, NAFTA and the "new regionalism"', *Pacific Affairs*, 70, 219–33.

Bowles, P. and MacLean, B. (1996), 'Regional trading blocs: will East Asia be next?', *Cambridge Journal of Economics*, 20(3), 393–412.

Breusch, T. (1978), 'Testing for autocorrelation in dynamic linear models', *Australian Economic Papers*, 17, 334–55.

Briguglio, L. (1995), 'Small island developing states and their economic vulnerabilities', *World Development*, 23(11), 1615–32.

Briguglio, L. (1998), 'Towards the construction of an economic vulnerability index: recent literature with special reference to small island developing states', paper presented at the ESRC IESG Study Group Small States in the International Economy Conference, University of Birmingham, 16 and 17 April, mimeo.

Bühner, R. (1993), *Strategie und Organisation, Analyse und Planung der Unternehmensdiversifikation mit Fallbeispielen*. 2.Ed. Wiesbaden.

Bune, P. (1987), 'Vulnerability', *EC-ACP Courier*, 4, 85–7.

Butcher, K. and A. Case (1994), 'The effect of sibling sex composition on women's education and earnings', *Quarterly Journal of Economics*, 109(3), 531–63.

Cammack, P., (1999), 'Interpreting ASEM: interregionalism and the new materialism', *Journal of the Asia Pacific Economy*, 4(1), 13–32.

Cammack, P. (1999), 'Interpreting ASEM, inter-regionalism and the new materialism', *Journal of the Asia Pacific Economy*, 4(1), 13–32.

Canagarajah, S. and H. Coulombe (1998), Child Labor and Schooling in Ghana, *mimeo*, World Bank.

Carl, V. (1989), *Problemfelder des Internationalen Managements*, Munich, Barbara Kirsch.

Cassen, R. (1976), 'Population and development: a survey', *World Development*, 4(10/11), 785–830.

Castells, M. (1992), 'Four Asian tigers with a dragon head, a comparative analysis of the state, economy, and society in the Asian Pacific rim', in R.P. Aelbaum and J. Henderson (eds.), *States and Development in the Asian Pacific Rim*, London: Sage, 33–70.

Central Bank and the Philippines (various years), *Statistical Bulletin*, Manilla: Government of the Philippines.

Central Bureau of Statistics (1987), *Sensus Pertanian 1983*, Seri I, Sampel Pendapatan Petani, Jakarta: Central Bureau of Statistics.

Central Bureau of Statistics (1994), *Penduduk Miskin dan Desa Tertinggal 1993*, Metodologi dan Analisis, Jakarta: Central Bureau of Statistics.

Central Bureau of Statistics (1995), *Sensus Pertanian 1993*, Seri D1, Pendapatan Rumahtangga Pertanian dan Indikator Sosial Ekonomi, Jakarta: Central Bureau of Statistics.

Central Bureau of Statistics (1996), *Sistem Neraca Sosial Ekonomi Indonesia 1993*, Jakarta: Central Bureau of Statistics.

Centre for Proactive Marketing Research (ed.) (1996), *Trends in the Southern African Vehicle Market*, Area A. Bryanston.

Chen, S., G. Dutt and M. Ravallion (1994), 'Is poverty increasing in the developing world?', *Review of Income and Wealth*, 40(4), 359–76.

Cheung, P. and Vasoo, S. (1992), 'Ageing population in Singapore: a case study', in Phillips (ed.) 1992.

Chhibber, A. and C. Leechor (1995), 'From Adjustment to growth in Sub-Saharan Africa: the lessons from the East Asian experience applied to Ghana', *Journal of African Economies*, 4(1), 83–114.

Chiu, S. and Lui, T.-L. (1998), 'The role of the state in economic development', in G. Thompson (ed.) *Economic Dynamism in the Asia-Pacific*, London: Routledge, 137–61.

Choi, Sung-Jae (1992), 'Ageing and social welfare in South Korea', in Phillips (ed.) 1992.

Cohen, B. (1998), 'The emerging fertility transition in Sub-Saharan Africa', *World Development*, 26(8), 1431–1461.

Cole D.C. and B.F. Slade (1997), 'Speeding Up by Slowing Down: a market-building approach to financial sector reform', in Wallace, L (ed.), *Deepening Structural reform in Africa; Lessons from East Asia*, Washington: International Monetary Fund.

Coleman, J.S. (1990), *Foundations of Social Theory*, London: Belknap Press.

Collier, P. and Gunning, J.W. (1995), 'Trade policy and regional integration: implications for the relations between Europe and Africa', *World Economy*, 18(3), 387–410.

Commander, S. (ed.) (1989), *Structural Adjustment and Agriculture: Theory and Practice in Africa and Latin America*, London: Heinemann.

Commonwealth Secretariat (1996), *Small States: Economic Review and Statistics*, Annual Series, 2, London: Commonwealth Secretariat.

Commonwealth Secretariat (1998), *A Study on the Vulnerability of Developing and Island States: A Composite Index*, Final Report, presented at the Islands and Small States Conference, Wilton Park, 26–28 February, mimeo.

Connolly, M.B. and D. Taylor, (1979), 'Exchange rate changes and neutralization: a test of the monetary approach applied to developed and developing countries', *Economica*, 46(183), 281–94.

Cook, P. and C. Kirkpatrick (1997), 'Globalisation, regionalisation and third world development', *Regional Studies* 31(1), 55–66.

Corden, W. (1996), 'Regionalism in world trade', in I. Elbadawi (1997), 'The impact of regional trade and monetary schemes on intra-Sub Saharan Africa Trade', in A. Oyejide and I. Elbadawi (eds.), *Regional Integration and Trade Liberalization in Sub-Saharan Africa, Framework, Issues and Methodological Perspectives*, London: Macmillan, 210–55.

Corden, W.M. and P. Neary (1982), 'Booming sectors and deindustrialisation in small open economies', *Economic Journal*, 92(368), 825–48.

Cornia, G.A., R. Jolly and F. Stewart (eds.) (1987), *Adjustment with a Human Face, Protecting the Poor and the Vulnerable and Promoting Growth*. Oxford: Oxford University Press.

Cuddington, J.T. (1987), 'Macroeconomic Determinants of Capital Flight: An Econometric Investigation, in Lessared D.R. and J. Williamson (eds) *Capital Flight and Third World Debt*. Washington DC: Institute for International Economics.

Cutler, D.M., J.M. Porteba, L.M. Sheiner and L.H. Summers (1990), 'An ageing society, opportunity or challenge', *Brooking Papers on Economic Activity*, 1, 1–74.

Das Gupta, M. (1987), 'Selective discrimination against female children in rural Punjab, India', *Population and Development Review*, 13(1), 77–100.

Davidson, R. and J. MacKinnon (1993), *Estimation and Inference in Econometrics*, New York: McGrawHill.

De Janvry, A. (1986), 'Integration of agriculture in the national and world economy: implications for agricultural policies in developing countries', *Agriculture in a Turbulent World Economy*, Proceedings of the Nineteenth International Conference of Agricultural Economists, Aldershot: Gower.

De Janvry, A. (1994), 'Structural adjustment and agriculture: African and Asian experiences', *FAO Economic and Social Development Paper*, Roe.

Deininger, K. and L. Squire (1996), 'A new data set measuring income inequality', *World Bank Economic Review*, 10(3), 565–91.

Dekle, R. and M. Pradhan (1997), 'Financial liberalisation and money demand in ASEAN countries: implications for monetary policy', *IMF Working Paper*, WP/97/36.

Demas, W.G. (1965), *The Economics of Development in Small Countries, with Special Reference to the Caribbean*, Montreal: McGill University Press.

De Melo, J. and A. Panagariya (1993), *New Dimensions in Regional Integration*, Cambridge: Cambridge University Press.

Department of the Interior (1996), *Report on the State of the Islands*, Washington DC: US Government.

Devos, S. (1985), 'An old-age security incentive for children in the Philippines and Taiwan', *Economic Development and Cultural Change*, 33(4), 793–814.

Diabré, Z. (1997), 'World Bank and IMF-supported programmes: a Burkina Faso perspective' in L. Wallace *Deepening Structural Reform in Africa: Lessons from East Asia*, Washington: IMF.

Dixon, R.J. and A.P. Thirlwall (1975), 'A model of regional growth rate differentials along Kaldorian lines', *Oxford Economic Papers*, 27, 201–14.

Djuhari Wirakartakusuma, M. (1993), 'Demographic transition in Indonesia and its implications in the 21st century', *Proceedings of the International Population Conference* 2, 259–77, Montreal: International Union for the Scientific Study of Population.

Dohner, R. and S. Haggard (1994), *The Political Feasibility of Adjustment in the Philippines*, Paris, OECD Development Centre.

DRI/McGraw-Hill (ed.) (1996a), *Asian Automotive Industry Forecast Report*, Autumn 1996, Lexington, MA.

DRI/McGraw-Hill (ed.) (1996b), *World Car Industry Industry Forecast Report*, November 1996, Lexington, MA.

Durlauf, S.N. (1996), Controversy on the convergence and divergence of growth rates – an introduction, *Economic Journal*, 106(3), 1016–18.

Durlauf, S.N. and D.T. Quah (1998), 'The new empirics of economic growth', *Centre for Economic Performance Discussion Paper*, no. 384.

Edwards, S. (1986), 'The pricing of bonds and bank loans in international markets: an empirical analysis of developing countries' foreign borrowing' *European Economic Review*, 30, 565–89.

Eijffinger, S.C.W. (ed.) (1997), *Independent Central Banks and Economic Performance*, Cheltenham: Edward Elgar.

Ekpenyong, S., O.Y. Oyeneye and M. Peil (1986), *Reports on Study of Elderly Nigerians*, Centre for West African Studies, University of Birmingham.

Ellis, M.A., (1996), 'External debt and fiscal adjustment in anti- inflation programs', *Journal of Macroeconomics*, 18(4), 727–33.

Engelmann, F.C. and Walz, U. (1995), Industrial centers and regional growth in the presence of local inputs, *Journal of Regional Science*, 35(1), 3–27.

Entwise, B. and C.R. Winegarden (1984), 'Fertility and pension programs in IDCs, a model of mutual reinforcement', *Economic Development and Cultural Change*, 32(2).

Evans, P. (1995), *Embedded Autonomy, States and Industrial Transformation*, Princeton NJ, Princeton University Press.

Evans, P. and G. Karras (1996), 'Convergence revisited', *Journal of Monetary Economics*, 37, 249–65.

Fair, R.C. (1970), 'The estimation of simultaneous equation models with lagged endogenous variables and first order serially correlated errors', *Econometrica*, 38, 507–16.

FAO (1990), *Agrostat Database*, FAO, Rome.

Fare, R., S. Grosskopf and C.A.K. Lovell (1994a), *Production Frontiers*, Cambridge: Cambridge University Press.

Fare, R., S. Grosskopf, M. Abrris, and Z. Zhang (1994b) 'Productivity growth, technical progress, and efficiency change in industrialised countries', *American Economic Review*, 84(1), 66–83.

Fei, J.C.H., G. Ranis and S.W.Y. Kuo (1979), *Growth with Equity: The Taiwan Case*, New York: Oxford University Press.

Ferderer, J.P., (1996), 'Oil price volatility and the macroeconomy', *Journal of Macroeconomics*, 18(1), 1–26.

Fernandez, R. (1997), 'Returns to regionalism: an evaluation of nontraditional gains from regional Trade arrangements', *World Bank Policy Research Paper No. 1816*, Washington DC: World Bank.

Fine, J. and Yeo, S. (1997), 'Regional integration in sub-Saharan Africa: dead end or a fresh start?', in A. Oyejide and I. Elbadawi (eds.), *Regional Integration and Trade Liberalization in Sub-Saharan Africa: Framework, Issues and Methodological Perspectives*, London: Macmillan, 428–74.

Fischer, S. (1996), 'Central banking: the challenges ahead maintaining price stability', *Finance and Development*, 34–7.

Folkers-Landau, D. and T. Ito (1995), *International Capital Markets: Developments, Prospects, and Policy Issues*, Washington DC: World Economic and Financial Surveys, International Monetary Fund.

Forder, J. (1998), 'Central bank independence – conceptual clarifications and interim assessment', *Oxford Economic Papers*, 50(3), 307–34.

Foroutan, F. (1993), 'Regional integration in Sub-Saharan Africa: past experience and future prospects', in J. De Melo and A. Panagariya (eds.), *New Dimensions in Regional Integration*, Cambridge: Cambridge University Press, 234–77.

Franco-Rodriguez, S., M. McGillivray and O. Morrissey (1998), 'Aid and the public sector in Pakistan: evidence with endogenous aid', *World Development*, 26(7), 1241–50.

Frey, B. and R. Eichenberger (1994), 'The political economy of stabilization programmes in developing countries', *European Journal of Political Economy*, 10(1), 169–90.

Frisvold, G. and K. Ingram (1995), 'Sources of agricultural productivity growth and stagnation in Sub-Saharan Africa', *Agricultural Economics*, 13, 51–61.

Frisvold, G.B. and E. Lomax (1991), 'Differences in agricultural research and productivity among 26 countries', *Agricultural Economic Report No. 644*, United States Department of Agriculture.

Fry, M.J., (1995), *Money, Interest and Banking in Economic Development*, Baltimore and London: The Johns Hopkins University Press.

Fry, M.J. (1998), 'Assessing central bank independence in developing countries: do actions speak louder than words?', *Oxford Economic Papers*, 50, 512–29.

Fry, M.J., CA.E. Goodhart and A. Almeida. (1996), *Central Banking in Developing Countries: Objectives, Activities and Independence*, London: Routledge.

Fulginiti, L.E. and R.K. Perrin (1997), 'LDC agriculture: non- parametric Malmquist productivity index', *Journal of Development Economics*, 53, 373–90.

Fulginiti, L.E. and R.K. Perrin (1998), 'Agricultural productivity in developing countries', *Agricultural Economics*, 19, 45–51.

Furnivall, J.S. (1943), *Educational Progress in Southeast Asia*, New York: Institute of Pacific Relations.

Galor, O. (1996), 'Convergence? Inferences from Theoretical Models', *Economic Journal*, 106, 1056–69.

Gang, I.N. and H.A. Khan (1991), 'Foreign aid, taxes and public investment', *Journal of Development Economics*, 24, 355–69.

Gangopadhyay, P. (1998), 'Patterns of trade, investment and migration in the Asia-Pacific region', in G. Thompson (ed.), *Economic Dynamism in the Asia-Pacific*, London, Routledge, 20–54.

Garnaut, R. and Drysdale, P. (eds.) (1994), *Asia Pacific Regionalism: Readings in International Economic Relations*, Pymble, NSW: Harper Educational.

Gerdes, W.D. (1993), 'The demand for money in socialist Tanzania', *Atlantic Economic Journal*, 18(3), 68–73.

Gereffi, G. (1993), 'International subcontracting and global capitalism: reshaping the Pacific Rim', in R.A. Palat (ed.), *Pacific-Asia and the Future of the World-System*, Westport, CT: Greenwood Press, 67–81.

Gereffi, G. (1996a), 'Commodity chains and regional divisions of labor in East Asia', *Journal of Asian Business*, 12(1), 75–112.

Gereffi, G. (1996b), 'The elusive last lap in the quest for developed- country status', in J. Mittelman (ed.), Globalization: Critical Reflections, Boulder: Lynne Rienner, 53–81.

Ghatak, S. (1995), *Monetary Economics in Developing Countries*, London: Macmillan.

Giersch, H. (1995), 'Freihandel und Ordnungspolitik', in *Nach der Reform der Welthandelsordnung*, Bonn: Dokumentation 13 der Herbert Quandt – Stiftung, 1995.

Gilpin, R. (1987), *The Political Economy of International Relations*, Princeton NJ: Princeton University Press.

Godfrey, L. (1978), 'Testing against general autoregressive and moving average error models when the regressors include lagged dependent variables', *Econometrica*, 46, 1293–1302.

Goldfeld, S.M. (1973), 'The demand for money revisited', *Brookings Papers on Economic Activity*, 3, 577–638.

Goold, M., A. Campbell and M. Alexander (1994), *Corporate-level Strategy: Creating Value in the Multi-business Company*, New York. John Wiley.

Greene, W.H. (1997), *Econometric Analysis*, New Jersey: Prentice-Hall.

Grifell-Tatje, E. and C.A.K. Lovell (1996), 'Deregulation and productivity decline: the case of Spanish banks', *European Economic Review*, 40, 1281–1303.

Grifell-Tatje, E. and C.A.K. Lovell (1997), 'A DEA-based analysis of productivity change and intertemporal managerial performance', *Annals of Operations Research*, 73, 177–89.

Grifell-Tatje, E. and J. Lopez Sintas (1995), Total factor productivity, technical efficiency, bias and technical change in the European textile-clothing industry, 1980–1989', *Management Report Series No. 210*, Rotterdam: Erasmus Universiteit.

Grosskopf, S. (1993), 'Efficiency and productivity', in H.O. Fried, C.A.K. Lovell and S.S. Shelton (eds.), *The Measurement of Productive Efficiency: Techniques and Applications*, New York: Oxford University Press.

Grossman, G.M and E. Helpman (1995), 'The politics of free-trade agreements', *American Economic Review*, 85(4), 667–84.

Gruat, J.-V. (1990), 'Social security schemes in Africa: current trends and problems', *International Labour Review*, 129(4), 405–21.

Grubel, H.G. (1968), 'Internationally diversified portfolios, welfare gains and capital flows', *American Economic Review*, 58, 1299–1314.

Guitian, M. (1973), 'Credit versus money as an instrument of control, *IMF Staff Papers*, 20, 785–800.

Gylfason, T. (1987), 'Credit policy and economic activity in developing countries with IMF stabilization programs', *Princeton Studies in International Finance, no. 60*.

Haas, E.B. (1968), *The Uniting of Europe, Political, Social and Economic Forces, 1950–1957*, Stanford, CA: Stanford University Press.

Hafer, R.W. and D.W. Jansen (1991), 'The demand for money in the United States: evidence from cointegration tests', *Journal of Money Credit and Banking*, 23(2), 155–68.

Haggard, S. (1990), *Pathways from the Periphery: The Politics of Growth in the Newly Industrializing Countries*, Ithaca NY: Cornell University Press.

Haggard, S., J.-D. Lafay and C. Morrisson (1995), *The Political Feasibility of Adjustment in Developing Countries*, Paris: OECD Development Centre.

Hallman, J.J., R.D. Porter and D.H. Small (1989), 'M2 per unit of Potential GNP as an Anchor for Price Level', *Board of Governors of the Federal Reserve System Staff Study*, No. 157.

Hamel, G. and C.K. Prahalad (1994), *Competing for the Future*, Boston MA: Harvard Business School Press.

Hammer, J.S. (1986), 'Children and savings in less developed countries', *Journal of Development Economics*, 23, 107–118.

Hansson, P. and M. Henrekson (1994), 'What makes a country socially capable of catching up?', *Weltwirtschaftliches Archiv*, 130(4), 747–59.

Haque, N. and P. Montiel (1989), 'Consumption in developing countries: tests for liquidity constraints and finite horizons', *Review of Economics and Statistics*, 408–15.

Haque, N., M.S. Kumar, N. Mark *et al.* (1996), 'The economic content of indicators of developing country creditworthiness', *IMF Staff Papers*, 43(4), 688–724.

Harden, S. (1985), *Small is Dangerous: Micro States in a Macro World*, London: Pinter.

Harrigan, K.R. (1985), 'An application of clustering for strategic group analysis', *Strategic Management Journal*, 6, 55–73.

Harrold, P., M. Jayawickrama and D. Bhattasali (1996), 'Practical Lessons for Africa from East Asia in Industrial and Trade Policies', *World Bank Discussion Papers*, Africa technical department series, 310.

Hatch, W. and K. Yamamura (1996), *Asia in Japan's Embrace: Building a Regional Production Alliance*, Cambridge: Cambridge University Press.

Hayami, Y. (1997), *Development Economics: From the Poverty to the Wealth of Nations*, Oxford and New York: Clarendon Press.

Hayami, Y. and T. Kawagoe (1987), 'An inter-country comparison of agricultural production efficiency', in *Productivity Measurement and Analysis: Asian Agriculture*, Tokyo: Asian Productivity Organisation.

Hayami, Y. and V.W. Ruttan (1979), 'Agricultural growth in four countries', in Y. Hayami Y. V.M. Ruttan and H.M. Southworth, (eds), *Agricultural Growth in Japan, Taiwan, Korea and the Philippines*, Honolulu, APO and East-West Centre: The University Press of Hawaii.

Hayami, Y. and V.W. Ruttan (1985), *Agricultural Development: An International Perspective*, Baltimore and London: The Johns Hopkins University Press.

Heller, P.S. (1975), 'A model of public fiscal behaviour in developing countries: aid, investment and taxation', *American Economic Review*, 65, 429–45.

Henderson, J. (1998), 'Danger and opportunity in the Asia-Pacific', in G. Thompson (ed.), *Economic Dynamism in the Asia-Pacific*, London: Routledge, 356–84.

Henderson, D.W. and J. Kim (1998), 'The choice of a monetary policy reaction function in a simple optimizing model', *International Finance Discussion Papers*, Board of Governors of the Federal Reserve System, no. 10.

Higgott, R. (1998a), 'The international political economy of regionalism: the Asia-Pacific and Europe compared', in W. Coleman and G. Underhill (eds.), *Regionalism and Global Economic Integration, Europe, Asia and the Americas*, London: Routledge, 68–80.

Higgott, R. (1998b), 'The Asian economic crisis: a study in the politics of resentment', *New Political Economy*, 3(3), 333–56.

Higgott, R. and R. Stubbs (1995), 'Competing conceptions of economic regionalism, APEC versus EAEC in the Asia-Pacific', *Review of International Political Economy*, 2(3), 516–35.

Hintjens, H.M. and M.D.D. Newitt (1992), *The Political Economy of Small Tropical Islands: The Importance of Being Small*, Exeter: University of Exeter Press.

Ho, Samuel P.S. (1978), *Economic Development of Taiwan, 1860–1970*. New Haven: Yale University Press.

Ho, P.S. (1986), 'Off-farm employment and farm households in Taiwan' in R.T. Shand (ed.) (1986), *Off-farm Employment in the Development of Rural Asia*, Canberra: National Centre for Development Studies, Australian National University

Hodrick, R.J. and E.C. Prescott (1980), 'Post-war US business cycles, an empirical investigation', *Discussion Paper, Carnegie-Mellon University, No. 451.*

Hodrick, R.J. and E.C. Prescott (1997), 'Post-war US business cycles: an empirical investigation', *Journal of Money, Credit and Banking*, 29(1), 1–16.

Hoffman, D.L. and R.H. Rasche (1997), *Aggregate Money Demand Functions: Empirical Applications in Cointegrated Systems*, Boston: Kluwer Academics.

Holden, M. (1996), 'Economic integration and trade liberalization in Southern Africa', *World Bank Discussion Paper No. 342*, Washington DC, World Bank.

Holmes, F. (1976), 'Development problems of small countries', in L.V. Castle and F. Holmes (eds.), *Cooperation and Development in the Asia Pacific Region: Relations Between Large and Small Countries*, Tokyo: Japan Economic Research Centre, 43–66.

Hopkins, R. (1995), 'Disentangling the performance of Latin American Agriculture, 1980–92' in Weeks (1995).

Hufbauer, G.C. and J.J. Schott (1994), *Western Hemisphere Economic Integration*, Washington DC: Institute for International Economics.

Huff, W.G. (1994), *The Economic Growth of Singapore*, Cambridge: Cambridge University Press.

Hunter, B. (ed) (1996), *The Statesman's Yearbook 1995/96*, London: Macmillan.

Hurt, S. (1997), 'Options and dilemmas for post-apartheid South Africa in a changing global order', Paper presented at the conference on 'Globalisation versus Regionalisation, New Trends in World Politics', University of Warwick, 4 December (*mimeo*)

International Labour Office (ed.) (1996), *Yearbook of Labour Statistics*, Geneva: ILO

International Monetary Fund (1993), *World Economic Outlook*, Washington DC: IMF.

International Monetary Fund (1997), *International Financial Statistics*, L, 6, Washington DC.

Islam N. (1995), 'Growth Empirics: A Panel Data Approach', *Quarterly Journal of Economics*, 110, 1127–170.

Jaeger, W.K. (1992), 'The effects of economic policies on African agriculture', *World Bank Discussion Papers No 147*.

Jahnke, H.E., D. Kirschke and J. Lagemann (1987), *The Impact of Agricultural Research in Tropical Africa: A Study of Collaboration between the International and National Research Systems*, Washington DC: World Bank.

Jebuni, C. (1997), 'Trade liberalization and regional integration in Africa', in A. Oyejide and I. Elbadawi (eds.), *Regional Integration and Trade Liberalization in SubSaharan Africa: Framework. Issues and Methodological Perspectives*, London: Macmillan, 353–69.

Jensen, P. and H.S. Nielsen (1996), 'Child labour or school attendance? Evidence from Zambia', *Working Paper 96–14*, Centre for Labour Market and Social Research, University of Aarhus and Aarhus School of Business.

Johansen, S. (1988), 'Statistical analysis of cointegrating vectors', *Journal of Economic Dynamics and Control*, 12, 231–54.

Johansen, S. and K. Juselius (1990), 'Maximum likelihood estimation and inference on cointegration – with applications to the demand for money', *Oxford Bulletin of Economics and Statistics*, 52, 169–210.

Johnson, C. (1982), *MITI and the Japanese Miracle*, Stanford: Stanford University Press.

Johnson, C. (1987), 'Political institutions and economic performance: the government-business relationship in Japan, South Korea, and Taiwan', in F. Deyo (ed.), *The Political Economy of the New Asian Industrialism*, Ithaca NY: Cornell University Press, 136–64.

Johnson, C. (1995), *Japan Who Governs?: The Rise of the Developmental State*, New York: W.W.Norton.

Jomo, K.S. (ed.) (1992), *Child Labor in Malaysia*, Kuala Lumpur: Varlin Press.

Joshi, H. and M. Saggar (1995), 'The demand for money in India: stability revisited', *Reserve Bank of India Occasional Papers*, 16(2), 79–100.

Judd, J.P. and J.L. Scadding (1982), 'The search for a stable money demand function: a survey of the post-1973 literature', *Journal of Economic Literature*, 20, 993–1023.

Kaldor, N. (1970), 'The case for regional policies', *Scottish Journal of Political Economy*, 17, 337–47.

Kamas, L. (1986), 'The balance of payments offset to monetary policy, monetarist, portfolio balance, and Keynesian estimates for Mexico and Venezuela', *Journal of Money, Credit and Banking*, 18(4), 467–81.

Karmokolias, Y. (1990), 'Automotive industry trends and prospects for investment in developing countries', *Discussion Paper No. 7* Washington DC: International Finance Corporation.

Kaskarelis, I.A. and E.G. Varelas (1996), 'Permanent income and credit rationing in the open economy multiplier/accelerator model: an exercise for the developing countries case', *Journal of Macroeconomics*, 18(3), 531–49.

Kendig, H., A. Hashimoto and L.C. Coard (1992), *Family Support for the Elderly: the International Experience*, Oxford: Oxford University Press.

Kenen, P.B. (1989), *The International Economy*, London: Prentice-Hall.

Khan, H.A. and E. Hoshino (1992), 'Impact of foreign aid on the fiscal behaviour of LDC governments', *World Development*, 20(10), 1481–8.

Khoman, S. (1993), 'Education policy', in Peter Warr (ed.), *The Thai Economy in Transition*, Cambridge: Cambridge University Press.

Kikonyogo, C.N., *Experiences under Stabilisation and Structural Adjustment Programmes in Uganda*, Kampala: Bank of Uganda.

Killick, T. (1995), 'Flexibility and Economic Progress', *World Development*, 23(5), 721–34.

Kirkpatrick, C. (1994), 'Regionalisation, regionalism and East Asian economic cooperation', *World Economy*, 17(2), 191–202.

Kisanga, E.J. (1991), *Industrial and Trade Cooperation in Eastern and Southern Africa*, Aldershot: Avebury.

Knight M., N. Loayza and D. Villanueya (1993), 'Testing the neoclassical theory of economic growth', *IMF Staff Papers*, 40(3), 512–41.

Knox, A.D. (1967), 'Some economic problems of small countries', in B. Benedict (ed.), *Problems of Smaller Territories*, London: Athlone Press, 35–45.

Koh, A.T. (1987), 'Saving, Investment and Entrpreneurship in Krause', L.B., A.T. Koh and T.Y. Lee, *The Singapore Economy Reconsidered*, Singapore: Institute of South-East Asian Studies.

Koray, F. and P.P. Chan (1991), 'Government spending and the exchange rate', *Applied Economics*, 23(9), 1551–8.

Krugman, P.R. (1991), 'Is bilateralism bad?' in E. Helpman and A. Razin (eds.), *International Trade and Trade Policy*, Cambridge, MA: MIT, 9–23.

Krugman, P.R. (1997), 'What should trade negotiators negotiate about?', *Journal of Economic Literature*, 35(1), 113–20.

Krugman, P.R. and A.J. Venables (1995), 'Globalization and the inequalities of nations', *Quarterly Journal of Economics*, 60(4), 857–80.

Kuhlmann, M. (1992), 'Welche Zulieferstruktur hat die besten Marktchancen? Bauen wir für die Zukunft das richtige Auto?', *Automobilhersteller und Zulieferer in*

Anpassungszwang technischer und ökologischer Forderungen, Konferenzunterlagen, Landsberg, Lech.

Kuroda, Y. (1997), 'Research and extension expenditures and productivity in Japanese agriculture, 1960–1990', *Agricultural Economics*, 16, 111–24.

Kuznets, S. (1960), 'The economic growth of small states', in E.A.G. Robinson (ed.), *The Economic Consequences of the Size of Nations*, London: Macmillan, 14–32.

Kwong, P. and C. Gouxuan (1992), 'Ageing in China: trends, problems and strategies, in Phillips (ed.) (1992).

Lall, S. (1994), 'The East Asian miracle: does the bell toll for industrial strategy?', *World Development*, 22(4), 645–54.

Leff, N. (1969), 'Dependency rates and savings rates', *American Economic Review*, 59(5), 886–96.

Leibenstein, H. and S. Maital (1992), 'Empirical estimation and partitioning of x-inefficiency: a data envelopment approach', *American Economic Review*, 82, 428–33.

Lessard, D.R. (1985), 'Principles of international portfolio selection', in D.R. Lessard (ed.), *International Financial Management, Theory and Application*, New York: John Wiley.

Levin, A. and C.F. Lin (1993), 'Unit root tests in panel data: new results', *Working Paper No. 93–56*, University of California, San Diego.

Levine, R. (1996), 'Financial development and economic growth: views and agenda', *Journal of Economic Literature*, 35, 688–726.

Levine, R. and D. Renelt (1992), 'A sensitivity analysis of cross- country growth regressions', *American Economic Review*, 82(4), 942–63.

Lim, C.Y. and Associates (1988), *Policy Options for the Singapore Economy*, Singapore: McGraw-Hill.

Lipsey, R.G. and K. Lancaster (1956/57), 'The general theory of second best', *Review of Economic Studies*, 24(1), 11–32.

Lipumba, N. and L. Kasekende (1991), 'The record and prospects of the preferential trade area for Eastern and Southern African states', in A. Chhibber and S. Fischer (eds.), *Economic Reform in Sub-Saharan Africa*, Washington DC: World Bank, 233–44.

Lizondo, J.S. (1993), 'Real exchange rate targeting under imperfect asset substitutability', *IMF Staff Papers*, 40(4), 829–51.

Lloyd, C.B. (1993), 'Fertility, family size and structure – consequences for families and children', *Proceedings of a Population Council Seminar*, New York, 9–10 June (1992), New York, the Population Council.

Lucas, R.E. Jr. (1977), 'Understanding business cycles', in K. Brunner and A.H. Meltzer: (ed.), *Stabilization of the Domestic and International Economy*, Carnegie-Rochester Conference Series on Public Policy, Amsterdam: North Holland, 5, 7–29.

Lucas, R.E. Jr. (1990), *Understanding Business Cycles: Studies in Business Cycle Theory*, Cambridge, MA: MIT Press.

Lusigi, A. (1998), *Productivity in African Agriculture, Measuring and Explaining Growth*, PhD dissertation, University of Reading, UK.

Lusigi, A. and C. Thirtle (1997), 'Total factor productivity and the effects of R&D in African agriculture', *Journal of International Development*, 9, 529–38.

Lusigi, A., J. Piesse and C. Thirtle (1998), 'Convergence of per capita incomes and agricultural productivity in Africa', *Journal of International Development*, 10, 105–15.

Lyakurwa, W., A. McKay, N. Ng'eno and W. Kennes (1997), 'Regional integration in Sub-Saharan Africa, a review of experiences and issues', in A. Oyejide and I. Elbadawi (eds.), *Regional Integration and Trade Liberalization in Sub-Saharan Africa: Framework, Issues and Methodological Perspectives*, London: Macmillan, 159–209.

MacBean, A.I. and D.T. Nguyen (1987), *Commodity Problems, Prospects and Policies*, London: Croom Helm.

Macharzina, K. (1993), *Unternehmensführung, das internationale Managementwissen: Konzepte – Methoden – Praxis*. Wiesbaden: Gabler.

Mansoor, A. and A. Inotai (1991), 'Integration efforts in Sub-Saharan Africa: failures, results and prospects – a suggested strategy for achieving efficient integration', in A. Chhibber and S. Fischer (eds.), *Economic Reform in Sub-Saharan Africa*, Washington DC: World Bank, 217–32.

Marcy, G. (1960), 'How far can foreign trade and customs agreements confer upon small nations the advantages of larger nations?', in E.A.G. Robinson (ed.), *The Economic Consequences of the Size of Nations*, London: Macmillan, 265–81.

Markowitz, H. (1952), 'Portfolio selection', *Journal of Finance*, 7, 77–91.

Masson P., B. Tamim and S. Hossein (1995), 'Saving behaviour in industrial and developing countries', *World Economic and Financial Surveys: Staff Studies for the World Economic Outlook*, Washington DC: Research Department of the International Monetary Fund, 1–27.

Maxfield, S. (1997), *Gatekeepers of Growth: The International Political Economy of Central Banking in Developing Countries*, Princeton, NJ: Princeton University Press,

McCarthy, C.L. (1994), 'Regional integration of developing countries at different levels of economic development – problems and prospects', *Transnational Law and Contemporary Problems*, 4, 1–20.

McGillivray, M. (forthcoming), 'Aid and public sector fiscal behaviour in developing countries', *Review of Development Economics*.

McGillivray, M. and O. Morrissey (eds.) (1999), *Evaluating Economic Liberalisation*, London, Macmillan.

McKay, A., O. Morrissey and C. Vaillant (1997), 'Trade liberalisation and agricultural supply response: issues and some lessons', *European Journal of Development Research*, 9(2), 129–47.

Meerman, J. (1997), 'Reforming agriculture: the World Bank goes to market', *World Bank Operations Evaluation Study*, Washington DC: World Bank.

Mehrotra, S. (1998), 'Social Development in High-Achieving Countries: Common Elements and Diversities' in Mehrotra, S. and R. Jolly, *Development with a Human Face: Experiences in Social Achievement and Economic Growth*, Oxford: Clarendon Press.

Messkoub, M. (1999), 'Crisis of ageing in less developed countries: too much consumption or too little production?', *Development and Change*, 30(2), 217–35.

Midgley, J. (1984), *Social Security, Inequality, and the Third World*, Chichester, UK: John Wiley and Sons.

Miller, S.M. (1991), 'Monetary dynamics: an application of cointegration and error-correction modeling', *Journal of Money Credit and Banking*, 23(2), 139–54.

Milner, C. and T. Westaway (1993), 'Country size and the medium term growth process: some country size evidence', *World Development*, 21(2), 203–12.

Milner, C. and O. Morrissey (1999), 'Measuring trade liberalisation', in McGillivray and Morrissey (1999), 60–82.

Milner, C., O. Morrissey and N. Rudaheranwa (1999), 'Protection, trade policy and transport costs: effective taxation of Ugandan exporters', University of Nottingham: *CREDIT Research Paper 98/13*.

Ministry in the Office of the President (1995), *A Poverty Profile of South Africa*, Pretoria.

Mistry, P. (1995), 'Open Regionalism: Stepping Stone or Milestone Toward and Improved Multilateral System?', in J.J. Teunissen, (ed.) *Regionalism and the Global Economy: The Case of Latin America*, The Hague: FONDAD.

Mistry, P. (1996a), 'Regional dimensions of structural adjustment in Southern Africa', in J. Teunissen (ed.), *Regionalism and the Global Economy: The Case of Africa*, The Hague: Forum on Debt and Development, 165–289.

Mistry, P. (1996b), *Regional Integration Arrangements in Economic Development: Panacea or Pitfall?*, The Hague: Forum on Debt and Development.

Mkandawire, T. and C.C. Soludo (1999), *Our Continent, Our Future: African Perspectives on Structural Adjustment*, Dakar: Codesria.

Morgan, R. (1991), 'Social security in the SADCC states of Southern Africa: welfare programmes and the reduction of household vulnerability', in E. Ahmad *et al.* (1991), 415–65.

Morrissey, O. (1999a), 'The emperor is fully clothed if a little ragged: East Asian miracles and crises', *Journal of the Asia Pacific Economy*, 4(2), 214–32.

Morrissey, O. (1999b), 'Political dimensions of economic policy reform', in M. McGillivray and O. Morrissey (1999), 83–102.

Morrissey, O. and D. Nelson (1998), 'East Asian economic performance, miracle or just a pleasant surprise?', *World Economy*, 21(7), 855–79.

Mosley, P., J. Hudson, S. Horrell (1987), 'Aid, the Public Sector and the Market in Less Developed Countries', *Economic Journal*, 97(387), 616–41.

Mosley, P., J. Harrigan and J. Toye (1991), *Aid and Power: The World Bank and Policy-based Lending*, Volume 2: *Case Studies*, London: Routledge.

Mosley, P., T. Subasat and J. Weeks (1995), 'Assessing adjustment in Africa', *World Development*, 23(9), 1459–73.

Mundle, S., 'Financing Economic Development: Some Lessons from Advanced Asian Countries', *World Development*, 26(4), 659–72.

Musinguzi, P. and P. Smith (1998), 'Structural Adjustment and Poverty: a study of rural Uganda', *Discussion Papers in Economics and Econometrics*, 98(13), UK: University of Southampton.

Myint, H. (1967), 'The inward and outward-looking countries of South East Asia', *Malayan Economic Review*, XII (1), April, 1–13.

Myrdal, G. (1957), *Economic Theory and Under-developed Regions*, London: Allen & Unwin.

National Statistical Coordination Board (various years), *Philippine Statistical Yearbook*, Manila: Government of the Philippines.

Ndlela, D. (1993), 'Regional economic integration and intra-African trade, issues for development', in G. Hansson (ed.), *Trade, Growth and Development: The Role of Politics and Institutions*, London: Routledge, 303–28.

Niehof, A. (1995), 'Ageing and the elderly in Indonesia: identifying key issues', *Bijdragen tot de Taal-, Land-, en kenkunde* 151 (III), 422–38.

Noorbakhsh, F. and A. Paloni (1998), 'Structural adjustment programmes and export supply response', *Journal of International Development*, 10(4), 555–73.

Nyong, M.O.(1993), 'Income and interest elasticities of the demand for money in South Africa: comments and extensions', *Indian Economic Journal*, 41(1), 83–9.

Oberender, P. and F. Daumann (1995), *Industriepolitik*, Munich Vahlen.

Obstfeld, M. (1983), 'Exchange rates, inflation, and the sterilization problem', Germany: 1975–1981, *European Economic Review*, 21, 161–89.

Odén, B. (1996), 'Regionalization in Southern Africa', *WIDER Working Paper*, Helsinki: WIDER.

ODI-IDS (1995), *Development Research Insights for Policymakers*, 16.

OECD (1997), *Geographical Disbursement of Financial Flows to Aid Recipients, 1992–96*, Paris: OECD.

Olivera, J.H. (1967), 'Money, prices, and fiscal lags: a note on the dynamics of inflation', *Banca Nazionale Del Lavoro Quarterly Review*, 20, 258–67.

Olson, M. (1990), 'Autocracy, democracy and prosperity', Department of Economics, University of Maryland, mimeo.

Onafowora, O. and O. Owoye (1998), 'Can trade liberalization stimulate economic growth in Africa', *World Development*, 26(3), 497–506.

Onchan, T. (1990), *A Land Policy Study*, Bangkok: Thai Development Research Institute Foundation.

Onitiri, H. (1997), 'Changing political and economic conditions for regional integration in Sub-Saharan Africa', in A. Oyejide and I. Elbadawi (eds.), *Regional Integration and Trade Liberalization in Sub-Saharan Africa: Framework, Issues and Methodological Perspectives*, London, Macmillan, 398–421.

Organisation for Economic Co-operation and Development (OECD) (1997), 'Table 44, GNP and Population of Developing Countries and Territories', http://www.oecd.org/dac/htm/table44.htm.

Organization of African Unity (OAU) (1981), *The Lagos Plan of Action for Economic Development of Africa, 1980–2000*, Geneva: International Institute of Labour Studies.

Organization of African Unity (OAU) (1991), *Treaty Establishing the African Economic Community*, Abuja, Nigeria, OAU.

O.V. (1996), Institutional Investors Ranking, *Handelsblat*, 15 May 1996.

Palat, R. (1993), 'Introduction: the making and unmaking of Pacific- Asia', in R. Palat (ed.) *Pacific-Asia and the Future of the World-System*, Westport, CT: Greenwood Press, 3–20.

Panitch, L. (1996), 'Rethinking the role of the state', in J. Mittelman (ed.), *Globalization, Critical Reflections*, Boulder: Lynne Rienner, 83– 113.

Pant, Y.P. (1974), *Problems of Development of Smaller Countries: A Study in the Problems and Prospects of the Development Process*, New Delhi: Oxford University Press.

Pasuk P. and C. Baker (1995), *Thailand: Economy and Politics*, Kuala Lumpur: Oxford University Press.

Pasula, K. (1994), 'Sterilization, Ricardian equivalence and structural and reduced-form estimates of the offset coefficient', *Journal of Macroeconomics*, 16(4), 683–99.

Patrinos, H. and G. Psacharopoulos (1997), 'Family size, schooling and child labor in Peru: An empirical analysis', *Journal of Population Economics*, 10, 387–405.

Perkins, D.H. (1994), 'There are at least three models of East Asian development', *World Development*, 22(4), 655–62.

Phillips, D.R. (ed.) (1992), *Ageing in East and South-East Asia*, London: Edward Arnold.

Phillips, P.C.B. (1986), 'Understanding spurious regressions in econometrics', *Journal of Econometrics*, 33, 311–40.

Phillips, P.C.B. and P. Perron (1988), 'Testing for unit roots in time series regression', *Biometrika*, 75, 335–46.

Phongpaichit, P. and C. Baker (1995), *Thailand, Economy and Politics*, Kuala Lumpur: Oxford University Press.

Platteau, J.-P. (1991), 'Traditional systems of social security and hunger insurance: past achievements and modern challenges', in E. Ahmad *et al.* (1991), 171–246.

Pomfret, R. (1986), 'The theory of preferential trading arrangements', *Weltwirtschaftliches Archiv*, 72, 439–65.

Porter, M.E. (1980), *Competitive Strategy, Techniques for Analyzing Industries and Competitors*, New York: Free Press.

Porter, M.E. (1987), 'Diversifikation – Konzerne ohne Konzept', *Harvard Manager*, 9, 30–49.

Porzecanski, A.C. (1979), 'Patterns of monetary policy in Latin America', *Journal of Money, Credit and Banking*, 11(4), 427–37.

Posen, A. (1998), 'Central bank independence and disinflationary credibility: a missing link', *Oxford Economic Papers*, 50(3), 335–59.

Prescott, E.C. (1986), 'Theory ahead of business-cycle measurement', *Carnegie-Rochester Conference Series on Public Policy*, 25, 11–44.

Pretzell, K.-A. (1996), 'Die APEC nach Osaka' in Ostasiatischer Verein e.V. (German Asia-Pacific Business Association) (ed.), *Asien Pazifik Wirtschaftshandbuch 1996*, 41.Ed. Hamburg. 25–30.

Price, S. and Insukindro (1994), 'The demand for Indonesian narrow money, long-run equilibrium, error correction, and forward looking behavior', *Journal of International Trade and Economic Development*, 3(2), 147–63.

Pritchett, L. (1997), 'Divergence, big time', *Journal of Economic Perspectives*, 11(3), 3–17.

Proff, H. (1994), *Auswirkungen der Politik der internationalen Finanzinstitutionen (IWF und Welt bank) auf importintensive und exportorientierte Unternehmen in Ghana*, Saarbrücken: Gabler.

Proff, H. (1997), 'Hybride Strategien: Unternehmenstrategien zur Sicherung des Überlebens', *Wirtschaftswissenschaftliches Studium (WiSt)*, 26, (6), 305–7.

Proff, H. and H.V. Proff (1996), 'Auswirkung der Regionalisierung der Weltwirtschaft auf die Geschäftsbereichsstrategien international tätiger Unternehmen', *Zeitschrift für Betriebswirtschaft*, (1996), 823–60.

Proff, H. and H.V. Proff (1997), 'Möglichkeiten und Grenzen hybrider Strategien – dargestellt am Bei- spiel der deutschen Automobilindustrie', *Die Betriebswirtschaft*, 6/97.

Proff, H.V. (1993), 'The North American Trade Region', *Intereconomics*, 28, 279–84.

Proff, H.V. (1994), *Freihandelszonen in Nordamerika, Ursachen und ökonomische Auswirkungen*, Wiesbaden: Gabler.

Putnam, R.D. with R. Leonardo and R.Y. Nanetti (1993), *Making Democracy Work, Civic Traditions in Modern Italy*, Princeton: Princeton University Press.

Quibria, M.G. and J.M. Dowling (1996), 'An Overview', in M.G. Quibria and J.M. Dowling, (eds.), *Current Issues in Economic Development: An Asia Perspective*, New York: Oxford University Press.

Raffée, H., J. Effenberger and W. Fritz (1994), 'Strategieprofile als Faktoren des Unternehmenserfolgs', *Die Betriebwirtschaft* (DBW), 54, 383–96.

Rajapatirana, S. (1995), 'Macroeconomic crisis and adjustment', *Finance and Development*, 48–51.

Ranis, G. and F. Stewart (1993), 'Rural non-agricultural activities in development: theory and application', *Journal of Development Economics*, 40, 75–101.

Ranis, G., F. Stewart and E. Angeles-Reyes (1990), *Linkages in Developing Economies: A Philippine Study*, San Francisco: International Center for Economic Growth.

Rao, V.V. Bhanoji (1996), 'Income inequality in Singapore: facts and policies' in Lim Chong Yah (ed.), *Economic Policy Management in Singapore*, Singapore: Addison-Wesley Publishing Company.

Ravenhill, J. (1998), 'The growth of intergovernmental collaboration in the Asia-Pacific region', in A. McGrew and C. Brook (eds.), *Asia-Pacific in the New World Order*, London: Routledge, 247–70.

Read, R. (1998), 'Small states and the case for special and differential treatment under the WTO', *mimeo*.

Roberts, R. (1994), *Offshore Financial Centres*, London: Edward Elgar.

Rodrik, D. (1994), 'King Kong meets Godzilla, the World Bank and the East Asian miracle', in A. Fishlow *et al.*, *Miracle or Design?, Lessons from the East Asian Experience*, New York: Overseas Development Council, 13–53.

Rodrik, D. (1995), 'Getting interventions right, how South Korea and Taiwan grew rich', *Economic Policy*, 20, 55–107.

Rojas-Suarez, L. (1990), 'Risk and capital flight in developing countries', *IMF Working Papers*, No. 64.

Romer, P. (1990), 'Endogenous Technological Change', *Journal of Political Economy*, October, S71–S102.

Romer, C.D. and D.H. Romer (1998), 'Monetary policy and the well-being of the poor', *NBER Working Paper Series*, No. 6793.

Rudner, M. (1994), 'Colonial education policy and manpower underdevelopment in British Malaya' in M. Rudner (ed), *Malaysian Development: A Retrospective*, Ottawa: Carleton University Press.

Salvatore, D. (1994), *International Economics*, 5th edn, New York: Prentice-Hall.

Salvatore, D. (1995), *International Economics*, Englewood Cliffs: Prentice-Hall.

Schiff, M. and C.E. Montenegro (1995), 'Aggregate agricultural supply response in developing countries: a survey of selected issues'. Washington DC: World Bank.

Schott, J.J. (1990), 'Is the world developing into regional trading blocs?' in E. Kantzenbach and O.G. Mayer (eds.), *Perspektiven der wirtschaftlichen Entwicklung und ihre Konsequenzen für die Bundesrepublik Deutschland*, Hamburg: Weltarchiv, 36–54.

Scitovsky, T. (1960), 'International trade and economic integration as a means of overcoming the disadvantages of a small nation', in E.A.G. Robinson (ed.), *The Economics Consequences of the Size of Nation*, London: Macmillan, 282–90.

Sen, K. (1995), *Ageing*, London: Zed Press.

Shand, R.T. (ed.) (1986), *Off-farm Employment in the Development of Rural Asia*, Canberra: National Centre for Development Studies, Australian National University.

Sideri, S. (1997), 'Globalisation and regional integration', *European Journal of Development Research*, 9(1), 39–82.

Singh, A. (1998), 'Growth, its sources and consequences', in G. Thompson (ed.), *Economic Dynamism in the Asia-Pacific*, London: Routledge, 55–82.

Smith, P. (1997), *Poverty Alleviation Strategies for Uganda: a report for the Bank of Uganda*, Kampala: Bank of Uganda.

Smith, P. (1998), *A Tale of Two Cities: Evaluating the Quality of Life in Singapore and Kampala*, Conference on the Quality of Life in Cities, National University of Singapore.

Smith, P. and A.M. Ulph (1995), 'A Comparative Study of Flexibility in the Response of National economies to the Oil-Price Shocks', in Killick, T. (ed.), *The Flexible economy: Causes and Consequences of the Adaptability of National Economies*, London: Routledge.

Stein, H. (ed.) (1994), *Asian Industrialisation and Africa: studies in policy alternatives to structural adjustment*, London: Macmillan.

Stiglitz, J. (1996), 'Some lessons from the East Asian miracle', *World Bank Research Observer*, 11(2), 151–77.

Stiglitz, J.E. and M. Uy (1996), 'Financial markets, Public Policy and the East Asian Miracle', *The World Bank Research Observer*, 11(2), 249–76.

Streeten, P. (1993), 'The special problems of small countries', *World Development*, 21(2), 197–202.

Stubbs, R. (1998), 'Asia-Pacific regionalism versus globalization: competing forms of capitalism', in W. Coleman and G. Underhill (eds.) *Regionalism and Global Economic Integration, Europe, Asia and the Americas*, London: Routledge, 68–80.

Suhariyanto, K. (1999), *Productivity Growth, Efficiency and Technical Change in Asian Agriculture: A Malmquist Index Analysis*, PhD dissertation, University of Reading, UK.

Sum, N.-L. (1997), ' "Time-space embeddedness" and "geo- governance" of cross-border regional modes of growth, their nature and dynamics in East Asian cases', in A. Amin, and J. Hausner (eds.), *Beyond Market and Hierarchy*, Cheltenham: Edward Elgar, 159–98.

Summers, L. (1991), 'Regionalism and the world trading system', in L. Summers (ed.), *Policy Implications of Trade as Currency Zones*, Kansas City: Federal Reserve Bank.

Summers, L. and A. Heston (1988), 'A new set of international comparisons of real product and price level estimates for 130 countries, 1950–1985', *Review of Income and Wealth*, 34(1), 1–25.

Tanzi, V. (1978), 'Inflation, Real Tax Revenue, and the Case for Inflationary Finance: Theory with an Application to Argentina', *IMF Staff Papers*, 25, 3.

Tanzi, V. (1986), 'Fiscal policy responses to exogenous shocks in developing countries', *American Economic Review*, 76(2), 88–91.

Targetti, F. and A. Foti (1997), 'Growth and productivity: a model of cumulative growth and catching-up', *Cambridge Journal of Economics*, 21(1), 27–43.

Tatom, J.A. (1991), 'The 1990 oil price hike in perspective', *Federal Reserve Bank of St Louis*, November/December, 3–18.

Tavlas, G.S. (1989), 'The demand for money in South Africa a test of the buffer stock model', *South African Journal of Economics*, 57(1), 1–13.

Temple, J. (1999), 'The new growth evidence', *Journal of Economic Literature*, 37(1), 112–56.

Tesang, W. and R. Corker (1991), 'Financial liberalisation, money demand, and monetary policy in Asian countries', *IMF Occasional Paper, No. 84.*

Theil, H. (1952), *Economic Forecasts and Policy*, 2nd edn, Amsterdam: North Holland.

Thirtle, C. (1998), 'The Hesitant Recovery of African Agriculture', Editor's introduction to Policy Arena, *Journal of International Development*, 10(1), 71–3.

Thirtle, C., D. Hadley and R. Townsend (1995), 'A multilateral Malmquist productivity index approach to explaining agricultural growth in sub- Saharan Africa', *Development Policy Review*, 13, 323–48.

Thomas, I. (1982), 'The industrialisation experience of small countries', in B. Jalan (ed.), *Problems and Policies in Small Economies*, London: Croom Helm, 103–24.

Tinakorn, P. (1995), 'Industrialization and welfare, how poverty and income distribution are affected' in M. Krongkaew (ed.), *Thailand's Industrialization and its Consequences*, London, Macmillan.

Tinbergen, J. (1952), *On the Theory of Economic Policy*, 2nd edn, Amsterdam: North Holland.

Tolley Publishing Co. (1993), *Tolley's Tax Havens*, Croydon: Tolley Publishing Co., 2nd edition.

Tongroj, O. (1990), *A Land Policy Study*, Research Monograph No. 3. Bangkok: the Thai Development Research Institute Foundation.

Tout, K. (1989), *Ageing in Developing Countries*, Oxford: Oxford University Press.

Tseng, W.A.C.R. and R. Corker (1991), Financial liberalization, money demand, and monetary policy in Asian countries, *IMF Occasional Paper*, Washington DC, No. 84.

Tsurumi, E.P. (1977), *Japanese Colonial Education in Taiwan, 1895–1945*, Cambridge, MA: Harvard University Press.

Tsurumi, E.P. (1984), 'Colonial education in Korea and Taiwan', in R. Myers and M. Peattie (eds.), *The Japanese Colonial Empire*, Princeton: Princeton University Press.

Tulkens, H. and P. Vanden Eeckaut (1995), 'Non-parametric efficiency, progress and regress measures for panel data: methodological aspects', *European Journal of Operational Research*, 80, 474–99.

Twomey, M. and A. Helwege (1991), *Modernisation and Stagnation: Latin American Agriculture into the 1990s*, Westport, CT: Greenwood Press.

UN (1995), *World Population Prospects: The 1994 Revision*, New York, UN. (Serial No., ST/ESA/SER.A/145).

UN (1997), *1995 Demographic Yearbook*, New York: UN. (Serial No., ST/ESA/SER.R/26).

UNCTAD (1997), *The Vulnerability of Small Island Developing States in the Context of Globalization: Common Issues and Remedies*, Geneva, UNCTAD, SIDS.

Underhill, G. (1998), 'International financial markets and national economic development models, global structures versus domestic imperatives', Paper presented to the conference on 'From Miracle to Meltdown, the End of Asian Capitalism?, Murdoch University, 20–22 August.

United Nations Development Programme (UNDP) (1997), *Human Development Report 1997*, New York.

UNDP (1997b), *Uganda Human Development Report 1997*, Kampala: United Nations Development Programme.

USDA (1990), *World Agriculture, Trends and Indicators*, Washington DC: USDA.

Vernon-Wortzel, H. and L.H. Wortzel (1990), *Global Strategic Management: The Essentials*. 2nd edn, New York: John Wiley.

Vlassoff, M. and C. Vlassoff (1980), 'Old age security and the utility of children in rural India', *Population Studies*, 34, 487–89.

Vlassoff, M. and C. Vlassoff (1990), 'The value of sons in an Indian village: how widows see it', *Population Studies*, 44, 5–20.

Vyas, V.S. and W.E. James (1988), 'Agricultural development in Asia: performance, issues and policy options', in S. Ichimura (ed.), *Challenge of Asian Developing Countries: Issues and Analyses*, Hong Kong: Asian Productivity Organisation.

Wade, R. (1990), *Governing the Market: Economic Theory and the Role of the Government in East Asian Industrialisation*, Princeton, NJ: Princeton University Press.

Wade, R. (1992), 'East Asia's economic success, conflicting perspectives, partial insights, shaky evidence', *World Politics*, 44(2), 270–320.

Webb, S. and K. Shariff (1992), 'Designing and implementing adjustment programmes', in V. Corbo, S. Fischer and S. Webb (eds.), *Adjustment Lending Revisited: Policies to Restore Growth*, Washington, DC: World Bank.

Weeks, J. (1995), *Structural Adjustment and the Agricultural Sector in Latin America and the Caribbean*, London: Macmillan.

Weltbank (1995), *Weltentwicklungsbericht 1996: Vom Plan zum Markt*. Washington DC: World Bank.

Weltbank (1996), *Weltentwicklungsbericht 1995: Arbeitnehmer im weltweiten Integrationsprozeß*, Washington DC: World Bank.

Woo, J. H. (1991), 'Education and economic growth in Taiwan: a case of successful planning', *World Development*, 19(8), August, 1029–44.

Wood, D.P.J. (1967), 'The small territories, some political considerations', in B. Benedict (ed.), *Problems of Smaller Territories*, London: Athlone Press, 23–34.

World Bank (1983), *World Development Report 1983*, New York: Oxford University Press for the World Bank.

World Bank (1984), *World Development Report 1984: Population Change and Economic Development*, Oxford: Oxford University Press for the World Bank.

World Bank (1987), *Philippines: A Framework for Economic Recovery*, Washington DC: World Bank Country Study, World Bank.

World Bank (1989), *Sub-Saharan Africa: From Crisis to Sustainable Growth*, Washington DC: World Bank.

World Bank (1990), *Adjustment Lending for Sustainable Growth*, Washington DC: Country Economics Department, World Bank.

World Bank (1991), *World Development Report 1991*, New York: Oxford University Press.

World Bank (1993), *The East Asian Miracle, Growth and Public Policy*, Washington DC: Oxford University Press.

World Bank (1994), *Averting the Old Age Crisis: Policies to Protect the Old and Promote Growth*, Oxford: Oxford University Press.

World Bank (1994), *Adjustment in Africa: Reforms Results and the Road Ahead*, Washington DC: World Bank.

World Bank (1995), *Global Economic Prospects and the Developing Countries*, Washington DC: World Bank.

World Bank (1996), *The Uruguay Round: Statistics on Tariff Concessions Given and Received*, Washington DC, World Bank.

World Bank (1997), *Private Capital Flows to Developing Countries*, Washington DC: Oxford University Press.

World Bank (1997b), *World Development Report 1997*, New York: Oxford University Press for the World Bank.

World Bank (1998), *World Development Indicators* on CD-ROM.

World Bank (1999), *World Development Report 1998–1999* New York: Oxford University Press for the World Bank.

Yamada, S. (1987), 'Agricultural growth and productivity in selected Asian countries', in *Productivity Measurement and Analysis: Asian Agriculture*, Tokyo: Asian Productivity Organisation.

Yamazawa, I. (1998), 'Economic integration in the Asia-Pacific region', in G. Thompson (ed.), *Economic Dynamism in the Asia-Pacific*, London: Routledge, 163–84.

Yoshida, M. and I. Akimune (1994), 'Regional economic integration in East Asia: special features and policy implications', in V. Cable and D. Henderson (eds.), *Trade Blocs? The Future of Regional Integration*, London: Royal Institute of International Affairs, 59–108.

Young, A. (1995), The Tyranny of Numbers: Confronting the Statistical Realities of the East Asian Growth Experience, *Quarterly Journal of Economics*, 110(3), 641–89.

Yu, T.F.L. (1998), 'Adaptive Entrepreneurship and the Economic Development of Hong Kong', *World Development*, 26(5), 897–911.

Index